Picasso: The Cubist Portraits of Fernande Olivier

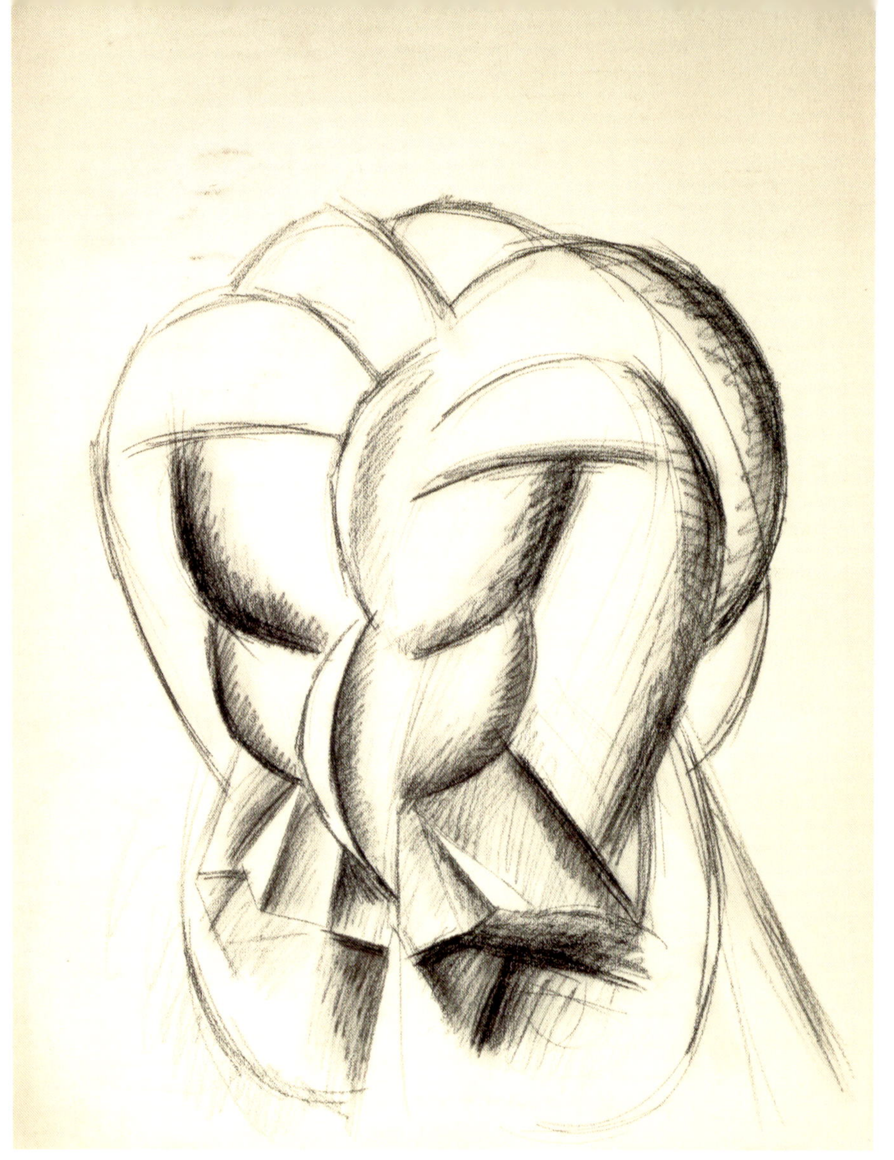

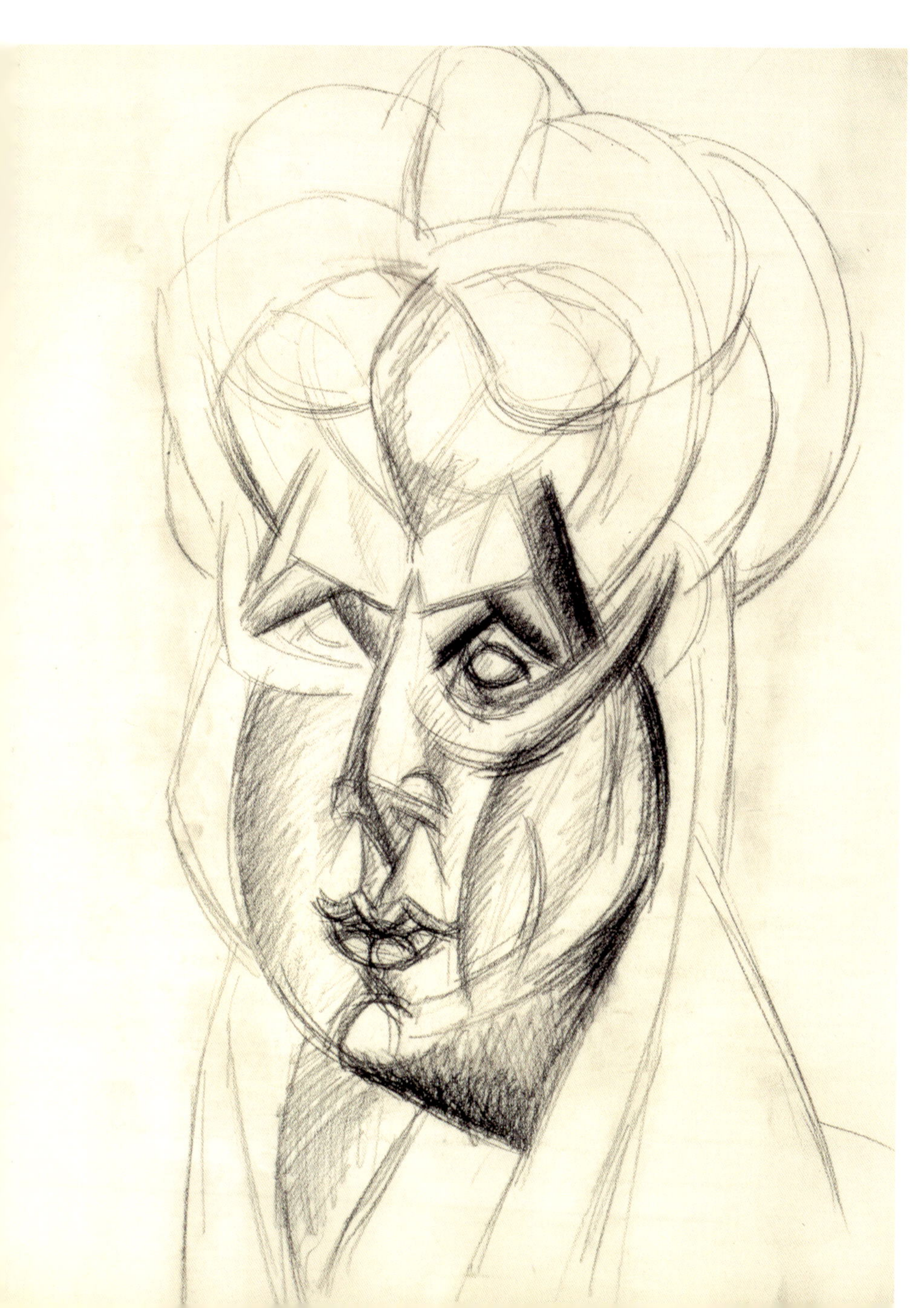

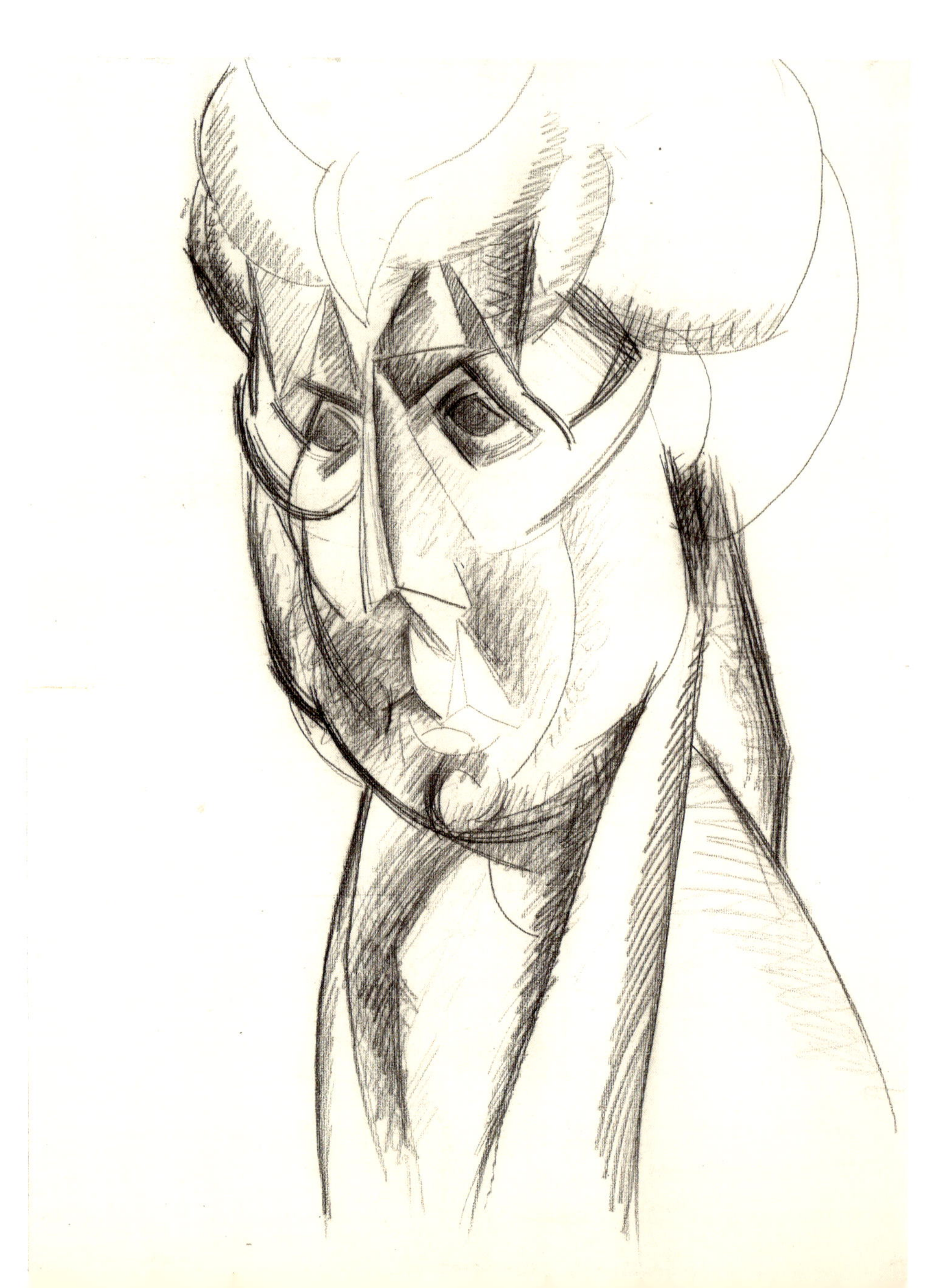

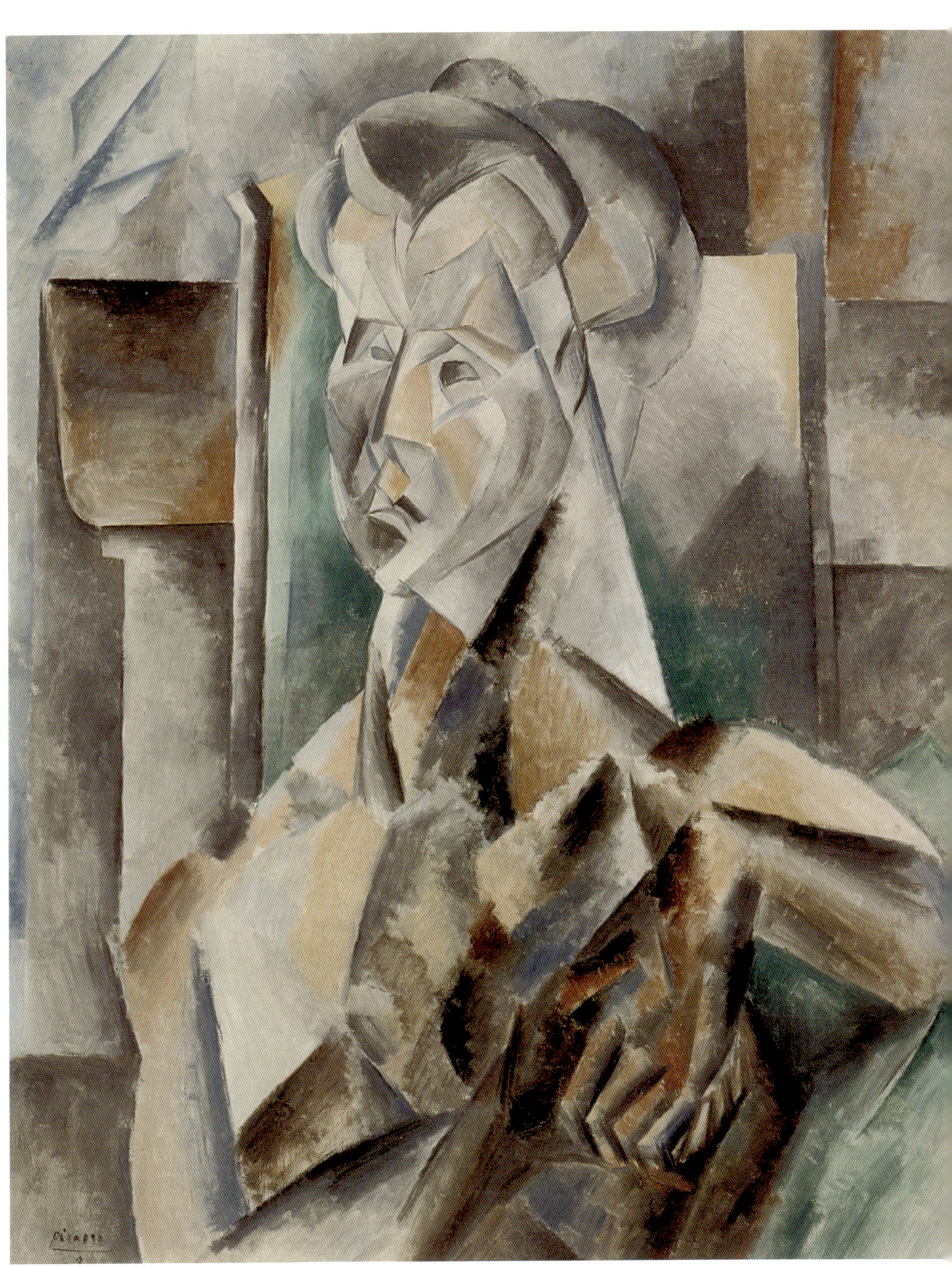

Jeffrey Weiss

Valerie J. Fletcher

Kathryn A. Tuma

National Gallery of Art, Washington

Princeton University Press, Princeton and Oxford

Picasso

The Cubist Portraits of Fernande Olivier

The exhibition was organized by the National Gallery of Art, Washington

---

National Gallery of Art
1 October 2003–18 January 2004

Nasher Sculpture Center, Dallas
15 February–9 May 2004

The exhibition is supported by an indemnity from the Federal Council on the Arts and the Humanities, Washington, DC.

Produced by the Publishing Office, National Gallery of Art, Washington
www.nga.gov

Editor in Chief, Judy Metro
Edited by Ulrike Mills
Designed by Margaret Bauer

Typeset in Sabon and Interstate. Printed by Cantz, Germany, on Scheufelen Phoenix Motion Xantur, 150 gsm.

Cover illustrations

Front: The studio at Horta de Ebro, summer 1909, original photographic print, Private collection (cat. 57)

Back: *Woman with Pears* (detail), Horta de Ebro, summer 1909, The Museum of Modern Art, New York, Florene May Schoenborn Bequest, 1996 (cat. 35)

Endsheets: *Nude in an Armchair* (detail), Horta de Ebro, summer 1909, Private collection (cat. 45)

Library of Congress
Cataloging-in-Publication Data

Weiss, Jeffrey S.
Picasso : the cubist portraits of Fernande Olivier / Jeffrey Weiss, Valerie J. Fletcher, Kathryn A. Tuma.
p. cm.
Catalog of an exhibition at the National Gallery of Art, Wash., D.C., Oct. 1, 2003–Jan. 18, 2004 and at the Nasher Sculpture Center, Feb. 15–May 9, 2004. Includes bibliographical references.

ISBN 0-89468-308-X
(softcover: alk. paper)
ISBN 0-691-11741-1
(trade hardcover: alk. paper)

1. Picasso, Pablo, 1881–1973—Exhibitions.
2. Picasso, Pablo, 1881–1973—Criticism and interpretation.
3. Olivier, Fernande—Portraits—Exhibitions.
4. Cubism—France—Exhibitions.
I. Title: Cubist portraits of Fernande Olivier. II. Fletcher, Valerie J. III. Tuma, Kathryn A. IV. Picasso, Pablo, 1881–1973. V. National Gallery of Art (U.S.) VI. Nasher Sculpture Center. VII. Title.

N6853.P5A4 2003 759.6—DC21
2003011885

Copublished in hardcover in 2003 by Princeton University Press

Princeton University Press
41 William Street
Princeton, New Jersey 08540
www.pupress.princeton.edu

In the United Kingdom:
Princeton University Press
3 Market Place
Woodstock, Oxfordshire
OX20 1SY

10 9 8 7 6 5 4 3 2 1

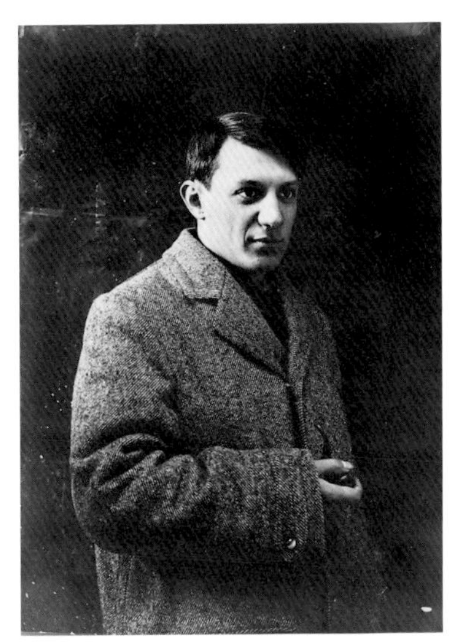

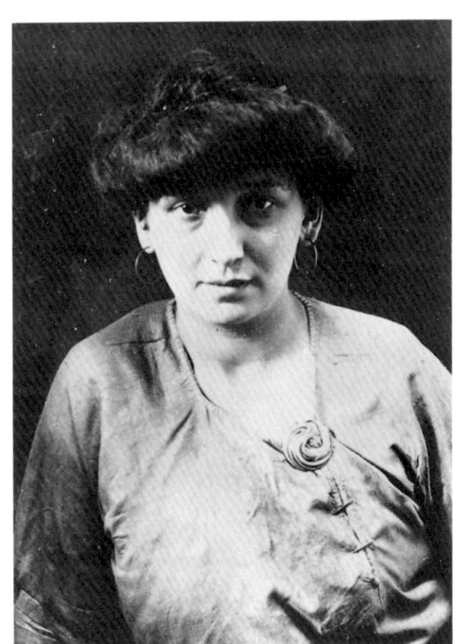

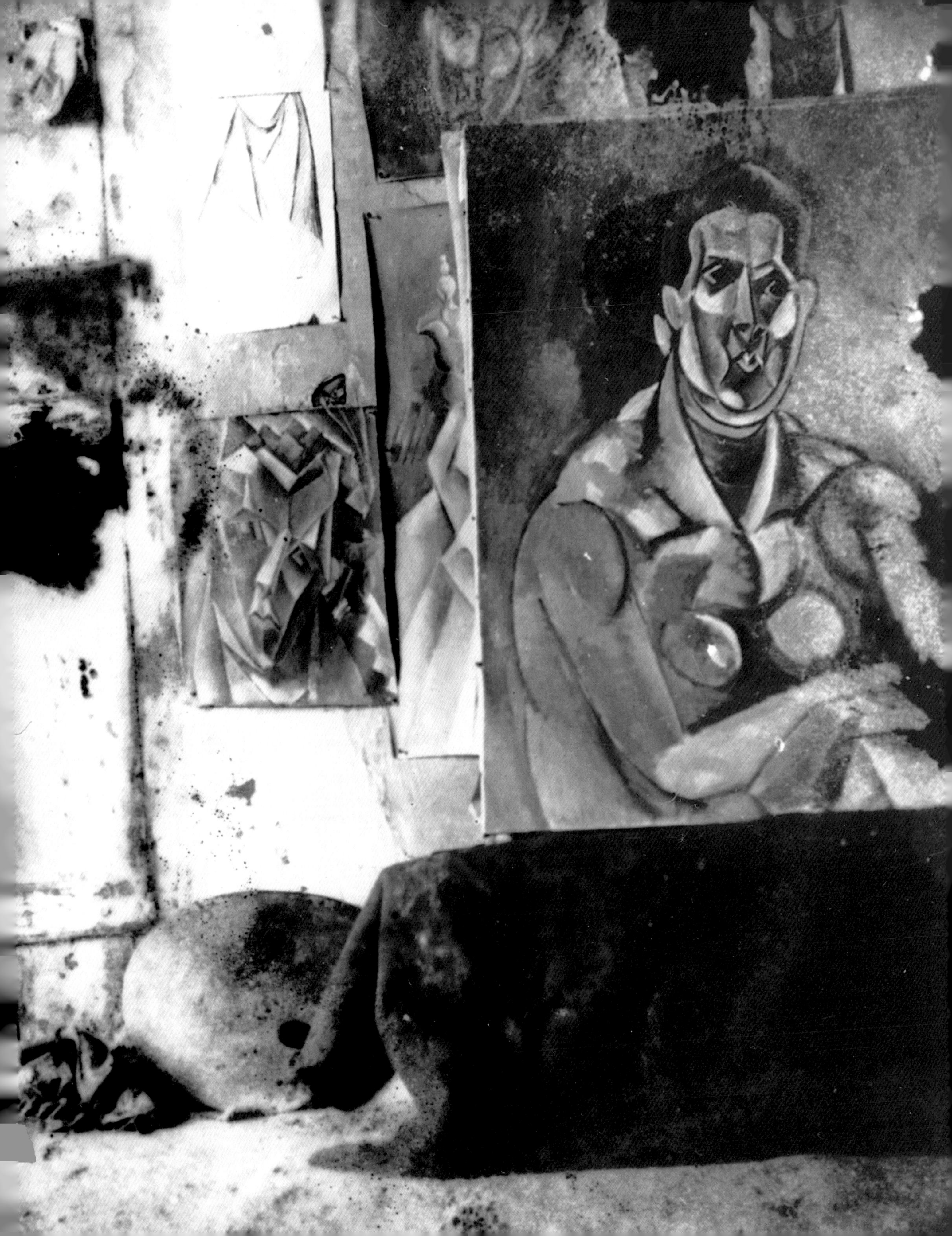

Contents

This exhibition was motivated by the acquisition of an early cast of Picasso's sculpture *Head of a Woman (Fernande)*, which entered the collection of the National Gallery of Art in 2002. The result is a project that honors an important work: in this setting, it becomes both a centerpiece and an object of serious study. In bringing scholarly expertise to bear on the way in which we represent works in our collection, an exhibition such as this one allows us to reach both a broad public and an audience of specialists and scholars in the field. It is this ambition that, we feel, serves the work, addressing it in ways that reflect its historical significance and its richness of meaning.

Picasso's career is, of course, vast and complex, and it has been the subject of innumerable exhibitions and books. Showing a small part of his oeuvre in unusual depth will, we hope, cast new light on one narrow but meaningful aspect of the artist's work. In an age when exhibitions are increasing in frequency and consequently place increasing demands on lenders, we have been fortunate to win the support of numerous collectors and institutions, each of whom recognized that the success of a project such as this would depend on our ability to comprehensively assemble these works. The lenders all deserve our profound gratitude for parting with so many precious objects, making it possible to show them together for the first time. We are especially pleased to be able to acknowledge the artist's heirs and the Musée Picasso in Paris, the repository for many works that the artist kept throughout his life. To them and to the other museums and private collectors who have supported our efforts, we are enormously indebted. We are delighted that a select version of this exhibition will travel to the Nasher Sculpture Center in Dallas. The Nasher plaster *Head of a Woman (Fernande)* is an essential work in the show, and the Nasher Center is therefore a fitting venue for this project. Thanks go to Ray Nasher and to Steve Nash, director of the Center, for their close collaboration. I am also eager to extend special recognition to Mitchell Rales, whose generosity helped make possible the acquisition of *Head of a Woman (Fernande)*, which we celebrate on this occasion.

Earl A. Powell III
Director, National Gallery of Art

Lenders to the Exhibition

Albertina, Vienna
The Art Institute of Chicago
Centre Georges Pompidou, Paris, Musée national d'art moderne / Centre de création industrielle
Galerie Jan Krugier, Ditesheim & Cie, Geneva
Gemeentemuseum Den Haag, The Hague
Joanne and Roberto de Guardiola
Jan and Marie-Anne Krugier-Poniatowski
Kunstsammlung Nordrhein-Westfalen, Düsseldorf
Latner Family Collection, Toronto
B.G.G. Merivale-Austin Esq.
Musée Picasso, Paris
Museo Nacional Centro de Arte Reina Sofía, Madrid
Museum Ludwig, Cologne
The Museum of Modern Art, New York
Narodni muzej, Belgrade
Raymond and Patsy Nasher Collection, Dallas, Texas
National Gallery of Art
Nichido Museum, Kasama
Marina Picasso
Private collection courtesy Galerie Gmurzynska, Cologne
Private collection Germany, courtesy Galerie Haas, Zurich
Private collections
Städelscher Museums-Verein e.V., Frankfurt am Main
The State Hermitage Museum, Saint Petersburg
Van Abbemuseum, Eindhoven
Tate

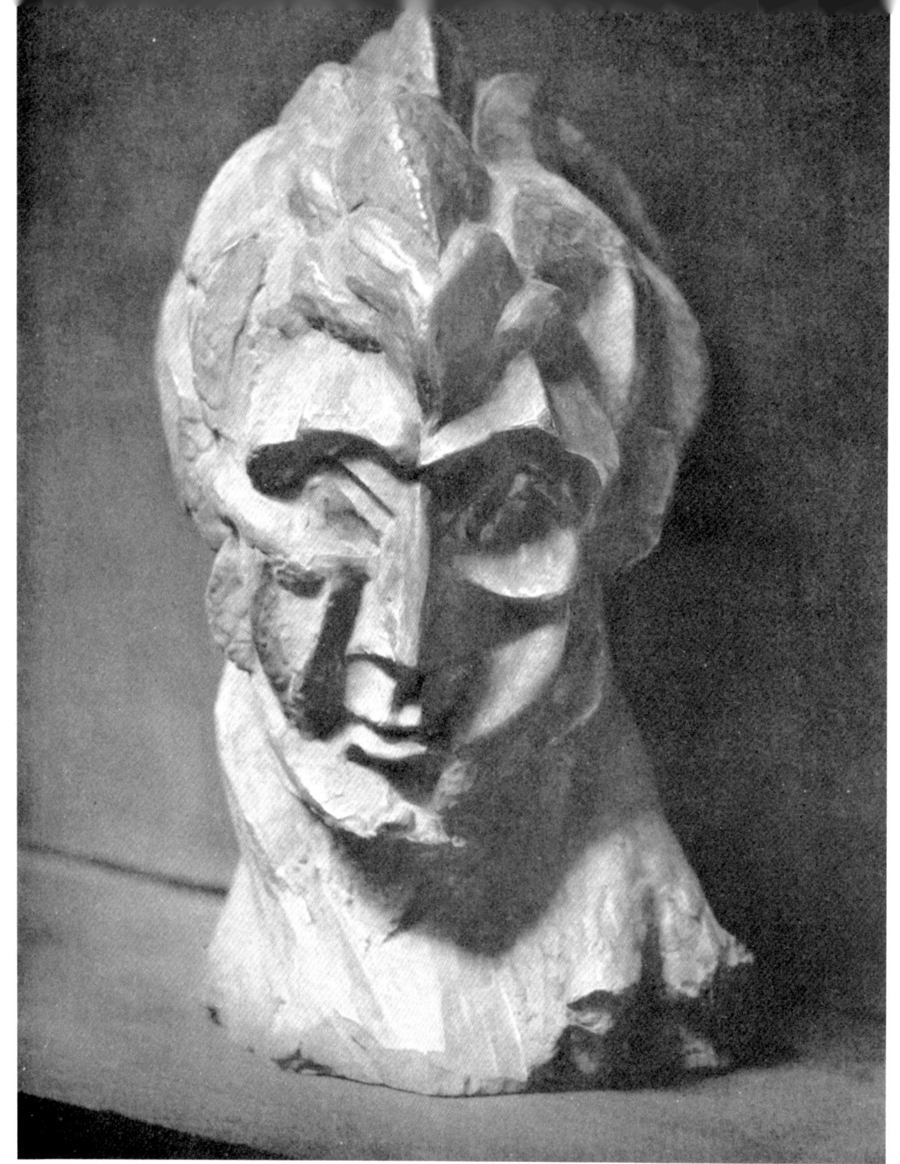

Preface

To say that this exhibition is devoted to process is to make a claim not only for its content, but also for the degree to which the methodology of the project—its own process—represents a form of interpretation. While it may not be possible to examine Picasso's Fernande portrait series as if there were no such thing as cubism, it is surely useful to attempt to engage these works in a way that defamiliarizes them, thereby constellating elements or qualities that may have managed to escape the definitions of cubism we have come to take for granted. This is achieved, somewhat ironically, by assembling the series in as near a complete form as the known whereabouts and availability of the objects have permitted. A handful of these objects have been repeatedly examined by historians of cubism. They have, however, only rarely and inconclusively been identified as belonging to a larger body of closely related works.

The narrative of the exhibition, which is intended to be a primarily formal one, is based on the premise that the character of Picasso's art during this period is, at times, embedded less in individual paintings, drawings, or sculptures—and least of all in isolated masterpieces—than in their nature as constituents of the group as a whole. In this regard, the Fernande series is allowed to define itself; no comparable attention is devoted by Picasso to a single landscape or still-life subject during the prewar period. Suspending the selective approach that is generally applied in histories of Picasso's cubism in favor of an inclusive one further reflects the conviction that certain essential abstract principles of the oeuvre can be accounted for only by observing the individual works in their fullest expression as multiple permutations of a single idea—a process of dilation rather than of progress or advance. This single idea is a formal problem that internalizes an associative one. Many works in the Fernande series are often loosely identified as "portraits" of Fernande Olivier, but they are rarely described as being psychologically charged. It is one ambition of the catalogue (as it complements the exhibition) to reconcile abstract formal principles with the striking affect and rare gravitas that saturate Picasso's treatment of this subject. The character of the actual sitter—and of her relationship to Picasso—has some bearing on the way in which she is portrayed by the artist in 1909. But the power of these images exceeds the contents of biography. In contrast to their sheer strangeness as convulsive reformulations of human physiognomy, the works demonstrate an apposite relationship to inherited, centuries-old iconographical conventions, such as those relating to the portrayal of melancholy. Affect is grounded in this relationship, which might finally be said to show Picasso placing experimental principles of form in the service of allegory.

Many colleagues have contributed to the preparation of this exhibition and its catalogue. For their expertise, resourcefulness, patience, and good will, we warmly thank the following: Nicholas Acquavella, Chris Adams, Stephanie D'Alessandro, Jean-Louis Andral, Carment Fernández Aparicio, Eva Avloniti, Anne Baldassari, Andrea Begel, Guy Bennett, Olivier Berggruen, Christiane Berndes, Ernst Beyeler, Marianne Biville, Hubert Boisselier, Stacy Bomento, Tanja Bosnjak, Antonella Bragaglia, Gilberte Brassaï, Marta Braun, Jeff Burch, Jacklyn Burns, Margaret Burri, Verónica Castillo, Linda Claremon, Ralph Colin Jr., Ina Conzen, Harry Cooper, Rachel Crognale, Pierre Daix, Barbara Dossi, Dominique Dupuis-Labbé, Bernd Dütting, John Elderfield, Dietmar Elger, Jonieke van Es, Alfred Fischer, Sabine Fopin, Larry Gagosian, Pamela Hatchfield, Mallory Hathaway, Jodi Hauptman, Hélène Klein, Laurie Klein, Anders Kold, Nancy Kuhl, Elizabeth Kujawski, Diana Kunkel, Leonard Lauder, Brigitte Léal, Laurent LeBon, Serge Lemoine, Pierre Levai, Jeremy Lewison, Sarah Linford, Kristin Makholm, Daniel Malingue, Duncan MacGuigan, Suzanne McCullagh, Charles Moffett, Pia Müller-Tamm, David Nash, Marta Gonzalez Orbegozo, Suzanne Pagé, Ivan Phillips, Joelle Pijaudier-Cabot, Laura Polson, John Richardson, Jennifer Ritchie, Cora Rosevear, Daniel Schulman, Sabine Schulze, Werner Spies, Margaret Stuffman, John Tancock, Kirk Varnedoe, Junko Watanabe, Ingeborg Weber, Hope Winter, and Wolfgang Wittrock. Emily Braun, Pepe Karmel, Marilyn McCully, and Michael Raeburn have lent special expertise and logistical support at various stages of the project. Mathias Rastorfer deserves particular credit for his devoted persistence in locating several works.

Valerie Fletcher, who has written the technical essay on the sculpture *Head of a Woman (Fernande)* in this catalogue and has been researching the *Head* for many years, has been a generous source of information and guidance in ways that contributed broadly to the exhibition. Her essay is the first serious treatment of its kind. In it, many vexing questions concerning the technical development of the *Head* are addressed with new expertise. Conversations with Kathryn Tuma contributed deeply to my own interpretation of the material. I am indebted to her for producing, in her essay, that rare thing: a wholly original treatment of an established topic in Picasso studies, and one that lies at the heart of the Fernande series—the artist's *cézannisme*.

At the National Gallery, I would like to thank director Earl A. Powell III and deputy director Alan Shestack for their continued support. Shelley Sturman, head of object conservation, was instrumental in our acquisition of *Head of a*

Woman (Fernande). Jay Krueger, senior conservator of modern paintings, provided indispensable counsel. Jennifer Cipriano, Alicia Thomas, and Jennifer Overton, working with Dodge Thompson, head of the department of exhibitions, managed the myriad organizational details relating to the budget, the indemnity, and the complex processing of loans. Donna Kirk and Jame Anderson, working with Gordon Anson and Mark Leithauser, head of the department of installation and design, coordinated the plans for our installation of the exhibition. Michelle Fondas and Melissa Stegeman were the expert registrars. In the library, Ted Dalziel and Tom McGill enabled us to assemble crucial research materials.

In the publishing office, Ulrike Mills, working with editor in chief Judy Metro, was a sympathetic and patient editor. Margaret Bauer developed and produced the design of the book with, as always, gratifying sensitivity to the material and original, precise style. Sara Sanders-Buell and Ira Bartfield were instrumental in assembling the photographic material for this catalogue.

In my own department of modern and contemporary art, Anna Lakovitch was a tireless assistant on the project; she was preceded by Kerry Roeder, for whose contribution I am also grateful. Lindsay Macdonald also provided valuable research. Jessica Stewart, research associate, devoted ingenuity, resourcefulness, good judgment, and unflagging attention to every aspect of the exhibition and the catalogue; her contribution to the project from beginning to end has been essential. Her careful chronology in this catalogue also contributes a useful biographical account of Picasso and Fernande in 1909.

Jeffrey Weiss
Curator, Modern and Contemporary Art,
National Gallery of Art

Fleeting and Fixed: Picasso's Fernandes

Jeffrey Weiss

When we invented cubism we had no intention whatever of inventing cubism. PICASSO

In 1911 Picasso began inscribing his paintings. These inscriptions took the form of short words or word fragments extracted from ready-made sources—typography from the masthead of a newspaper, for example, or stenciled lettering from the window of a café. Among the earliest inscriptions is the complete phrase *ma jolie,* an endearment that was probably lifted from the refrain of a popular song (fig. 1). It is said to have been used here to address the artist's own lover (soon to be referred to in other pictures as "*jolie* Eva"); she, in turn, is presumed to be the subject of the painting so inscribed.[1] This is what we infer, and while the motivation of the word (as a device) in Picasso's painting has been much debated, what motivates our inference in this case is that these particular words—*ma jolie*—label a painting that evokes, however obscurely, the image of a seated figure. Picasso's inscriptions from this period possess various meanings and motivations, but *ma jolie* serves a distinct function: it serves to name.

1. The identification of the phrase *ma jolie* originated with Gertrude Stein. See Gertrude Stein, *The Autobiography of Alice B. Toklas* (London, 1933), 122.

"Words present to us a little picture of things," wrote Marcel Proust, "clear and familiar, like the pictures hung on the walls of schoolrooms.... But names present to us—of persons, and of towns which they accustom us to regard as individual, as unique, like persons—a confused picture...." In what amounts to a theory of naming from the final chapter of his book *Du côté de chez Swann* (1913), Proust characterizes the "place name," in particular, as a kind of cue—the marker for an object not of memory, but of longing and imagination. For young Marcel, Proust's protagonist, it is the name alone—the very act of pronouncing the name—that provokes the image of an unknown place, an impression or exotic "simulacrum," as he puts it, that had been constructed from books and hearsay rather than firsthand experience: Giotto's Florence, Stendhal's Parma, or the Norman town of Balbec, with Gothic architecture described to him by Swann and "cliffs of Death" pounded by turbulent seas. "I thought of names," Marcel explains, "not as an inaccessible ideal but as a real and enveloping atmosphere into which I was about to plunge, the life not yet lived...." The power of the name becomes less abstractly clear (even as it approaches the realm of the "inaccessible ideal") when Marcel turns from place to person—specifically, to the person of Gilberte, Swann's daughter, with whom Marcel would fall in love. Marcel recalls encountering Gilberte for the first time and overhearing a friend utter her name:

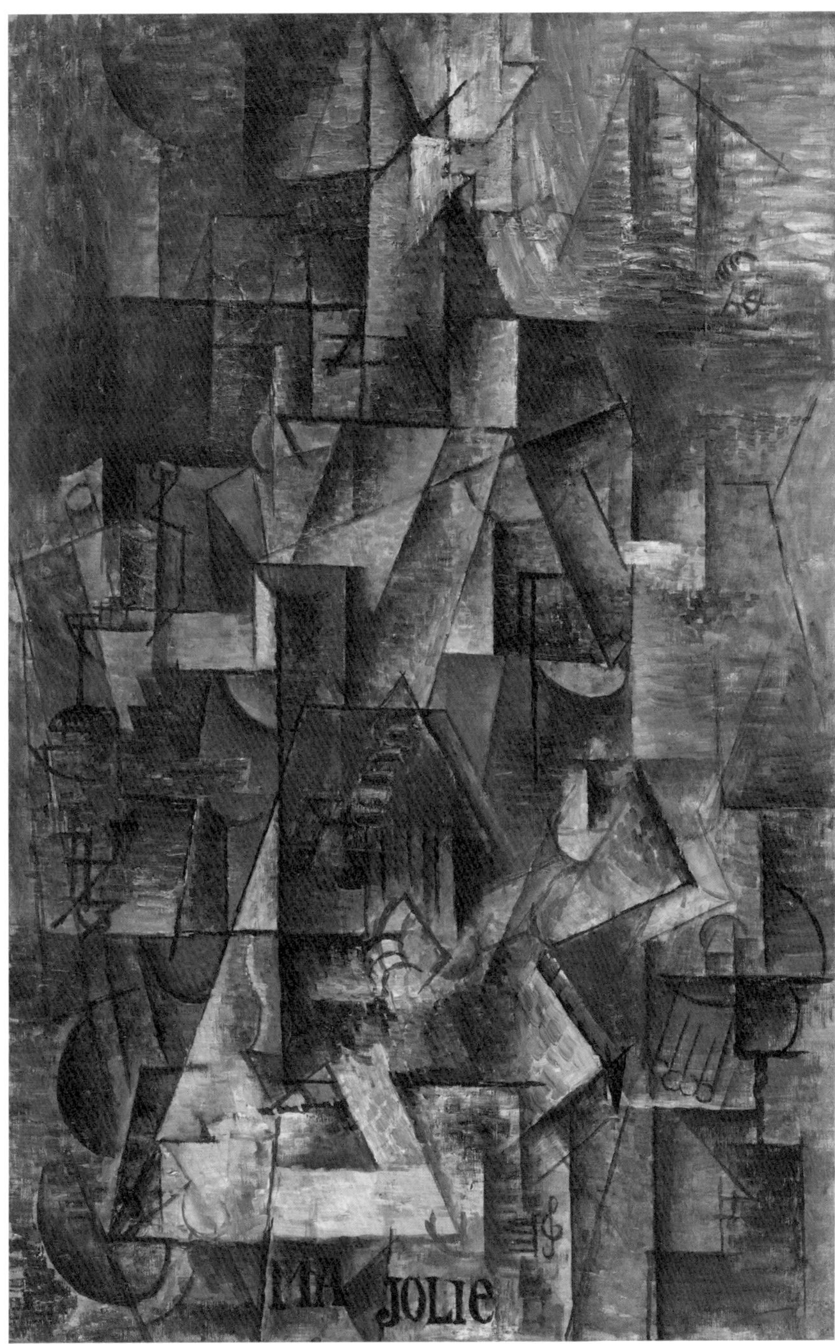

1

Pablo Picasso, *"Ma Jolie" (Woman with a Zither or Guitar)*, Paris, winter 1911–1912, oil on canvas, The Museum of Modern Art, New York, Acquired through the Lillie P. Bliss Bequest

The name Gilberte passed close by me, evoking all the more forcefully the girl whom it labeled in that it did not merely refer to her, as one speaks of someone in his absence, but was directly addressed to her; it passed thus close by me, in action so to speak, with a force that increased with the curve of its trajectory and the proximity of its target—carrying in its wake, I could feel, the knowledge, the impressions concerning her to whom it was addressed that belonged not to me but to the friend who called it out....

For the "enforced simplicity" of the image conjured by the place name (which could "hold" only two or three attributes of the unvisited place), Proust's Marcel substitutes a rapturous imagining instigated by the suddenly disclosed name of an object of longing, present but as yet unknown.[2]

The inscribed painting, "*Ma Jolie,*" possesses two registers—visual and lexical—but the visual one, the painted image, is difficult to grasp. Fragments of shadow and illumination as well as lines delineate the outer reaches of form: in place of likeness, there is only the vague appearance of a body occupying pictorial space, dispersed and unknowable. The words *ma jolie* were clearly intended to complement the image, but the concrete flatness of the inscription manages to throw the image's elusiveness—like its shadowy apparition of shallow depth—into striking relief. As a label, *ma jolie* identifies not just the figure represented by the painting but the painting itself. By 1911 Picasso's process had resulted in the dissolution of the object. If intense scrutiny of both the world and the mechanics of picture-making had brought him beyond the brink of likeness, then we can rightly ask whether the name *ma jolie* signifies absence rather than presence—whether, on some level, it figures loss. Years later, in the third volume of his great work, *A la recherche du temps perdu,* Proust had words for this, too: "a person scattered in space and time," he wrote, speaking more of jealousy now than of newly awakened desire (of Albertine, not Gilberte), "is no longer a woman but a series of events on which we can throw no light, a series of insoluble problems...."[3]

. . .

In 1909 Picasso created a group of works devoted to a single subject, that of his companion, Fernande Olivier. Quantifying the Fernande sequence depends on defining it—establishing to what degree Picasso is representing a particular sitter or, instead, a "type" derived from attributes identifiable with her. In other words, in order to characterize the works as "portraits," we would be required to extend our definition of the genre. The obvious paintings, those in which the subject is clearly

2. For passages cited, see Marcel Proust, *In Search of Lost Time, vol. 1: Swann's Way,* trans. C.K. Scott Moncrieff and Terence Kilmartin (New York, 1981), 416–428.

3. Marcel Proust, *In Search of Lost Time, vol. 3: The Captive,* trans. C.K. Scott Moncrieff and Terence Kilmartin (New York, 1981), 99–100. This passage is cited in Mieke Bal, *The Mottled Screen: Reading Proust Visually,* trans. Anna-Louise Milne (Stanford, Calif., 1997), 225, from whose discussion of Proust and photography I draw in this essay.

Fernande, number close to one dozen. Extrapolating from these core works to include images of women in various formats—head, bust, half-length, and full-length—that clearly possess Fernandesque attributes, the number grows, surprisingly, to some five dozen objects, all produced within an eight- to ten-month period of time. They encompass virtually every medium but printmaking: oil, gouache and watercolor, charcoal and graphite, sculpture, and photography, with which Picasso recorded certain paintings and drawings in his studio during the summer of 1909, when he and Fernande spent several months in the remote Spanish village of Horta de Ebro. We cannot say for certain whether Fernande actually "sat" for any of the works, something that obviously has an acute bearing on the larger role of the portrait genre (and the assault to which it was subjected by Picasso in 1909). Considering the restricted range of formats as well as the inclusion of all mediums, such intense devotion to repeated representations of a single "portrait" subject is exceedingly rare in his oeuvre and does not exist prior to 1909.

There are, of course, other cases in which Picasso poured himself into a single project, including two important paintings that predate the Fernande sequence: *Les Demoiselles d'Avignon,* in 1907, and *Three Women,* in 1908, both preceded by numerous drawings and painted sketches. But these examples differ from those of 1909 in several key characteristics. Above all, prior to 1909, the relationship of preparatory works to a finished product had been essentially conventional: works on paper were produced in order to develop single figures or to plan the structure of a final composition; this process culminated in a large, complex canvas with multiple figures interacting on a narrative or allegorical plane. Conversely, while some sketches and study drawings are included among the portraits of Fernande, many of these images were never realized on canvas. The rest of the Fernande sequence is composed of individual paintings and works on paper—repetitions or permutations in a formal narrative that possesses no obvious goal or final work. In many respects, therefore, the sequence is serial in nature:[4] it contains multiple "solutions" often nearly identical in form, and while they do not cohere as a programmatic whole (in the fashion of, for example, Monet's *Rouen Cathedral* paintings), they constitute a tight, self-perpetuating succession of consecutive speculations about one thing. In this regard, the Fernande group represents an unremarked prototype for later examples of seriality in Picasso's oeuvre. Indeed, it may even be possible to claim that seriality begins here. Yet, beyond the objectivity of form, seriality in 1909 can also be said to represent a quality of fixation. Series are, after all, largely repetitive (or

4. The serial nature of the Fernande portraits produced at Horta has been observed; see Pierre Daix, "Portraiture in Picasso's Primitivism and Cubism," in William Rubin, ed., *Picasso and Portraiture: Representation and Transformation* [exh. cat., The Museum of Modern Art] (New York, 1996), 276. The implications of seriality, however, remain misrepresented as methodical progress and the "evolution" of "style"; see Elizabeth Cowling, *Picasso: Style and Meaning* (New York, 2002), 211–213.

relational) rather than developmental by nature. Since systematic patterns of change are often difficult or even impossible to discern in the Fernande portraits, the body of work requires us to consider other, less conventional criteria of meaning and method. The addition of sculpture as well as photography not only intensifies the level of labor and conceptual attention Picasso devoted to this body of work but also further aggravates its lack of center.

The key works devoted to Fernande were created at Horta, a place Picasso had known from his youth. These paintings openly depict a recognizable individual, and from them we can extract specific elements or features that allow us to identify related images produced before and after the summer. Fernande often wore her hair in a distinctive coiffure that featured a coil and a topknot, although hair sometimes spills down the back, loose or in a long braid; her body type was somewhat robust, and the lower half of her face, especially around the jaw, possesses a pronounced bulge; the depression in the center of her upper lip is deep and well-defined. All these characteristics can be clearly observed in Picasso's numerous, much more voluptuous images of Fernande in 1906, especially the portraits he produced during the summer they spent together in Gósol (fig. 2), a mountain village in the Spanish Pyrenees. We rely on these elements as cues, of course, because the formal language of Picasso's work during 1909 was increasingly unsuited to the representation of likeness. It is in 1909, however, that a prominent new characteristic appears: the repeated downward-turning rotation of the head.

. . .

The entire sequence of works, which was created roughly between spring 1909 and winter 1909–1910, breaks down into a number of distinct but overlapping groups. The first appearance of the Fernande type in 1909 occurs with four heads executed in watercolor and gouache (cats. 2–5); these share masklike features, a technique of long, thin, parallel brushstrokes, sharply delineated areas of light and dark, and a certain volumetric simplicity that can be traced back through Picasso's work of the previous year. The heads can also be compared to the painting of a bust-length image (cat. 1) with which they share a relatively featureless face. Three sketches of female nudes probably also date from this phase; here the Fernande type is identifiable through the coiffure and the tilted head, and the bodies reveal a pronounced, albeit schematic definition of musculature. Five large works on paper (cats. 6–10), also dating from the spring, are executed in various combinations of watercolor,

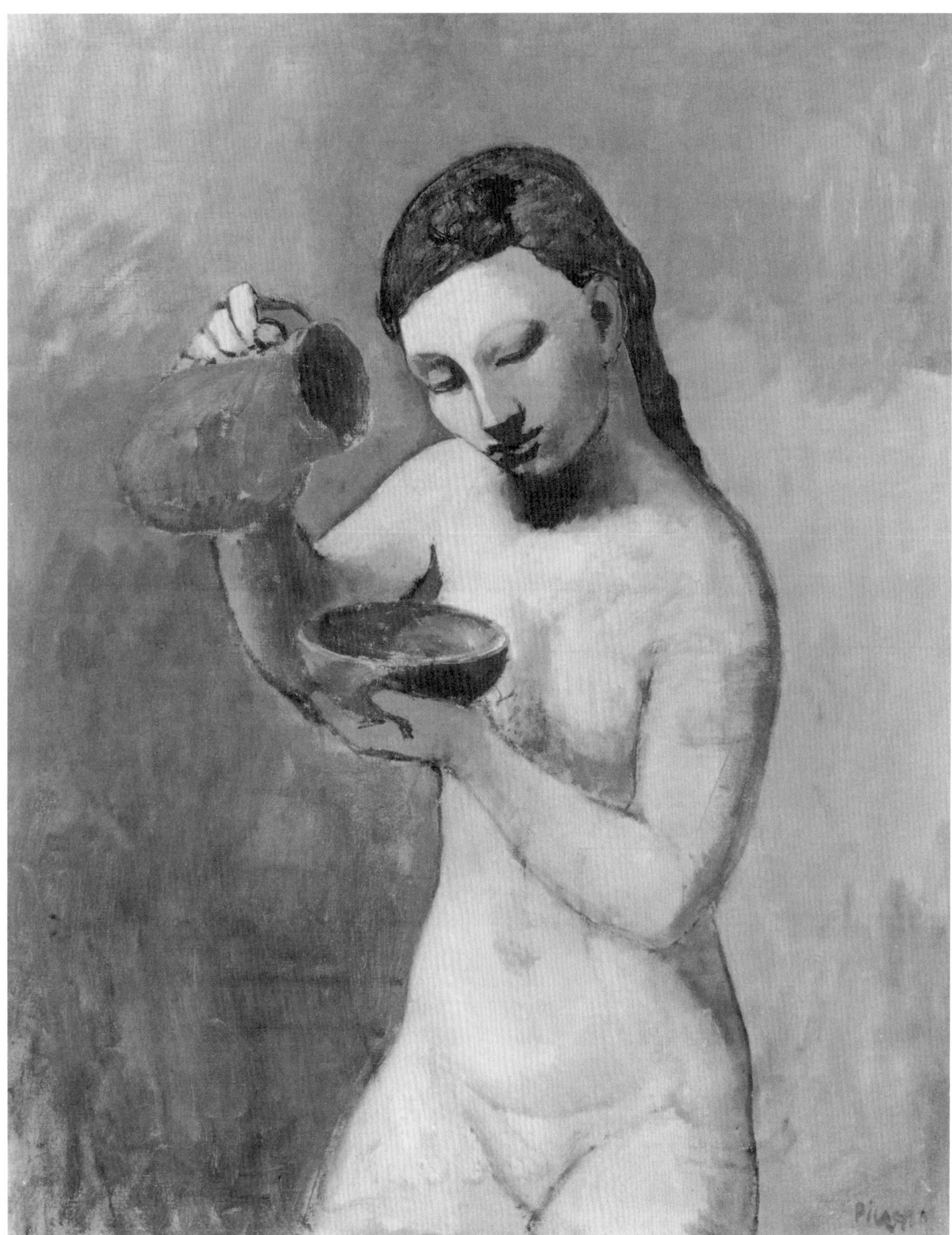

2

Pablo Picasso, *Girl with a Pitcher*, Gósol, summer 1906, oil on canvas, The Art Institute of Chicago, Gift of Mary and Leigh Block

5. Pierre Daix and Joan Rosselet, *Picasso: The Cubist Years, 1907–1916* (Boston, 1979), discussion of cats. 284, 285.

gouache, ink, and charcoal; these are virtually identical in structure, format, and dimension, showing the head turned toward the right and inclined between 10 and 15 degrees (an axis that can be traced between the upper right and lower left corners of the sheet). All the images depict cropped views of the subject's shoulders in positions that help establish the torsion of the neck; two display arms, one raised behind the head in a bather or odalisque pose, the other bent so that a supporting hand can rest beneath the chin. All these permutations can also be observed in the three smaller sketches of nudes.

Following the five heads, we can identify five sketches of seated nudes (cats. 14–18) that are also nearly identical in format. These may be related to the other nude sketches, with which they share elements of anatomy and aspects of posture. Similarities within this sequence are remarkable: both the pose and the placement of the body on the sheet are the same; differences among them are slight and primarily pertain to the degree of detail and finish in the face and torso. In four of the five drawings, even the top of the head is slightly cropped, and the hands—which rest on the thighs—fall just short of the bottom edge. These four drawings possess the same dimensions; curiously, in the fifth Picasso adds a strip of paper to the top, presumably in order to accommodate a fuller treatment of the head and face. As a type, this head—in structure, physiognomy, and tilt—is the subject of a separate drawing (cat. 19), which in turn is clearly the prototype for two paintings that appear in photographs of the Horta studio. One of these canvases shows a single head (cat. 20); the other, which depicts three heads from slightly different vantages, was subsequently cut in half and sold as two separate works (cats. 21, 22).[5] It is difficult to say whether the series of five seated-nude drawings predates the trip to Horta. What seems likely, however, is that the two (now three) paintings of heads in this manner—which trace back to the seated nudes—were the first Fernande portraits Picasso produced there.

The eight paintings from Horta that constitute the heart of the Fernande portrait sequence—and are featured as such in the studio photographs—can be separated into two groups. Each represents Fernande in a well-calibrated progression of distances, from half-length to close-cropped head or bust. The first group incorporates three works (cats. 27–29) distinguished by a relatively fleshy treatment of the face, which appears somewhat bloated and shows a double chin (Fernande was apparently quite ill at Horta, and that fact might be reflected here). In the largest canvas, Fernande is shown with folded arms; the rounded anatomy in this painting is very close in treatment to the sequence of five drawings of seated female nudes. Two precise, stiffly hieratic drawings (cats. 32, 33)—a frontal image of the face and a bust-length portrait—appear to be transitional: the swelling delineation of muscles in the shoulder and chest belongs to the first group, yet we observe that the eyes, which had been almond-shaped, are squared off, a characteristic (tracing back to images from the spring) that Picasso will now repeat in subsequent works. In the frontal drawing, the bilateral division of the forehead has become faceted and hard. The second group of paintings from Horta consists of five canvases (cats. 35, 36, 38, 39, 45), one of which has been destroyed in a fire. These images trade the softer anatomy of the preceding type for a construction that is articulated by blade-like edges and angular, interlocking forms. Some of the works oppose an illuminated figure against a dark ground (which is largely the case in the preceding group), while others are more evenly lit throughout, strengthening the impression of a shallower pictorial space. Picasso reactivates the motif of the inclined head that he had temporarily abandoned in the first group, in which Fernande's posture is erect. Between the first and second groups, Fernande's head is slightly turned in opposing directions—to the right in the first, left in the second. While the works in the first group are all interiors, three paintings from the second include landscape elements. The second group is accompanied by three known drawings (cats. 34, 37, 44), including structural sketches of the neck and upper body. These sketches bear features that are shared throughout the group as a whole, although each can probably be assigned to specific paintings, for which they would have served as studies. Some of them appear in the photographs, where they are shown pinned to the studio wall. The massive, bifurcated neck is a distinguishing element in Picasso's representation of Fernande at Horta; he had begun to develop this feature with the sequence of nude sketches, but the neck reaches imposing girth during the summer.

Various images from the summer depart from the core works. One painting (cat. 31), which probably falls between the two groups discussed above, shows Fernande seated in a stocky chair. Both the painting and the chair appear together in one of the Horta studio photographs (cat. 56) (in which the leftmost edge of this painting can be glimpsed jutting out from behind another Fernande canvas); the posture is erect, and the hair is worn in a long braid. This facial type, an exaggeration of physiognomic torque from the Chicago portrait (cat. 28), also appears in a large, related drawing (cat. 30). Much less idiosyncratic are two paintings of a seated female nude (cats. 47, 48), for which there is a related sketch (cat. 46); despite a

6. See John Richardson with Marilyn McCully, *A Life of Picasso, 1907–1917*, 2 vols. (New York, 1996), 2:139.

7. For a complete technical account of *Head of a Woman (Fernande)*, see the essay by Valerie Fletcher in this volume.

somewhat ambiguous sitting or standing pose, the figure, on closer inspection, is clearly seated in an armchair. These works, one of which is also visible in a Horta studio shot (cat. 54), possess a greater degree of allover faceting than the other paintings. They are, however, directly related to *Nude in an Armchair* (cat. 45), with which they share a number of elements: the pose, the structure of the shoulder muscles, the form of the chair itself, and the folds of the mantle that frames the figure. These traits allow us to identify the works as images of Fernande. One painting known as *Head of a Woman in a Mantilla* (cat. 43), also visible in multiple studio photographs (cats. 51–55), resembles the seated nudes in its treatment of faceted planes, which have here attained a state of greater geometric definition. This work appears to be accompanied by three sketches, quasi-architectonic studies for isolated facial features such as the nose and mouth (cats. 40–42). A lost painting of a standing nude (cat. 50), seen from the back with her arms raised, and three related sketches, one drawn on two sheets (cat. 49), appear in studio photographs (cats. 58, 51); here, the identification with Fernande is admittedly tentative.

Picasso's eight studio photographs from Horta (cats. 51–58) record various works he had produced there, including a number of paintings and sketches from the Fernande series. In some of these, the same works are seen differently juxtaposed. Since each of the photographs reproduces paintings that appear to date from both the beginning and end of the summer, it is clear that they were taken—probably in one day—toward the close of the season. The photographs were not, therefore, intended to account for "progress" so much as to compare permutations of a single motif or (in images including landscape and still-life paintings) applications of the Horta "style" to various subjects.

Following their return to Paris at the end of the summer, Picasso and Fernande moved from the Bateau Lavoir studio to an apartment on the Boulevard de Clichy. It was probably sometime in September 1909 that Picasso produced the original version of his sculpture, now known as *Head of a Woman (Fernande)*. This was executed in clay, apparently in the studio of the sculptor Manolo (Manuel Hugué), a close friend.[6] The piece would first be cast in bronze in 1910 (cat. 66). Two plaster versions (cats. 64, 65) were created specifically in preparation for the bronze edition: one would have been a "master" and the other a "working model." They were fabricated from the 1909 clay original, which was destroyed in the process.[7]

One image seems to correspond directly to Picasso's work on the original *Head*. This drawing in watercolor (cat. 63) is particularly close in its treatment of

8. See Roland Penrose, *The Sculpture of Picasso* [exh. cat., The Museum of Modern Art] (New York, 1967), 19.

Fernande's coiffure, which is one of the most striking aspects of the sculpture. The arcing lines in this image are now assumed to reflect Picasso's later remark to Roland Penrose concerning his ambition, in 1909, to execute a version of the sculpted *Head* using wire elements; the result would have been to open the solid mass, which means that the wires—and the lines in the present drawing—can be interpreted as the edges of circular planes. ("I thought that the curves you see on the surface should continue into the interior," Picasso is quoted as saying.[8]) The effect is that of a mass being sequentially un-leaved. Four standing nudes (cats. 59–62), all works on paper, can be grouped together through their near-identical pose: a figure in contrapposto leaning for balance on one folded arm (the nudes also share a strongly elongated left arm and distorted hand). One of the figures is a variant, with the head lowered and a hand raised to the chin. These drawings can, in turn, be linked to the Fernande portraits through the obvious resemblance of the head and face in the largest sheet (cat. 62) to portrait heads from the fall, including the sculpture.

One imposing bust-length painting of Fernande (cat. 70) was probably produced during the fall, shortly after the *Head*. Here Picasso returns his subject to an erect posture, now including folded arms and powerful, clasped hands. Two large, highly finished drawings (cats. 68, 69) are clearly studies for this painting. Indeed, the head and neck in the painting, which is sharp in its definition of line and edge, are virtually transcribed from what must be the second of these two sheets (the Albertina drawing); as such, they are wholly at odds with the softer representation of the shoulders and bust, which have been executed with a much broader application of the brush. Picasso's approach to the structure of the face and hair show that, in this group of three works, the sculpture had now become an explicit model. In particular, several features distinguish all these works, including *Head of a Woman,* from the portraits at Horta: the crescentlike clump of hair above the forehead, the projecting lower orbital ridge, the rounded tendons of the neck, the rounded jaw, and the ball-like tip of the chin. In the drawings, bold chiaroscuro clearly implies that the image was produced from the direct observation of a sharply illuminated object. A third charcoal drawing (cat. 67) can also be said to belong to this sequence of works derived directly from the *Head*. Exactly matching the dimensions of the other two drawings (the watermarks show that they were executed on the same kind of paper) and their handling of shadow and light, this strong, anomalous image has sometimes been identified as a back view

9. See Daix and Rosselet 1979, cats. 306–313.

of Fernande's knotted hair. Matching certain passages to the sculpture, however, indicates instead that it probably represents a lowered head seen from the top.

One drawing from around this period shows a quasi-naturalistic image of Fernande (cat. 71); Picasso created a handful of works that stand out in this way. The drawing can be dated to the fall or winter specifically by matching the other elements in the composition—an apple and a casket—to cubist still-life paintings that obviously belong to this period of work.[9] This sketch of Fernande's face appears to be the prototype for at least one bust-length painting (cat. 72) presumed to date from late in the year. A drawing of a head leaning on a supporting hand (cat. 74) is more difficult to date; it shares the long, scalloped hair with the apple/casket drawing, while its broadly faceted and folded structure seems to correspond to paintings from the winter (cat. 73).

Three large canvases dating from late 1909 or early 1910, each representing a seated nude (cats. 75–77), clearly draw on the paintings from the summer and early fall. The first is identifiable as Fernande. Facial features in the other two images have been almost completely dissipated by a new extreme of planarity and fragmentation. These can be related to the first through format and pose, with bent arms forming a kind of broken loop. All three paintings show the familiar engineering of the muscles and tendons of the neck and, most importantly, a slightly rotated and inclined head—the last remaining vestiges of the Fernande type.

. . .

It is conventional to characterize Picasso's process during the prewar period in terms of a narrow pursuit of certain formal problems. In some respects, the nature of his painting lends itself to this approach since the works appear to develop through a series of well-defined phases. Between 1908 and 1911, Picasso established an intuitive system for addressing the representation of mass and space in a manner that manages to retain an impression of weight and depth while reconciling the metaphorical conceit of representation with the surface of the canvas, which is concretely flat. An object or figure and its environment were together recorded as a topography of planes, a dense, allover structure packed into a shallow pictorial space. The planes were illuminated from multiple directions, heightening the ambiguity according to which they were distributed—along with passages of dark shadow—across the surface of the canvas and into an illusory depth. Over time, the ratio of depicted mass to depicted space underwent a gradual inversion, as

10. In this regard, the only challenge to the conventional narrative is T. J. Clark, "Cubism and Collectivity," in *Farewell to an Idea: Episodes from a History of Modernism* (New Haven and London, 1999), 169–223.

11. The subject of Fernande is characterized this way by Pierre Daix, "Portraiture in Picasso's Primitivism and Cubism," in exh. cat. New York 1976, 278.

the planar elements came to be dispersed through an implied, a priori structure that approximates a grid. According to these terms, what occurs in 1909—in landscape and still-life painting as well as in portraits and other figures—could be qualified as a period not only of transition, but also of maximum stress, where qualities that represent the coherence of mass stand in dynamic opposition to the encroaching dissolution of mass in the medium of space. With specific reference to the Fernande sequence, however, the implementation of both sculpture and photography—which Picasso had never before applied to a single body of work—signals a peculiar intensification of activity, as if this process not only exceeded the conditions of painting but also required various mediums to address one another critically.

Methodologically, historical narratives of cubist form have long implied two things: a tacit assumption that Picasso's work demonstrates the inexorable drive toward a single goal; and selectivity, according to which key works are identified and separated from the oeuvre in order to isolate formal elements that represent progress toward the goal.[10] While these biases possess a certain logic, selective, teleological accounts leave little room for, among other elements, the eruption of activity represented by the Fernande sequence as a whole: a great deal of alternately redundant or multidirectional work produced during a compressed period of time and related to a single portrait subject—a person whose intimate proximity would, at first, seem to be virtually anathema to Picasso's formalist concerns, which little lend themselves to the traditional elements (likeness, identity, character) of portraiture. Similarly, while portraiture as a genre had long engaged Picasso and would remain a chief preoccupation of his work (in contrast to Braque, for example, who created few portraits in his career), the incessant proliferation of "Fernandes" in 1909 should caution us not to address Fernande herself as a conventional portrait subject whose coordinates for the artist were primarily biographical; multiple sequences of works each represented by similar or identical "takes" reveal instead a process of extreme formalism. The undeniable intensity of the work does derive in part from the fact that the identity of an individual is at stake (that is, she is not merely a convenient formalist vehicle),[11] and our engagement with that individual is provoked or heightened by the process of relentless iteration. Yet the artist's general disavowal of anecdotal description ensures that the role of the sitter as object remains, in some fashion, internalized.

What interpretive or organizational model would serve as an adequate substitute for a strict narrative and allow for the complex series of pursuits represented

12. This topic is a significant one in the historiography of cubist painting. For one overview, see Clark 1999, 426 n.31. In his discussion of the Fernande portraits at Horta, Clark replaces the concept of the multiple view with a procedure of interlocking forms unfolding through and filling—ultimately buckling—the rectangle of pictorial space; see page 204. The present essay takes the metaphorics of cubist space in 1909 to be inseparable from a consideration of the application of multiple mediums, including sculpture and photography.

by the Fernande portraits? Perhaps one that, while accounting for an undeniable element of progress, would also acknowledge that repetition or seriality effectively overrides the developmental scheme and establishes a taxonomy for the works by suggesting instead that they be assigned in clusters to structural or iconographic—possibly even affective—centers, each holding a related yet distinct set of motivations or concerns.

One striking element, for example, that preoccupies a specific series of Fernande portraits is the structure of the neck. As previously noted, it suddenly emerges as a consideration in the second group at Horta (cats. 35, 36, 38, 39, 45) and is the object of intense focus in a discrete number of works. Picasso treats it as a complex volume composed of flat, folded planes that describe a massive external support structure and a gaping interior; the channel from the throat to the collarbone (the notched horizontal span across the upper torso) represents a plunging distance. Distortions of scale in Picasso's work from this period are sometimes attributed to the device of the multiple view: representing more of an object than is visible from a single vantage point in order to approximate the vision of a mobile observer.[12] Yet such a device, if it can even be said to have been systematically pursued by the artist, can hardly justify every formal development of this kind over the course of two or three years. It is, in any case, an insufficient rationale for the specific—and essentially grotesque—structure Picasso has devised at Horta. That this neck was invented for a particular formal and physiological purpose is confirmed by comparing these images of Fernande to the preceding group of portraits, which show erect heads, relatively normal proportions, and a soft representation of flesh and muscle. (These works may be said to reflect Picasso's attempt to reconcile certain descriptive conventions of portraiture with other schematic elements that had come to characterize his work during the spring.) If, however, the anatomical discrepancies of the new buttresslike structure challenge the habits of cubist formal analysis, such as multiple views or the penetration of closed form, then we might say instead that they were designed to accomplish something more precise: the magnified embodiment of two actions, rotation and tilt, using means that are at once anatomically and pictorially structural. The system of planes is potentially dynamic in convincing mechanical terms that can be traced back to actual physiology, yet firmly inserted into a closed pictorial matrix of interlocking forms, thereby bringing the object or body as a rounded mass close to the dimensionality (planar, rectilinear) of the canvas. These paintings are not, of course, "about" necks, but they are centered on that element, a massive fulcrum that pictorially transposes the mechanics of the downward turn—a gesture that is used to epitomize the condition of the body in a three-dimensional world. Further, what is generally ignored is that, in the context of portraiture, the full weight of this operation is also being made to turn on a motif—the lowered head—that draws undeniable affective power from a long iconographical and allegorical tradition, one pertaining above all to the representation of melancholy.

Such paintings are surely among the most powerful yet peculiar, even eccentric, images in the history of prewar art. They can be normalized through recourse to the narrative of cubism, but their seismic emergence in the summer of 1909 can also be implemented to alter that narrative. In relation to Picasso's work from 1908 to 1911, the entire Fernande portrait sequence represents a severe imbalance of attention (in quantity, narrow range, and the rare confluence of techniques). In that context, the most extreme paintings from Horta possess a quality that had been gathering since the spring: as devices of description or likeness vanish, affect remains, like a residue of human presence—much the way the works sustain an impression of manifest weight and depth despite the growing ambiguity of projecting and receding planes. Picasso embeds the quality of affect in a complex, increasingly dispersed yet gravity-stricken density of form, and it is by invoking this embeddedness that we will best be able to characterize his achievement. Yet form in the Fernande sequence is not specific to painting and drawing—not, in fact, specific to any single medium. It belongs, instead, to the reciprocal relationship the artist established among a multiplicity of mediums, including sculpture and photography.

. . .

Observing Picasso's *Head of a Woman (Fernande)* (cat. 66) is a topological challenge. While the overall character of the work is, in certain respects, conventionally representational, its individual elements both heighten and undermine the familiar structure of the face and skull. In this regard, viewed from any direction, the sculpture presents itself as a series of acts—efforts in massing that would appear to possess a sculptural logic of their own, one extrapolated from, more than strictly descriptive of, the givens of anatomy and physiognomy.

The most eccentric element of the *Head* is what lies atop: a coiffure composed of irregular, loamy chunks of faceted form—shaped like sections carved from a solid sphere—that rise in a rhythmic, roughly symmetrical formation from the

13. Maurice Gieure, *Initiation à l'oeuvre de Picasso* (Paris, 1951), 151–155. The author mistakenly refers to the *Head* as a *Tête d'homme*, however, and dates it 1907.

sitter's brow to the apex of her skull. Fanning out in this manner around both occipital lobes, these elements expand in size and drop in number when they reach the back, growing sinuously long and thick and arranging themselves according to a simpler symmetry, out and down from a center line that is occupied by a prominent scalloped crest. In the right-facing profile view, these forms largely radiate from the ear, like spokes; in the left-facing view, they move according to a vortex pattern. From the rear, the architectonic extrusion of thickset locks exaggerates the phallic elevation of the back of the skull, which is not just held up at its base but seemingly pushed up by the supporting action of the neck, a massive trunk that was kneaded into existence. This neck, a transcription from the portraits at Horta, is a furrowed quasi-pyramidal mass that opens in front like a turned-up collar; there it frames the throat, which is contained in a deep cavity beneath the lowered chin. The configurations of hair and neck join in the back to form an integrated upward flow that heightens the motion implied by the turned head, a clockwise rotation that is slight but appears to engage every element.

Most remarkable of all, physiognomy participates in these rhythmic patterns that course through the work. Flesh and bone structure are articulated through a series of soft ridges and faceted forms that are composed of tilted planes and sharp edges, or "arrises" (*arêtes*), to borrow terminology from the author Maurice Gieure, who has produced the most acute formal analysis of the *Head*.[13] Gieure characterizes the piece as being structured architecturally, in a manner that joins the face and brow to the composition of the hair; divided by a vertical axis slightly inclined toward the right, it takes the form of a *double ogive* (pointed arch) construction. The arch becomes a motif. It can be seen to govern the shape of the face, culminating in the front of the coiffure; it is also multiplied, as Gieure observes, through smaller forms: the double-brow, the eye sockets, and the shape of the eyes themselves. Yet between the two sides, a distinct opposition occurs: in the lower face, the left and right are, respectively, defined by swelling and void; similarly, the left eye takes the form of a blank protrusion while the right eye is hollow. The left jawbone is composed of a single flange; on the right, it is thickly delineated by two deep folds.

These elements create a pronounced bilateral disjunction in the structure of the face, something that has long been obscured by the fact that *Head of a Woman* is photographed and reproduced almost exclusively in a three-quarter view from the front-left side. Photographs of the *Head* probably play a significant role in its

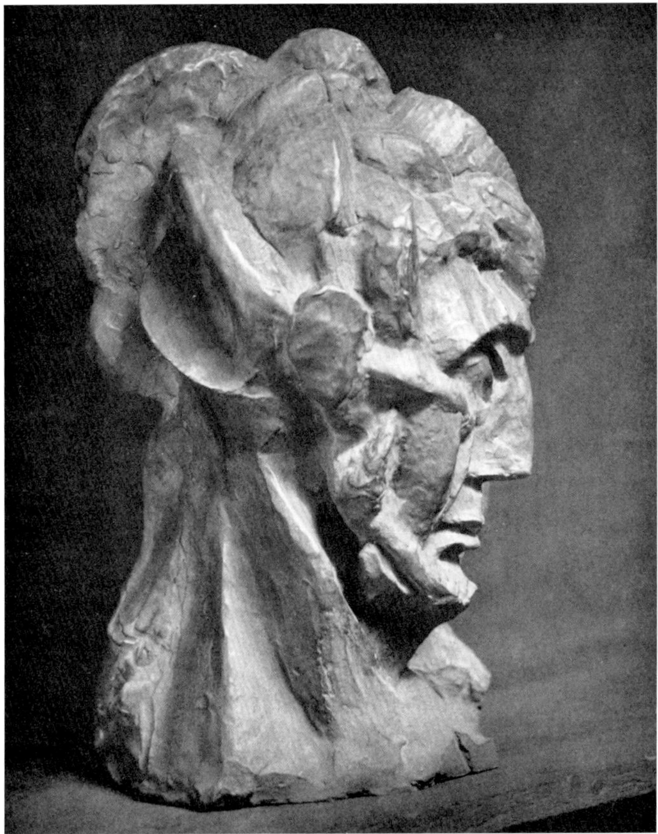

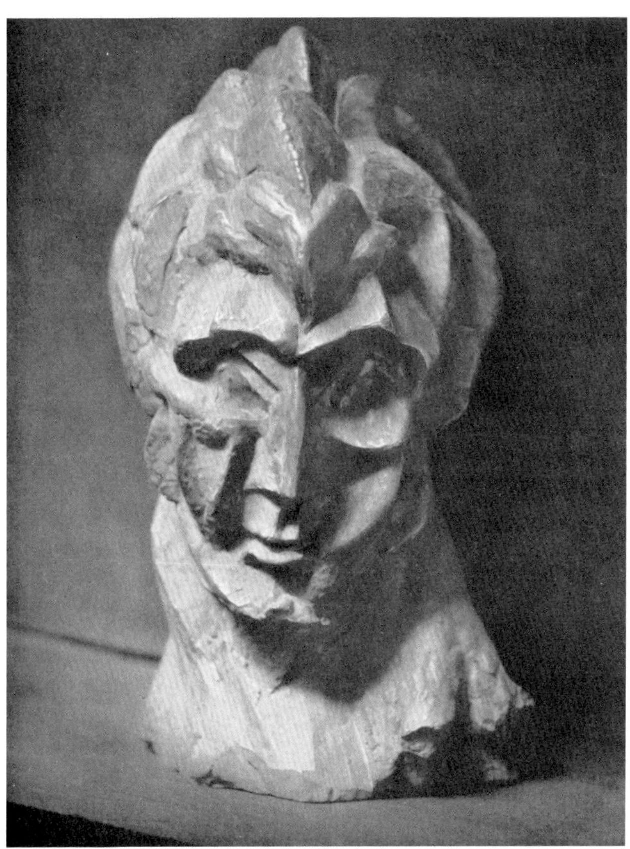

3 | 4
Alfred Stieglitz, *Picasso: Sculpture*, 1912, photographs, from *Camera Work*, special number (August 1912)

critical history. Only Alfred Stieglitz took pains to publish the work from two vantages—the front and left profile (figs. 3, 4). These remarkable photographs, reproduced in Stieglitz's periodical *Camera Work* in 1912, probably depict the bronze cast Stieglitz himself acquired in 1912, although the tonality of the images and the definition of form actually make the piece look more like a plaster than a bronze (it is highly unlikely, however, that these images were taken from one of the plaster models). More than any subsequent image of the work, these photographs represent the *Head* as an object that is strenuously unsettled in its surface and mass. After the 1930s, the most commonly used photograph has been a three-quarter view taken by Brassaï (fig. 5) (Brassaï shot the work from the front as well, but the two views were never reproduced together). Here, in utter contrast to the Stieglitz photographs, hard light evokes a flickering surface of hollows and protrusions—more abstract in its effect, yet for this reason less unsettling due to its diminished emphasis on physiognomic distortion. Both the Stieglitz and the

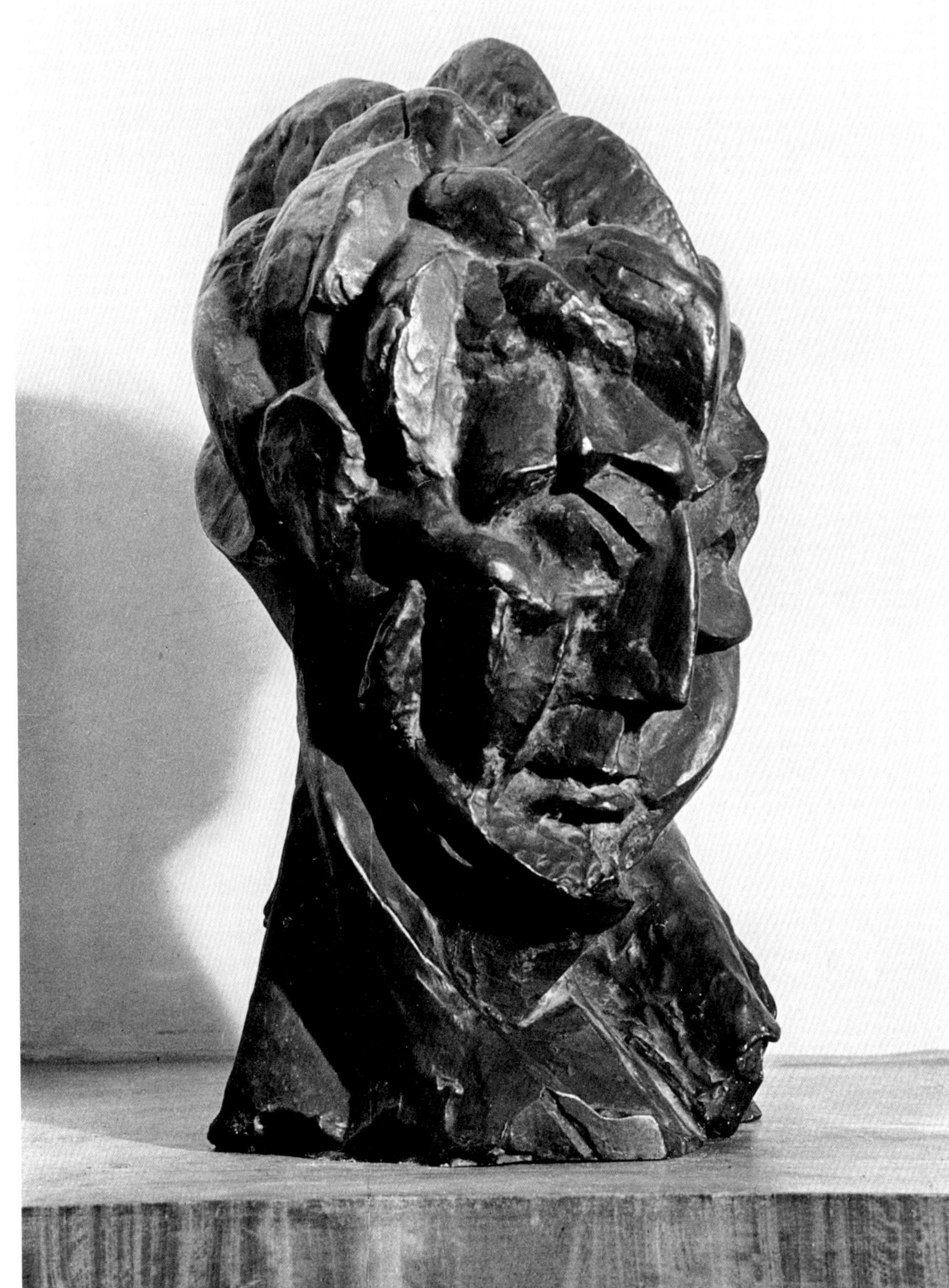

5
Brassaï, *Head of a Woman*, c. 1943, photograph, Estate Brassaï, Musée Picasso, Paris

Brassaï images are interpretations, of course, and it is the prevalence of Brassaï's photograph that has influenced our impression of the *Head* as a tempered object. In fact, the sculpture's disjunctive facial structure is best revealed by opposing frontal three-quarter vantages from the left and right: partial integrity of mass on one side and open structure on the other, with ensuing intimations of buckling or imminent collapse. The two views could almost be said to represent different individuals, an impression that is equally striking in opposing three-quarter views from the back. Seen full face, the disparity remains clear and reaches its maximum expressive pitch in the eyes, which are blindly unyielding (left) and alarmingly exposed (right).

Head of a Woman possesses a cumulative dynamic that courses around the surface and into the form. The turning and lowering of the sitter's head encourages the beholder to view the work from various points of view. This is a principle of gestural dynamism in sculpture of any period; here it is intensified by the turning of the forms themselves—the undulant neck, for example, and the plaits of hair—which maintain a ceaseless flow. Moreover, some forms literally describe the principle of rotation: in the left profile, a crescent—broken by the ear—extends from the cheekbone to the back of the skull; from the front, a raised line that begins at the base of the neck appears to coil around back and reemerge on the right side of the face. In this way, even as we are invited to circumnavigate the *Head*, single vantages are active in and of themselves, as arcs and troughs of unseen origin push their way into our line of sight. The work becomes gyratory.

How long can we discuss *Head of a Woman* without raising the topic of cubism? The *Head* represents, of course, an episode in the stylistic development of Picasso's work that is attributed to the history of cubism, evincing formal issues that belong more to painting (and drawing) than to sculpture—problems expressed in sculpture almost uniquely with the creation of the *Head*. In this context, early cubism is sometimes said to be inherently "sculptural": pictures seek to reconcile the flatness of the image with a palpable sensation of the figure as a body in space by employing reductive devices such as monochromy and planarity—the rendering of the head and body through sharply defined planes clearly illuminated in stark contrasts of light and dark. The paintings and drawings are also said to approximate sculpture's availability to the beholder as an object in ambient space. Taken together, however, the claims of the literature represent a tautological account according to which *Head of a Woman* is said by some authors to have been derived from paintings that are themselves so sculptural that they compelled the artist to pursue his subject in a sculptural medium, thereby creating an object described by others as essentially "painterly"—a faithful, even slavish, transcription of the painted works.[14]

Accordingly, *Head of a Woman* has been characterized as both a success and a failure. While it is sometimes acknowledged to be a bold, early sculptural approximation of (often vaguely described) cubist formal principles such as fragmentation or the decomposition of form, it is also understood to be compromised in this regard by its nature as an ultimately conventional, solid sculptural mass—conventional, that is, in that it falls short of the historical achievement represented by constructed sculpture beginning in 1912, when Picasso (possibly following Braque) replaced modeling and carving with lightly eliding planes of paper, cardboard, and sheet metal or wood that express mass through volume and open form. While a kind of penetrability is achieved in the *Head* through the gouging of so-called hollows or voids, this quality also demonstrates the work's adherence to solid mass—and, by extension, the inevitable limitations of traditional sculptural means. As histories of the *Head* have tended to implicate the whole history of cubism, the formalism of the piece is consequently subjected to interpretive anachronisms, a critique that concerns itself less with what the *Head* is than what it is not—in other words, with what it fails to accomplish in light of Picasso's later work. The conceptual condition of modern sculpture prior to 1912, however, offers other prospects.

. . .

The very problem of a distinction between the perceptual experience of painting and sculpture (and, by implication, the way in which such a problem impinges on works in either medium) broadly recurs in theoretical texts of the nineteenth century. The terms were established mid-century by Charles Baudelaire, in his notorious review of the Paris Salon of 1846. In this discussion, subtitled "Why Sculpture Is Boring," Baudelaire explained that sculpture is inferior to painting in that it is subject to accidents of beholding—disadvantageous points of view, unforeseen tricks of illumination, and other vagaries of setting and display. "Brutal and positive like nature, it is at the same time vague and elusive, because it presents too many faces at once." In direct contrast to painting, which is "exclusive and despotic" in being available to a single vantage, the experience of sculpture cannot be controlled in this way: "the spectator, who turns around the figure, can choose a hundred different points of view, except the correct one."[15] The legacy of such an argument can be traced

14. This conclusion occurs in some individual treatments of the work during summer and fall 1909, but is largely to be drawn from the literature as a whole. See especially Julio Gonzalez, "Picasso sculpteur," *Cahiers d'Art* 6–7 (1936), n.p.; Alfred H. Barr Jr., *Picasso: Fifty Years of His Art* [exh. cat., The Museum of Modern Art] (New York, 1946), 69; John Golding, *Cubism: A History and an Analysis, 1907–1914* (New York, 1959), 81–82; William Rubin, *Picasso in the Collection of the Museum of Modern Art* [exh. cat., The Museum of Modern Art] (New York, 1972), 61; Pierre Daix, "1909 ou l'an 1 du cubisme," and Helmut R. Leppien, catalogue entries, in Helmut R. Leppien, ed., *Der zerbrochene Kopf: Picasso zum 100. Geburtstag* [exh. cat., Hamburger Kunsthalle] (Hamburg, 1981), 25–29 and 52–60; Werner Spies with Christine Piot, *Picasso: Das Plastische Werk* (Stuttgart, 1983), 51, 55–56; Elizabeth Cowling and John Golding, *Picasso: Sculptor/Painter* [exh. cat., Tate Gallery] (London, 1994), 21.

15. Charles Baudelaire, "Pourquoi la sculpture est ennuyeuse," repr. in Baudelaire, *Curiosités esthétiques* (Paris, 1923), 187–188; author's translation.

16. Adolf Hildebrand, *The Problem of Form in Painting and Sculpture* (New York and London, 1907).

to the end of the century by way of the German sculptor Adolf Hildebrand, in his *The Problem of Form in Painting and Sculpture* (first published in German in 1893, this book appeared in English in 1907). Hildebrand maintained that viewing sculpture should be a controlled experience entailing the selection of a single, optimum vantage through which the full character of a given work would achieve maximum clarity. For Hildebrand, walking around a sculptural object and observing it from various distances results in perceptual fluctuations—multiple views and a variable grasp of the tactility of three-dimensional form—that detract from the kind of stability one achieves through a single, stable, "pictorial" impression.[16]

In the context of this problematic, what *Head of a Woman* may be said to represent is an attempt to reclaim sculpture's perceived "weakness" as the condition for an experience of instability that the artist could exploit, if not quite control—not a correction for the fallibility of sculpture, then, but an abetment of it. In observing that the act of beholding sculpture is not just subject to, but compromised by, changes in vantage and light, Baudelaire implicated figural statuary in a classical or realist mode. If, instead, a work is made to resist naturalistic coherence through formal ruptures that specifically address these vagaries of beholding, then the inherent nature of the object becomes one of dislocation. To borrow Baudelaire's own terminology, the sculpture presents "many faces at once" through a play of faces or parts of faces that conspire to disrupt the impression of a unified whole; the spectator's "hundred different points of view" are all equally incorrect since—thanks to the dynamic of waves and turns—no single one truly prevails. Terms are thereby reversed: elements that represent the elusiveness of sculpture—its inherent "inferiority"—are heightened and made to activate a changing experience of the sculptural object; this experience is now available not only by walking around the object but also by standing still. Thus *Head of a Woman* seeks to attain a critical relationship to the conventional condition of sculpture (as understood and theorized in the modernist context) by physically embedding rotation into its very mass. The intimate yet powerful torsion of the piece—the downcast turning of the head—is both a gestural cue that allegorizes aesthetic viewing as a process that occurs in actual space, and a structural principle extrapolated into the configuration of the head and face as a series of precincts and profiles that disrupt a coherent hierarchy of vantage points, thereby preventing any single view from being fully determined or ideal.

The Baudelairean legacy demonstrates that a critical vocabulary for the condition of sculpture will possess the key terms according to which the medium could be asked to transcend its own limitations. One figure brings us closer to this condition as it pertains to the period of early cubism. The work of Auguste Rodin has sometimes been cited as a stylistic source for *Head of a Woman*—that is, for the failure of the *Head* to constitute a true breakthrough for cubist sculpture.[17] Rodin's role, however, is complex. It is worth recalling that, with Rodin, modeled and cast sculpture attained a language of fragmentation, decenteredness, and convulsive figuration that profoundly transformed the sculptural body by attenuating sculpture's formal means, and that this transformation was still fully capable of inspiring a radical apprehension of sculptural form on the very eve of cubism. Specifically, two important essays about Rodin by Rainer Maria Rilke, published in 1903 and—moments before the inception of cubist painting—in 1907, serve to reorient our understanding of *Head of a Woman.*

Rilke's Rodin essays bore many implications for the sculptural "imaginary" around 1900, even as they anticipated issues relating to modernist sculptural practice well into the twentieth century.[18] Indeed, specifically with regard to *Head of a Woman,* Rilke's Rodin is uncannily apt. Two formal achievements are chiefly at stake: a "conquest" of the elements of light and space. According to Rilke, Rodin accomplished an actual dynamism (in addition to a depicted one) in his work through the abstract manipulation of light. While sculptors had employed gestural movement for centuries, Rilke wrote, "what is new is the kind of movement which light has been made to impart by means of the peculiar treatment of the surfaces, the inclines of which are so manifestly varied that light flows from them now slowly, now in a cascade, appearing now shallow and now deep, gleaming or dull." Specifically, Rodin had developed the means with which to control light, "which is no longer accidental in any of its effects." Instead, the sculpture—"the thing"—"takes possession of it and uses it as something of its own"; Rilke referred to this as an "acquisition and appropriation of light." He further claimed that Rodin had also managed to create an active relationship between sculpture and surrounding space. The artist arrived at this quality by a close observation of objects in the world, revealing "a mysterious geometry of space from which he learnt that if an object were really going to take its place in space...its contours must be arranged in the direction of certain planes inclining towards each other." The precise mechanics of this procedure, of course, remain obscure; Rilke's analysis of the object in space is an intuitive one that draws on recent developments in the language and ambitions of his own verse. "It is difficult," he confesses, "to express precisely what this

17. William Rubin in exh. cat. New York 1972, 61, "The cubist stylization to which it has been submitted does not obscure the work's direct continuity with nineteenth-century sculpture." Quoting Robert Goldwater, *What Is Modern Sculpture?* (New York, 1969), Rubin attributes the *Head* to "Rodin's art 'of the hollow and the lump,' with the lumps sharpened between increased hollows." He adds: "[The *Head*] does not constitute a break with the past comparable to that represented by the cubist painting which inspired it."

18. The phrase is from Alex Potts, who has recently given extended consideration to the historical significance of Rilke's texts on Rodin. See Potts, *The Sculptural Imagination: Figurative, Modernist, Minimalist* (New Haven and London, 2000), 77–101.

knowledge was." But he describes the dynamics of the relationship by remarking how it is put into practice: "With ever increasing decisiveness and assurance the given details are brought together in strongly marked surface-units, until finally they adjust themselves, as if under the influence of rotating forces, in a number of great planes, and we get the impression that these planes are part of the universe and could be continued into infinity."[19]

Absent a truly compelling contemporary characterization of Picasso's *Head of a Woman,* Rilke's treatment, which precedes it by two years, will certainly serve. It could be claimed, for example, that the eccentric serrated profile of the sculpture's coiffure and the hollows and protrusions of the face give purchase, by conceit at least, to surrounding space as well as absorbed and reflected light, while the "influence of rotating forces" precisely identifies an essential shaping principle at stake throughout the work's form and its spatial and temporal relationship to the beholder. Such comparisons are not merely coincidences of rhetoric. Throughout the Rodin essays, and with special attention in the essay of 1903, Rilke further identifies a unit, the "plane," which he describes as the irreducible element or "cell" of Rodin's art: "the exactly defined plane, of varying size and emphasis, from which all else must be made." This is the means by which Rodin "intensified the relationship of the atmosphere to his statue," forming the basis for the condition of the sculptural object in his work: "he made all things, plane for plane, in relationship to space...it now seemed as if space snatched them to itself."[20] This insight is significant, for the role of the plane characterizes that relationship as being simultaneously physical and optical: it is the means for creating a sculptural surface as well as evoking, through its contact with that surface, a heightened sensation—an optical impression—of something like tangible space. We recognize, in this regard, that the "plane" could equally qualify as a painterly or pictorial device, and it is precisely this term that Rilke applies to his description of technique in the paintings of Cézanne. In Rilke's writings on Rodin, "plane" appears in German as *die Fläche,* but in his letters from 1907, he actually specifies the French, *plan.* "Curiously," he goes so far as to explain, "[Cézanne] refers to them again and again with the same word Rodin used."[21] Of course, Picasso's work of 1908–1909 is premised on a close scrutiny of Cézanne, and the language of the plane—in its mutual relevance to both Cézanne and Rodin—brings the character of form in Rilke's Rodin closer to the intrinsic nature of early cubism, including the dynamic of painting-sculpture.

. . .

19. Citations are from a translated edition of "The Rodin-Book" (the publication of both essays as a single book in 1907) in Rainer Maria Rilke, *Where Silence Reigns: Selected Prose,* trans. G. Craig Houston (New York, 1978), 138–139.

20. Rilke 1978, 95, 124.

21. Rainer Maria Rilke, *Briefe aus den Jahren 1904 bis 1907* (Leipzig, 1939), 410–411; English translation from Rilke, *Letters on Cézanne,* trans. Joel Agee (New York, 1985), 39.

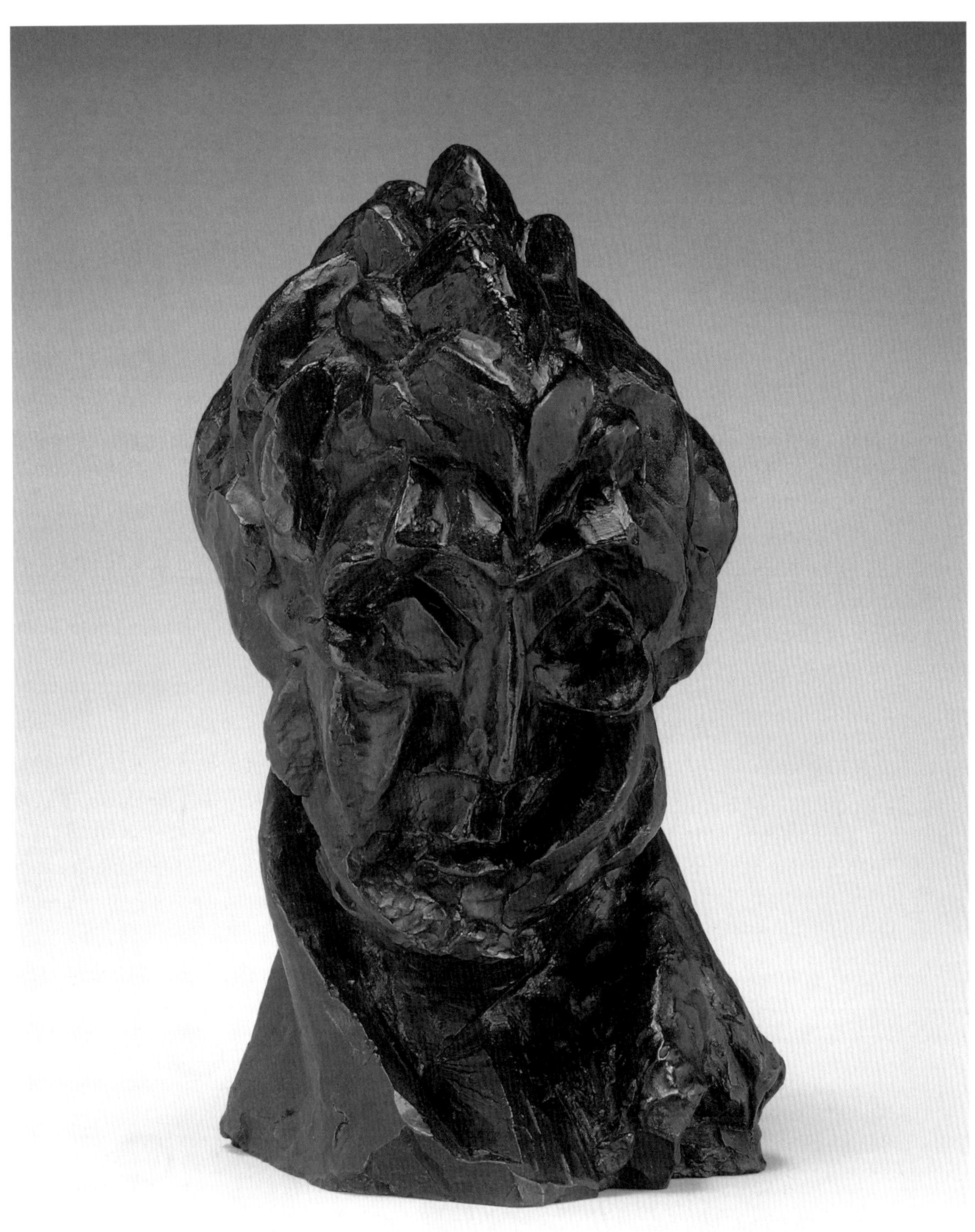

Head of a Woman (Fernande) (cat. 66)

Rilke's language confirms the Rodinesque nature of *Head of a Woman,* but the Rodin in question is an artist who rearticulates key issues of early cubism and demonstrates that they belong to multiple formal narratives after 1900. Virtually every serious critical and historical text about Picasso (and Braque) that addresses Cézanne's contribution to the development of cubism may be said, by implication, to confirm the relevance of Rodin—through Rilke's concept of the "plane"—to a cubist sculptural space. But the Rilkean version can also be traced through subsequent interpretations of the *Head.*

Focusing on the experience of light evokes the reflective property of cast bronze, and it is important to specify that the first bronze version of *Head of a Woman,* which was originally modeled in clay, was probably not cast until late 1910. We have no way of knowing whether Picasso originally intended the clay model to be produced in bronze.[22] This means that the role of light as an essential element in his conception of the *Head* must not be made to depend on the reflectivity of bronze. It is, however, a bronze cast to which Guillaume Apollinaire alluded in 1913, when he described the *Head,* in strictly Rilkean terms, as "a bronze in which [Picasso] concentrated the greatest possible quantity of light," a quality that, he continued, produces "dynamism" in the work.[23] Nearly all subsequent interpretations of the *Head* have described it specifically as a bronze, since the clay original was destroyed in the molding and casting process. The only extant alternative would have been the plaster models from which the casts were made. These have remained little known until recently, although they may not have been completely inaccessible: as early as 1915, a Russian, Ivan Aksenov, must have remembered seeing the plasters (or must have been alluding to someone else's recollection) when he mistakenly made reference in his book on Picasso to "a cycle of wax heads" from 1909. Aksenov explains that these preceded the paintings of heads (the Fernande portraits), which were executed in "the pale yellow of patinated wax," works that reduce the "problem" of the "sculptural investigations" to the "distribution of light and color harmony."[24] Yet we recall that, as a conceit, Rilke's own reference to the "acquisition and appropriation of light" in Rodin refers not to the reflected gleam of bronze sculpture but to the way in which illumination and shadow are collected through the manipulation of form in any medium (including bronze, as well as the plasters he observed in Rodin's studio)—that is, the way in which they are captured and dynamically controlled by the transformation of sculptural surface through a complex configuration of "planes."

22. In his interviews with Brassaï, Picasso remembered selling early sculptures to Vollard in order to raise money, explaining that it was Vollard's idea to cast them in bronze. This may have included the *Head,* although it is not among the works Picasso named. See Brassaï, *Conversations with Picasso,* trans. Jane Marie Todd (Chicago, 1999), 74.

23. LeRoy C. Breunig, ed., *Apollinaire on Art: Essays and Reviews, 1902–1918* (New York, 1988), 320. The reference occurs in Apollinaire's review of the Boccioni exhibition at the Galerie La Boétie in Paris.

24. Ivan Aksenov, *Picasso i okrestnosti* (Moscow, 1917), trans. and repr. in Marilyn McCully, ed., *A Picasso Anthology: Documents, Criticism, Reminiscences* (Princeton, N.J., 1981), 113.

Ultimately, serious consideration of the *Head* would have to wait until 1949, in a lengthy text about Picasso's sculpture by the art dealer Daniel-Henry Kahnweiler,[25] a pioneering historian and critic of cubism who addressed the work in these terms, claiming that the *Head* "takes to its extreme consequences the impressionist sculpture of Rodin and Medardo Rosso." For Kahnweiler, this sculptural pictorialism is paradoxical given the "sculptural" ambition of Picasso's paintings of 1908–1909, which, he claimed, had resulted in an optical impression of sculptural relief.[26] Kahnweiler does not pass over the development; claiming that the artist sought "to endow his bronze with created light, like that in a picture," he distinguishes the *Head* from previous sculpture (Picasso's own as well as certain historical conventions of sculpture in general). Now, "it is no longer the *form* of the head that is represented, but the objectivisation of light on that head." Parallel to Picasso's search for "pictorial means which would avoid modeling by chiaroscuro," the *Head* shows him replacing a sculptural "surface copied from natural bodies" with a kind of modeling that was "more insistent"—a means for "represent[ing] light instead of the solid body that had always been respected in European sculpture, which had created 'blocks.'" Kahnweiler does not take the example of Rodin (and Rosso) to prove the limitations of the *Head*. Instead, he means to characterize the work's extreme extrapolation of a particular structural and optical problem concerning cubism as a language of both painting and sculpture: specifically, the problem of managing light. In this case, he is addressing light as a pictorial element of representation that is itself being "represented" or "objectified" in both mediums, in the process of which both the sculptural body (the "block") and the pictorially depicted one are penetrated or compromised. Again, in post-Rilkean terms, it is not the reflectivity of bronze that concerns him, but the manipulation of light and space through the "insistent" handling of form.

As Kahnweiler shows, Rilke's sculptural space—and its implications for painting—came to occupy a place in twentieth-century formalist theory. If this were true beyond cubist studies, would it usefully reflect on Picasso's activity in 1909? During the 1930s, in an analysis largely devoted to medieval art, Henri Focillon posited a series of observations about space and light in sculpture based on principles that are, at the very least, implicitly Rilkean. In his landmark book *La Vie des formes*, Focillon distinguishes two principles for sculptural space: "space as a limit and space as an environment." In the first instance, "space more or less weighs on form and rigorously confines its expansion, at the same time as form presses against

25. Daniel-Henry Kahnweiler, *The Sculptures of Picasso* (London, 1949), n.p.

26. Addressing the optical character of early cubist painting as an approximation of relief sculpture has become a central, though disputed, metaphor in cubist formal analysis. Kahnweiler pursued the related problem of pictorial versus sculptural vision apart from cubism (with reference to Hildebrand, Rosso, and Rodin) in his essay, "L'Essence de la sculpture," originally published in German in 1919; see Daniel-Henry Kahnweiler, *Confessions esthétiques* (Paris, 1963), 84–102. Interestingly, in his essay on cubism from 1920, Kahnweiler passes over Picasso's work from 1909 (it is characterized as a "completion" of the new formal language of 1908, "without essential changes"); see Kahnweiler 1963, "Le Montée du cubisme," 28. For recent debates concerning the aptness of the bas-relief metaphor in the work of both Picasso and Braque, see William Rubin, "Cézannisme and the Beginnings of Cubism," in *Cézanne: The Late Work* [exh. cat., The Museum of Modern Art] (New York, 1977), 172–186; Leo Steinberg, "Resisting Cézanne," *Art in America* (November–December 1978), 125–131; Steinberg, "The Polemical Part," *Art in America* (March–April 1979), 119–123; Rubin, "Pablo and Georges and Leo and Bill," *Art in America* (March–April 1979), 131–136.

27. Henri Focillon, *The Life of Forms in Art*, trans. Charles Beecher Hogan and George Kubler (New York, 1989), 79–80.

space. . . ." In the second, "space yields freely to the expansion of volumes that it does not already contain." As a sculptural precept, space as limit restrains modeling (surface qualities that represent "the point at which the internal mass of sculpture meets with space") by reducing "undulations and disturbances" to "accent[s] and slight movement[s]" that do not "break the continuity of planes." Space as environment represents the contrary: "exactly as it delights in the scattering of volumes, in the interplay of voids, in sudden and unexpected perforations, so does it, in the modeling, welcome those multiple, tumbled planes that rend the light asunder." Space as limit applies not only to relief sculpture, but also to sculpture in the round, "over the masses of which it stretches a skin that guarantees solidity and density"; space as environment "not only clearly defines a certain way of making statues, but it also affects those reliefs that attempt to express by all manner of devices the semblance of a space wherein forms move freely." This can be traced to the "baroque state of all styles" in which the skin is "no longer an accurate mural envelope; it is quivering under the thrust of internal reliefs that seek to come up into space and revel in the light and that are evidence of a mass convulsed to its very depths by hidden movements."[27]

Focillon's distinction, which derives from his deeply material, quasi-organic theory of the genesis of aesthetic form, is meant to establish "general rules" in an "interpretation of space" and could be said to apply to virtually any instance of an opposition between sculpture that is reductive in profile and sculpture that is vigorously modeled or carved. The concept of space as environment, however, demonstrates how the legacy of a Rilkean apprehension of sculptural space could radicalize a broader analysis of the history of sculpture according to terms that once belonged to the avant-garde. Focillon flagrantly ignores the watershed of constructed sculpture: he insists that "the character of sculpture must, in one way or another, be that of a solid" (regardless of its nature as relief sculpture or freestanding object); that "its design does not and cannot suggest to us anything resembling a void." Nor is sculpture "an envelope" (instead, "it bears down with all the weight of density"). To the extent that these observations are intended to apply to sculpture as a medium in general, they deprive the history of sculpture of the cubist invention of constructed relief, which would indeed take the form of both envelope and void. Yet Focillon traces his principles of space—of "limit" and "environment"—from sculpture into painting in a fashion that otherwise verifies the relevance of this conceptual system to terms belonging to the historiography of cubist form. The equiva-

28. Focillon 1989, 76–77, 80–82.

29. Henri Focillon, *Art d'Occident: Le Moyen Âge, Roman et Gothique* (Paris, 1955), 247–248.

lent of these concepts in painting, he explains, can be addressed through the element of light: the way in which "painted space varies according to whether the light is outside the painting or within it"—whether a painting will appear to be "conceived as an object within the universe, lighted as other objects are by the light of day, or as a universe with its own inner light, constructed according to certain rules."[28] Exactly as stated here, the principle of internal light—which Focillon would elsewhere attribute to gold-ground Gothic painting and stained glass[29]—is a foundational tenet of cubist painting, as well as a fundamental one in the history of cubist formal analysis. Indeed, it applies above all to paintings by Picasso and Braque from late 1908 to 1911, in which the individual planar elements of a given object or body are represented as if having been "lit," within the painting's own space, from multiple directions. (By 1910 this technique will serve to defeat the integrity of the solid object, allowing form to be distributed through and across the ambient, grid-like coordinates of a shallow pictorial space.) Above all, Focillon's direct extrapolation from the concept of space as environment in sculpture to that of internal light in painting identifies a painting-sculpture dynamic we now begin to recognize as specifically relevant to Picasso's progress in 1909.

If Rilke's Rodin defamiliarizes cubism, it does so by inviting us to address *Head of a Woman*—and the relationship between painting and sculpture—without recourse to the prejudice of 1912. In so doing, we stress the elements of space and light, elements that are internal to the metaphorical nature of painting as a language of illusionism, but that belong to sculpture instead in an external, genuinely palpable way; it is with the fall of light and shadow and the movement of the beholder through actual space that the sculptural object is revealed to us. Efforts at controlling these two elements—to resist or correct Baudelaire's formulation of sculpture's "inferiority" to painting in this regard—represent a sculptural strategy during the late nineteenth and early twentieth centuries, as Kahnweiler implies when he lists both Rodin and Rosso in his treatment of *Head of a Woman*. Rosso was an Italian sculptor who had been living, working, and regularly exhibiting in Paris since 1884, and whose celebrity, albeit minor, was such that he was the subject of a serious monograph (written by Ardengo Soffici) in 1909. In his work, he attempted to create a kind of sculpture that could represent optical experience, as if the figures he portrayed had been glimpsed in motion or observed through the obscurity of night (fig. 6). To this end, the two sides of a sculpted face might even be subjected to distinctly different treatments in surface modeling or mass. Further, Rosso's sculp-

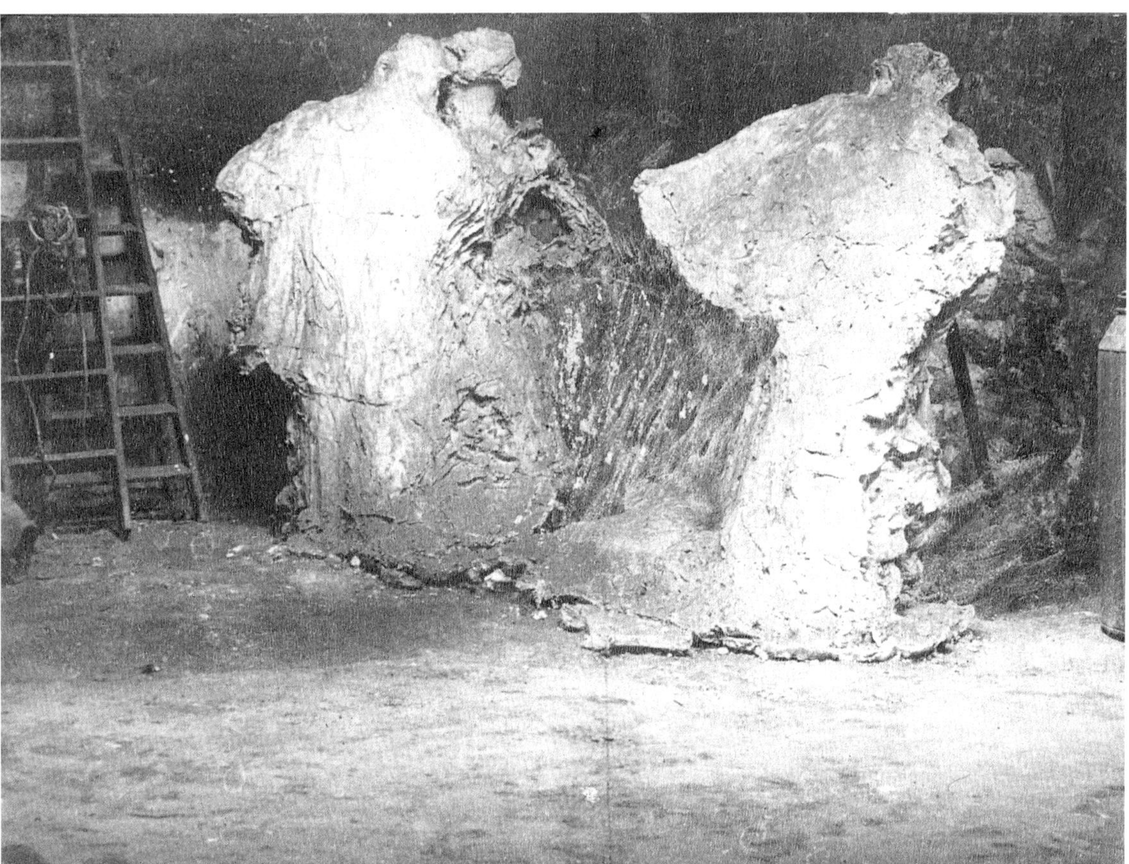

6

Medardo Rosso, *Impression on the Boulevard*, 1895–1896, photograph, Museo Rosso, Barzio

30. Margaret Scolari Barr, *Medardo Rosso* [exh. cat., The Museum of Modern Art] (Garden City, N.Y., 1963) 46, 49, 73 n.111.

31. John Coplans, "Brancusi as Photographer," in *Provocations: Writings by John Coplans* (London, 1996), 231.

32. The only serious treatment of Picasso's photography remains Anne Baldassari, *Picasso photographe 1901–1916* [exh. cat., Musée Picasso] (Paris, 1994); and Baldassari, *Le miroir noir* [exh. cat., Musée Picasso] (Paris, 1997).

33. Two letters from Picasso, written from Horta in June and August, promise photographs (the second specifies images of recent paintings); a third asks if they have arrived. The letters belong to the Stein Collection, Yale Collection of American Literature, Beinecke Rare Book and Manuscript Library.

tural objects were intended to be viewed from a single vantage, a pictorial (and Hildebrandian) conceit that he attempted to maintain through methods of display.[30] Rosso's sculptures were created to account for, rather than transcend, the contingency of perception. What Picasso's *Head* represents in this context is a sculptural object that seeks extreme means through which to internalize the conditions of its own viewing in light and space—and, by extension, through the element of time.

. . .

Two artistic mediums, as the critic John Coplans has written (in reference to Constantin Brancusi), explicitly correspond through their shared elements of light, space, and temporality: sculpture and photography.[31] The history of Picasso's work in 1909 includes photography; of special relevance are the studio images from Horta that record the painted portraits of Fernande. The true extent of Picasso's camera work during the prewar years is a fairly recent discovery; as a result, the photograph has played virtually no role in the historiography of cubism.[32] Yet in the Fernande sequence, photographs do not simply record the paintings; they constitute nothing less than a separate body of work.

Picasso's own letters indicate that the photographs at Horta may have been produced partly in order to share his new work—or the progress of his work—with his inner circle, including Gertrude and Leo Stein (to whom he promised and sent images of the paintings he had been producing that summer).[33] But the nature of Picasso's photography obviously raises a number of other issues concerning the way in which he used the camera to visualize and conceptualize his own work. It is significant, above all, that the photographs at Horta precede Picasso's momentous return to sculpture. While photography has provoked and absorbed artists in all mediums since its invention, it is the sculptor more often than the painter who has made experimental or strategic use of the photograph specifically as a means of recording his own work in the setting of the studio. Rodin, Rosso, Brancusi, and Alberto Giacometti share this interest; each produced, supervised, or facilitated a staging of his work for the camera. The photograph pictorializes sculpture as an object situated in space and revealed by light, allowing the artist to control the conditions according to which it is viewed (sometimes heightening those conditions to theatrical effect). It also allows multiple objects to engage one another within the restricting or flattening device of the frame, creating a play of formal correspondences that go unnoticed when the works are viewed from within actual space. If the modernist rapport between sculpture and photography is a natural one, this is because the photographic image can, at once, be evidentiary and self-conscious—a record of the work and a means of interrogating its condition as a medium.[34] While Picasso was not a sculptor at Horta, the fact that he soon would be, coupled with the deep history of photography in the hands of sculptors, invites us to consider the motivation behind the Horta studio photographs with sculpture in mind. To this end, especially with regard to the Fernande canvases, we might begin by saying that, in certain respects, the photographs allowed Picasso both to record painting and to implement it.

Picasso shot various types of photographic images at Horta: landscape and rooftop views (one of which was first published by Gertrude Stein in 1928), portraits of townspeople, and multiple views of the studio. The studio images each show paintings and sketches Picasso produced during the summer, arranged in changing configurations. Among them are four landscape paintings and two still lifes, the *Bottle of Anís del Mono* and *Carafe, Jug, and Fruit Bowl*; the remainder, some twenty works, are images of Fernande. Five of the photographs (cats. 51–55) show works on canvas and paper relating to one another in a casual yet deliberate manner, leaning or tacked up against the wall and, in some cases, overlapping (only the edges of some paintings can be glimpsed). Two photographs each (cats. 56, 57) show a pair of Fernande paintings standing side by side. One other (cat. 58) is, remarkably, a deliberate double- or multiple-exposure image: the bilateral configuration is maintained, but each side is now superimposed (during the developing process through an overlay of separate negatives) with other canvases from the Fernande group. The paintings are "stacked" and viewable through one another—like transparent projections—in shallow space.[35]

The photographs show Picasso openly addressing the Fernande pictures as a body of work. Picasso had produced several similar studio photographs of multiple paintings prior to Horta in 1908 and early 1909;[36] there the implication is that he is using the photograph as a tool for comparing pictures and scrutinizing process. This also appears to be the case at Horta, but the staging is somewhat more developed: a greater number of objects are called into play, and while they are not arranged according to a chronological sequence, they are being sorted. To a certain degree, the result is a specific emphasis on seriality, something that Picasso would use photography to portray several years later when he recorded two sets of papiers-collés at his studio on Boulevard Raspail in 1912 (fig. 7). In addition, the camera is being

34. For related issues in the use of photography as a tool for recording and interpreting sculpture per se, see Geraldine A. Johnson, ed., *Sculpture and Photography: Envisioning the Third Dimension* (Cambridge, Mass., 1998); esp. Hélène Pinet, "*Montrer est la question vitale*: Rodin and Photography," 68–85, and Paul Paret, "Sculpture and Its Negative: The Photographs of Constantin Brancusi," 101–115. See also Elizabeth A. Brown, "Brancusi's Photographic In-Sights," in Dorothy Kosinksi, ed., *The Artist and the Camera: Degas to Picasso* [exh. cat., Dallas Museum of Art] (New Haven, 1999), 267–285.

35. For Picasso's photographic process, see Baldassari 1994, 25–26, 29, 34; specifically concerning the photographs at Horta: 177–179, 187, 192, 194.

36. Baldassari 1994, 146, 152.

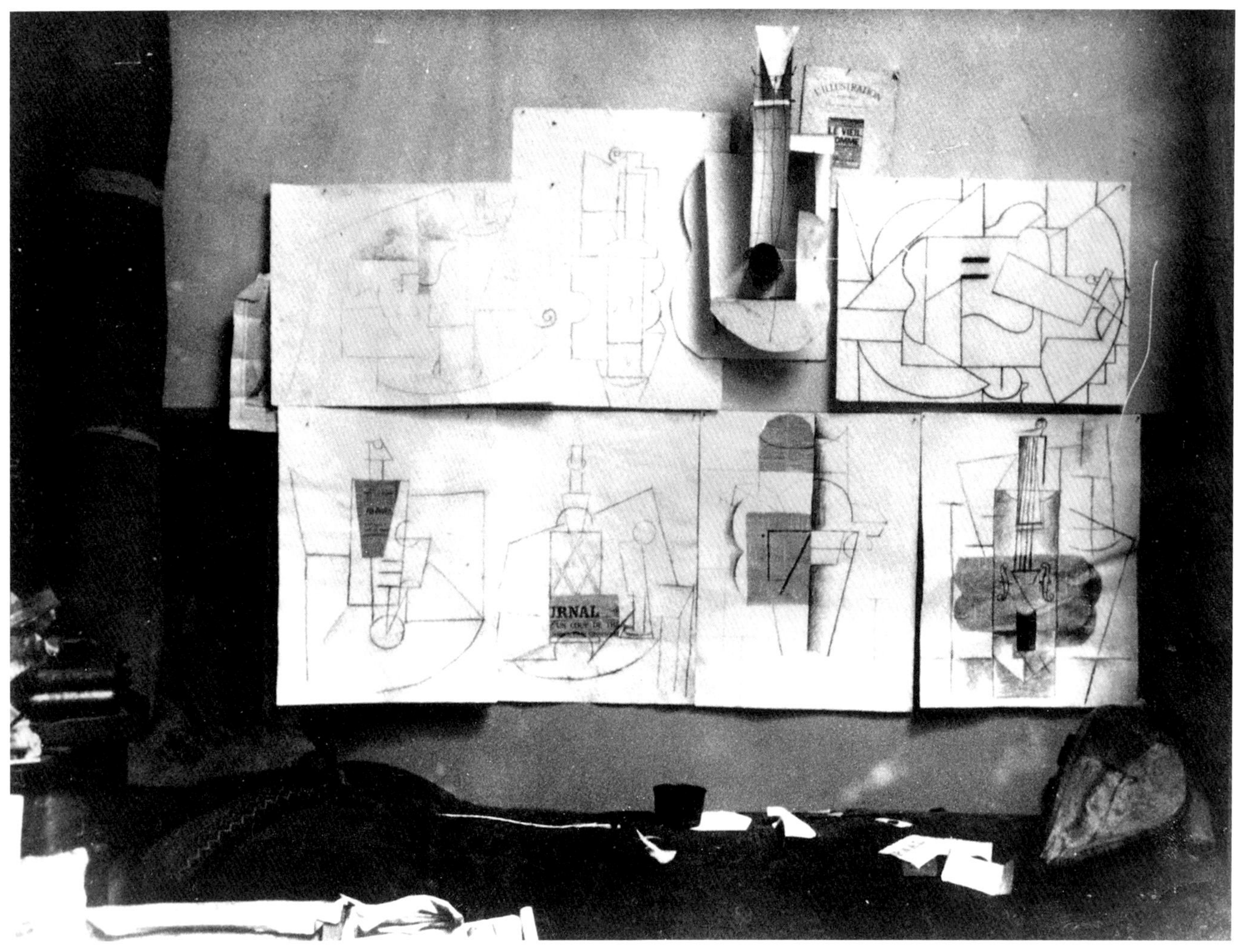

7

Pablo Picasso, Installation of papiers collés at the studio on Boulevard Raspail, Paris, winter 1912, photographic print from original negative, Archives Picasso, Musée Picasso, Paris

37. Baldassari 1994, 187, 192, 194.

38. Baldassari 1994, 194.

39. Such issues were broadly theorized during the period; see Mark Antliff, *Inventing Bergson: Cultural Politics and the Parisian Avant-Garde* (Princeton, N.J., 1993).

employed at Horta in order to classify works in the Fernande sequence according to stylistic or functional type. The same could be said for the images in which only two paintings are shown, although in this case, comparisons are more focused: one-to-one oppositions of format and setting, subtle distinctions in point of view, slight shifts in posture and expression, and modulations in the structural articulation of the head. In some respects, the multiple-exposure image could be said to intensify this approach to both seriality and collation.

The bilateral photographs have, on one occasion, been linked to stereoscopy.[37] Stereoscopic views are photographic cards that show the same subject in side-by-side images taken from two slightly different vantages; when viewed through a simple binocular device, they create an impression of tangible depth (collecting such cards was a common pastime during this period, and Picasso owned examples). Yet the concept of perceptual resolution, through which the stereoscopic image achieves depth, is completely foreign to Picasso's strategy. Further, while the "optical vibration" and "dispersion of elements" in the double-exposure image has been taken to resemble—even to anticipate—specific qualities that would come to characterize cubist painting through 1912,[38] this resemblance is at best accidental and superficial, and it obviously cannot account for Picasso's motivations. Significantly, multiple- and time-lapse exposure processes occupied a prominent role in avant-garde visuality during the early twentieth century. They were applied, for example, by the Italian futurist photographer Anton Giulio Bragaglia, whose *Cercando* (fig. 8) from around 1912 places the conventionally static portrait genre into a dynamic state that clearly means to seize qualities such as mobility and duration and to posit them as conditions of consciousness or the formation of personal identity.[39] The method would be adopted in Russia and Germany during the 1920s, when double exposure was deployed in portraiture to achieve multiple views and—with specific relevance to our discussion of Fernande—to depict the physical act of rotation (fig. 9). Based on this modernist convention, we can at least claim that some fusion of a spatial and temporal optic is inherent to the multiple exposure as it was implemented by the early avant-garde. Picasso's own multiple exposure confirms that strategies of opticality at Horta both anticipate and typify an avant-gardist mode. Given his medium-based concerns of the time, however, we can more precisely say that those strategies were being applied to the painting-sculpture dynamic that prevailed in his work in 1909.

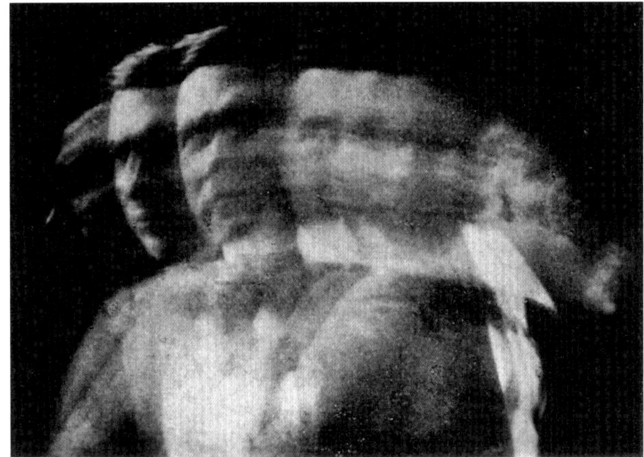

8

Anton Giulio Bragaglia, *Cercando* (photodynamic), 1912, photograph, Antonella Vigliani Bragaglia

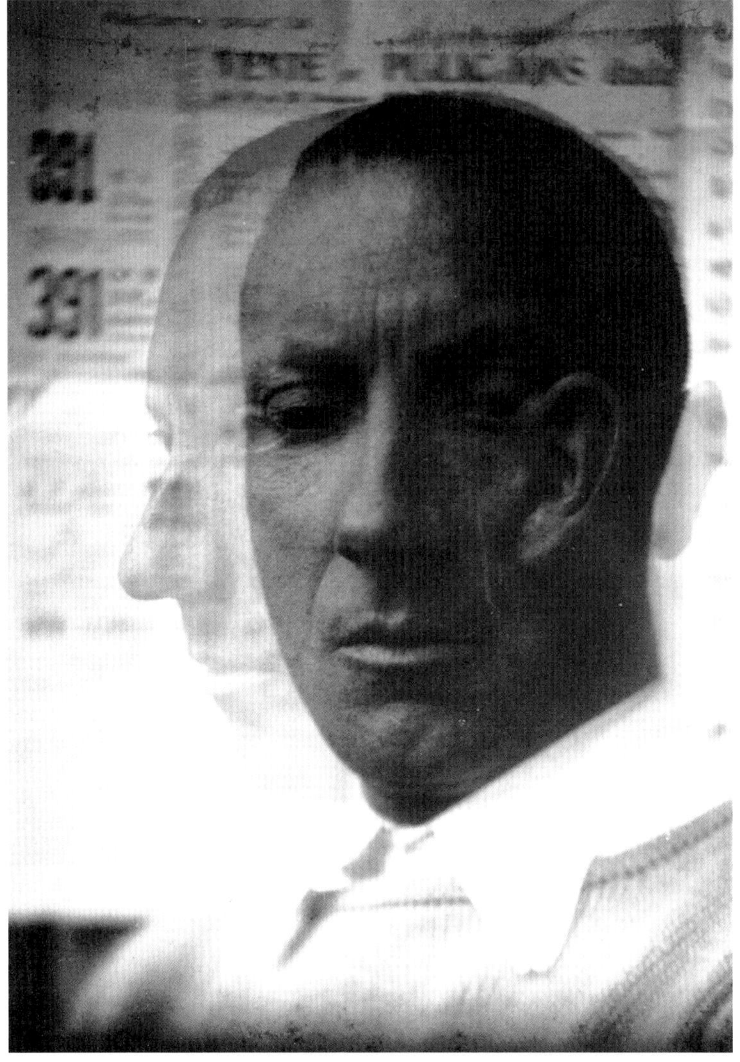

9

El Lissitzky, *Hans Arp,* 1924, gelatin silver print

40. Coplans 1996, 232.

41. For a discussion of this issue, see Potts 2000, 80–81, 84–88.

"Paintings finish at the edge of the frame," writes Coplans; "in comparison, sculpture is a contextual and temporal medium,"[40] experienced over time in variable conditions that can change the way it appears. Photographs also finish at the edge, but they record the object in light and space, and they preserve it within a continuum of time. All three of these elements are implicated in an expanded manner by Picasso's *surimpression,* in which the artist places his Fernande paintings into a photographic pseudo-space (a fictive realm of shallow depth created by a successive process of exposure and exchange) and thereby subjects them to contingent experience: they are multiple, transparently layered views of the same thing (heads, busts, and half-length images of Fernande) that resist the stability of optical resolution. The process of multiple exposure may well have suggested itself to Picasso by the very act of stacking and overlapping canvases; this is the manner in which he displays and records his work in each of the other Horta studio photographs, and it is indexed by the procedure of superimposing (stacking) the photographic negatives, much as the seriality of the Fernande portraits is thematized by the photograph as an image produced through mechanical repetition. Shuffling the canvases—paintings possessed of their own internal dynamics of light unrelated to the conceit of lighting from beyond the frame—within a shallow space that is simultaneously actual, depicted, and embodied by the medium, Picasso submits them to multiple forms of real and diagetic illumination. Light, again, is at stake. In this operation, the studio itself becomes a strategic domain, one that is distinctly sculptural: historically, sculpture before Rodin was largely situational—related to an architectural setting; beginning with Rodin, sculpture was essentially independent of architecture.[41] As a result, the proper setting of modern sculpture, if it has one at all, became that of the studio, a realm within which the sculptural object has otherwise become unfixed. At Horta, the photographic space of the multiple exposure is a construction that both designates and intensifies the studio as a contingent realm, but one that contains painting. In place of the concept of sculptural painting around 1909, then, the camera and the studio may be said to have made the paintings available to the equivalent of a sculptural apprehension.

If the serial nature of the Fernande sequence is new for Picasso, we might look specifically to the element of repetition for a principle that guides us through the reciprocity of mediums in 1909. Through doubling and multiplicity (both across space and within it), the Horta photographs portray the consecutiveness of the Fernande paintings without establishing whether the impact is intended to be cumula-

42. Rilke 1978, 137.

43. Focillon 1989, 78.

44. Proust 1981, 3:145; also cited in Bal 1997, 225.

tive or open-ended. In this way, both mechanical repetition and transparency, which are inherent to photography, not only parallel and even subtend the seriality of the Fernande paintings at Horta (or their latent seriality, which Picasso seems to be discovering for himself in the process of photographing the works); they also bear a spatial, temporal, and unexpectedly psychological relationship to the Baudelairean condition of the sculptural object—the multiple faces or hundred points of view. In Baudelaire's formulation, looking at sculpture is not understood to be a continual experience, but one broken down into the successive observation of static "profiles." By the turn of the century, this account has acquired an edge: Rilke wrote, in Baudelairean fashion, that Rodin studied the body in order "to know all the hundred profiles" and thereby comprehend his subject completely before producing the work. But the procedure bore other implications: "only then did the thing exist," Rilke added, "only then did it become an island separated on all sides from the continent of the uncertain."[42] Focillon would describe sculptural experience in these inherited terms, as a "collection of flat images, whose sequence or superposition elicits the concept of the solid only because the exigency already lies within ourselves";[43] in doing so, like Rilke, he represented the cumulative outcome of this sequential process of perception and apprehension as a matter of subjective urgency. This much is certainly true of the Proustian paradigm, in which the principle of multiple or successive vantages through space or time—relating to both visual and affective comprehension—is allegorized as a specifically photographic condition: "For I possessed in memory only a series of Albertines, separate from one another, incomplete, a collection of profiles or snapshots, and so my jealousy was restricted to a discontinuous expression, at once fleeting and fixed."[44] With Picasso's implementation of the camera, the Fernande paintings are both addressed as "sequence" and subjected to "superposition," a double operation at once photographic and, within the conceptual frame of modernist convention, inherently sculptural. As it turns out, it is also, according to that same convention, not without intrinsic implications—"exigency," "uncertainty," "incompleteness," "discontinuity"—relating to perceptual wholeness as an object of compulsion and distress. The reciprocity of mediums simply heightens the notion that the consequences of seriality at Horta are both fleeting and fixed.

. . .

Using photography, Picasso observed and addressed the paintings at Horta through a process of mediated vision and estrangement. His interest in photography would remain fairly consistent, as evidenced by his remarks to Christian Zervos in 1935, with whom Picasso discussed the photograph as a source of higher intuition: "It would be very interesting to preserve photographically, not the stages, but the metamorphoses of a picture." He refers to a serial or sequencing procedure (not specifying the movie camera, which would suggest something else), but his ambition has changed: "Possibly one might then discover the path followed by the brain in materializing a dream." Here the photograph acquires a capacity for inner truth, telling him something about his work that was at risk of being obscured by his own process: "But there is one very odd thing—to notice that basically a picture doesn't change, that the first 'vision' remains almost intact, in spite of appearances.... When the work is photographed, I note that what I put in to correct my first vision has disappeared, and that, after all, the photographic image corresponds with my first vision before the transformation I insisted on."[45]

Looking back on Horta, it is relevant that the practice of photographic imaging around 1900 included both x-rays and "spirit photography" (trick photographs depicting spirits of the deceased that were actually produced using a double-exposure process), which were both popularly understood to have placed the evidentiary implications of the photographic medium into the service of "invisible" truths.[46] Not surprisingly, the other function of photography represented in the studio images at Horta—the consecutiveness of sorting and quantification—directly corresponds to a separate, primarily technical (non-aesthetic) application of photography during the period, one that has been characterized as "statistical" or "archival."[47] This concept was both a model and an institutional practice implemented above all within the precincts of criminology throughout Europe (with implications for anthropology and eugenics) as a system for police intelligence devoted to the vast statistical compilation of photographic portraits of members of criminal society. Taxonomy of this kind was joined to typology when Sir Francis Galton, who published extensively on heredity and race during the late nineteenth century, developed the technique of the photographic "composite view" in which a single image was produced from a series of portraits of individuals, all drawn from a given ethnic category or social group, that were successively exposed on a single plate. Through this process of "pictorial statistics," shared features gained presence through superimposition while idiosyncratic deviations from the norm barely registered, resulting

45. "Statement by Picasso: 1935," in Alfred H. Barr Jr., ed., *Picasso: Forty Years of His Art* [exh. cat., The Museum of Modern Art] (New York, 1939), 15.

46. Early books and pamphlets on this subject are legion; see, for example, Jean Finot, *La Photographie transcendentale* (Paris, n.d.). For a historical analysis, see also Tom Gunning, "Phantom Images and Modern Manifestations: Spirit Photography, Magic Theater, Trick Films and Photography's Uncanny," in Patrice Petro, ed., *Fugitive Images: From Photography to Video* (Bloomington and Indianapolis, 1995), 42–71.

47. Allan Sekula, "The Body and the Archive," *October* (Winter 1986), 3–64.

10

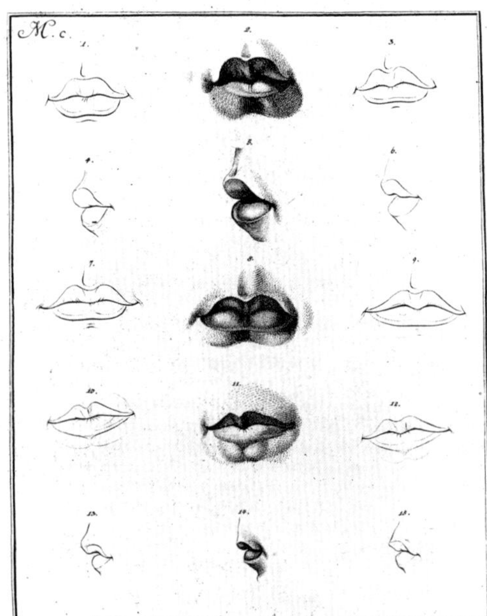

11

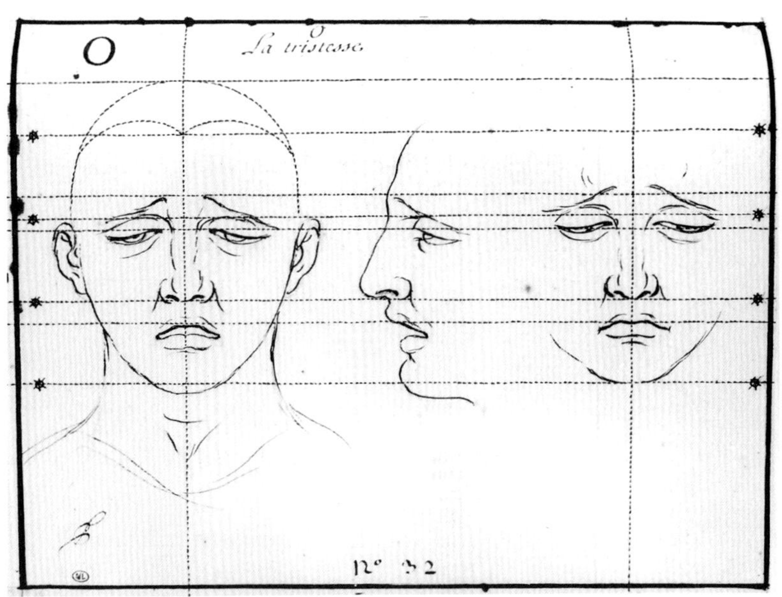

12

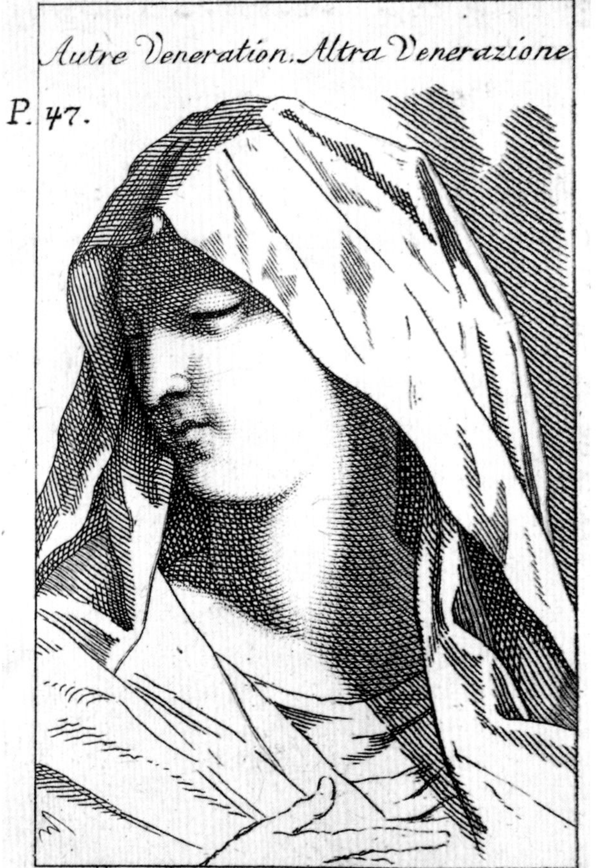

10

Johann Caspar Lavater, *Tableau mit Variationen fünfer Münder*, originally published in Johann Caspar Lavater, *Physiognomische Fragmente, zur Beförderung der Menschenkenntniss und Menschenliebe*, 4 vols. (Winterthur, 1775–1778)

11

Charles Le Brun, *La Tristesse (Sadness)*, seventeenth century, pen and ink, Musée du Louvre, Paris

12

Charles Le Brun, *Autre Veneration, Altra Venerazione*, seventeenth century, from Charles Le Brun, *Conferenza del signor Le Brun primo pittore del re di Francia… sopra l'espressione generale e particolare delle passione con le sue figure tradotta in italiano* (Verona, 1751)

in the photographic representation of a generic "type." In Galton's work, seriality and transparency are themselves superimposed, as are the concept of statistical quantification and the pretense—an ironic one, given the conceit of the camera as an innately empirical tool—of inner truth.

Extrapolating further, we also observe that the photographic "archive" was itself drawn from prephotographic systems of taxonomy and typology that, historically, had long belonged to the realm of the artist's studio[48]—methods for classifying anatomy and physiognomic expression that were originally devised during the late seventeenth and eighteenth centuries to support the practice of history painting.[49] Theories of expression were devoted to both deciphering the elements of physiognomy as outward signs revealing the inner character of an individual, and, in turn, extrapolating from individuals in order to establish a repertoire of categories or types. Separate facial features—a catalogue of eyes, noses, and mouths—were isolated and itemized according to a language of expression presumably derived from the observation of nature (fig. 10), while facial gestures, in turn, were codified, creating an artist's inventory for the representation of emotional character or states of mind (figs. 11, 12). By 1900 the pseudoscience of physiognomic expression had long been integrated into academic practice, with which any trained artist of the period would have been familiar, even as it was challenged by the rise of naturalism. Nonetheless, during the late nineteenth century, new authors such as Charles Henry would attempt to establish the abstract, schematic underpinnings of an expressive language of the face and body (something of serious interest to Georges Seurat, among other postimpressionist painters at the end of the century),[50] and such pursuits were given new life in other disciplines—including criminology and anthropology—by the mechanical facility of the camera as a device for recording on a vast scale.

Fernande did not sit for Picasso in Horta. This much seems clear from the long letters she wrote to Alice Toklas and Gertrude Stein in the summer of 1909, which make virtually no mention of Picasso's work. What the letters do broadcast is that Fernande was unhappy and unwell. Apparently afflicted with a kidney infection, she had occasion to complain at length of physical discomfort and emotional distress. At one point, she also believed she might be pregnant, openly implicating Picasso in her discontent. Pain, boredom, depression, and self-pity were alleviated by occasional periods of distraction, but the overall picture is fairly bleak: "I can promise you that if this goes on for another month it will all be over and I'll be dead."[51] As for Picasso, his extremely brief letters to the Steins reveal only that Fernande was suffering and bedridden, and that he was managing, nonetheless, to paint.

48. Sekula 1986, 11.

49. See, for example, Laurent Baridon and Martial Guédron, *Corps et arts: Physionomies et physiologies dans les arts visuels* (Paris, 1999).

50. See William Innes Homer, *Seurat and the Science of Painting* (Cambridge, Mass., 1964).

51. In a letter to Stein presumed to be from mid-July. Translation from Fernande Olivier, *Loving Picasso: The Private Journal of Fernande Olivier*, trans. Christine Baker and Michael Raeburn (New York, 2001), 243.

52. Stein 1933, 50.

53. Ambroise Vollard, *Cézanne* (Paris, 1924), 140.

54. For the metaphor of the *écorché*, see the essay by Kathryn Tuma in this volume.

Behind the question of the sitting exists a powerful mythology of modernist portraiture, one in which Picasso plays a prominent role. Gertrude Stein relates that Picasso's celebrated portrait of her from 1906 was produced over the course of some ninety sessions, after which the artist abandoned the painting until, months later, he wiped out the face and replaced it with a schematized mask.[52] The tale is almost certainly adapted from one the art dealer Ambroise Vollard tells about Cézanne, who painted his portrait in 1899, for which Vollard claims to have sat 115 times.[53] It makes little difference if the numbers are apocryphal; Cézanne is also said to have left the portrait of Vollard unfinished, and the moral of the story is that the painting dramatizes the act of observation in Cézanne's work as a profound condition of uncertainty or dread. Stein's version substitutes the reinvention of likeness through a striking epiphany of conceptual insight that occurs at observation's breaking point. The Fernande series is, then, almost a necessary construction: successive versions of a single portrait (achieved over the course of multiple sittings) are now peeled into a succession of separate, often nearly identical canvases. The result is a "portrait" practice that forfeits its grounding in likeness through observation but preserves the procedural connotations of persistence and multiplicity—and perhaps, by extension, the province of doubt.

In painting Fernande, who was close but absent, Picasso replaced likeness with a procedure for retaining features or personal qualities through the application of signs that could be depicted in a reductive manner: a well-defined, contracted mouth, hollowed or darkened eyes, a powerfully articulated brow, and a rotated and inclined head. Such elements, drawn from a typological scheme, are hardened representational cues that are adaptable to the constitution of pictorial and sculptural form in Picasso's work in 1909. It is important to observe that, throughout the Fernande series, Picasso had intermittent recourse to techniques of naturalism, especially in the first sequence of portraits at Horta, where the modeled representation of flesh and muscle marks a distinct shift away from the schematic works he had produced during the spring. Clearly, this quality—which, of course, disappears with the second group—was not viable given the direction of his work. It is not insignificant that subsequent paintings of Fernande from the summer have been loosely described over the years as resembling an *écorché,* the flayed figure that can be found in countless books of anatomy often produced for use by artists from the sixteenth century to the present day;[54] as a deindividualized type, the *écorché* offers a specifically structural version of the body—the muscles and ligaments behind the surface envelope—that lends itself directly to the planar articulation of the figure in 1909 and 1910. It is, in certain respects, a substitute model or archetype, one that maintains the integrated presence of the body while addressing it as an open rather than a closed form. Of course, while the *écorché* is a typological figure, it is far from being a mechanical one, and it also carries the potential for deep pathos. Similarly, in the second group of portraits from Horta, the representation of the head is clearly and specifically responsive to the structure of the human skull: one can discern the pronounced, broad hollow of the temporal fossa and the deep shadow cast by the lateral configuration of the zygomatic arch (which begins at the side of the occular orbit and terminates at the ear) (fig. 13). The formal language of the work can be seen to exploit selected elements from the inherent structure of muscle and bone, and this process, in turn, exerts an acute influence on meaning. It also places added pressure on an expanded definition of "cubism."

Although classification would appear to be anathema to early modernist reformulations of the face and body, it turns out to have offered an essential salvaging or preserving function. It is through the agency of the typological device that the most abstracted works in the Fernande series retain the dimension of a Fernande "type," a procedure that applies not only to physiognomy but also to identity or character. In fact, as Picasso substitutes a typological or structural language for a descriptive one, expression comes to be carried even less by facial features than by broader provinces: the plane of the brow, and the position of the head. In the sequence of large-scale, nearly identical drawings of heads from the early spring, the forehead was divided bilaterally using vertical hatching, bundles of long, parallel lines that schematize shadow and light while serving also to portray this area as the splayed surface of an articulated volume that has been unfolded and laid flat. The technique culminates at Horta in the now notorious "reversible cube," which is planted at the center of Fernande's brow (cats. 35, 36) and serves as the hinge for a multipart, ambiguously lit accordion fold that extends across her forehead and around the sides of her head. This device is an expression of the mobile or encompassing view of an object Picasso had been developing in his painting throughout the period. It was replicated in the *Head,* with its corrugated brow. The reversible cube is often said to figure "cubist" form (as a volume it can be read as both projecting and receding), but it also clearly belongs to a series of devices in the Fernande works that serve to gather density at the middle of the brow through a heightening of mass —the projection of planes that coalesce around a prowlike center. (This area of

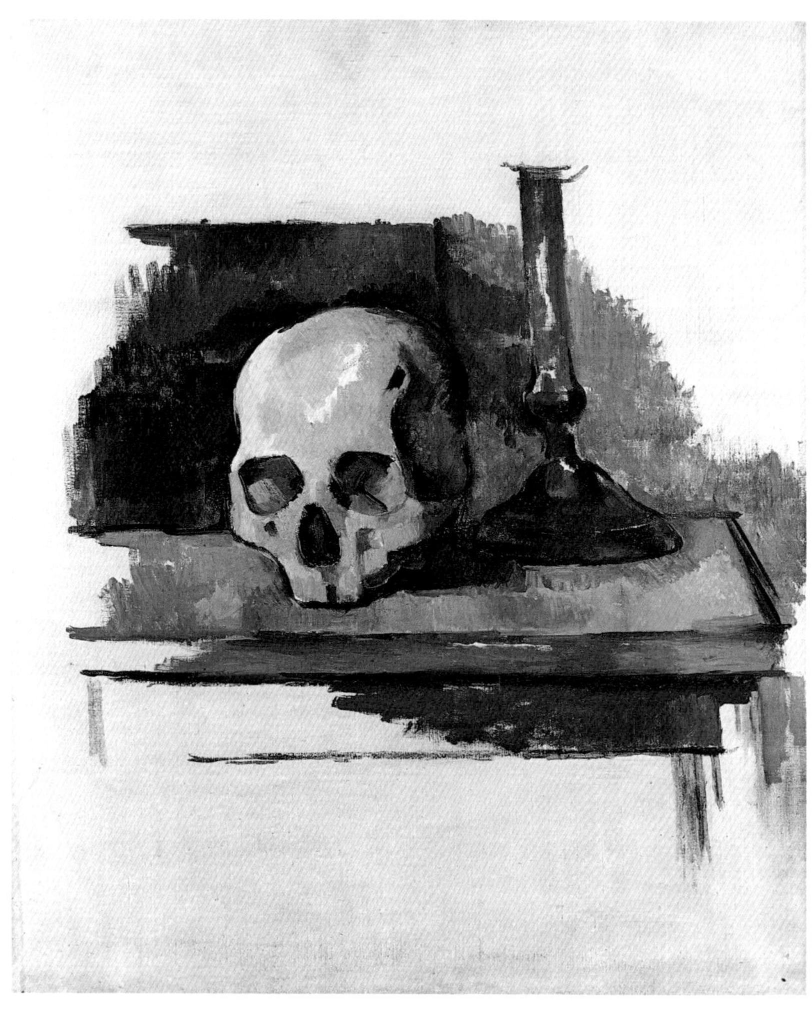

13

Paul Cézanne, *Still Life with Skull and Candlestick*, 1900, oil on canvas, Staatsgalerie Stuttgart

14

Malinconia, c. 1618, illustration from Cesare Ripa, *Nova iconologia di Cesare Ripa* (Padua, 1618)

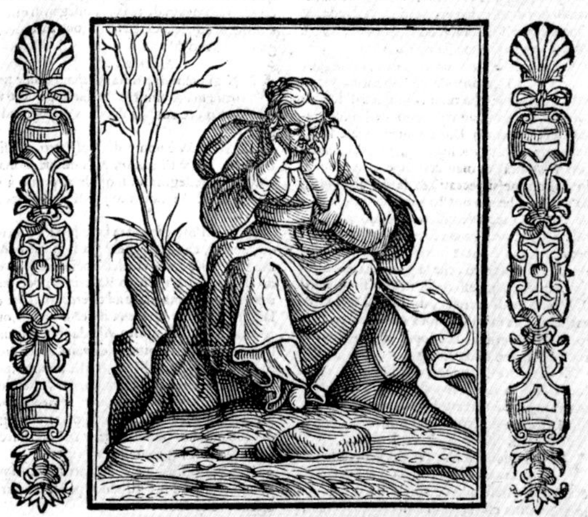

musculature at the center of the brow is, indeed, referred to as the "corrugator.") In relation to other features, the heavy, complex brow is a morpheme of deep, often afflicted, interiority and spiritual distress—a "natural" articulation that has been codified as such throughout the history of the physiognomic sign.

Beyond the brow, the position of the head itself is the salient indicator of affect in the Fernande series. This gesture—turning and inclining—has had a long life under the world-historical sign of melancholy (contemplation, psychic pain, madness, cosmic inspiration, genius); as such, it possesses both typological utility and semaphoric power (fig. 14). Curiously, the motif actually emerged as a sort of "pathos formula" in modernist sculpture.[55] It began with Rilke's Rodin, whom the poet credited with having developed a gestural language that expresses a quality he characterized as "turning-inward-upon-oneself," a "tense listening to inner depths"; the most extreme example, according to Rilke, is Rodin's *La Méditation* (fig. 15), the altered version of an earlier figure Rodin adapted to his monument for Victor Hugo. Inward-turning was, of course, centered on the fulcrum of the neck, "which stretches slightly upwards, as it rises from the body bent downwards and sideways, and holds the listening head...."[56] The modernist lineage of torque, tilt, and involution includes Rosso (fig. 16) and Brancusi—his repeated versions of *Mlle Pogany* (fig. 17)—as well as Picasso's *Head of a Woman.* It is a peculiar recurrence. We can claim that the gesture was probably a pantomime for symbolist interiority (the aesthetic conceit of a retreat from appearances), but it seems to have developed a formal currency in sculpture per se, where turning is a means for activating sculptural space. *Head of a Woman* was specifically interpreted in this way by Raymond Duchamp-Villon, whose *Horse* (fig. 18) (which was ultimately developed as a monumental bronze) is perhaps its most explicit progeny. More importantly, the downward rotation of the *Head* was Picasso's own prototype for the posture of the (in)animate *Absinthe Glass* (fig. 19), his return to bronze sculpture—serially executed as six individually painted casts—in 1914. This work turns out to be an important replay of several key issues pertaining to the *Head.* Above all, it reveals that, even after the advent of constructed sculptural relief in 1912, Picasso continued to pursue elements of light, space, and form specific to sculptural objects that were modeled and cast. Thus the *Absinthe Glass* interprets the earlier work by employing a dialectic of repetition and difference in relation to the dynamics of sculpture as mass, and it declares this function by explicitly adapting the *Head*'s gyratory tilt.[57]

55. The term *Pathosformel* was developed by the historian Aby Warburg beginning just after the turn of the century. It signifies a methodology by which certain motifs of, for example, gestural or physiognomic expression are said to survive and recur within the history of representation, often imported across national boundaries and long periods of time to take their place in works unrelated to the cultural milieu of the original. The thesis first appeared in print in 1905 and was elaborated by Warburg over the course of some twenty years. In referencing the "pathos formula," I mean to acknowledge a concept invented during the period of early modernism that could itself be said to represent a modernist system, one that is expressed through the reciprocity of form and melancholic pathos in modernist sculptural manifestations of rotation (although national or cultural boundaries are obviously not at stake in my adaptation of the concept). Melancholia was among Warburg's categories of pathos, and it was from a theory regarding the allegorical representation of melancholia propounded by Warburg and his circle that Walter Benjamin extrapolated his understanding of melancholy in German baroque *Trauerspiel.* See Raymond Kilbansky, Erwin Panofsky, and Fritz Saxl, *Saturn and Melancholy: Studies in the History of Natural Philosophy, Religion and Art* (London, 1964); E.H. Gombrich, *Aby Warburg: An Intellectual Biography* (London, 1970); and Max Pensky, *Melancholy Dialectics: Walter Benjamin and the Play of Mourning* (Amherst, 2001).

56. Rilke 1978, 103–104.

15

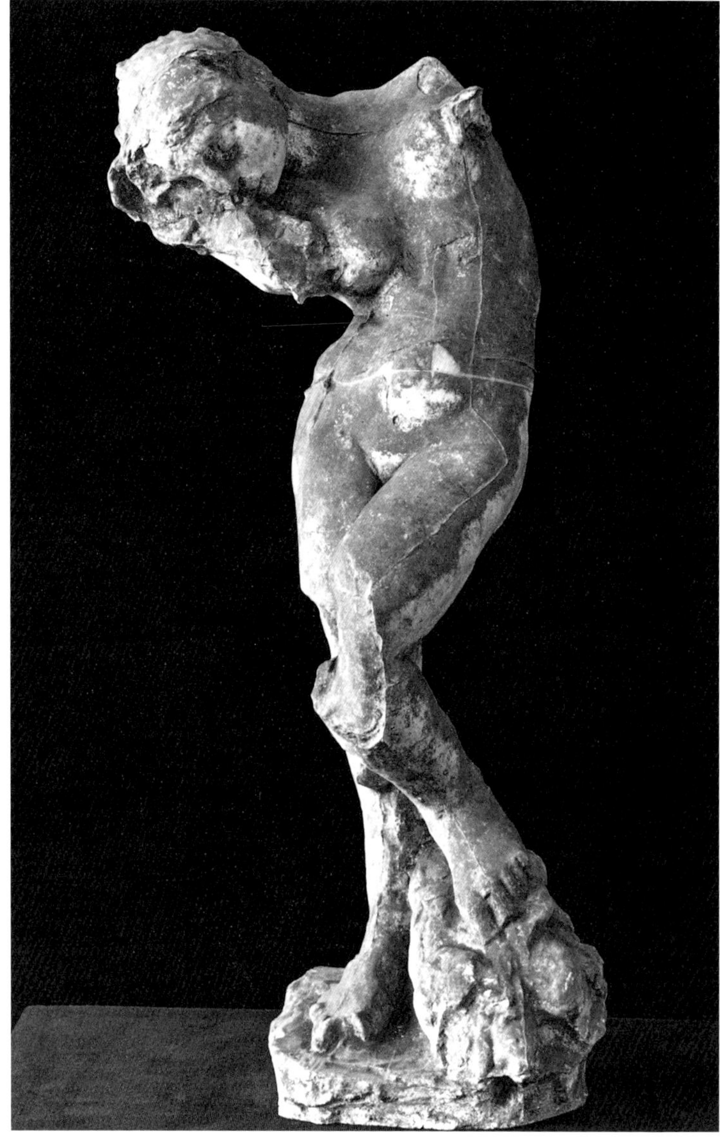

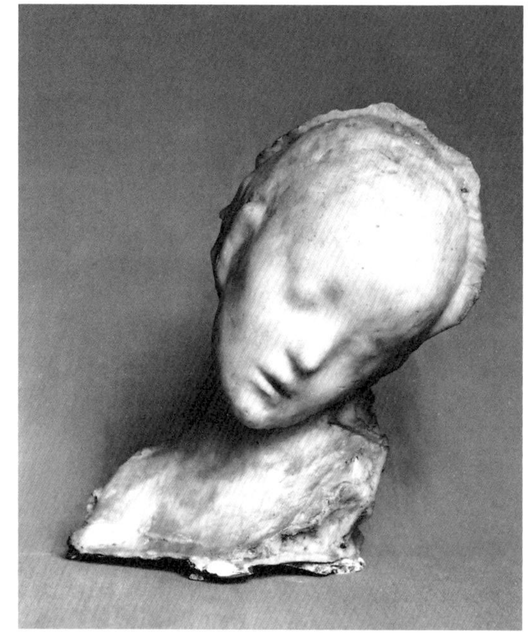

17

15

Auguste Rodin, *Meditation without Arms*, 1883–1884(?), plaster, Musée Rodin, Paris

16

Medardo Rosso, *Bambino malato*, 1889, wax over plaster, Staatliche Kunstsammlungen Dresden, Skulpturensammlung

17

Constantin Brancusi, *Mademoiselle Pogany (II)*, 1920, plaster, Musée national d'art moderne, Centre Georges Pompidou, Paris

18

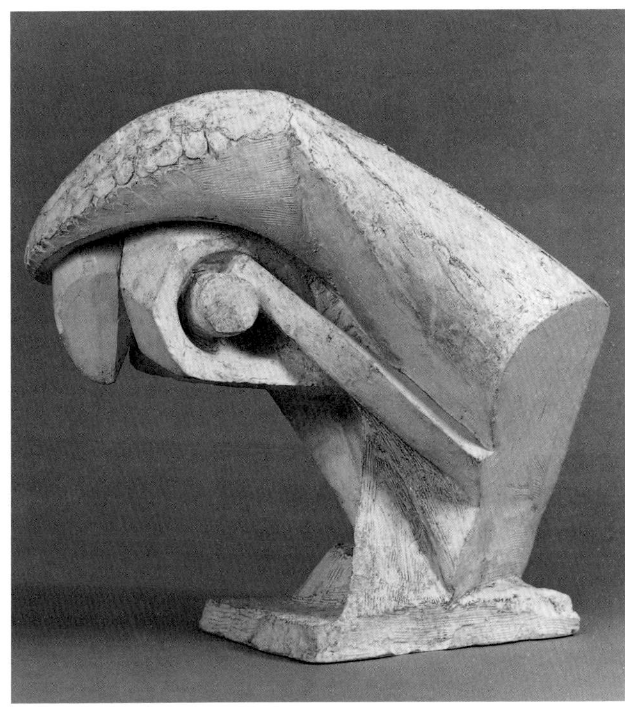

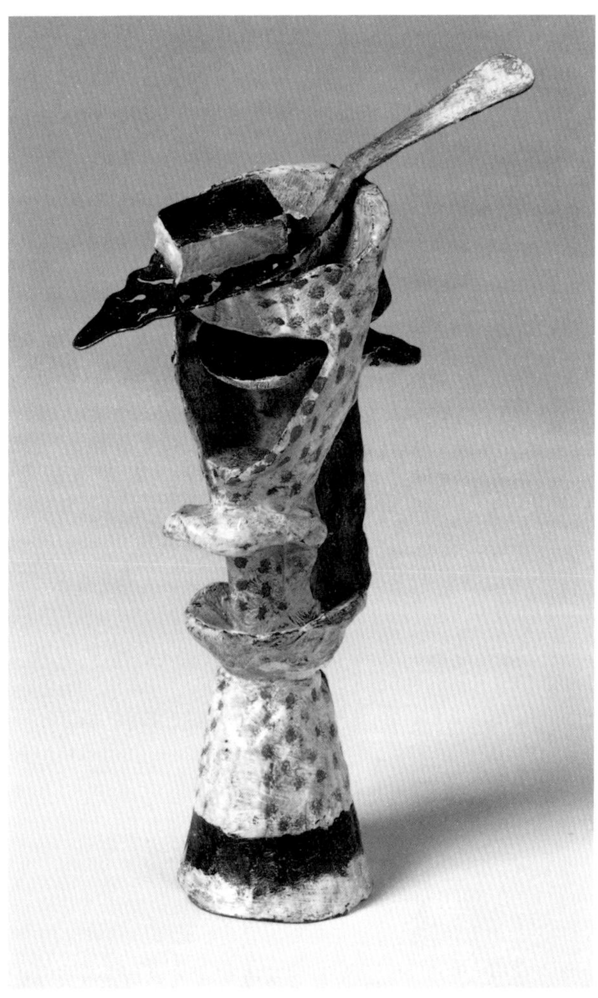

19

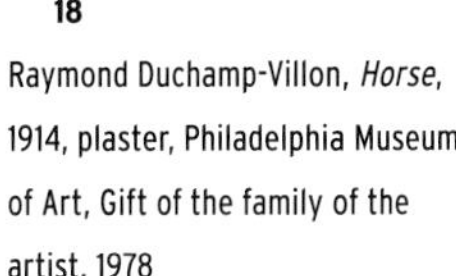

18

Raymond Duchamp-Villon, *Horse*, 1914, plaster, Philadelphia Museum of Art, Gift of the family of the artist, 1978

19

Pablo Picasso, *Absinthe Glass*, 1914, painted bronze, Philadelphia Museum of Art, A. E. Gallatin Collection

57. One further work that remains identifiable—albeit from an apparent distance—with *Head of a Woman (Fernande)* is the *Cube*, a sculpture created by Giacometti in 1934. Described by the artist as a "head," this thirteen-sided polyhedron (inscribed on its surface with a barely visible portrait of his just-deceased father) possesses a complex origin and relationship to Giacometti's oeuvre, including his *Tête cubiste (Tête crâne)*. See Georges Didi-Huberman, *Le Cube et le visage* (Paris, 1993). But its configuration of planar *faces*, which presents no primary vantage, implies a faceted rotation and, from certain positions, shows a distinctly relevant downward tilt. In some respects, *Head of a Woman (Fernande)* inhabits Giacometti's *Cube*. The *Cube* is also a transplanted instrument of affect, having been derived from the geometrical solid in Albrecht Dürer's engraving *Melancolia I*, the iconographical locus classicus of postmedieval melancholy.

58. Philippe Pinel, "Melancholia, or Delirium Upon One Subject Exclusively," in *A Treatise on Insanity* (London, 1806) (first published in French in 1801).

The mechanics of the Fernande series shift the locus of the image's affective share away from the motility of facial expression to individual features that have been converted into fixed signs. Sequencing and classification serve to abstract melancholy, taking for granted its long iconographic history as a disposition or humor (and one that had been gendered as an allegorical personification) in order to draw it through the structural matrix of the painting where, like a deposit, it collects and remains. The modernist typological recurrence of downward rotation is a further clue in fathoming this procedure. It could be said to represent a compression, possibly even the existence of a symbolic form—a cipher of pathos that simultaneously designates the province of a specifically sculptural space. Seriality, which is at once a visual and a physical act, broadens this dynamics of space and affect: repetition is a form of spatialization (as elements in a series, the canvases are made to occupy actual space, becoming "brutal and positive like nature," to quote Baudelaire's characterization of the sculptural object) as well as relentlessness or fixation. We recall the disquieting urgency of sculptural apprehension—that it is our own internal exigency which compels us to reconcile the hundred profiles of sculpture into a "concept of the solid" (Focillon), something stable and known. And we speculate: considering the fixation expressed by the persistent repetition of this motif in the Fernande series, could Fernande's "melancholy" chiefly be an indicator—a displacement or projection—of Picasso's own? The motto for such a conjecture would be drawn from an important early treatise on the classification of melancholia, in which the condition—less mood-state than madness—is characterized in these very terms: "Delirium Upon One Subject Exclusively."[58]

A final clue may be traced to two earlier depictions by Picasso. The downturned head was a common device in his work from 1901 to 1905 (the so-called Blue and Rose periods), where it is natural to the pervasive mood of fin-de-siècle ennui. But the most meaningful precursor to Fernande's pose in 1909 is a painting from 1906—often presumed to be a portrait of Fernande—in which Picasso shows his sitter from an angle that emphasizes the top of her lowered head (fig. 20). This image (which itself may have been derived from a drawing of Fernande engrossed in sewing) could be taken primarily as a quasi-fetishistic representation of hair, one that anticipates and even explains the eccentric drawing of plaited hair from fall 1909 (cat. 67). But the painting is also the striking double of a self-portrait that dates from this period, a drawing in which Picasso portrays himself (with a shaved head) in the identical pose (fig. 21), which is repeated twice, from frontal and

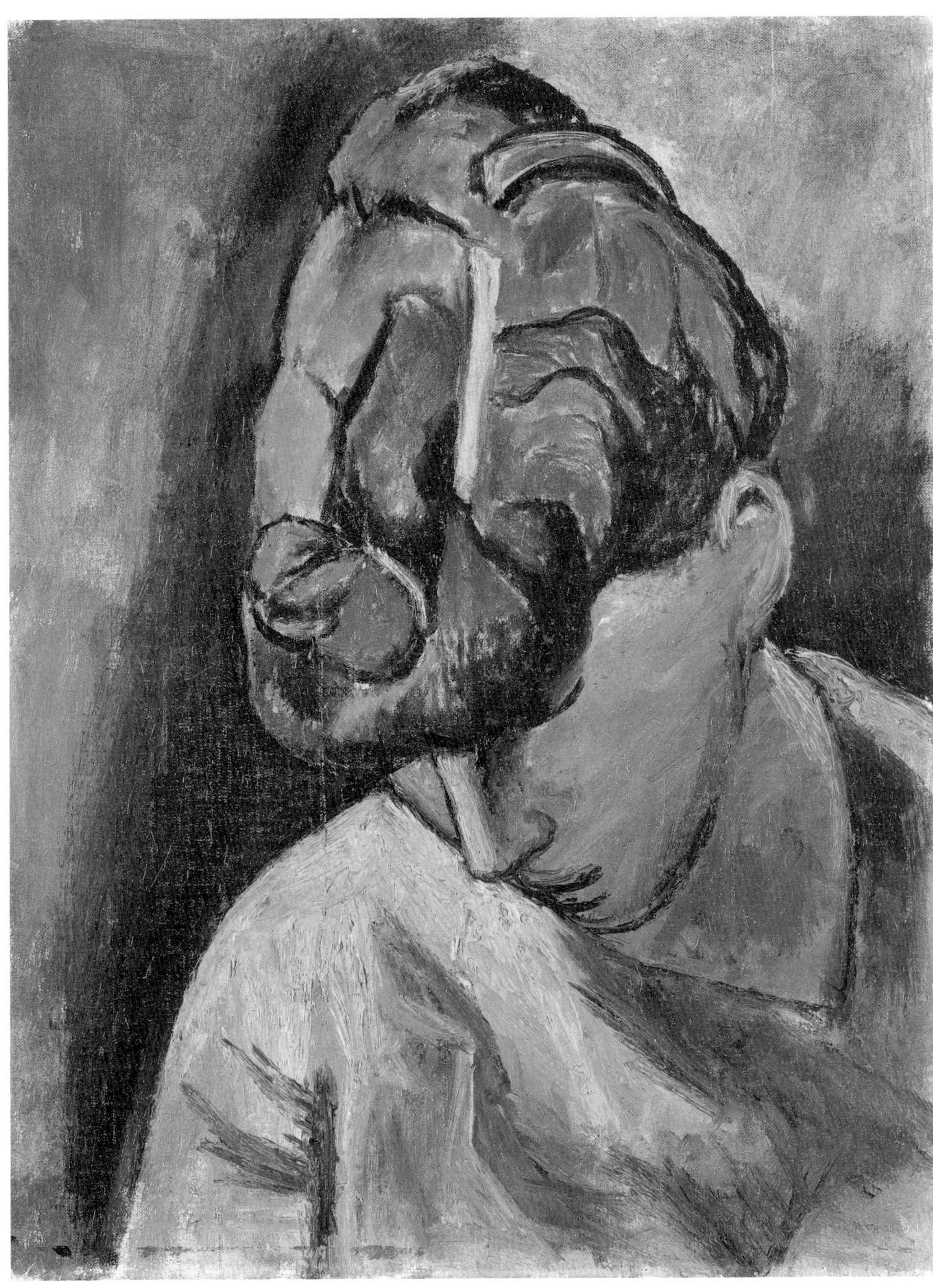

20
Pablo Picasso, *Woman with Her Head Bent*, Paris, early fall 1906, oil on canvas, Staatsgalerie Stuttgart

59. This sketch is a study for a painting (Philadelphia Museum of Art) in which Picasso finally chose to portray himself erect and staring. A second sketch (Musée Picasso, Paris) shows the transition to the final image.

profile views. The drawing depicts two glimpses of the artist deeply engrossed in his work: touching brush to palette on the left side of the sheet and (by implication through an overlay of images) pencil to page on the right side. Rapt absorption in the act of art-making is being matched by Picasso to the interiority he ascribed to Fernande.[59] It is the theme of absorption, a chief element of the melancholic disposition, through which the drawing allegorizes the very position of the head as a motif for the delirium of process. In any case, the coincident images of Picasso and Fernande expose the relevance of this allegorical dynamic to the condition—repetition and affect—of Picasso's work in 1909.

The end of the "Fernande series" is virtually the end of likeness even as a typological conceit (cats. 75–77). If, throughout 1909, Fernande had been object but not sitter, then here the figure—to the extent we can now even speak of Fernande—retains character through classification and trace: alone, the articulated brow and the downward rotation of the head resist the fate of disintegrated mass. Presence and pathos compensate for the slow migration and demise of likeness and identity. Picasso would attempt to revive the physiognomic cue later in 1910 with the portraits of Wilhelm Uhde and Kahnweiler. Compared to the impact of the last "Fernandes," however, identity had become merely anecdotal. These later paintings thoroughly prevent form from coalescing as integrated mass, rendering the schematic features disembodied and absurd. Portraiture had already passed by early 1910.

It is not just form but process that distinguishes the character and motivation of Picasso's art in 1909. The articulation of the body and the serialization of the work are both acts of dispersal. Distributed across a multiplicity of pictures and sorted as such by the camera, superimposed, grafted through sculpture and dispersed again within the frame of a single canvas, the object had become a series of events or insoluble problems—a person scattered in space and time. The power of a work will always reside in the extraction of gravity directly from means.
In 1906 it was accrued through accumulation; with the Fernande series, it was, instead, retained through acts of repetition. If scattering is in part a process of dispossession, then the affective gravity of the portrait was, with the final Fernandes, now a function of loss. Likeness being extrinsic, identity would soon be the burden of the name.

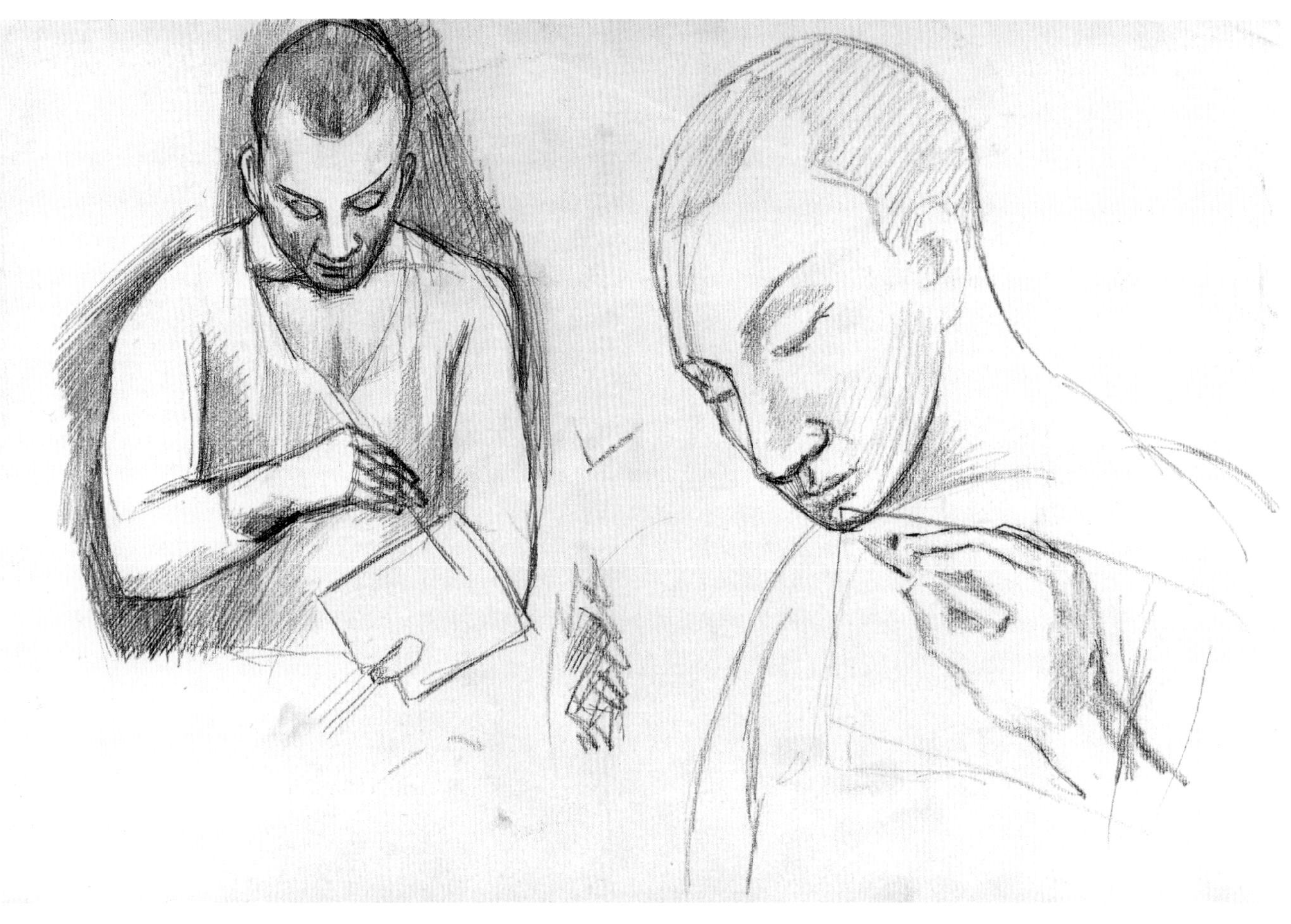

21

Pablo Picasso, *Studies for "Self-Portrait with Palette,"* Paris, 1906, pencil on paper, Musée Picasso, Paris

Catalogue

1
Bust of a Woman
Paris, spring 1909
oil on canvas
72.7 × 60 cm
28 5/8 × 23 5/8 in.
Tate, purchased 1949

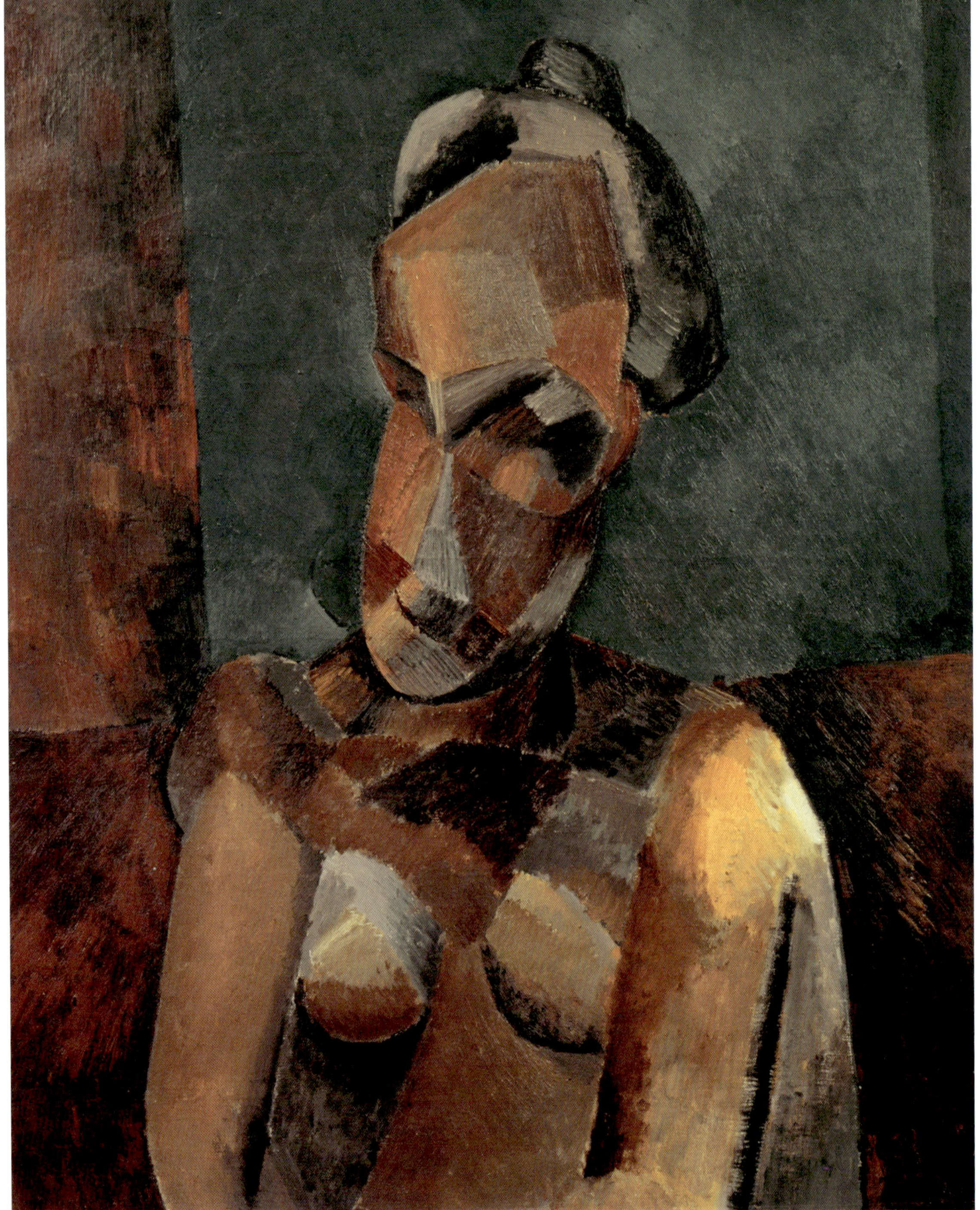

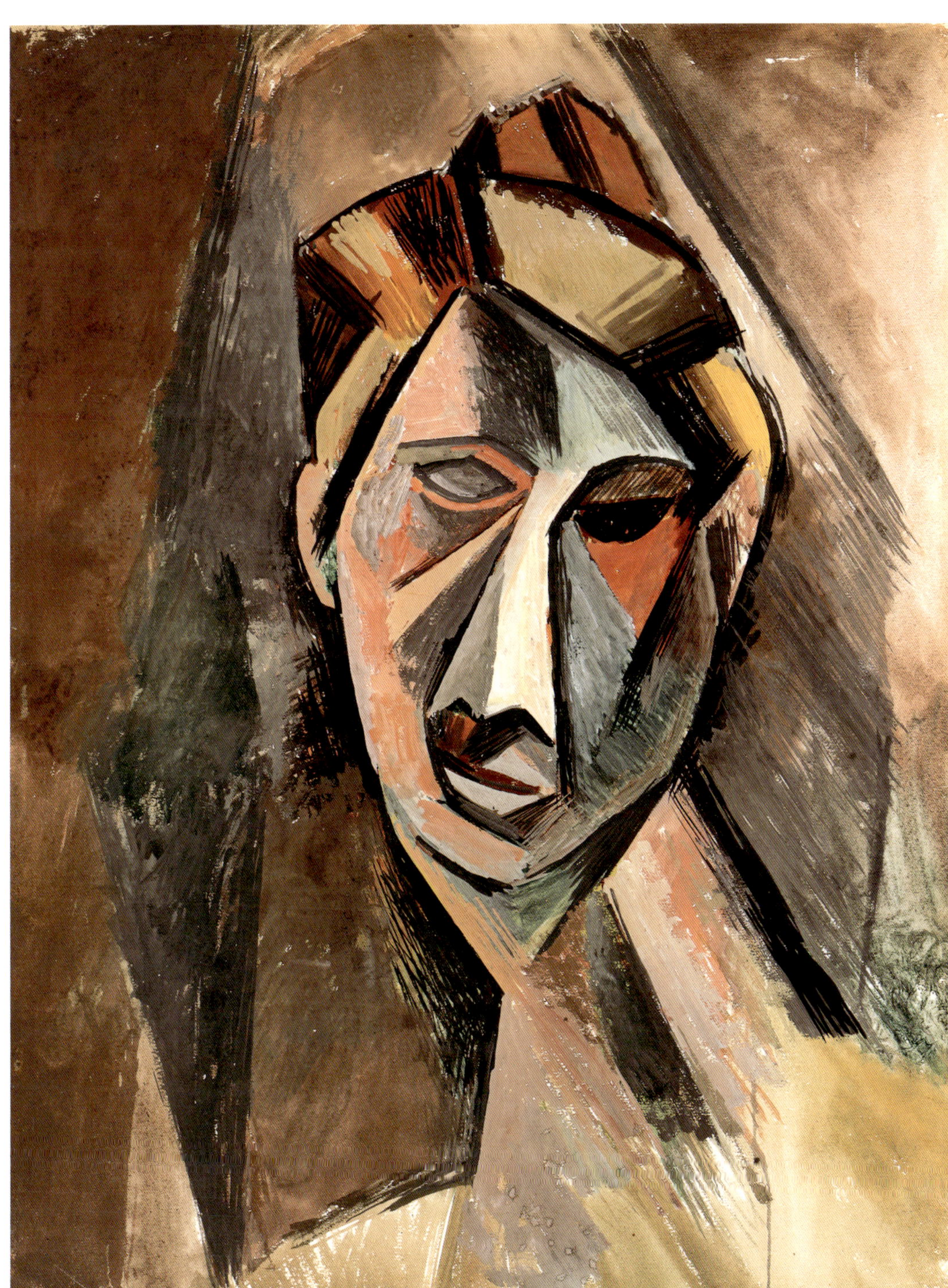

2
Bust of a Woman
Paris, spring 1909
gouache on paper
62.5 × 47 cm
24 5/8 × 18 1/2 in.
Private collection

3
Head of a Woman
Paris, spring 1909
watercolor on paper
60.3 × 47.6 cm
23 ¾ × 18 ¾ in.
Joanne and Roberto
de Guardiola

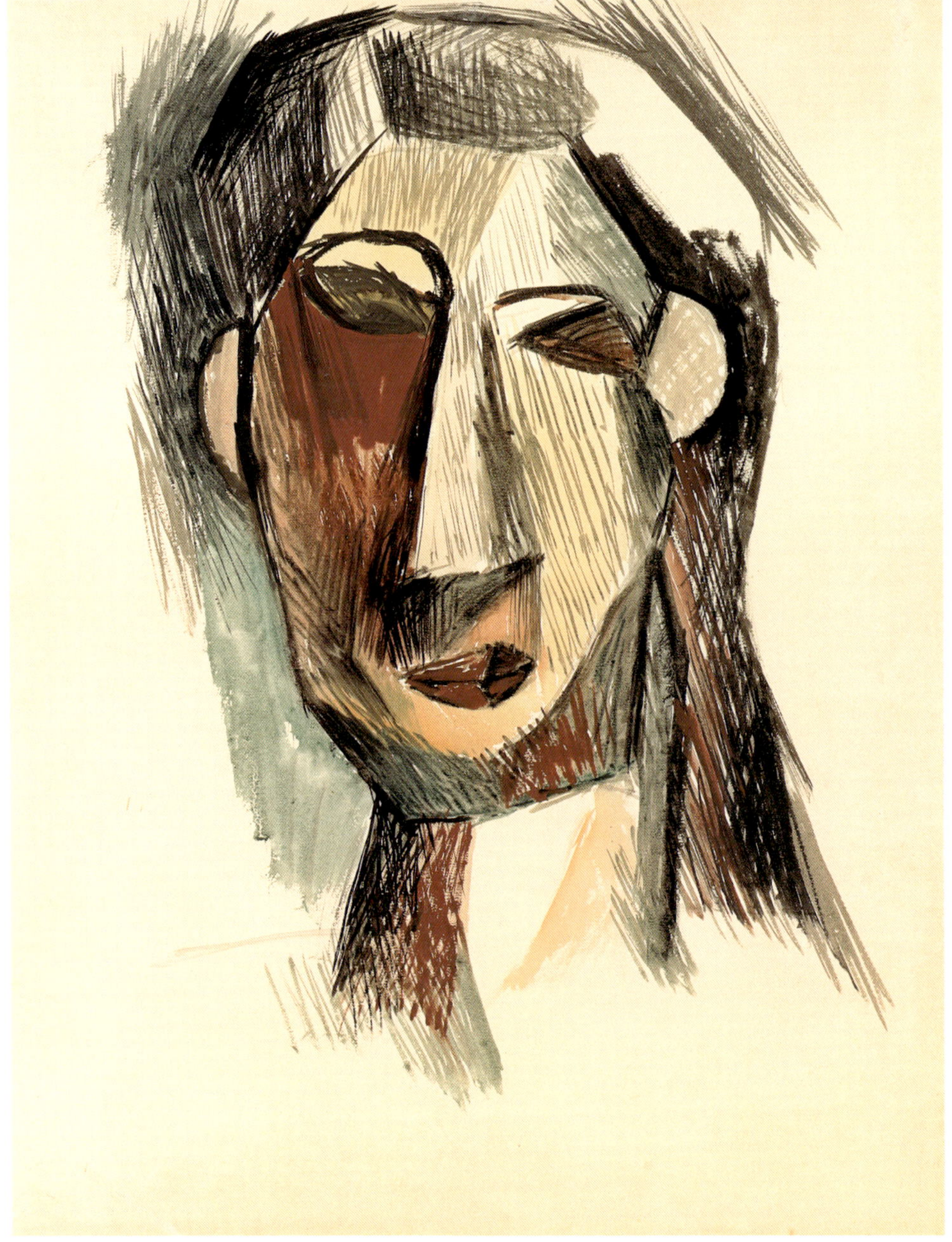

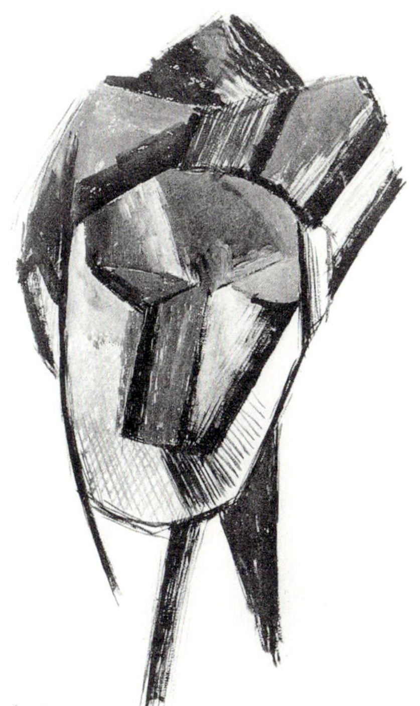

4
Head of a Woman
Paris, spring 1909
watercolor on paper
mounted on canvas
50 × 33 cm
19 11/16 × 13 in.
Location unknown

5
Head of a Woman
Paris, spring 1909
gouache on paper
62.2 × 48 cm
24 1/2 × 18 7/8 in.
The Museum of
Modern Art,
New York, Gift of
Mrs. Saidie A. May

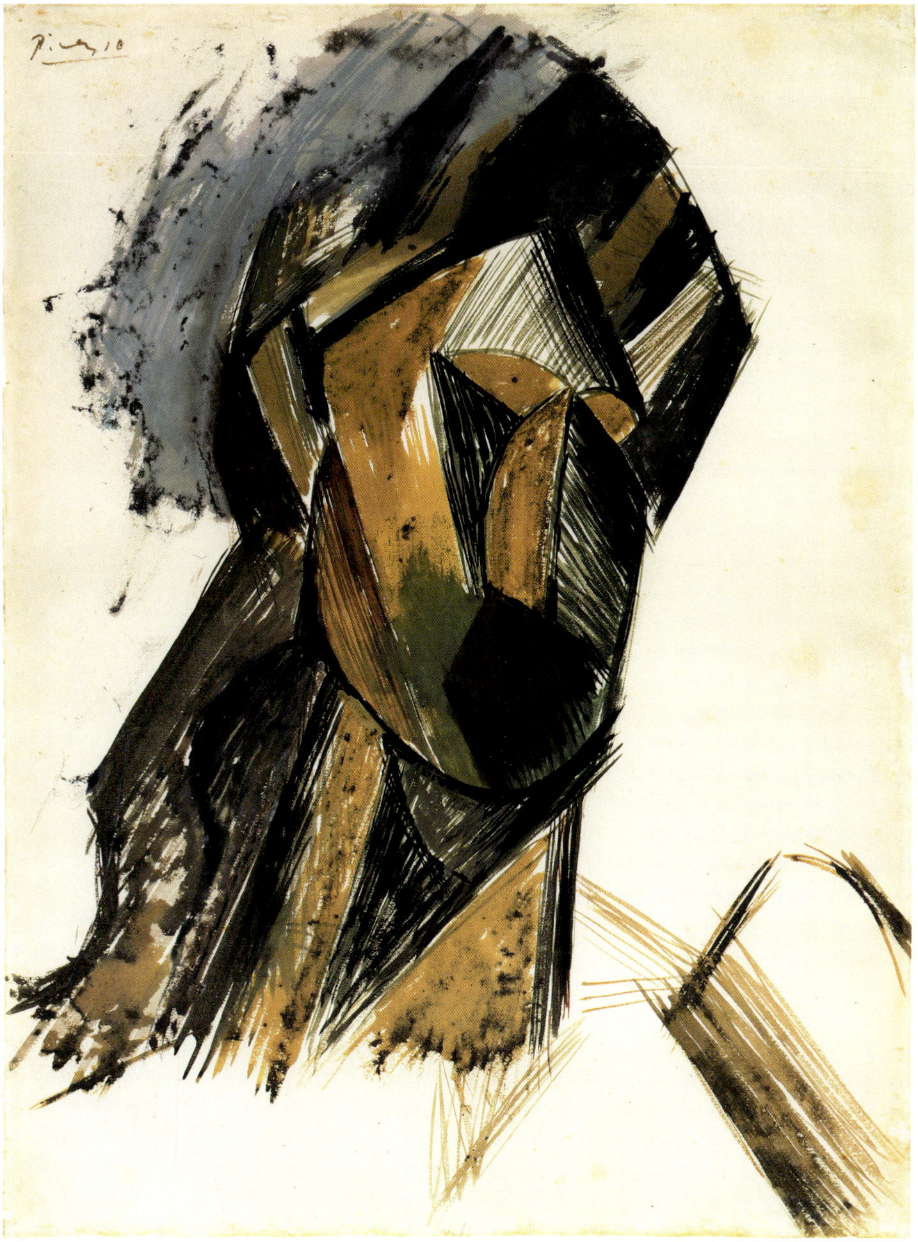

6
Head of a Woman
Paris, spring 1909
pen and brown ink on paper
63.3 × 48.3 cm
$24\frac{15}{16}$ × 19 in.
Private collection Germany, courtesy Galerie Haas, Zurich

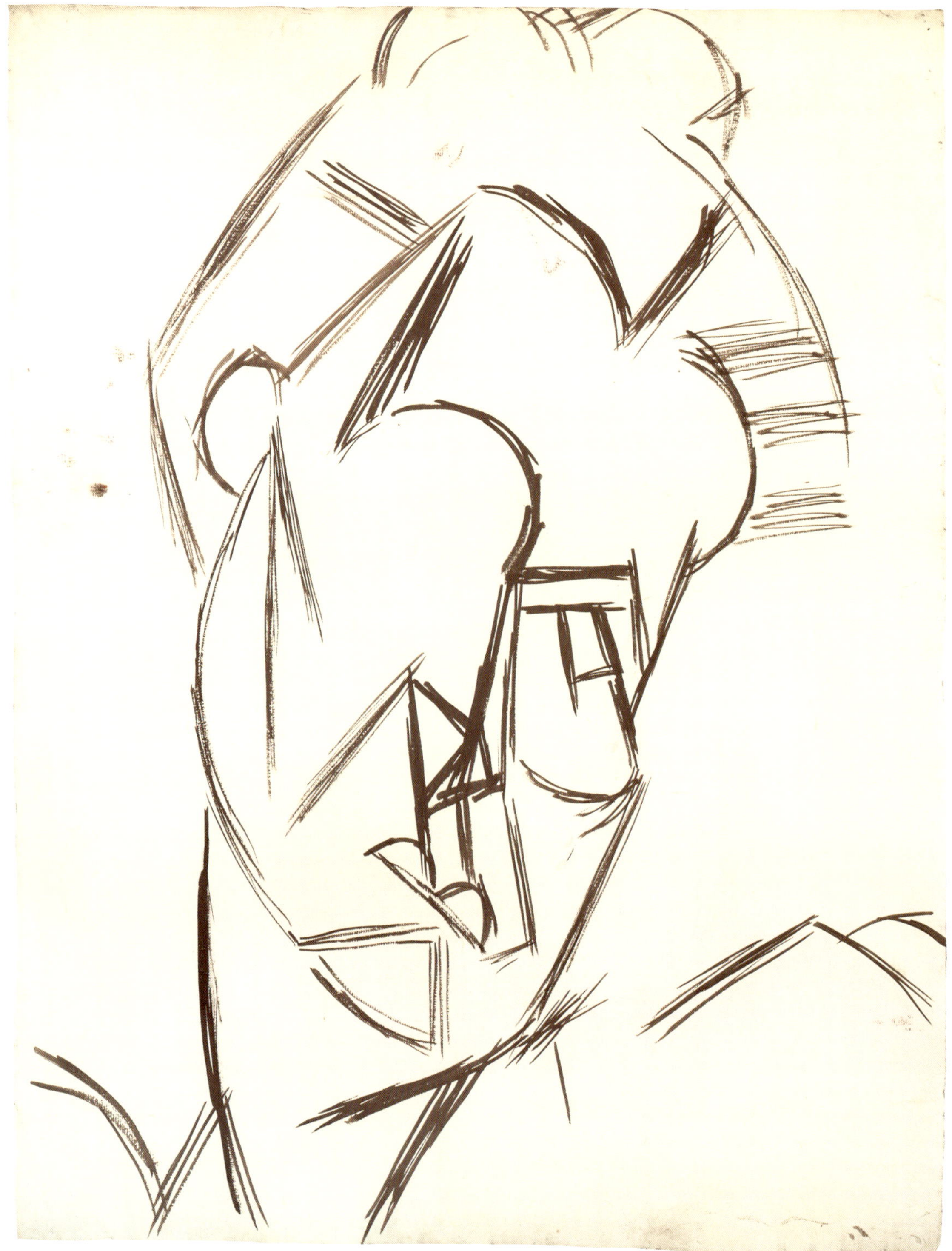

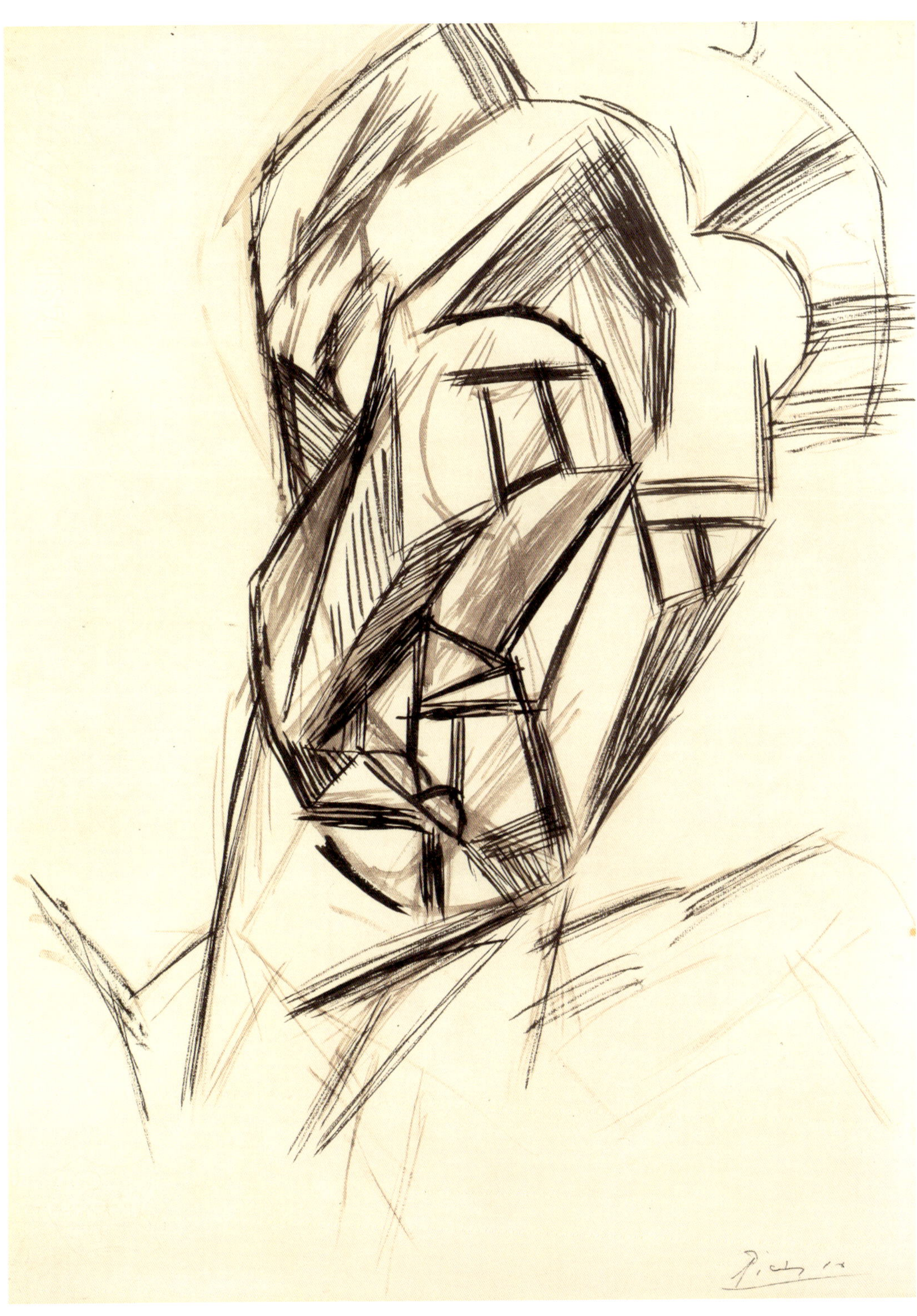

7
Head of a Woman
Paris, spring 1909
pen and ink on paper
62.5 × 46.5 cm
24 5/8 × 18 5/16 in.
Museum Ludwig,
Cologne (Ludwig
Donation)

9
Head of a Woman
Paris, spring 1909
ink and charcoal on paper
62.2 × 46.4 cm
24 1/2 × 18 1/4 in.
Location unknown

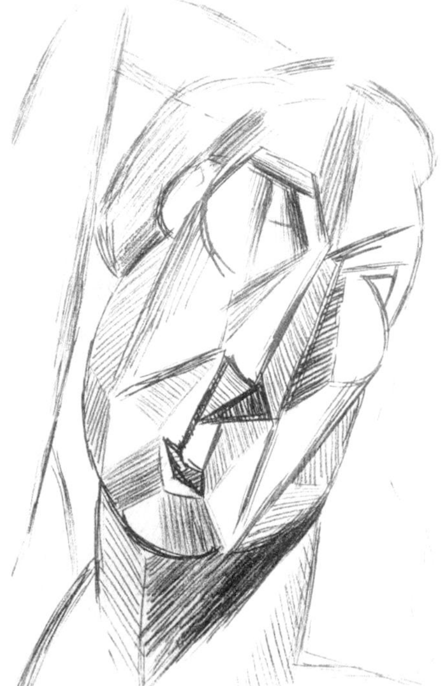

8
Head of a Woman
Paris, spring 1909
india ink on paper
63 × 48 cm
24 13/16 × 18 7/8 in.
Location unknown

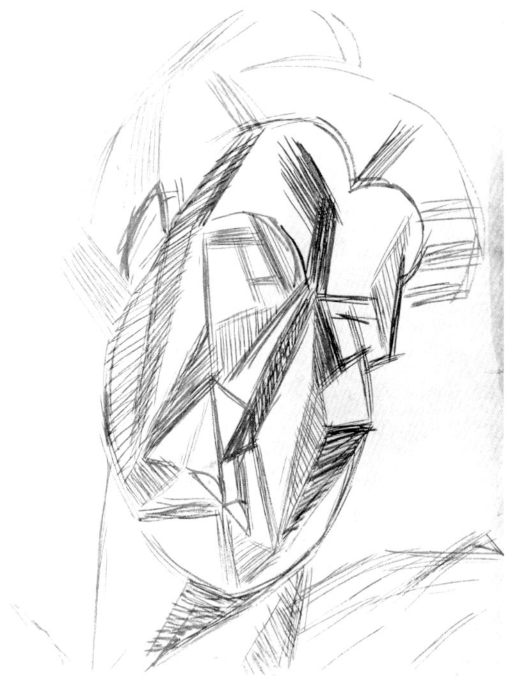

10
Head of a Woman
Paris, spring 1909
gouache and watercolor with charcoal and red chalk, stumping and erasing, on ivory laid paper
61.8 × 47.8 cm
24 5/16 × 18 13/16 in.
The Art Institute of Chicago, Edward E. Ayer Endowment in memory of Charles L. Hutchinson

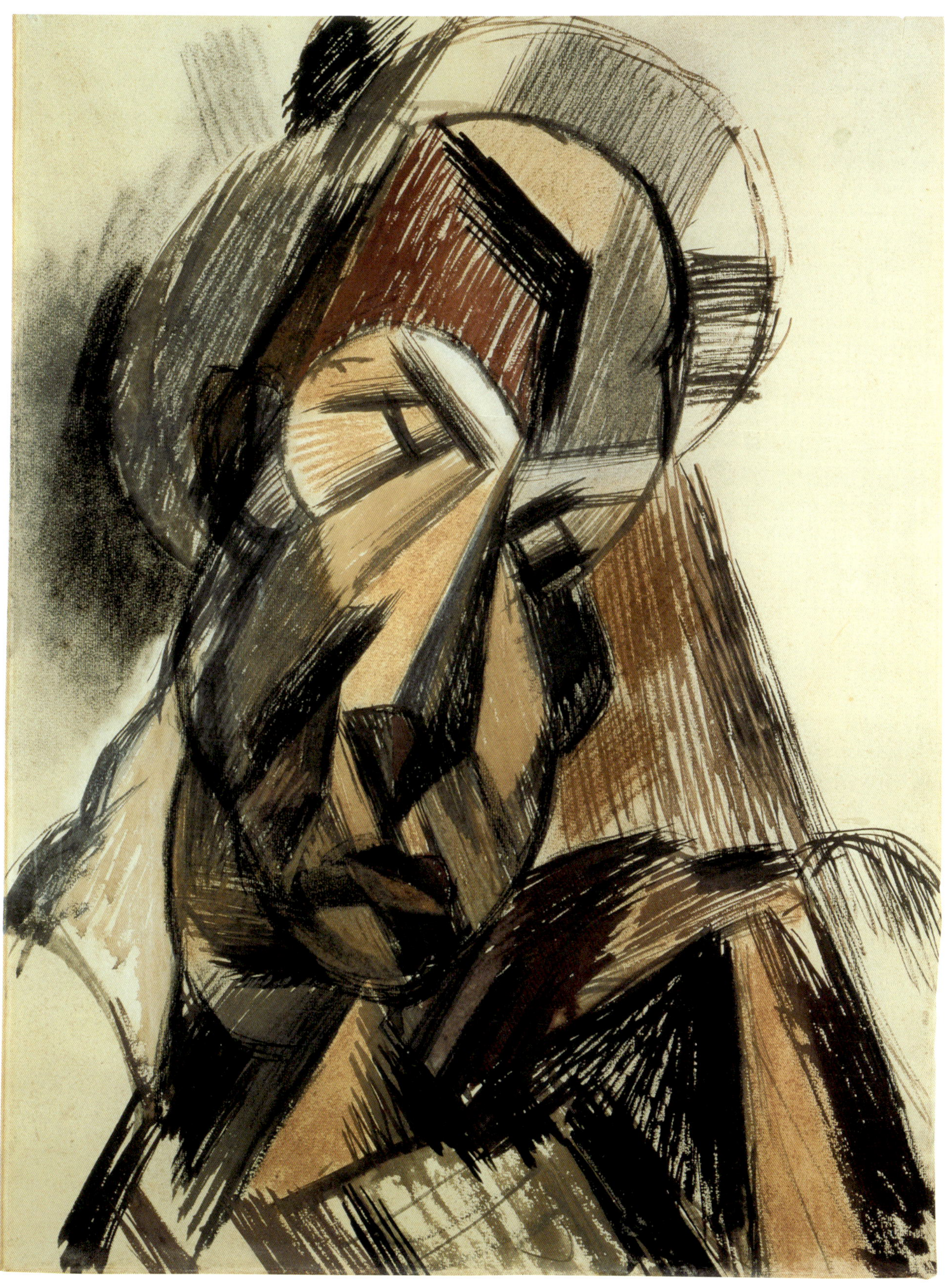

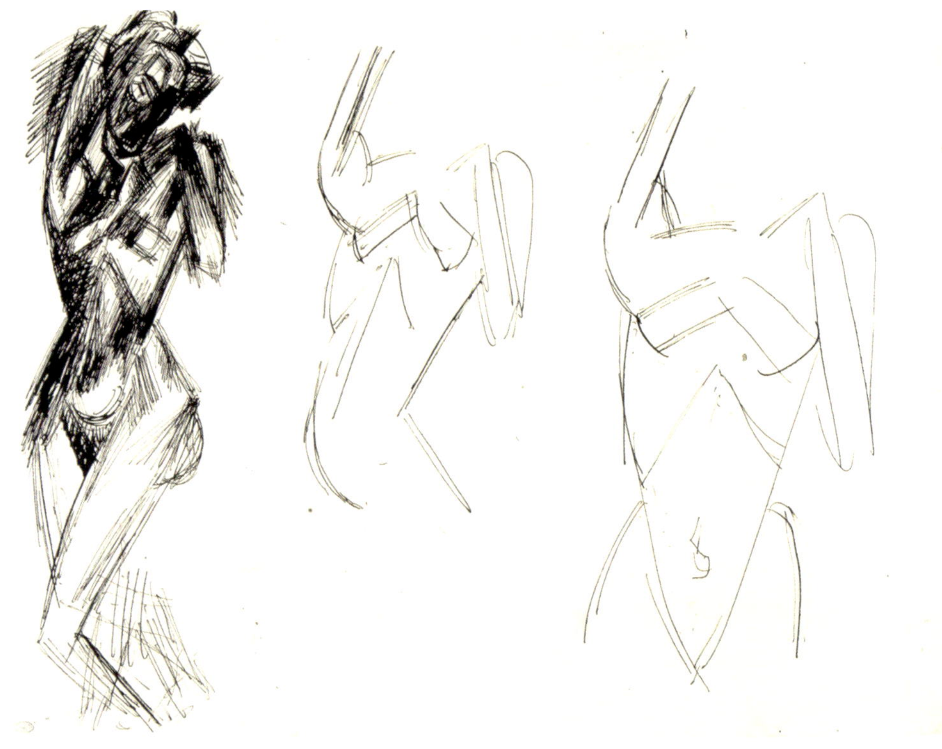

11
Three Studies of a Female Nude
Paris, early 1909
pen and ink on paper
31.5 × 48.5 cm
12 3/8 × 19 1/8 in.
Musée Picasso, Paris

12
Female Nude with Raised Arm
Paris, early 1909
pen, ink, and wash on paper
31.7 × 23.6 cm
12 1/2 × 9 5/16 in.
Musée Picasso, Paris

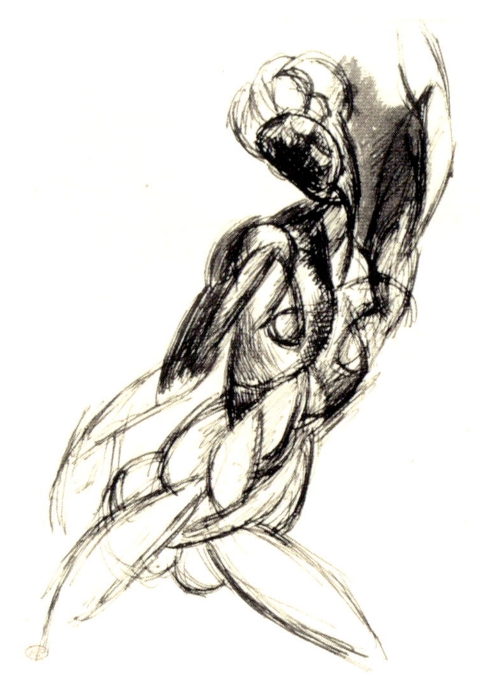

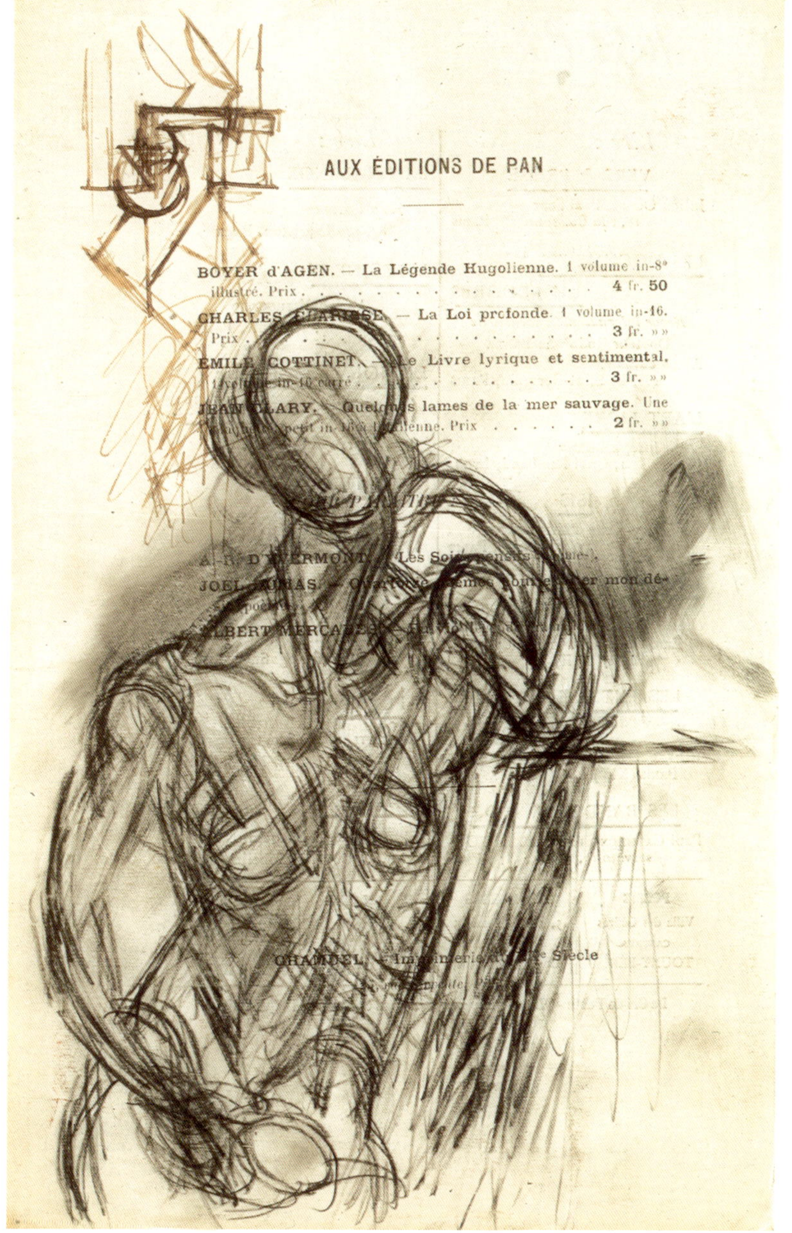

13
Study of a Woman
Paris, early 1909
charcoal on a page from the periodical *Pan*
26 × 16.5 cm
10¼ × 6½ in.
Collection Marina Picasso; Courtesy Galerie Jan Krugier, Ditesheim & Cie, Geneva

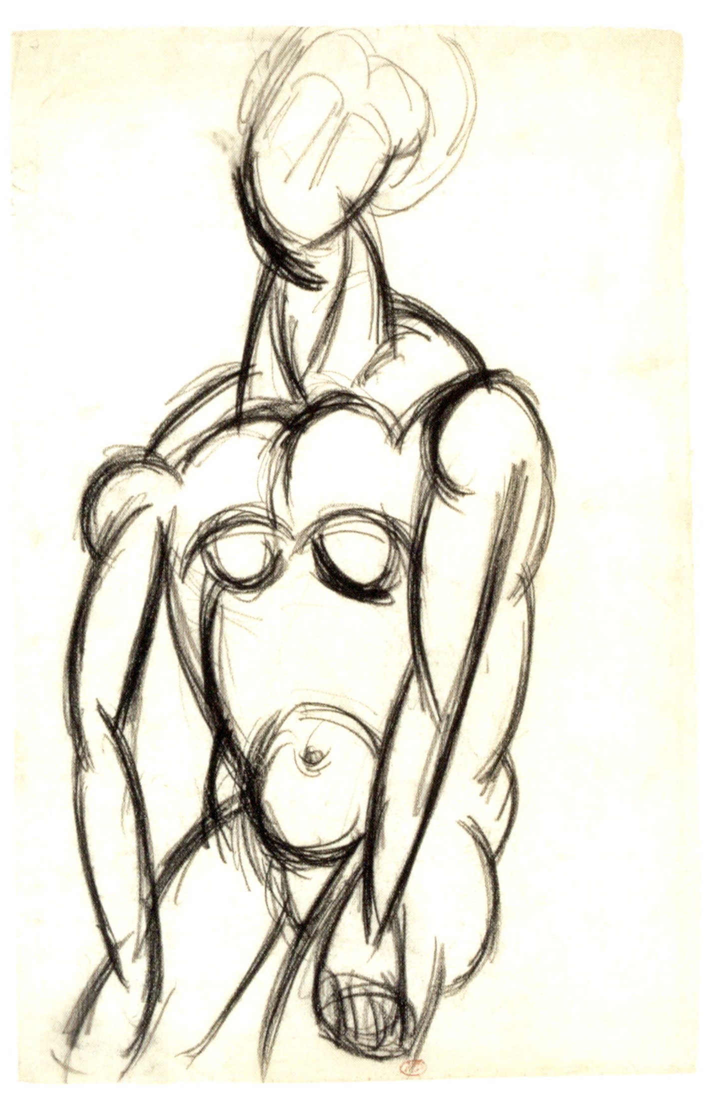

14
Seated Nude
Paris, early 1909
black pencil on paper
32.3 × 21.6 cm
12 11/16 × 8 1/2 in.
Musée Picasso, Paris

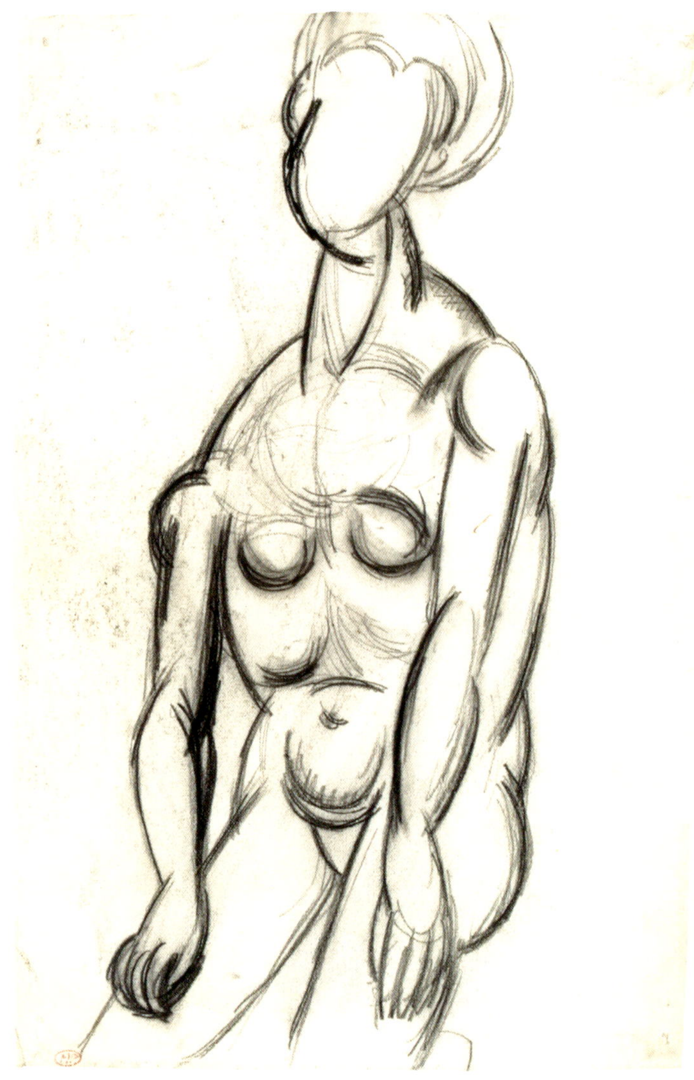

15
Seated Nude
Paris, early 1909
black pencil on paper
32.3 × 21.3 cm
12 11/16 × 8 3/8 in.
Musée Picasso, Paris

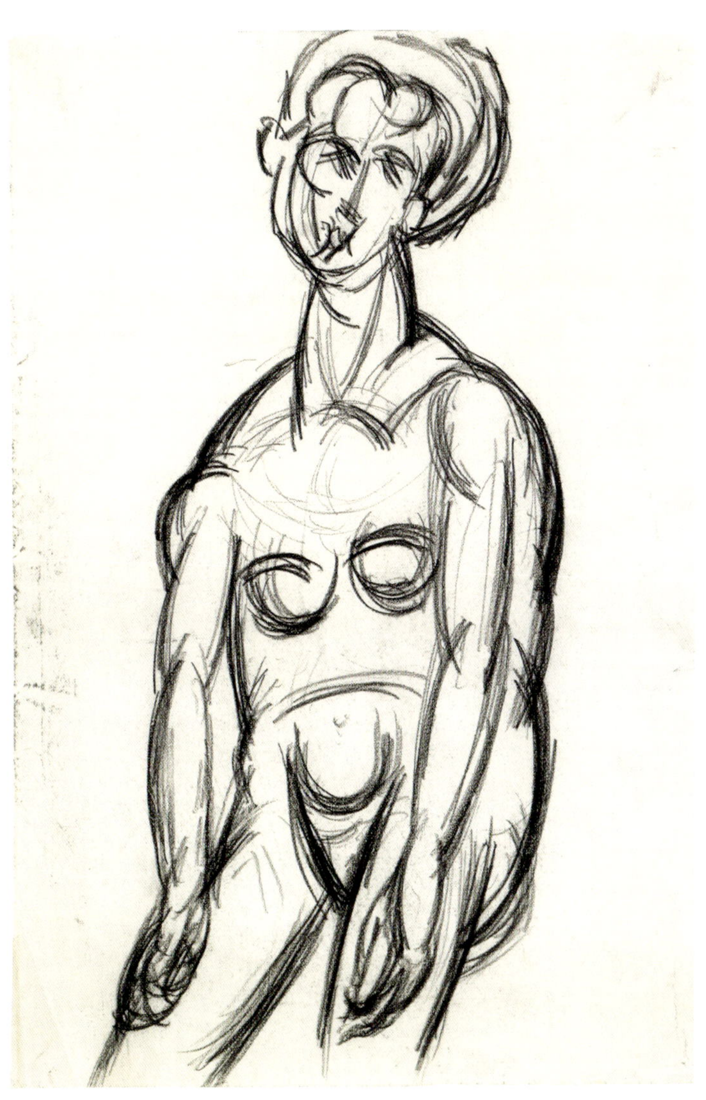

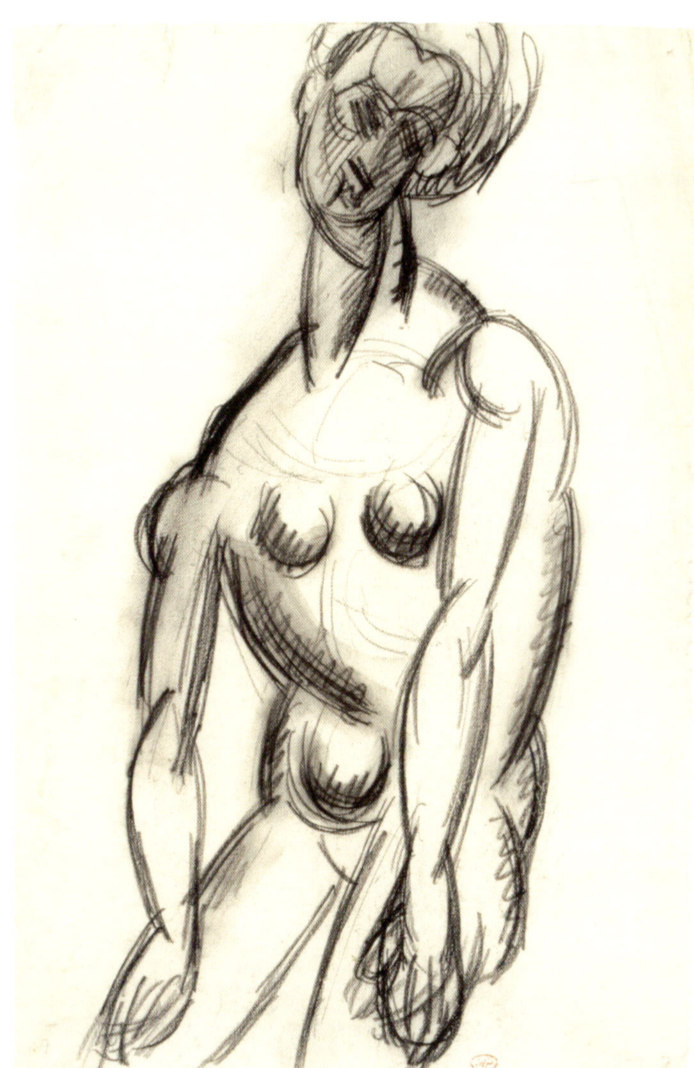

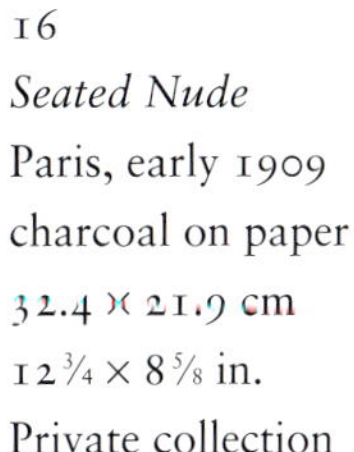

16
Seated Nude
Paris, early 1909
charcoal on paper
32.4 × 21.9 cm
12¾ × 8⅝ in.
Private collection

17
Seated Nude
Paris, early 1909
black pencil on paper
32.6 × 21.4 cm
12 13/16 × 8 7/16 in.
Musée Picasso, Paris

18
Seated Nude
spring–summer 1909
charcoal on one sheet of paper, torn and pinned
41.9 × 21.9 cm
16½ × 8⅝ in.
Private collection

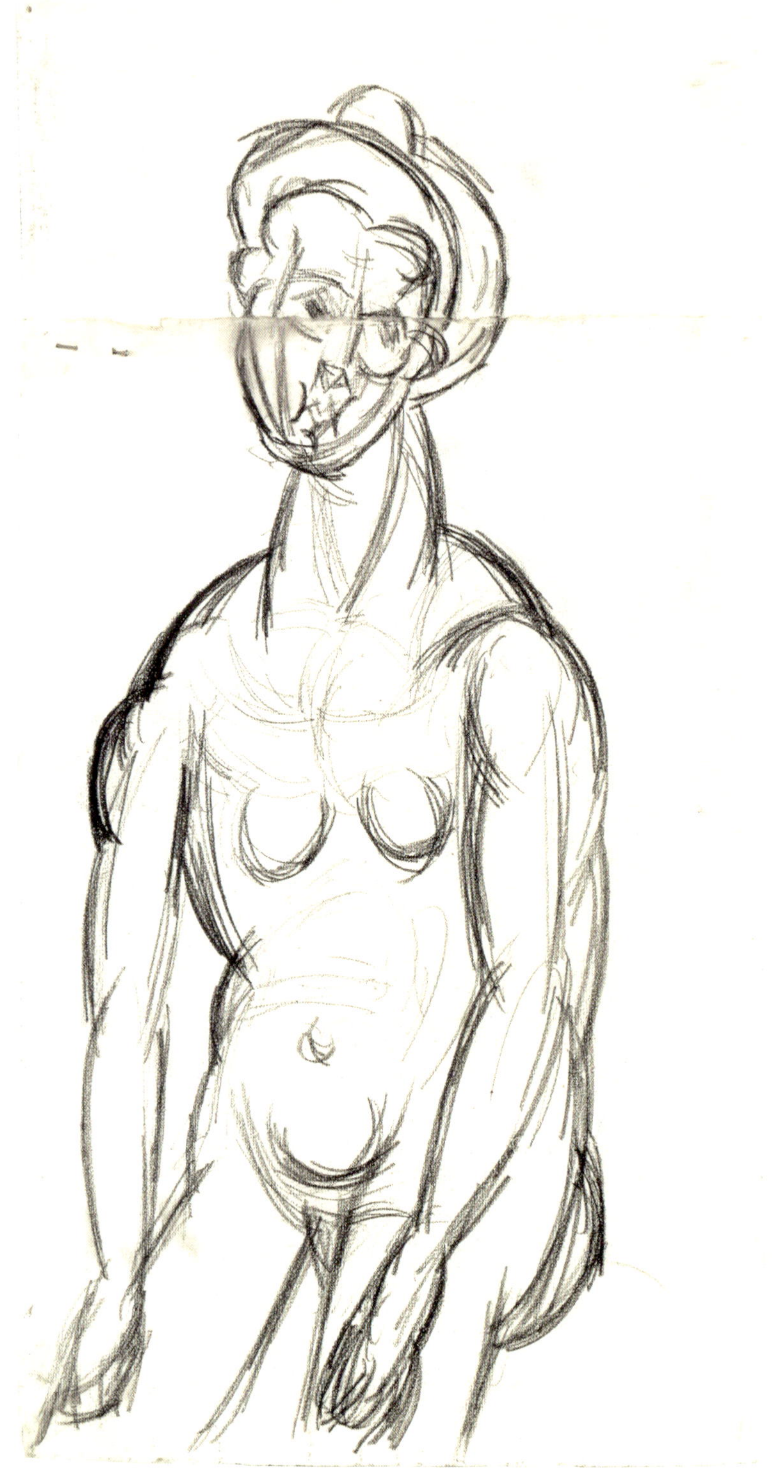

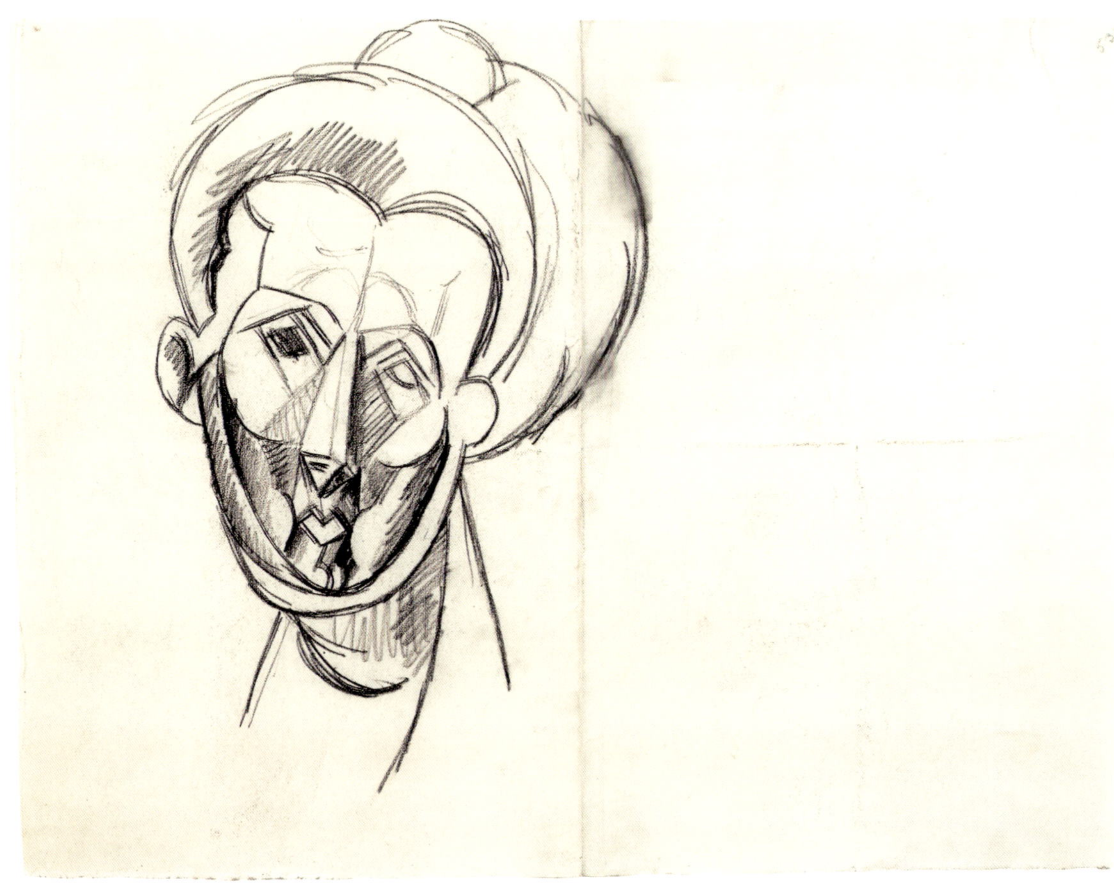

19
Head of a Woman
spring–summer 1909
charcoal on paper
32.4 × 43.2 cm
12¾ × 17 in.
Private collection

20
Head of a Woman
Horta de Ebro,
summer 1909
oil on canvas
59 × 50 cm
23 1/4 × 19 11/16 in.
Narodni muzej,
Belgrade

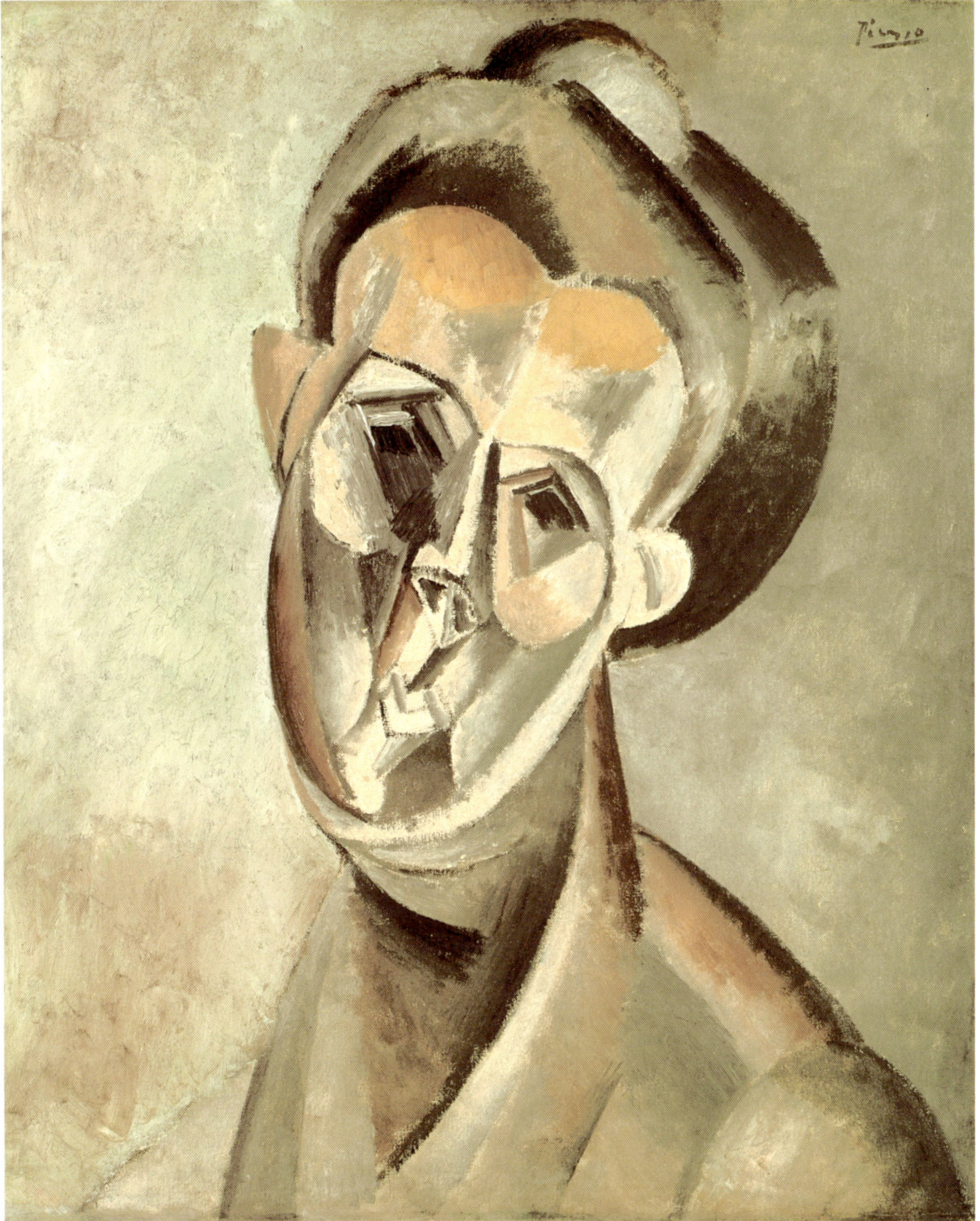

Studio photographs (see cat. 55) show that cats. 21 and 22 originally formed a single work.

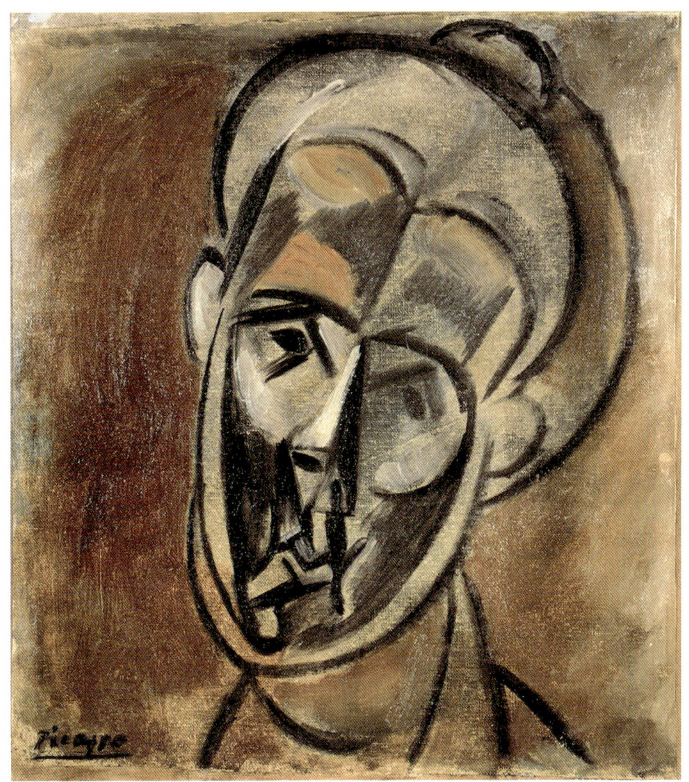

21
Head of a Woman
Horta de Ebro,
summer 1909
oil on canvas
35 × 32 cm
13 ¾ × 12 ⅝ in.
Nichido Museum,
Kasama

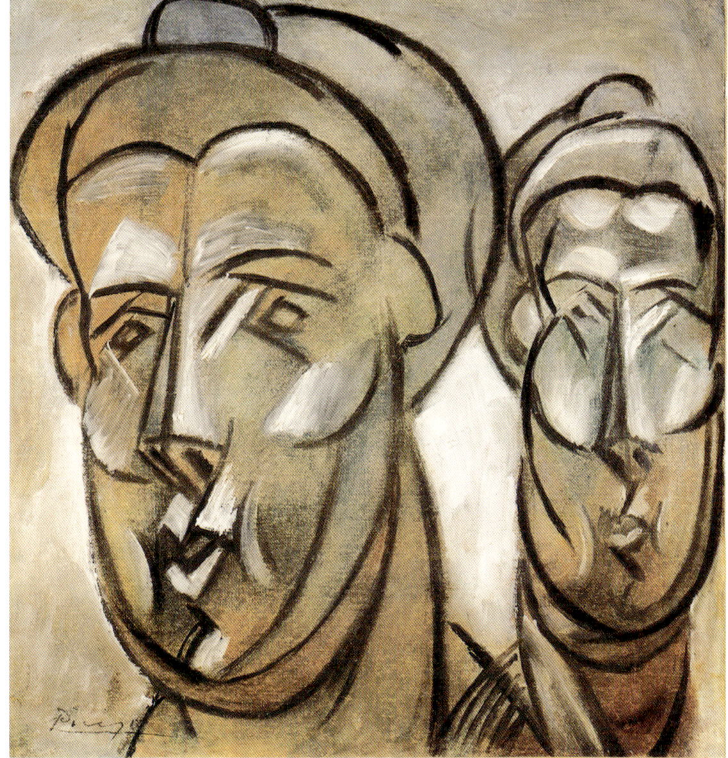

22
Two Heads
Horta de Ebro,
summer 1909
oil on canvas
36 × 35 cm
14 3/16 × 13 ¾ in.
Courtesy Galerie
Gmurzynska,
Cologne

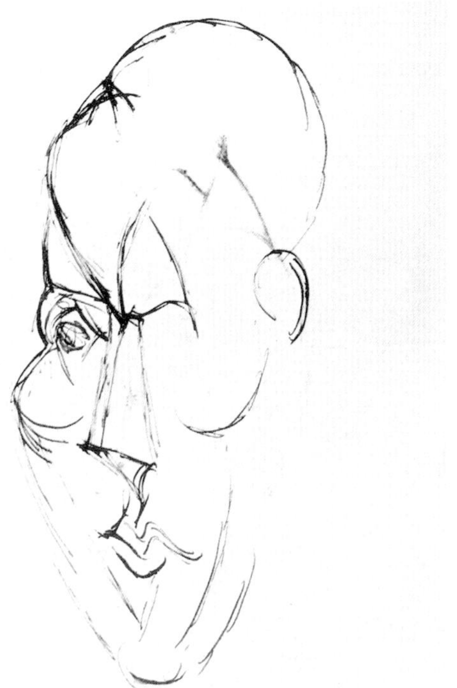

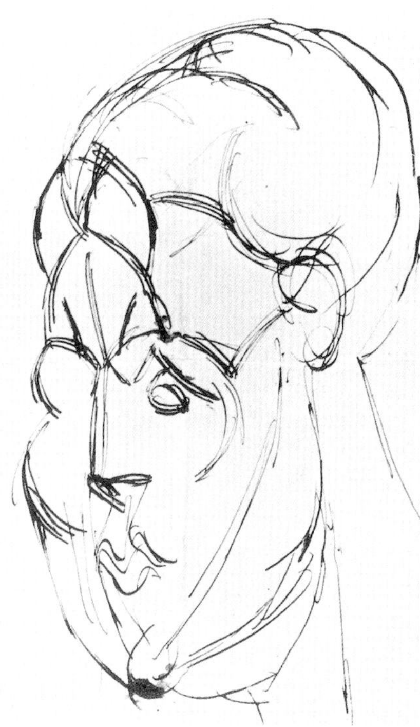

23
Head of a Woman
Horta de Ebro,
summer 1909
india ink on paper
21.6 × 16.5 cm
8 ½ × 6 ½ in.
Heirs of the artist

24
Head of a Woman
Horta de Ebro,
summer 1909
india ink on paper
21.6 × 16.5 cm
8 ½ × 6 ½ in.
Heirs of the artist

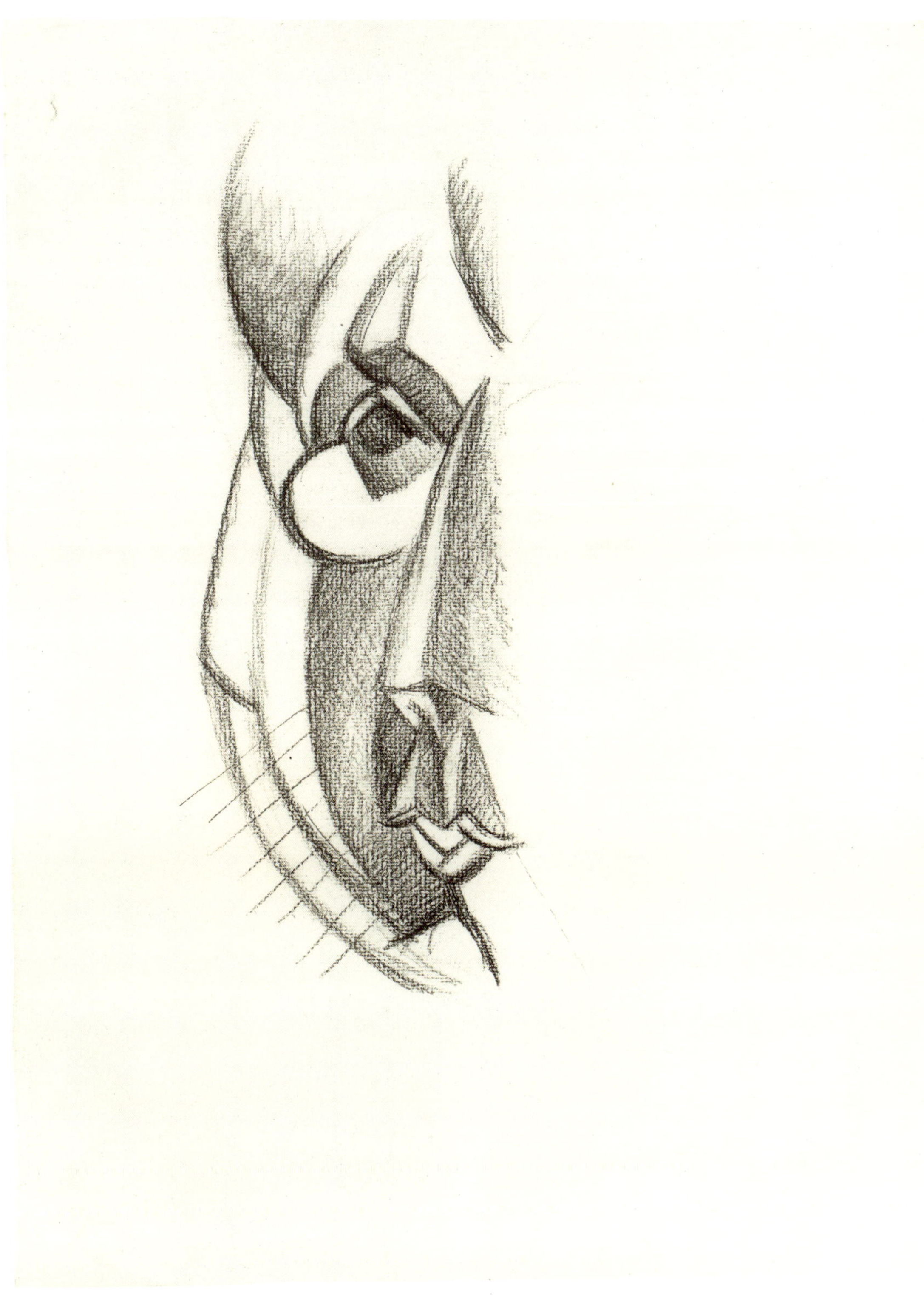

25
Study for
Head of a Woman
Horta de Ebro,
summer 1909
charcoal on paper
32 × 24.5 cm
12⅝ × 9⅝ in.
Jan and Marie-Anne
Krugier-Poniatowski
Collection

26
Head of a Woman
Horta de Ebro,
summer 1909
ink on paper
10.8 × 13.3 cm
4 ¼ × 5 ¼ in.
Heirs of the artist

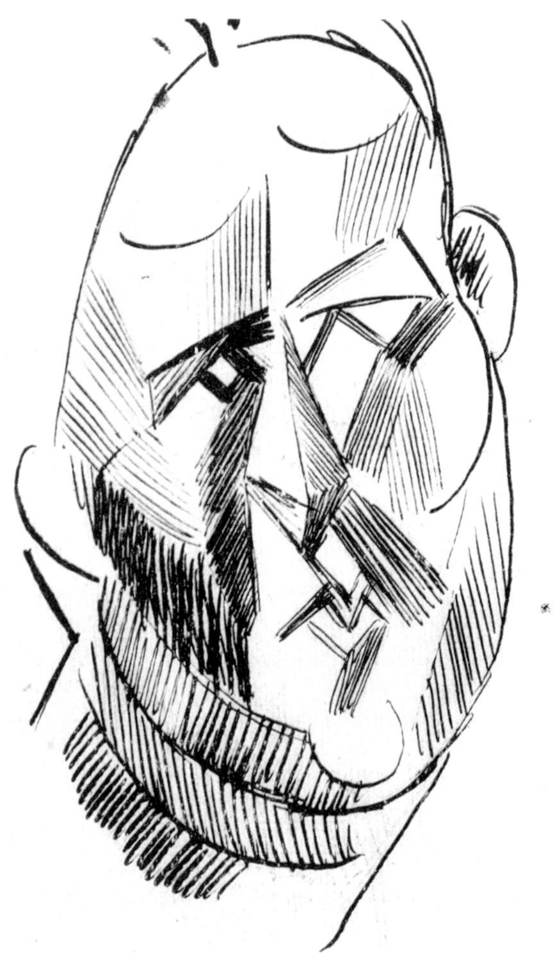

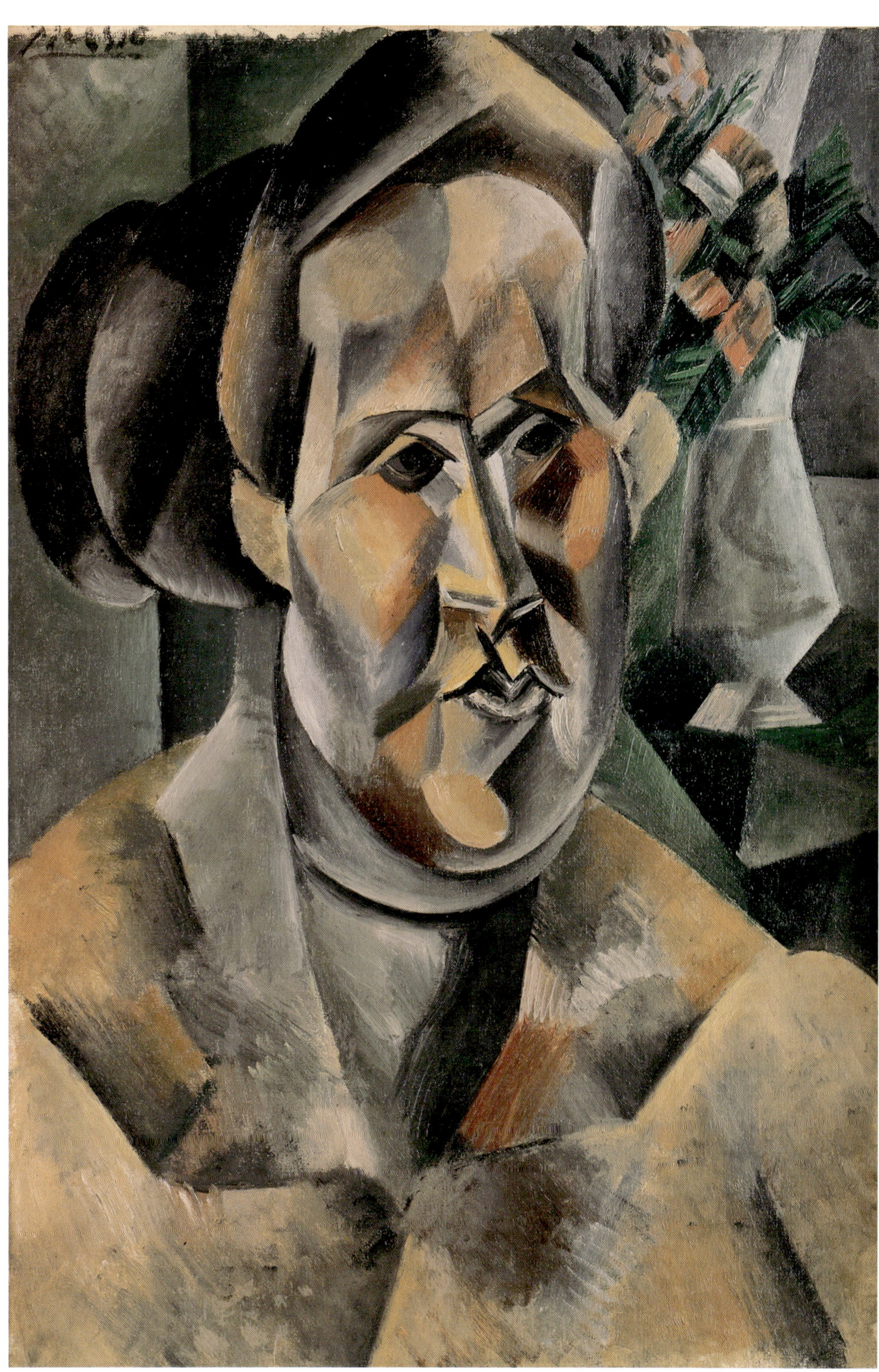

27
Portrait of Fernande
Horta de Ebro,
summer 1909
oil on canvas
61.8 × 42.8 cm
24 5/16 × 16 7/8 in.
Kunstsammlung
Nordrhein-Westfalen,
Düsseldorf

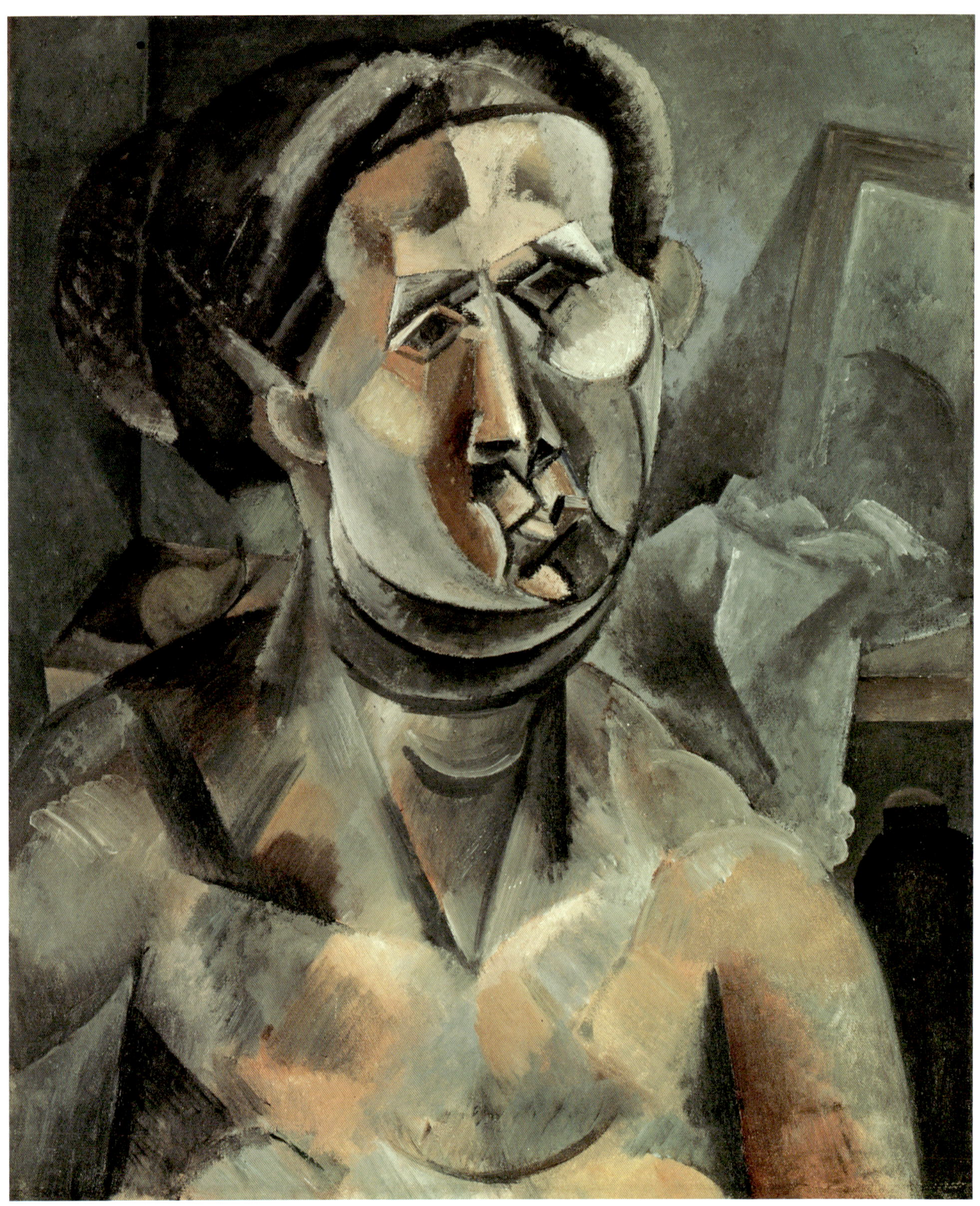

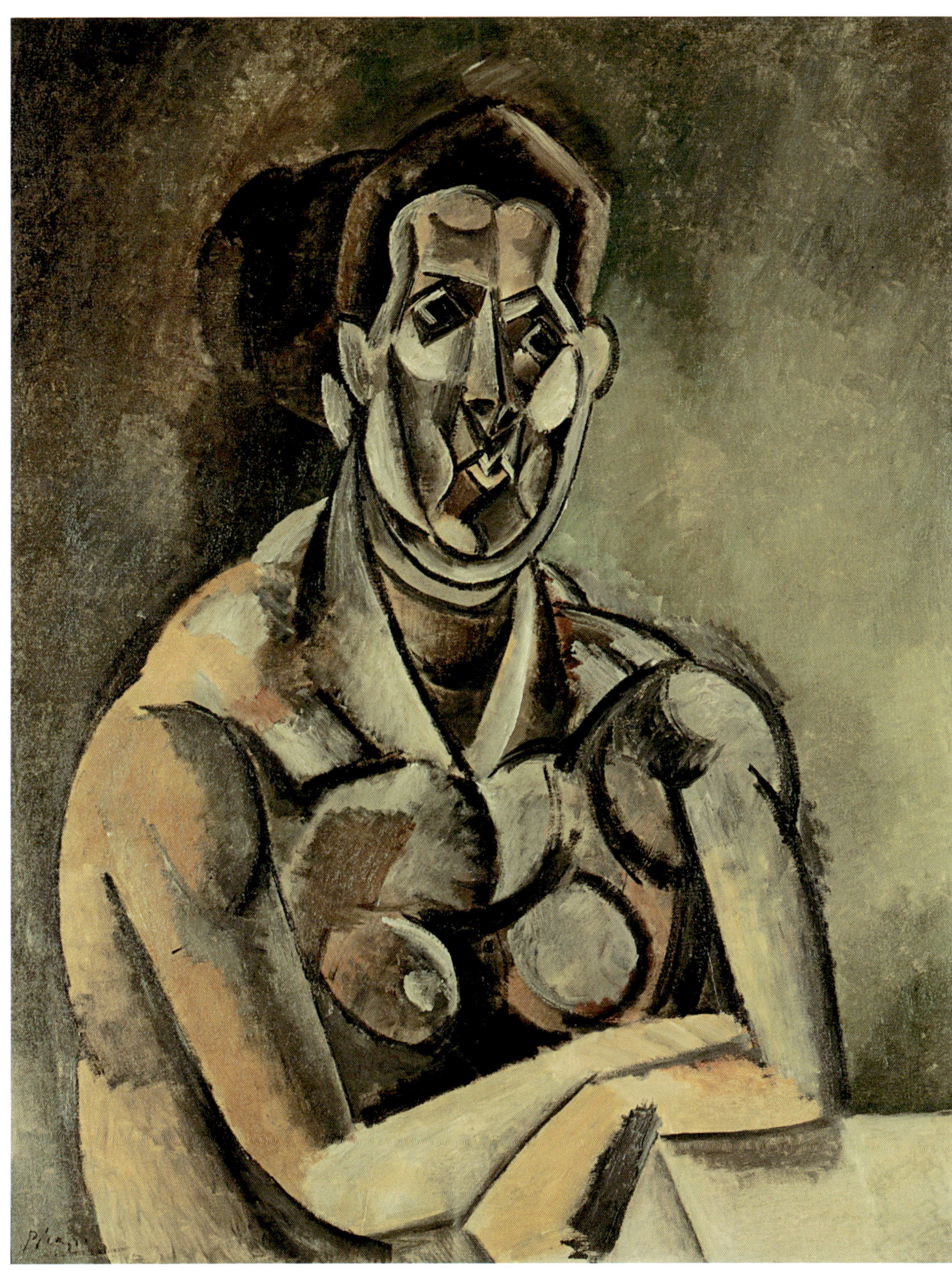

28
Head of a Woman (Fernande)
Horta de Ebro, summer 1909
oil on canvas
60.6 × 51.3 cm
23 7/8 × 20 3/16 in.
The Art Institute of Chicago, Joseph Winterbotham Collection

29
Bust of a Woman
Horta de Ebro, summer 1909
oil on canvas
93 × 74 cm
36 5/8 × 29 1/8 in.
Hiroshima Museum of Art

30
Head of a Woman (Fernande)
Horta de Ebro, summer 1909
black chalk and gray wash on paper
64.1 × 47 cm
25 ¼ × 18 ½ in.
Private collection

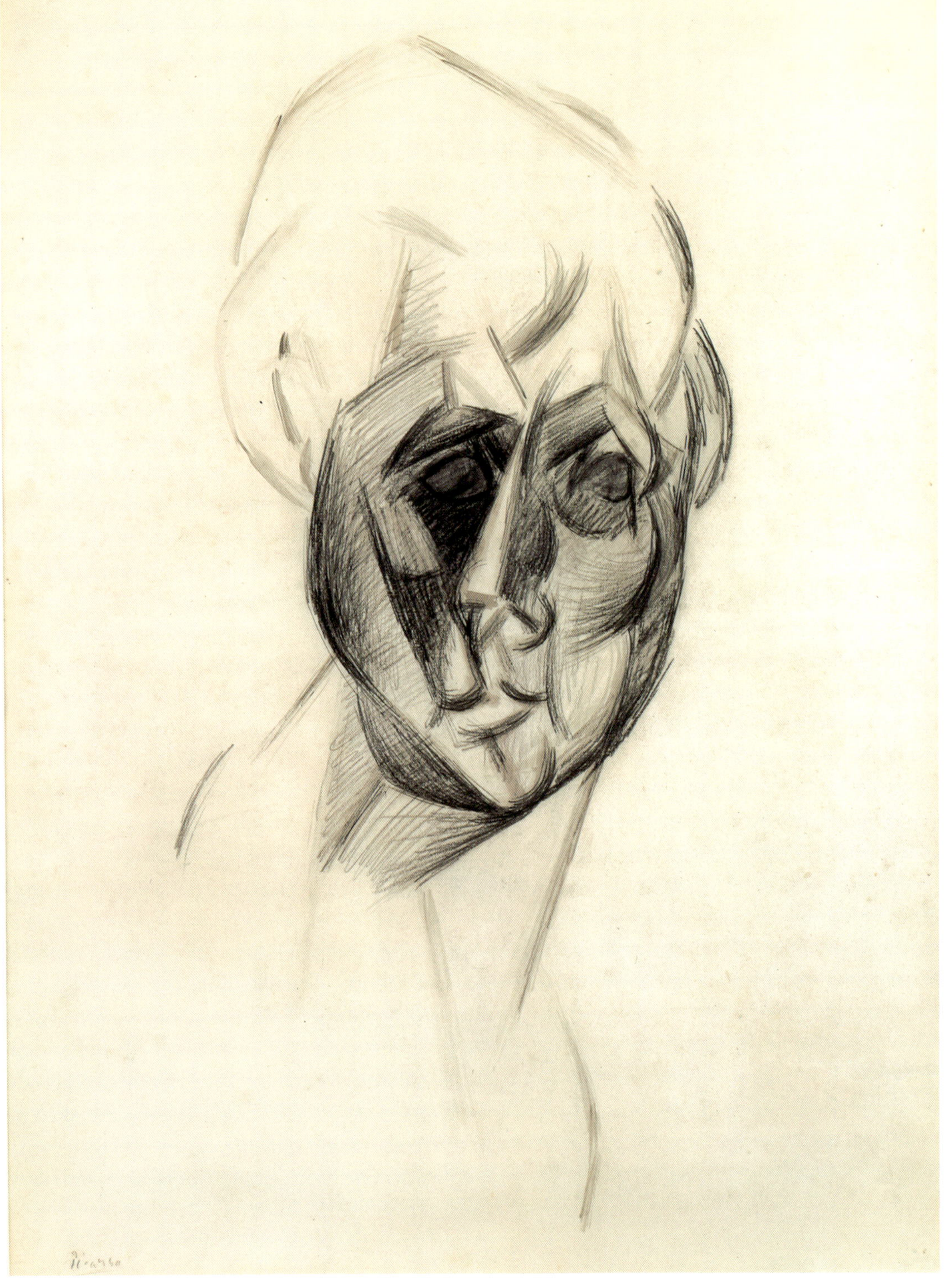

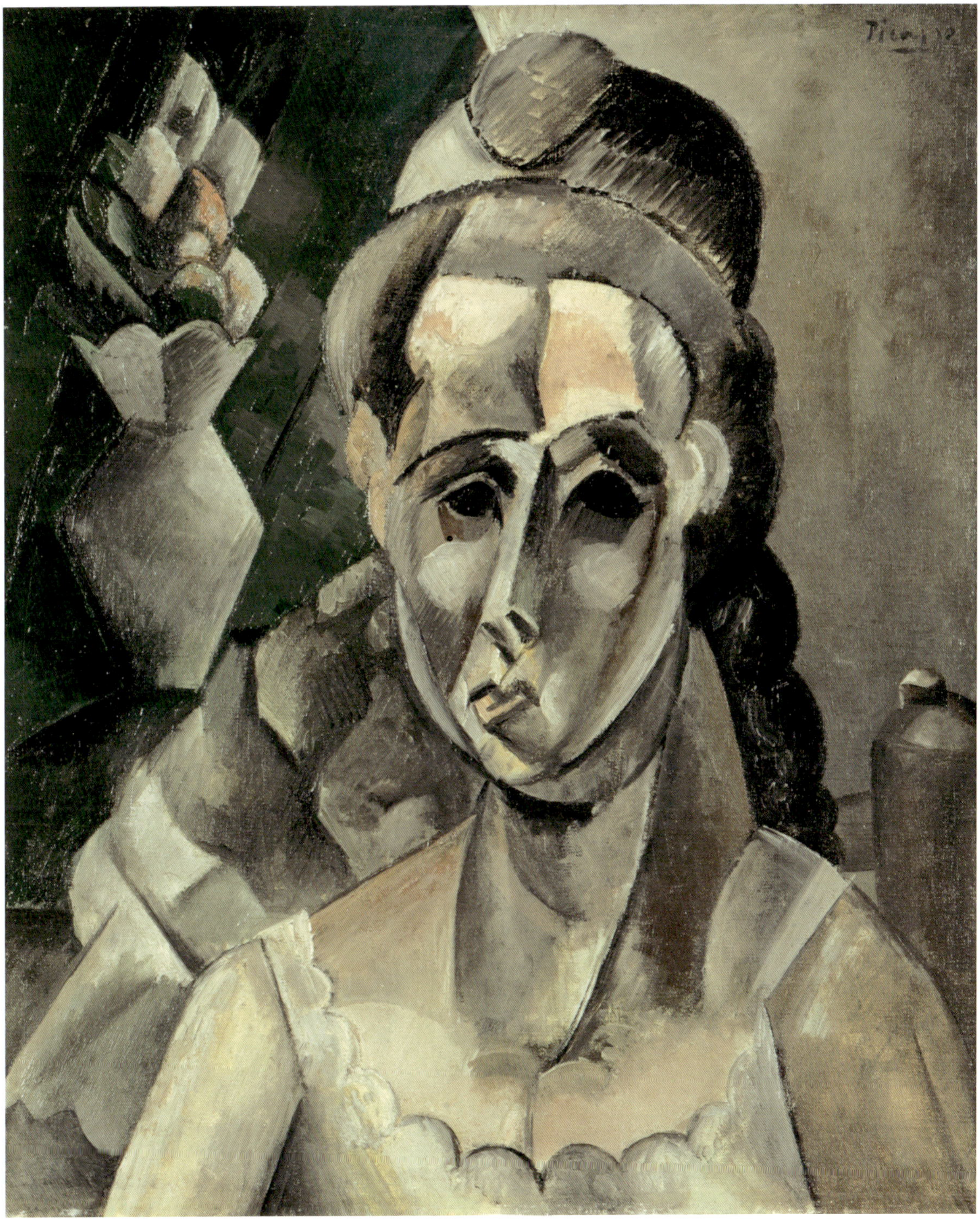

31
Woman with a Vase of Flowers
Horta de Ebro, summer 1909
oil on canvas
61 × 52 cm
24 × 20½ in.
Stiftung Sammlung Bernhard Sprengel, Sprengel Museum Hannover

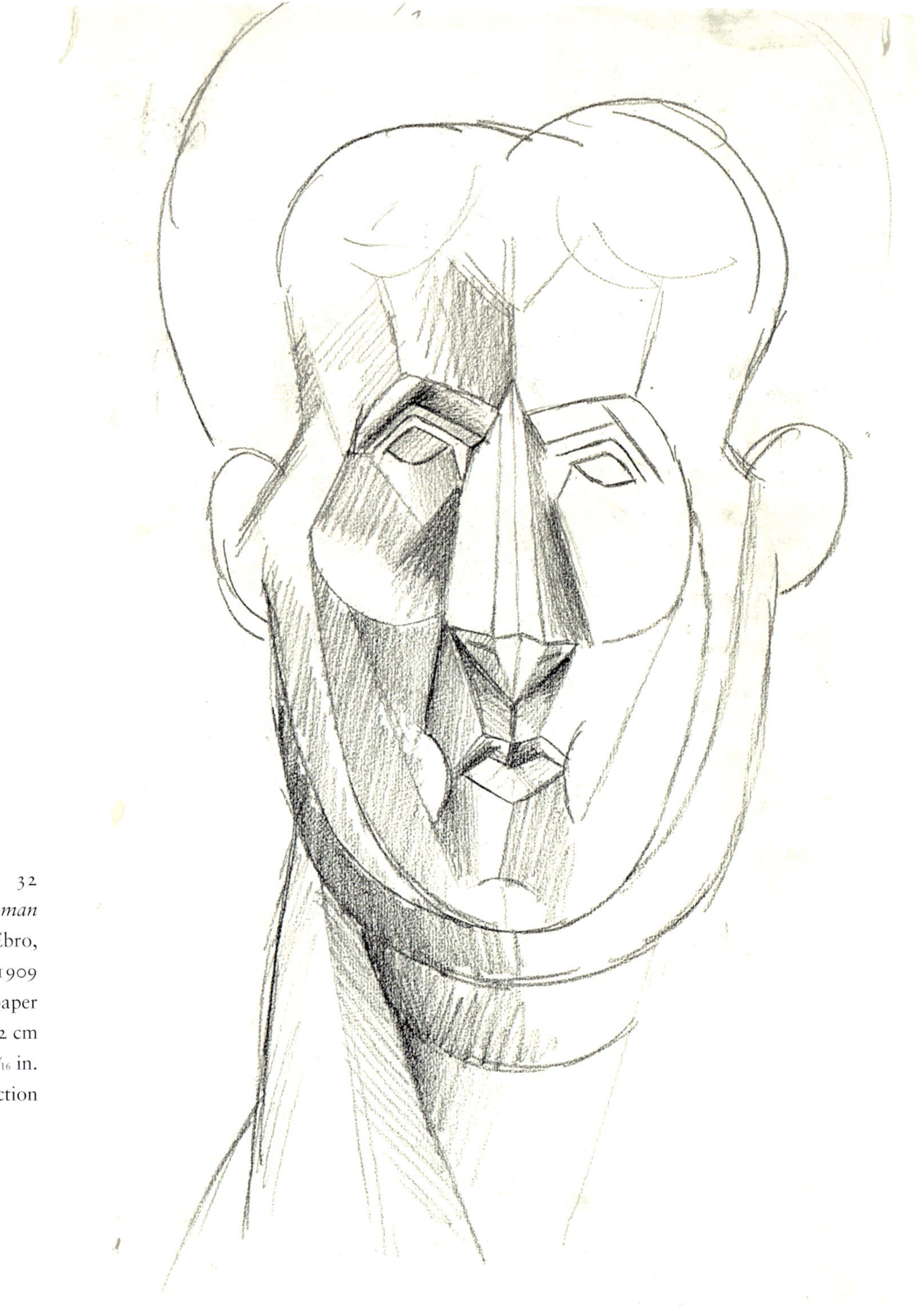

32
Head of a Woman
Horta de Ebro,
summer 1909
charcoal on paper
32.5 × 22 cm
12 13/16 × 8 11/16 in.
Private collection

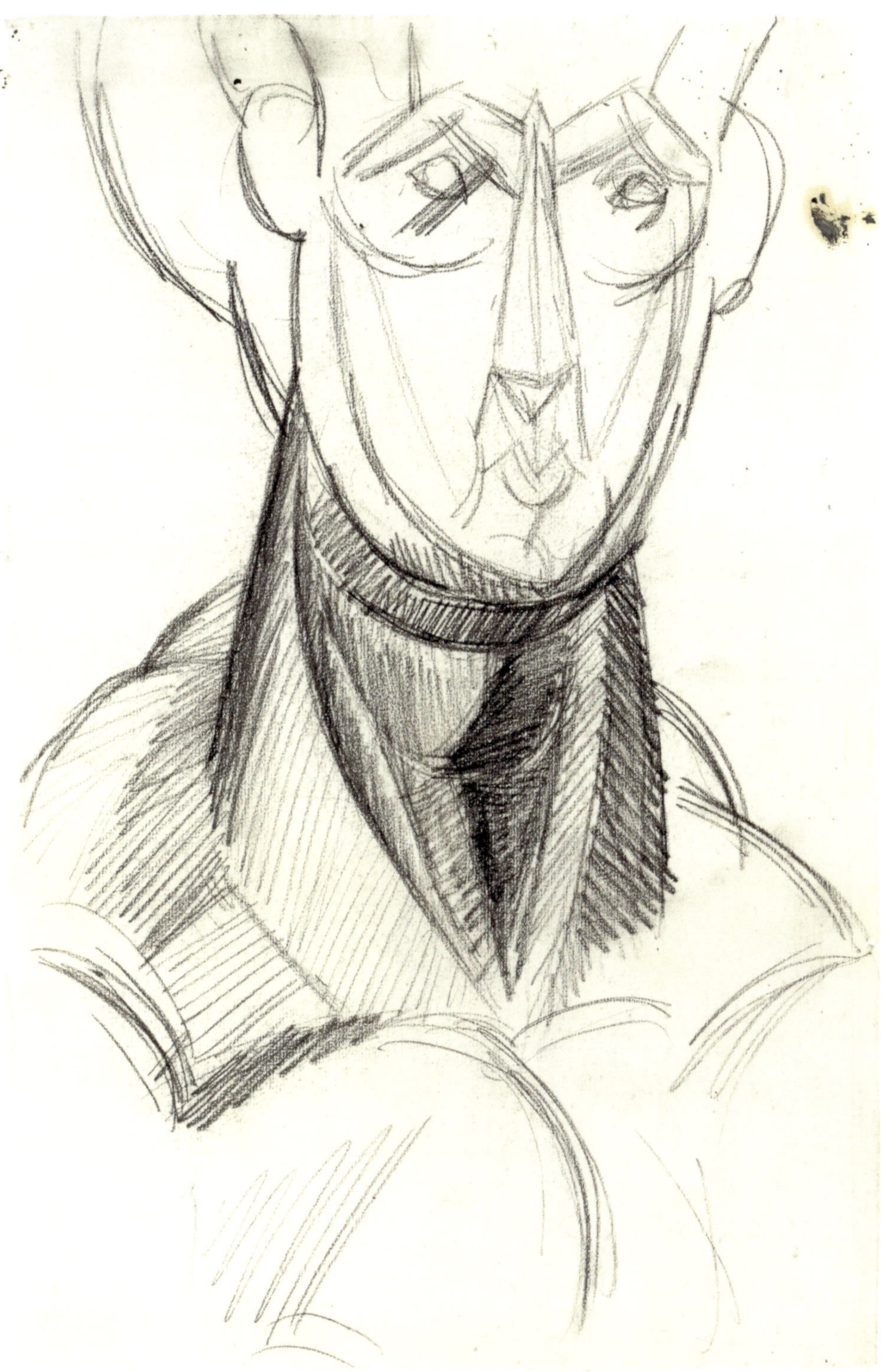

33
Bust of a Woman
Horta de Ebro,
summer 1909
charcoal on paper
32.5 × 22 cm
12 13/16 × 8 11/16 in.
Private collection

34
Study (Woman's Neck)
Horta de Ebro,
summer 1909
charcoal on paper
32.4 × 21.9 cm
12 3/4 × 8 5/8 in.
Heirs of the artist

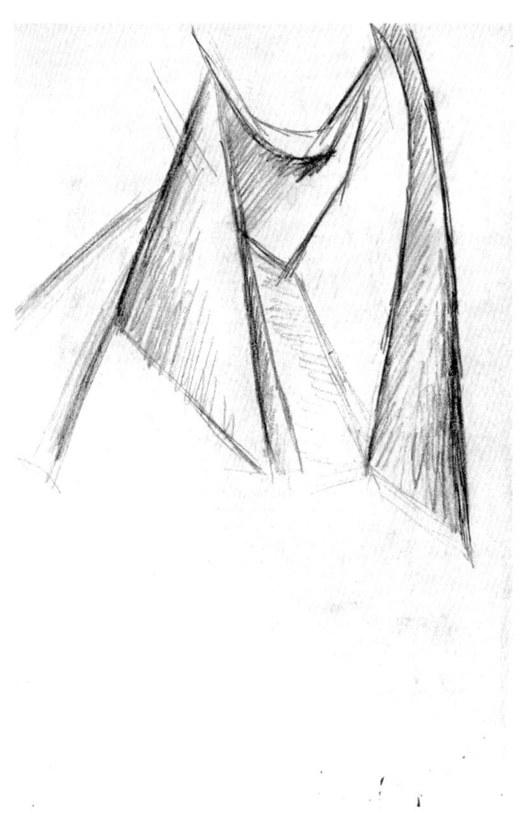

35
Woman with Pears
Horta de Ebro,
summer 1909
oil on canvas
92.1 × 70.8 cm
36 1/4 × 27 7/8 in.
The Museum of
Modern Art, New
York, Florene
May Schoenborn
Bequest, 1996

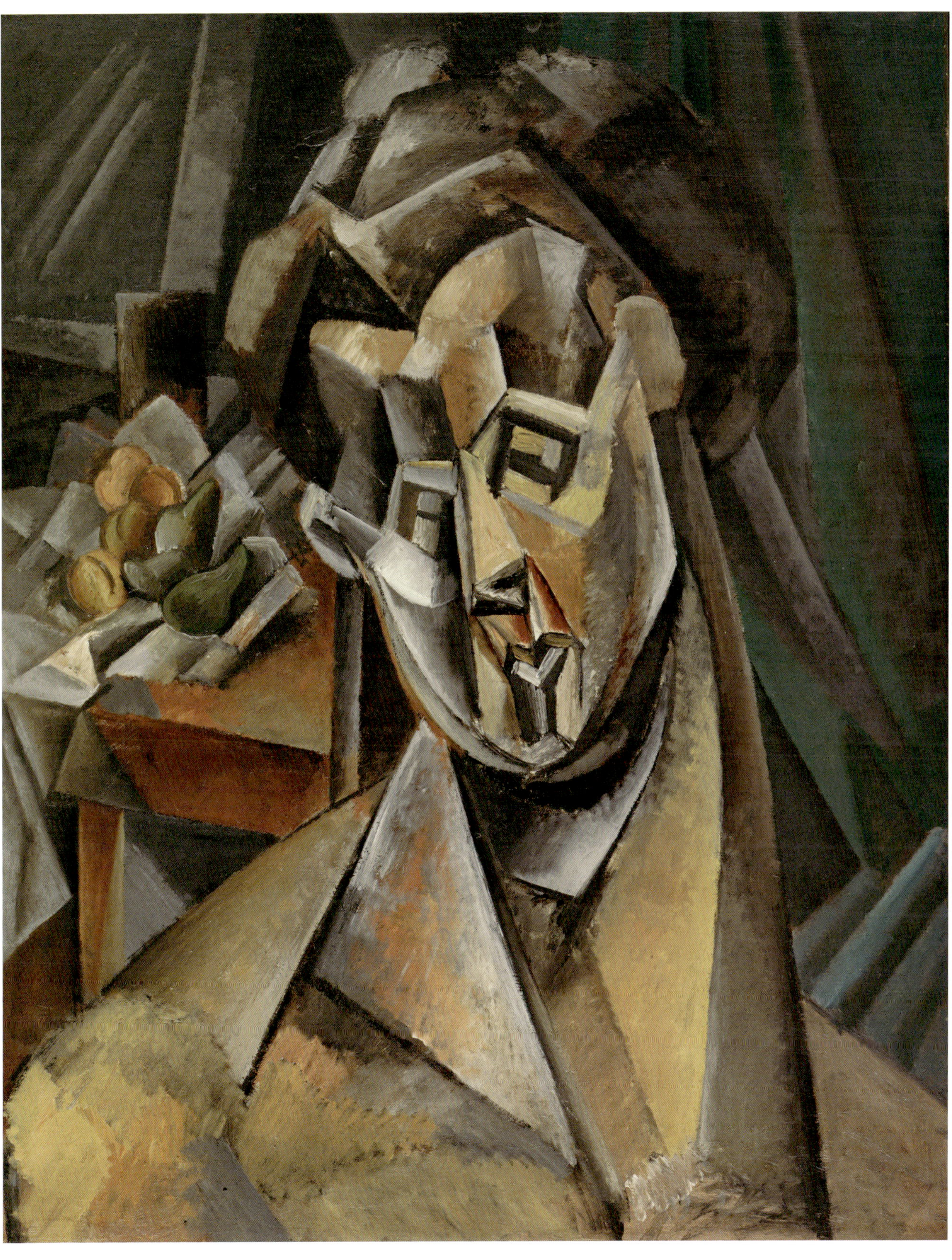

36
Head of a Woman (Fernande)
Horta de Ebro, summer 1909
oil on canvas
65 × 54 cm
$25\frac{9}{16} \times 21\frac{1}{4}$ in.
Formerly Museu de Arte Moderna, Rio de Janeiro; this painting was destroyed in 1978

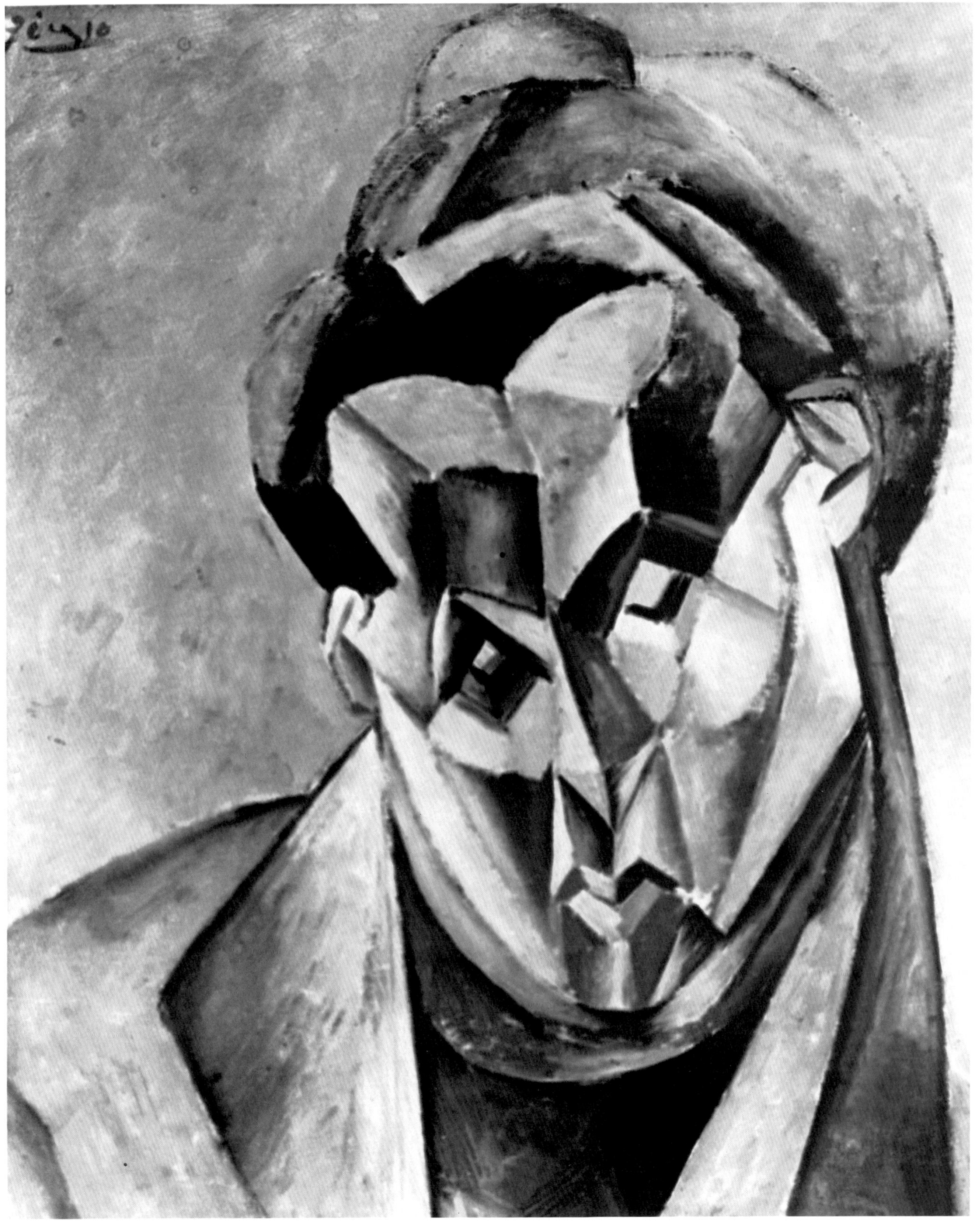

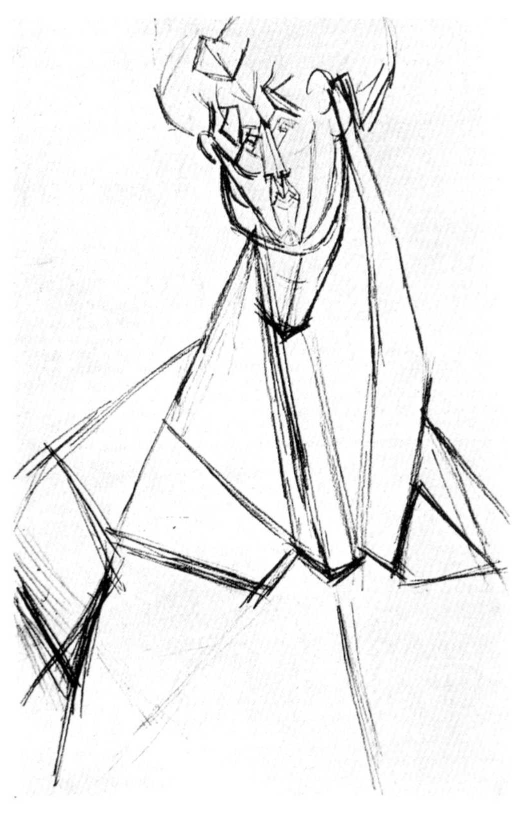

37
Study (Bust of a Woman)
Horta de Ebro, summer 1909
charcoal on paper
32.4 × 21.9 cm
12 ¾ × 8 ⅝ in.
Heirs of the artist

38
Seated Woman
Horta de Ebro, summer 1909
oil on canvas
81 × 65 cm
31 ⅞ × 25 9/16 in.
Private collection

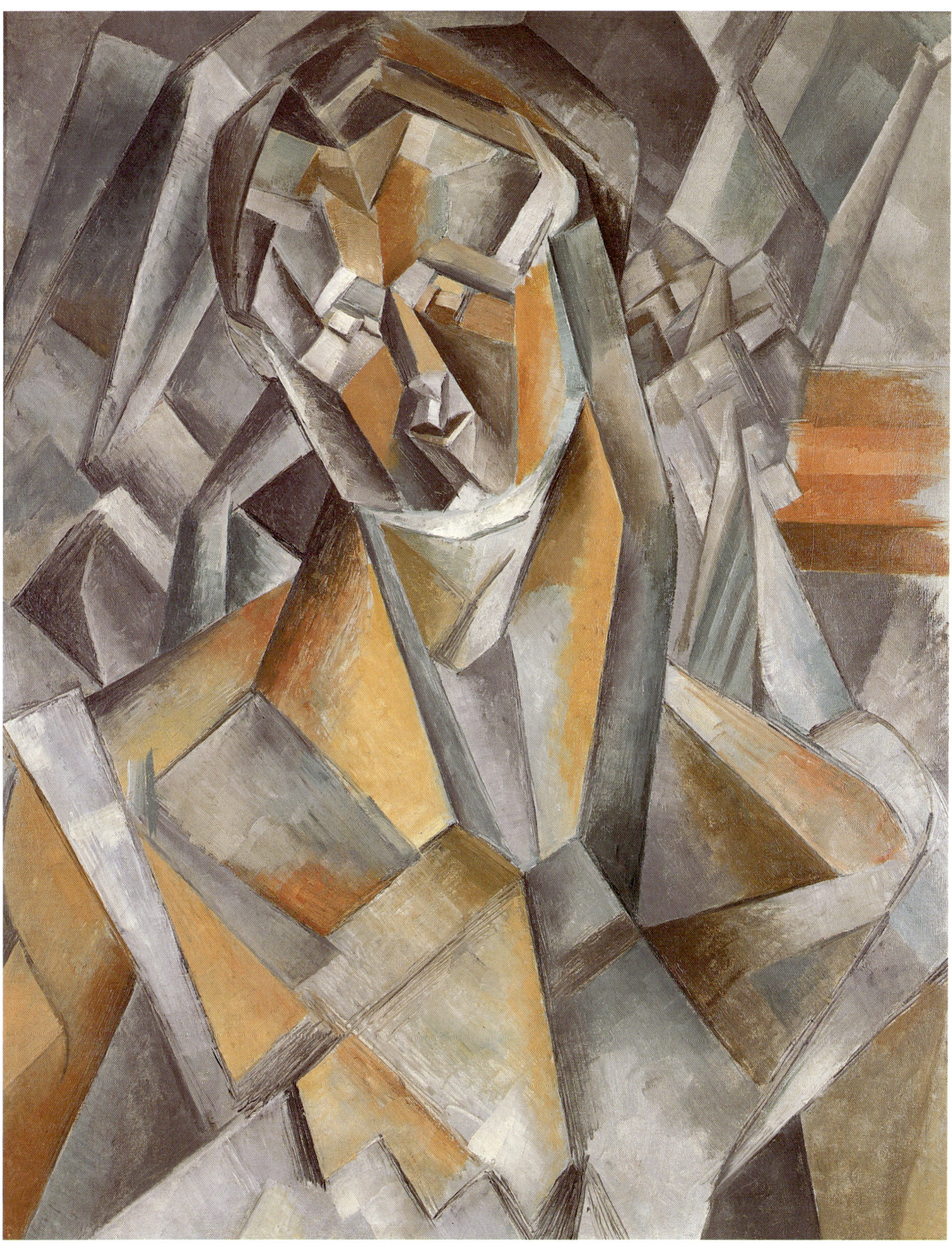

39
Head of a Woman
(Fernande Olivier)
Horta de Ebro,
summer 1909
oil on canvas
65 × 54.5 cm
25 9/16 × 21 7/16 in.
Städelscher Museums-
Verein e.V.,
Frankfurt am Main

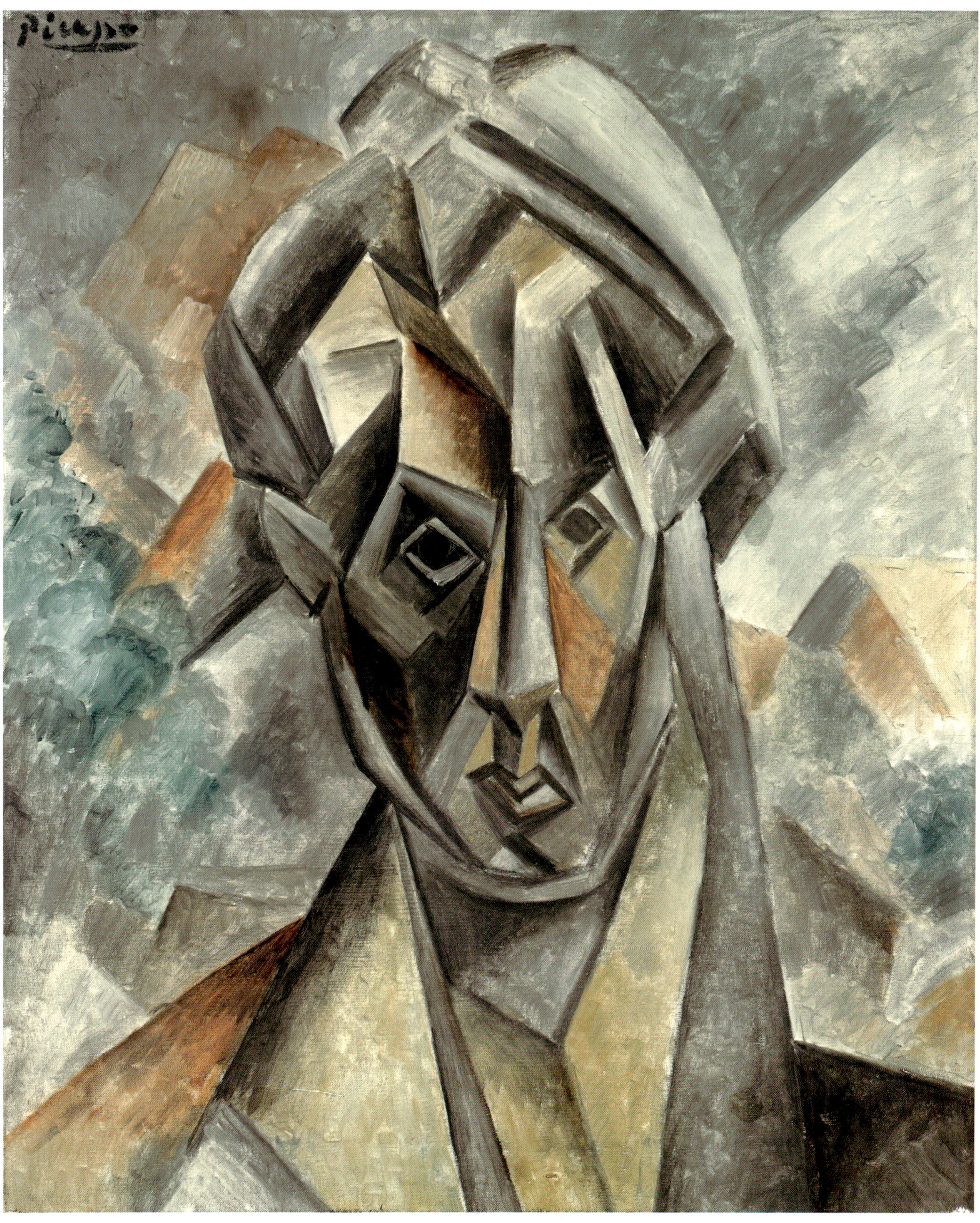
Picasso

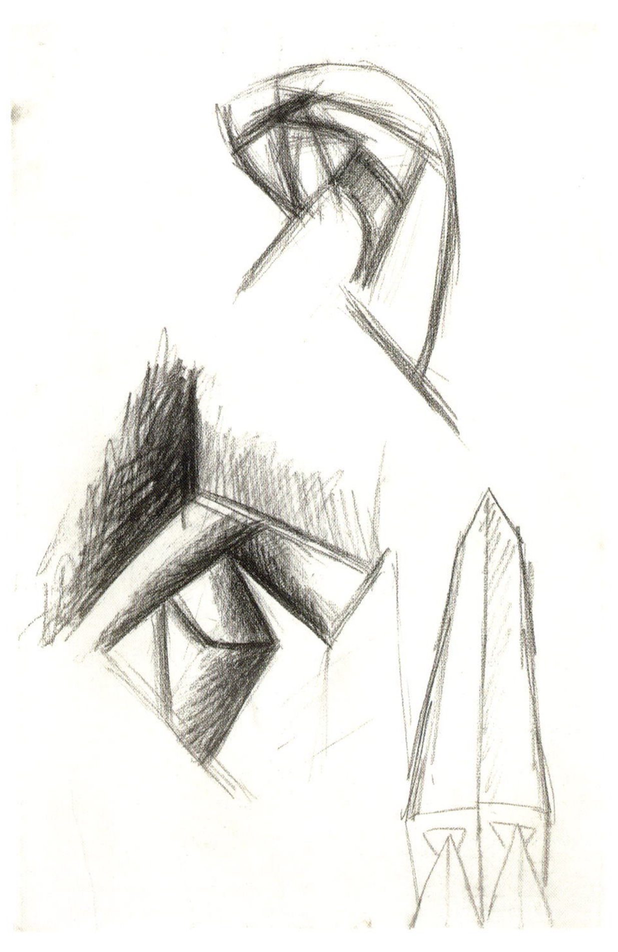

40
Study (Ear, Eye, Nose)
Horta de Ebro,
summer 1909
charcoal on paper
32.5 × 22 cm
12 13/16 × 8 11/16 in.
Private collection

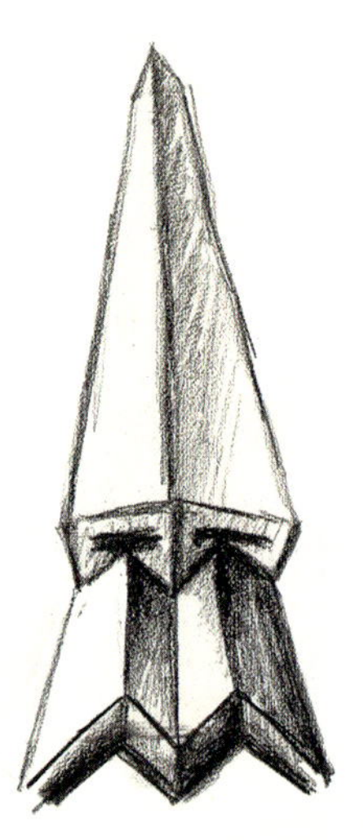

41
Study (Nose)
Horta de Ebro,
summer 1909
charcoal on paper
32.5 × 21.5 cm
12 13/16 × 8 7/16 in.
Private collection

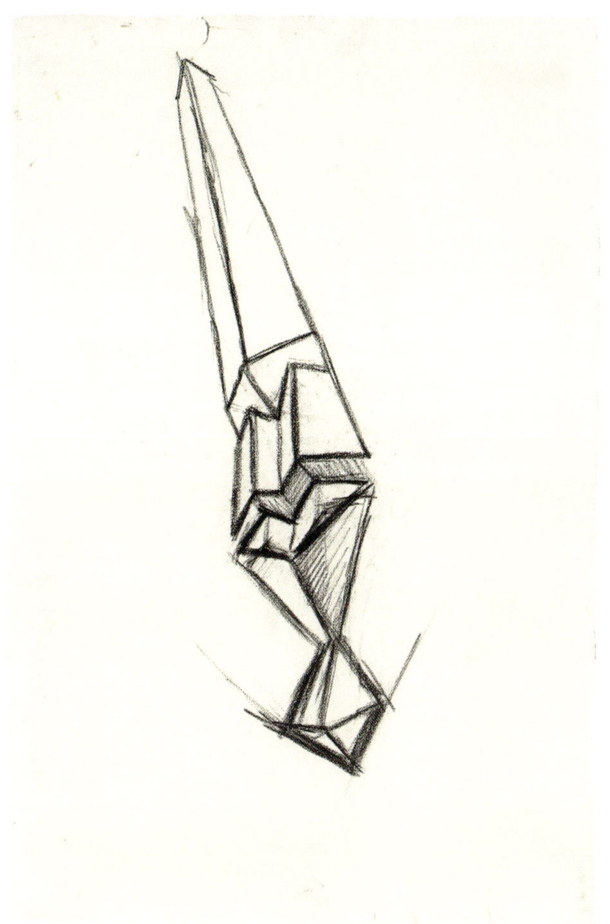

42
Study (Nose and Mouth)
Horta de Ebro,
summer 1909
charcoal on paper
32.5 × 22 cm
12 13/16 × 8 11/16 in.
Private collection

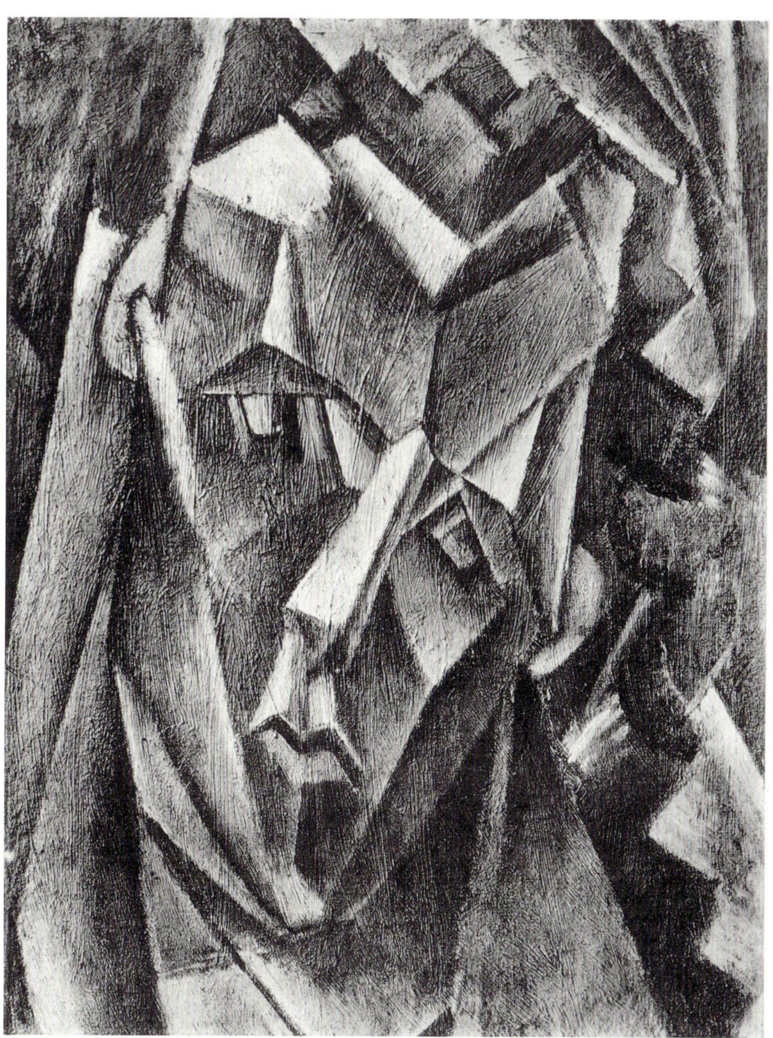

43
Head of a Woman in a Mantilla
Horta de Ebro,
summer 1909
oil on canvas
39 × 30 cm
15 3/8 × 11 13/16 in.
Location unknown

44
Study (Torso of a Woman)
Horta de Ebro, summer 1909
charcoal on paper
32.5 × 21.5 cm
12 13/16 × 8 7/16 in.
Collection Marina Picasso; Courtesy Galerie Jan Krugier, Ditesheim & Cie, Geneva

45
Nude in an Armchair
Horta de Ebro, summer 1909
oil on canvas
92.7 × 74.9 cm
36 1/2 × 29 1/2 in.
Private collection

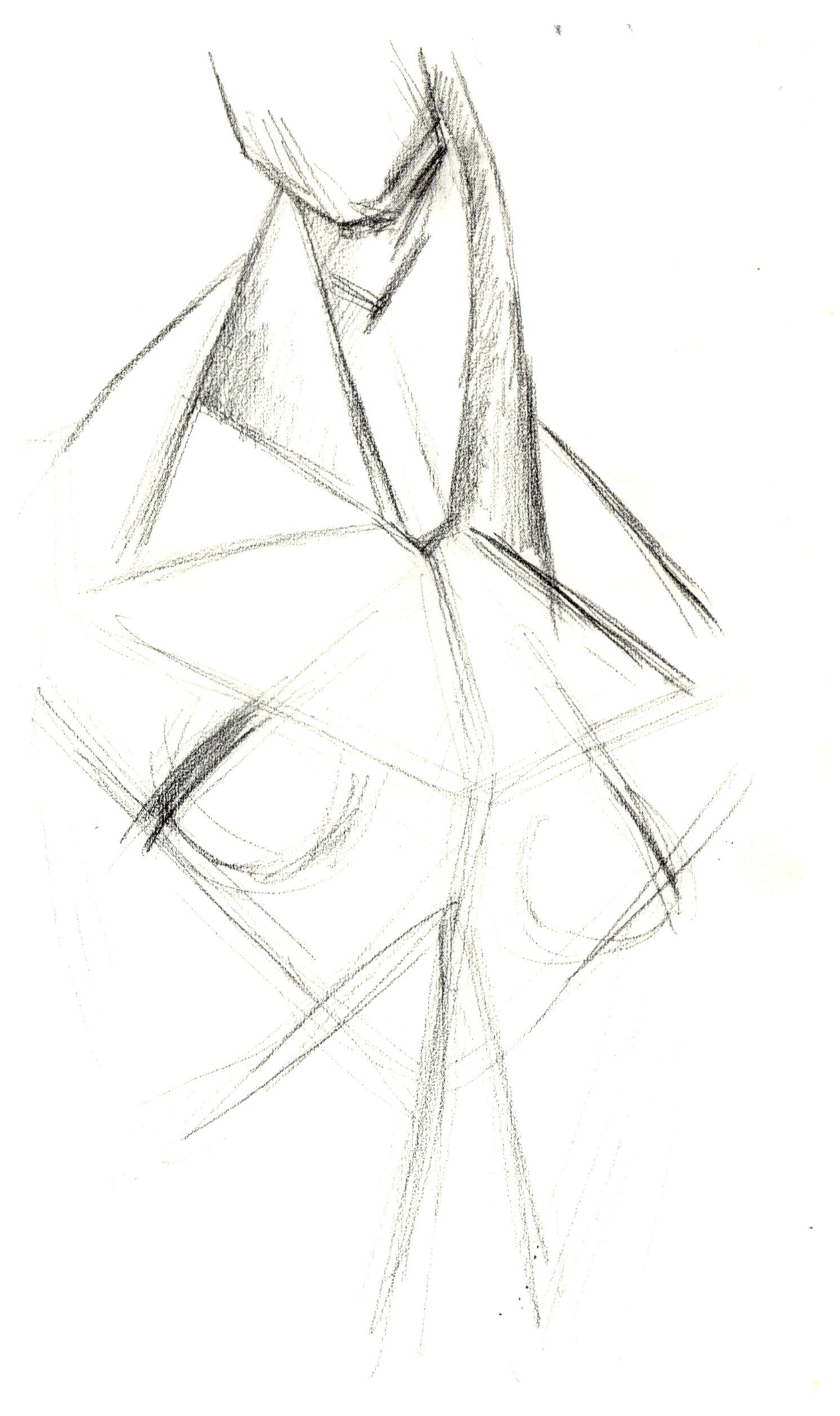

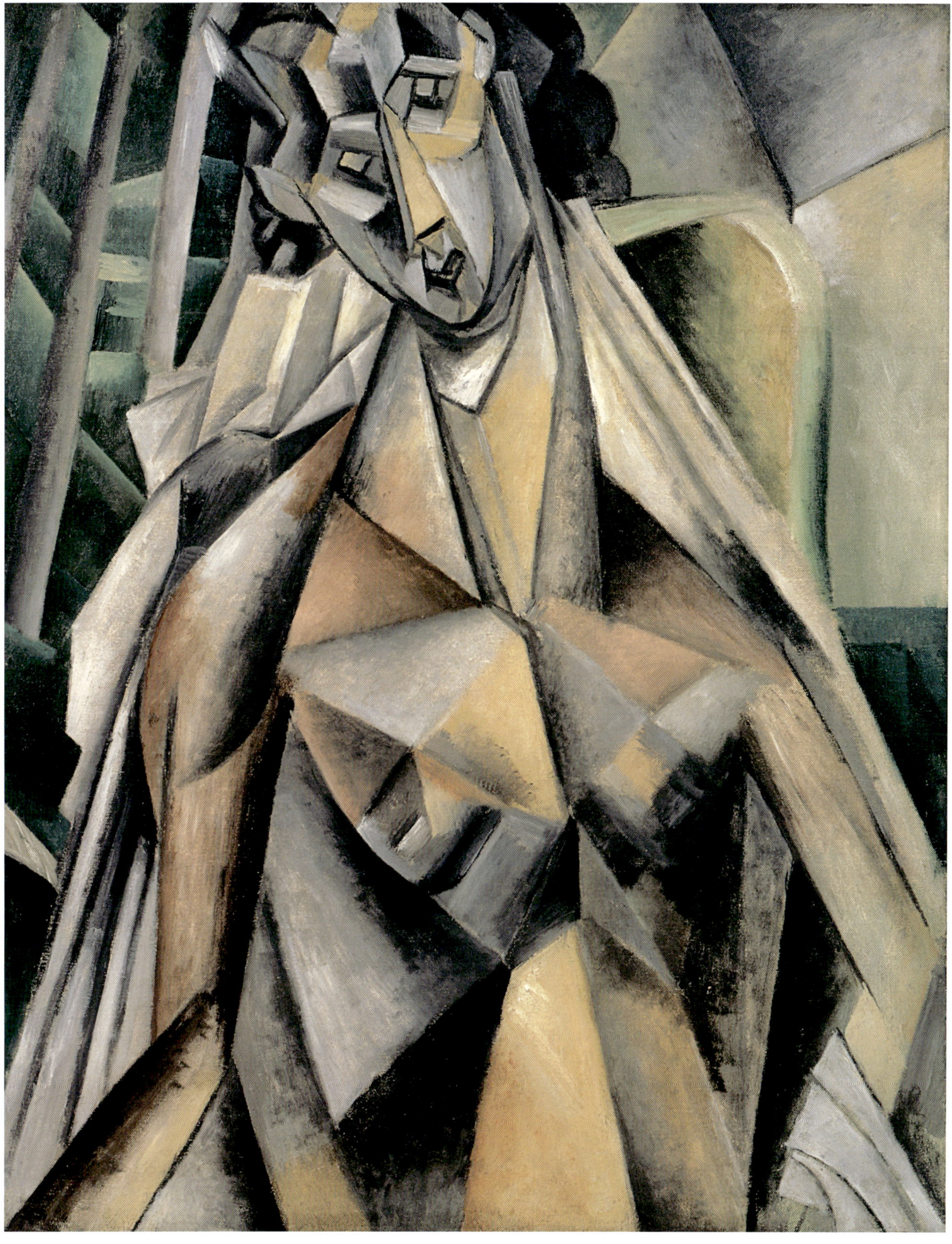

46
Study (Female Nude)
Horta de Ebro,
summer 1909
charcoal on paper
32.5 × 22 cm
12 13/16 × 8 11/16 in.
Collection Marina
Picasso; Courtesy
Galerie Jan Krugier,
Ditesheim & Cie,
Geneva

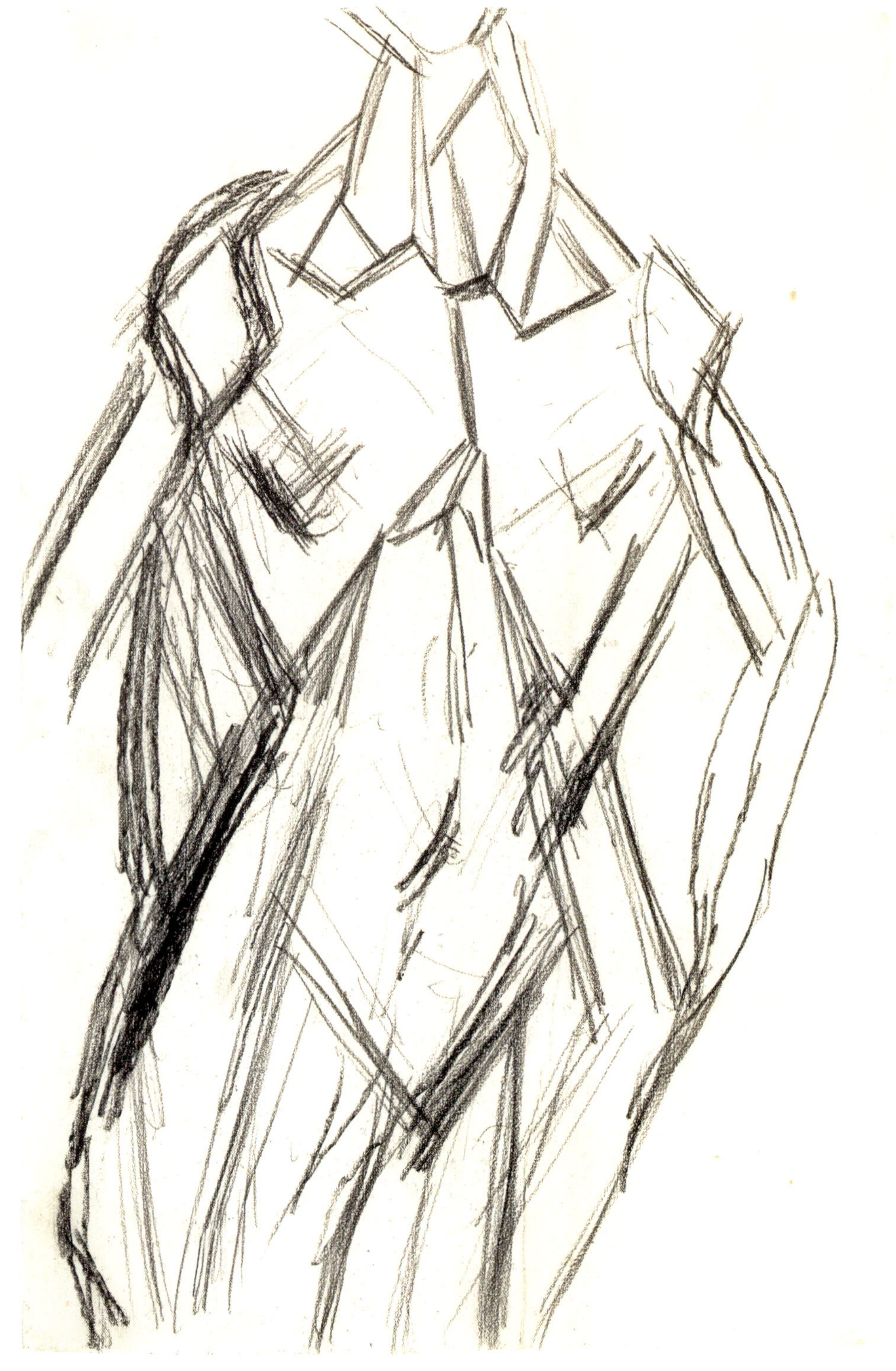

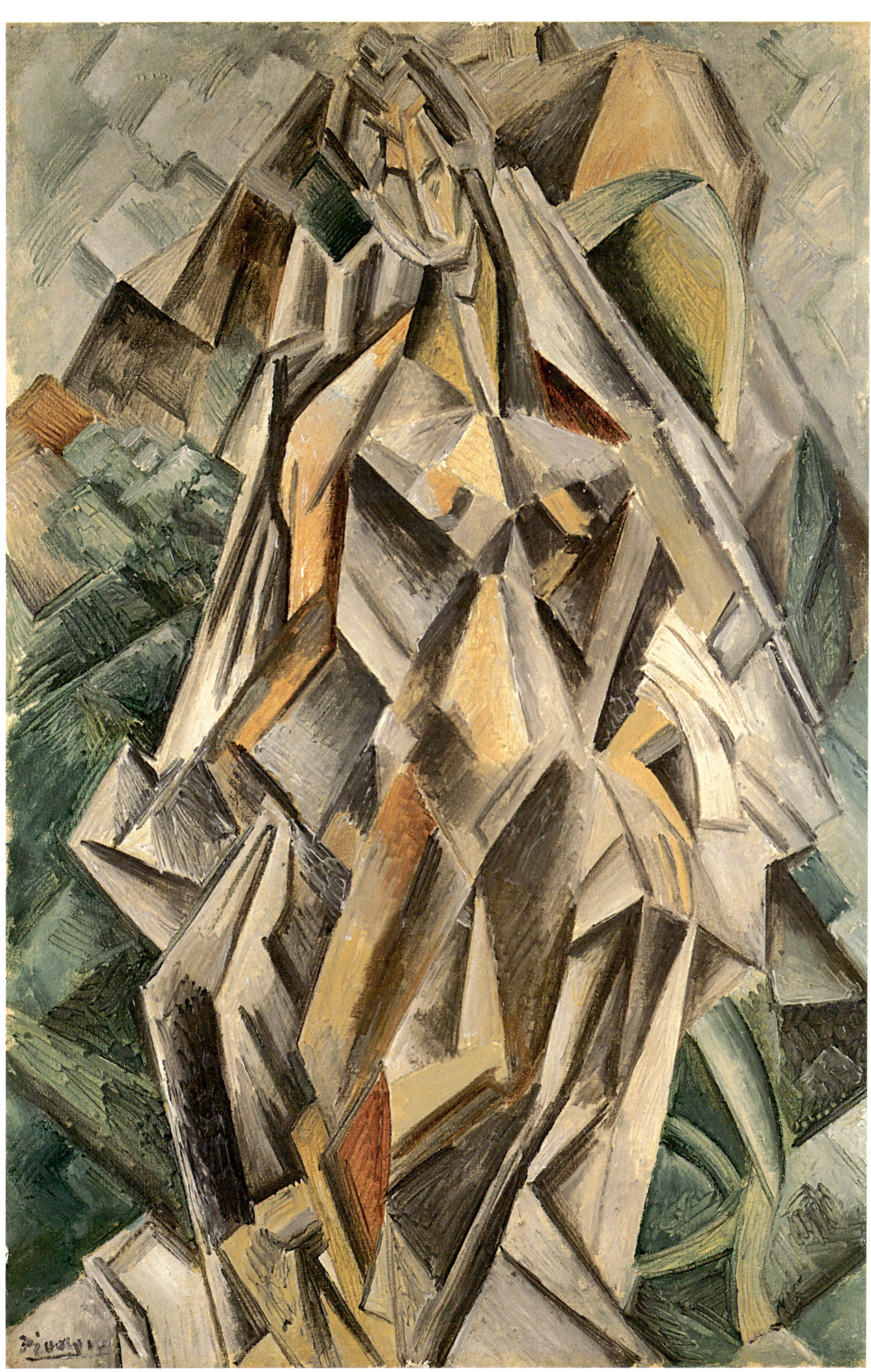

47
Female Nude
Horta de Ebro,
summer 1909
oil on canvas
92.5 × 63 cm
36 7/16 × 24 13/16 in.
POLA Museum of Art,
Kanagawa

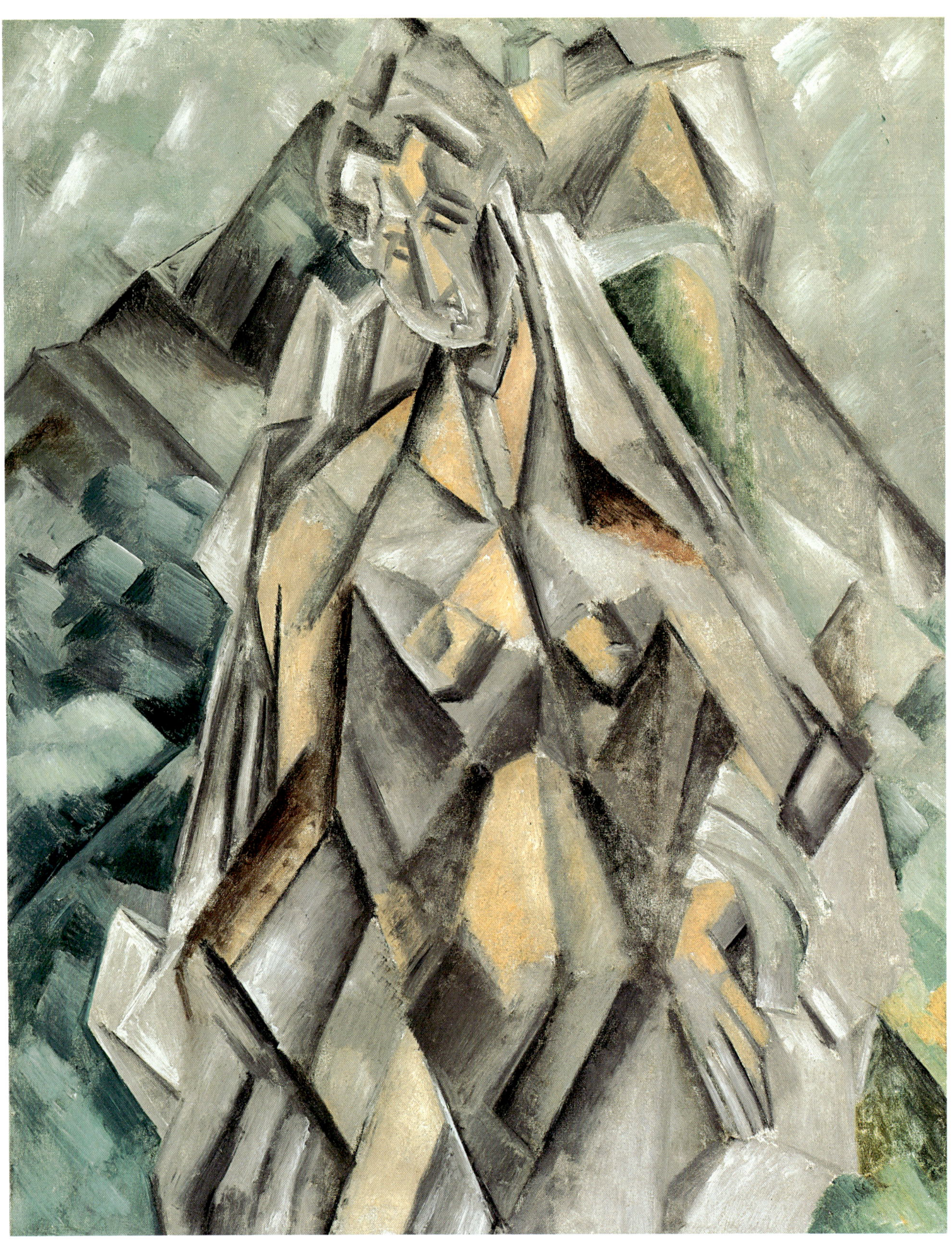

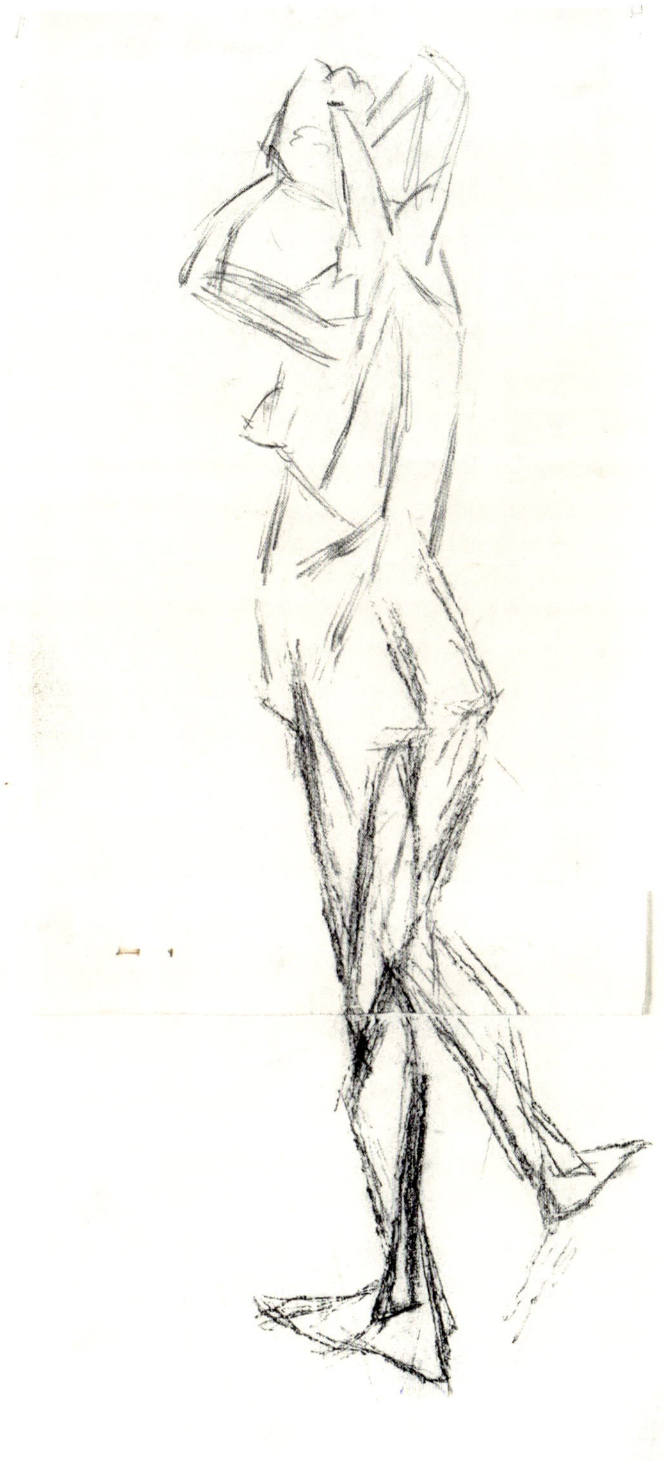

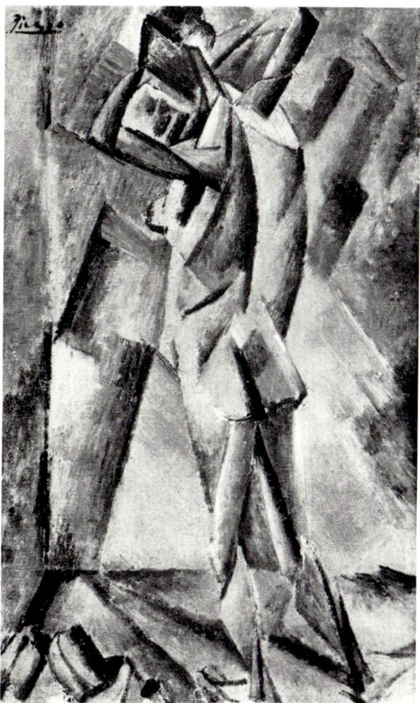

48
Female Nude
Horta de Ebro,
summer 1909
oil on canvas
88.9 × 71.4 cm
35 × 28⅛ in.
Private collection

49
Study (Standing Nude with Raised Arms)
Horta de Ebro,
summer 1909
charcoal on paper
47.5 × 22 cm
18 11/16 × 8 11/16 in.
Private collection

50
Standing Nude with Raised Arms
Horta de Ebro,
summer 1909
oil on canvas
61 × 38 cm
24 × 14 15/16 in.
Location unknown

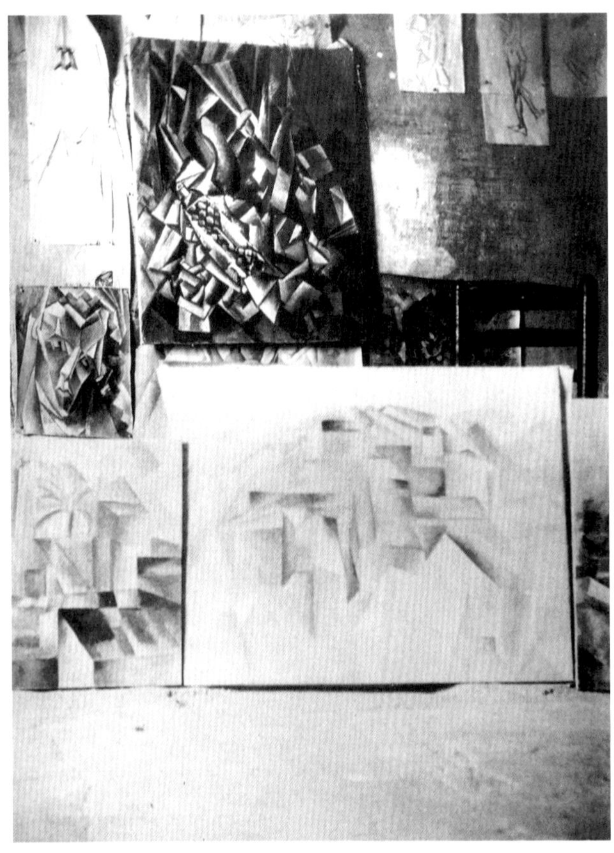

51
The studio at
Horta de Ebro
summer 1909
original
photographic print
11 × 8.2 cm
4 5/16 × 3 1/4 in.
Private collection

Photograph depicts clockwise from upper right: study for *Standing Nude with Raised Arms;* cat. 49; second study for *Standing Nude with Raised Arms; Landscape (Santa Bárbara Mountain)* (Daix 276); *The Reservoir, Horta de Ebro* (Daix 280); *Houses on the Hill, Horta de Ebro* (Daix 278); *Factory at Horta de Ebro* (Daix 279); cats. 43, 34, 41, 40, 33; at center: *Bottle of Anís del Mono* (Daix 299); underneath, *Carafe, Jug, and Fruit Bowl* (Daix 298)

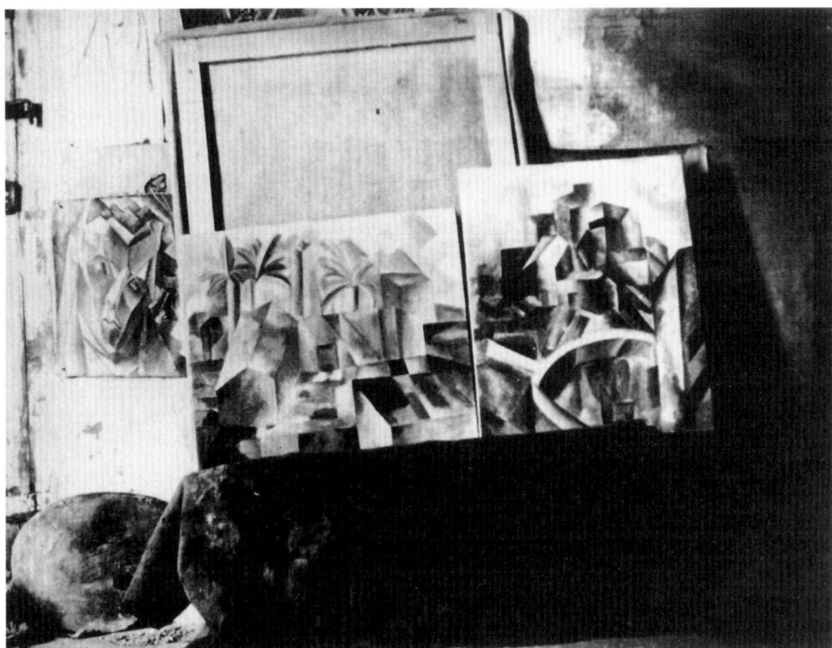

52
The studio at
Horta de Ebro
summer 1909
original
photographic print
8.6 × 11 cm
3 3/8 × 4 5/16 in.
Private collection

Photograph depicts clockwise from lower right: *The Reservoir, Horta de Ebro* (Daix 280); *Factory at Horta de Ebro* (Daix 279); cats. 43, 34, 21 and 22 (as single work)

53
The studio at
Horta de Ebro
summer 1909
original photographic print
11 × 8.8 cm
4 5/16 × 3 7/16 in.
Private collection

Photograph depicts clockwise from upper right: cats. 21 and 22 (as single work); cat. 29; *Carafe, Jug, and Fruit Bowl* (Daix 298); cats. 43, 34, 41

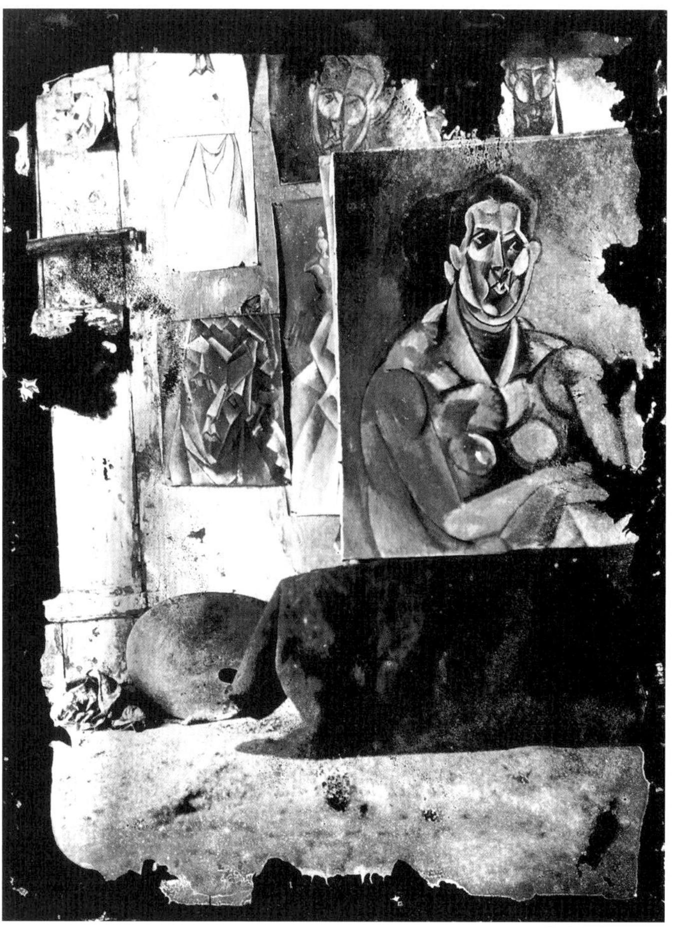

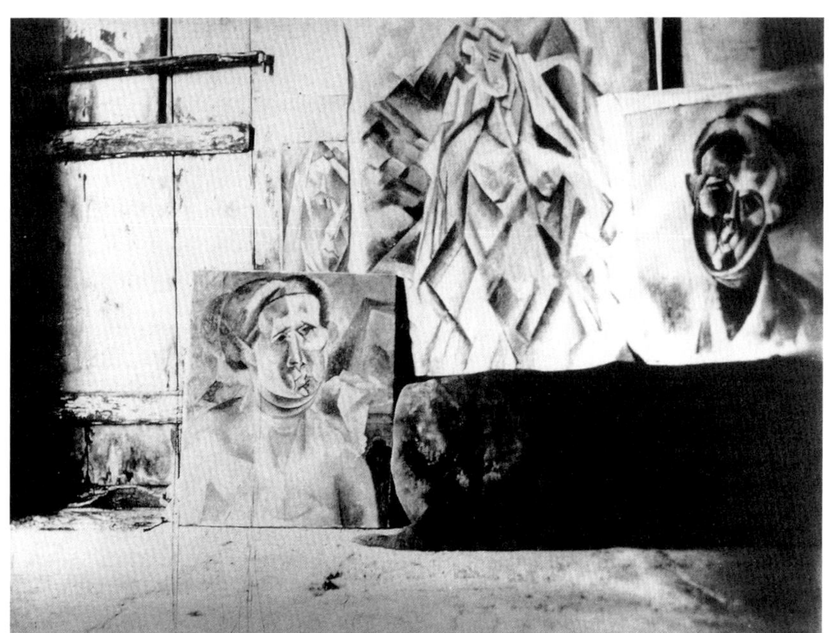

54
The studio at
Horta de Ebro
summer 1909
original
photographic print
8 × 11 cm
3 1/8 × 4 5/16 in.
Private collection

Photograph depicts left to right: cats. 28, 43, 48, 20

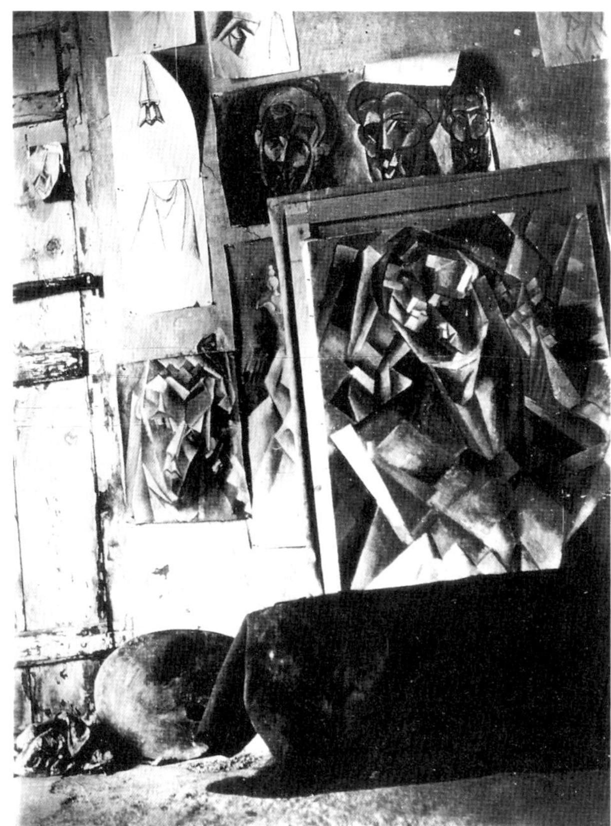

55
The studio at
Horta de Ebro
summer 1909
original
photographic print
10.8 × 8.3 cm
4 ¼ × 3 ¼ in.
Private collection

Photograph depicts clockwise from upper right: study for *Standing Nude with Raised Arms;* cat. 38; *Carafe, Jug, and Fruit Bowl* (Daix 298); cats. 43, 34, 41, 44, 40, 21 and 22 (as single work)

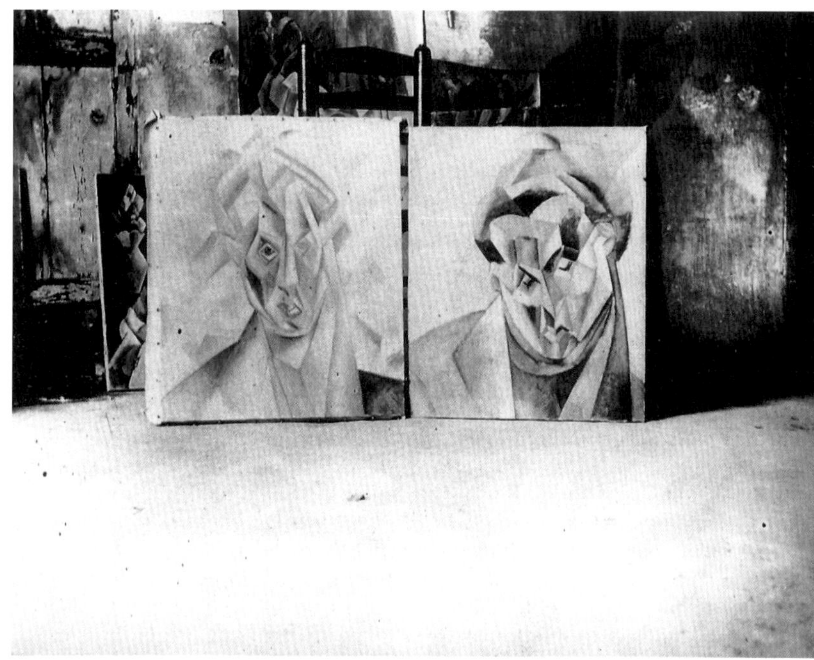

56
The studio at
Horta de Ebro
summer 1909
original
photographic print
11 × 8.7 cm
4 5/16 × 3 7/16 in.
Private collection

Photograph depicts left to right, front: cats. 39, 36; left to right, back: cat. 31; *Carafe, Jug, and Fruit Bowl* (Daix 298); *Landscape (Santa Bárbara Mountain)* (Daix 276); *Bottle of Anís del Mono* (Daix 299)

57
The studio at
Horta de Ebro
summer 1909
original
photographic print
8.3 × 11 cm
3 1/4 × 4 5/16 in.
Private collection

Photograph depicts left to right, front: cats. 45, 35; back: cats. 34, 21 and 22 (as single work); *Carafe, Jug, and Fruit Bowl* (Daix 298)

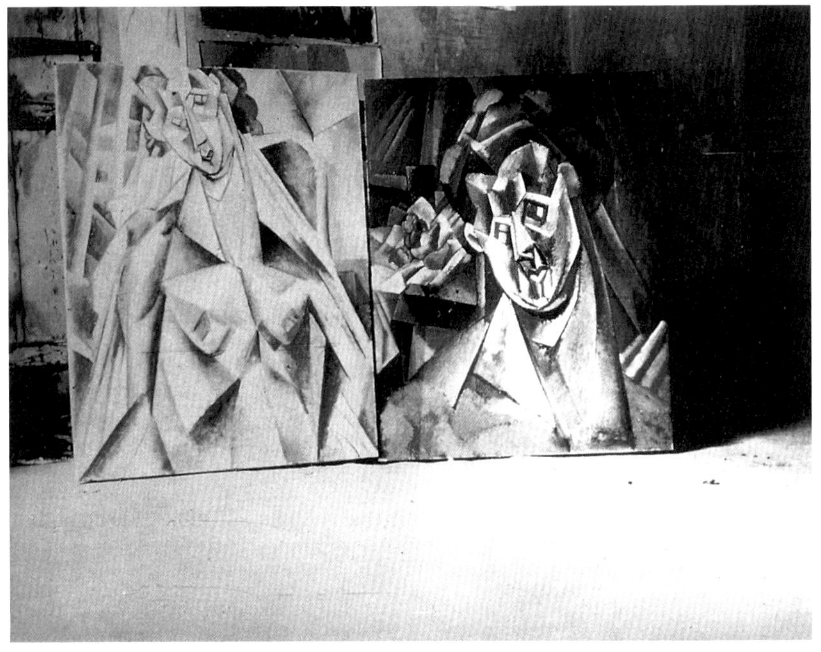

58
The studio at Horta de Ebro
summer 1909
original photographic print
8.1 × 10.2 cm
3 3/16 × 4 in.
Private collection

The following works can be discerned in this multiple-exposure photograph: cats. 45, 35, 48, 50, 28, 31

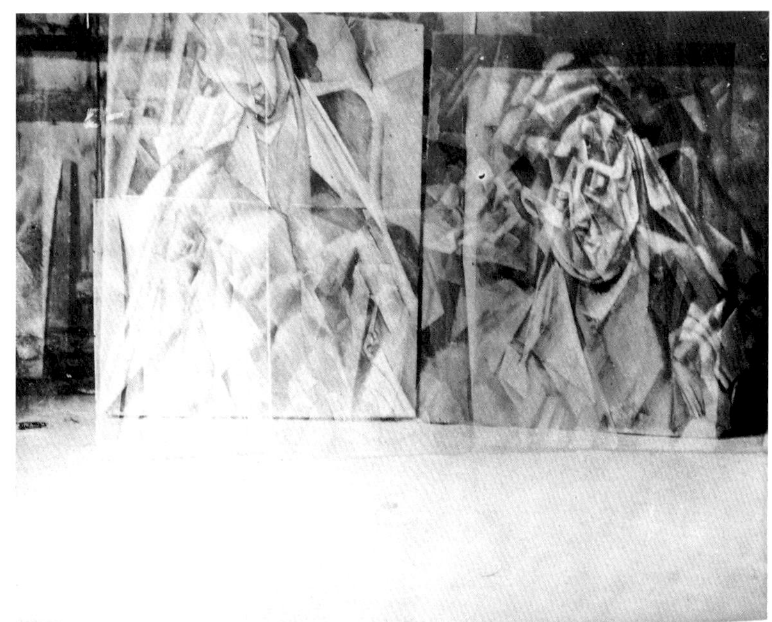

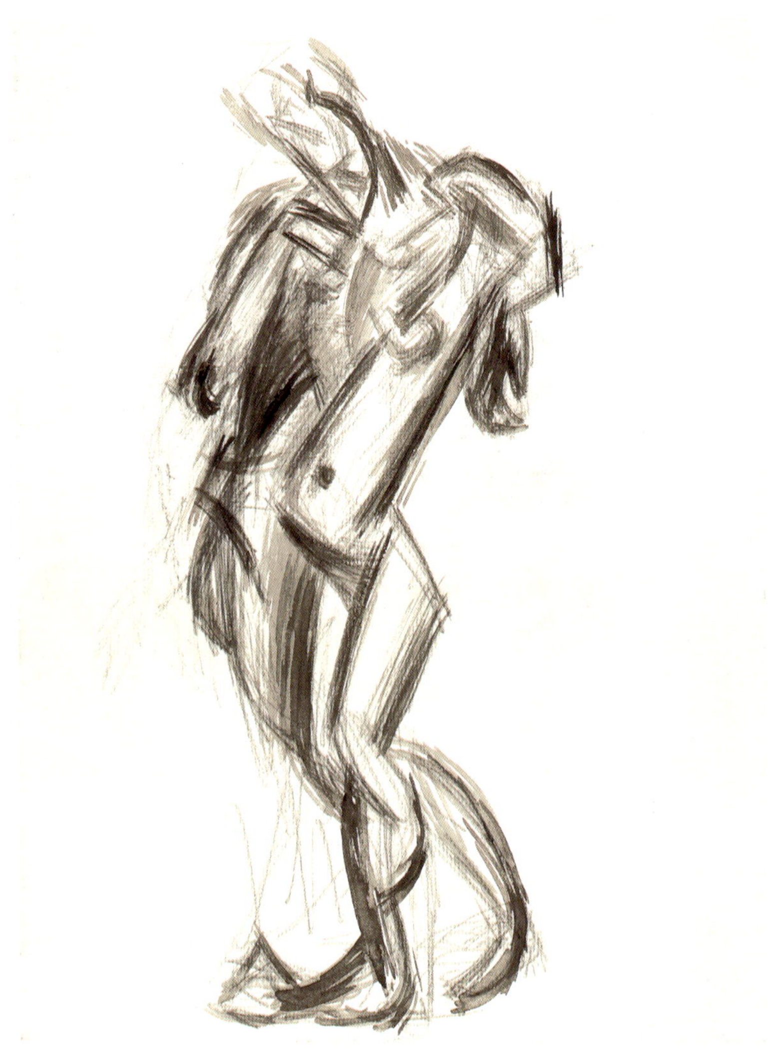

59
Standing Nude
Paris, fall 1909
watercolor and pencil
on paper
31.5 × 24 cm
12 3/8 × 9 7/16 in.
Private collection

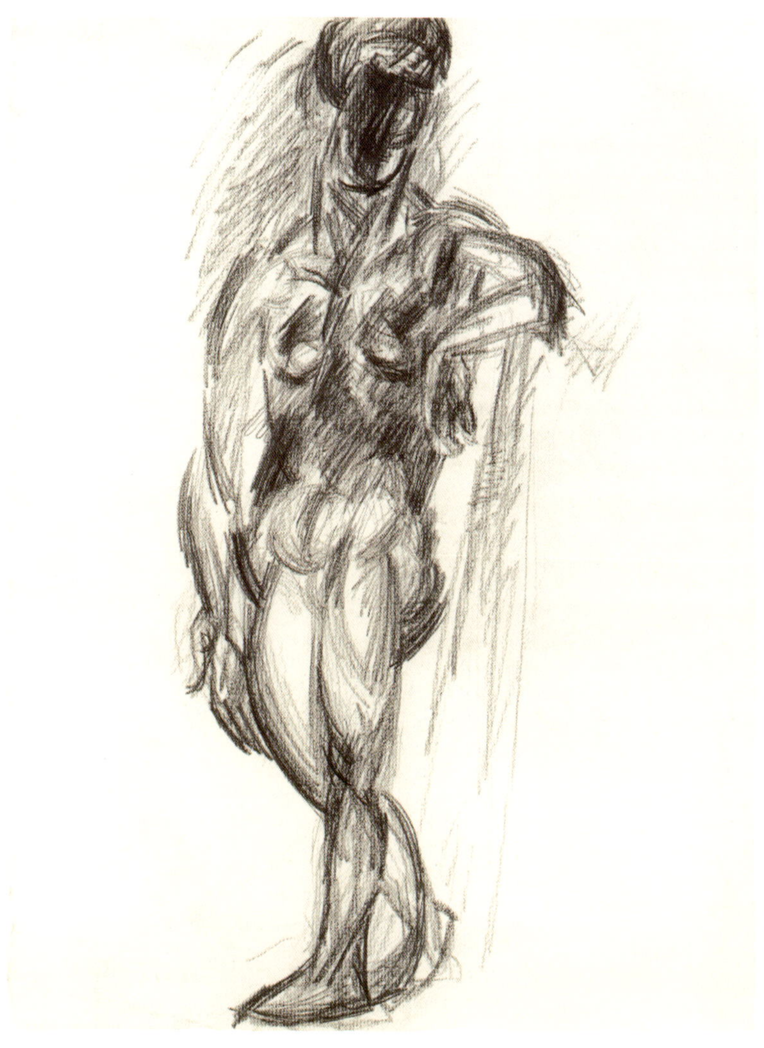

60
Standing Nude
Paris, fall 1909
pencil on paper
30.5 × 24 cm
12 × 9 7/16 in.
Collection Marina Picasso; Courtesy Galerie Jan Krugier, Ditesheim & Cie, Geneva

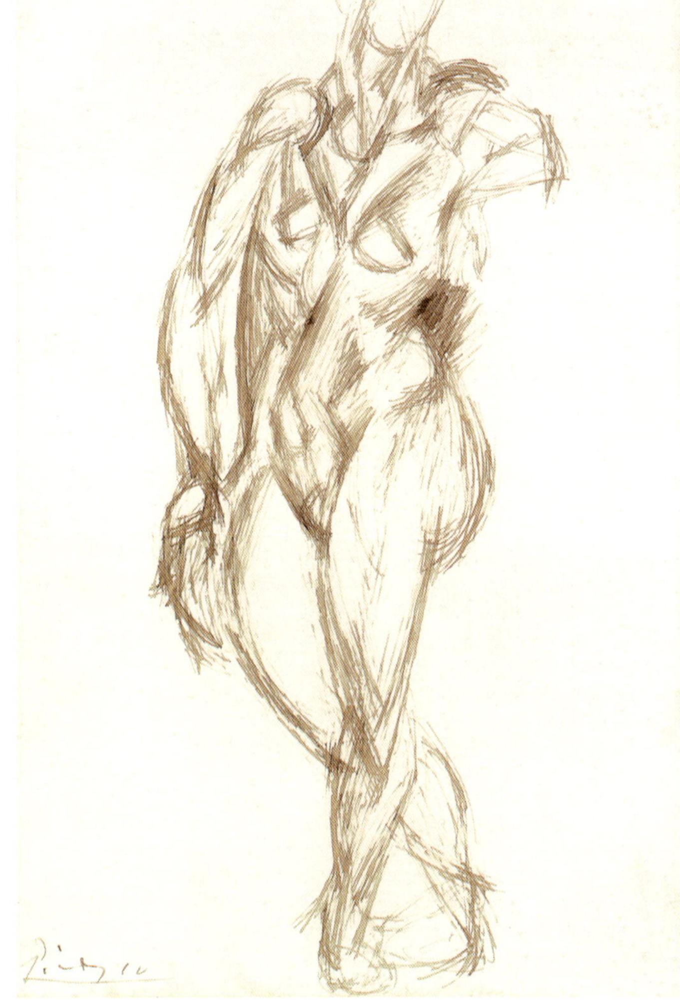

61
Standing Nude
Paris, fall 1909
pen and ink on paper
32 × 21 cm
12 5/8 × 8 1/4 in.
B.G.G. Merivale-Austin Esq.

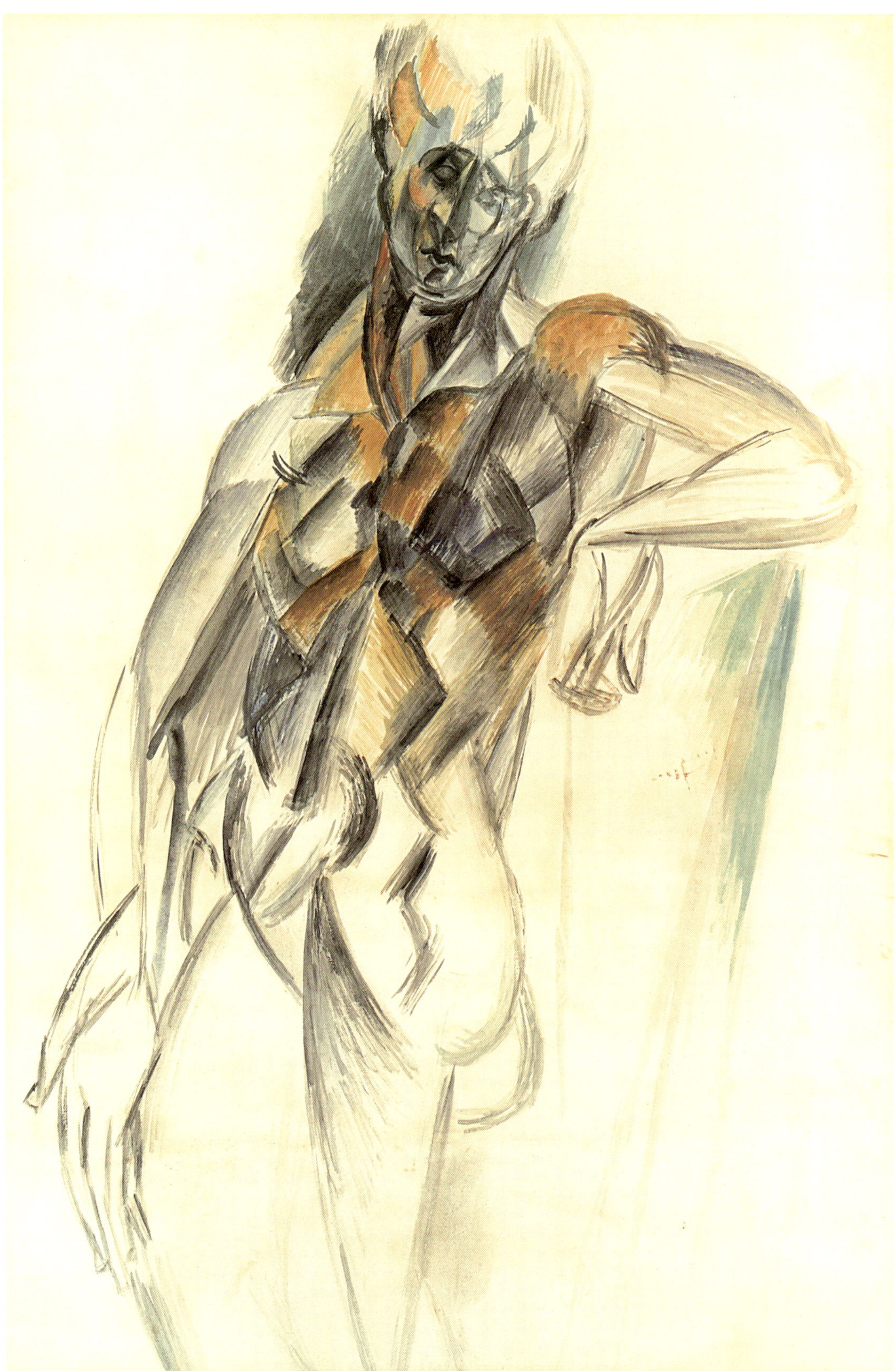

62
Standing Female Nude
Paris, fall 1909
watercolor on paper
62 × 42 cm
24 7/16 × 16 9/16 in.
Private collection

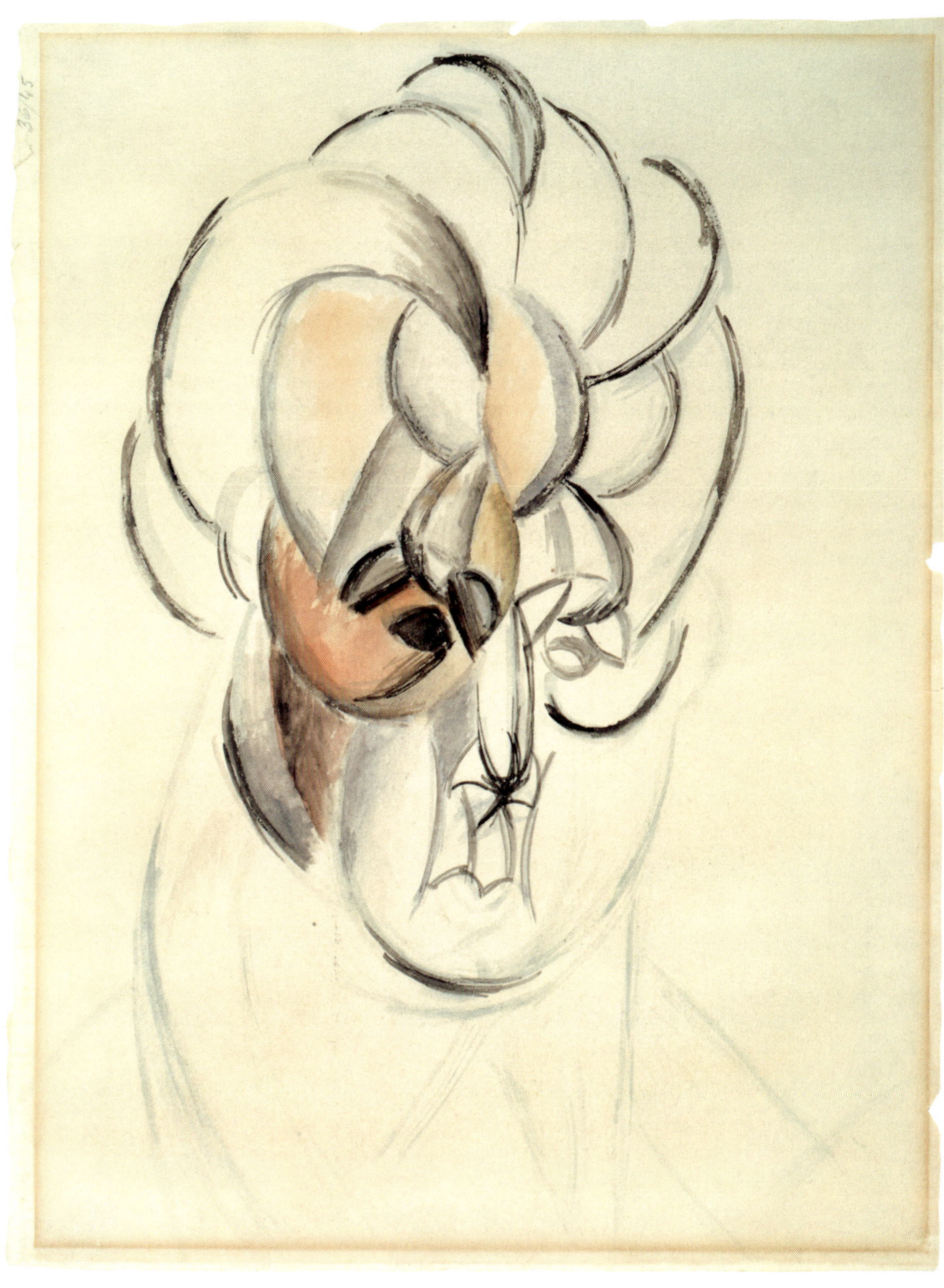

63
Study for Head of a Woman
Paris, fall 1909
watercolor on tan wove paper
33.2 × 25.6 cm
13 1/16 × 10 1/16 in.
The Art Institute of Chicago, Alfred Stieglitz Collection

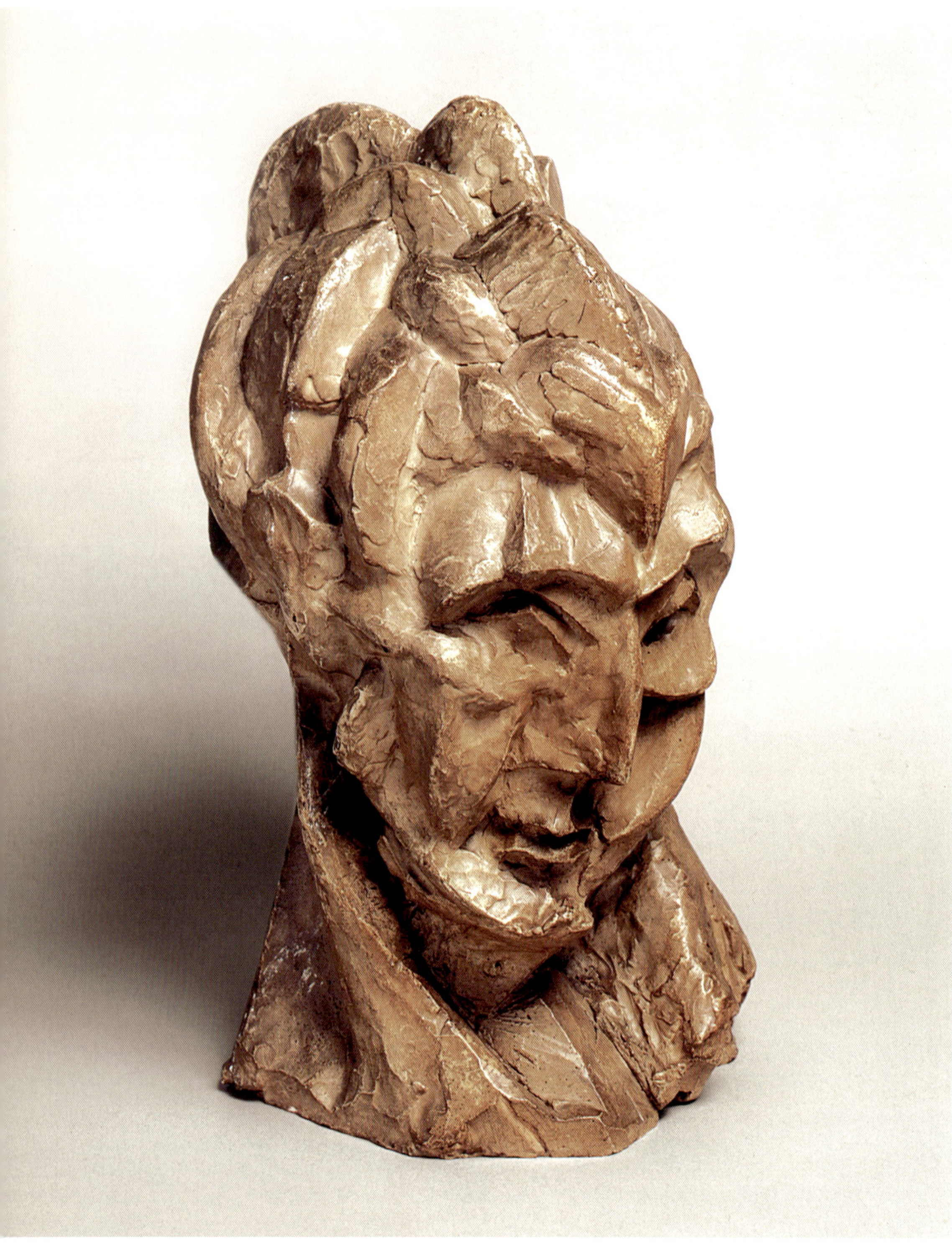

64
Head of a Woman (Fernande)
Paris, fall 1909
plaster
41.9 × 25.4 × 29.2 cm
16½ × 10 × 11½ in.
Latner Family Collection, Toronto

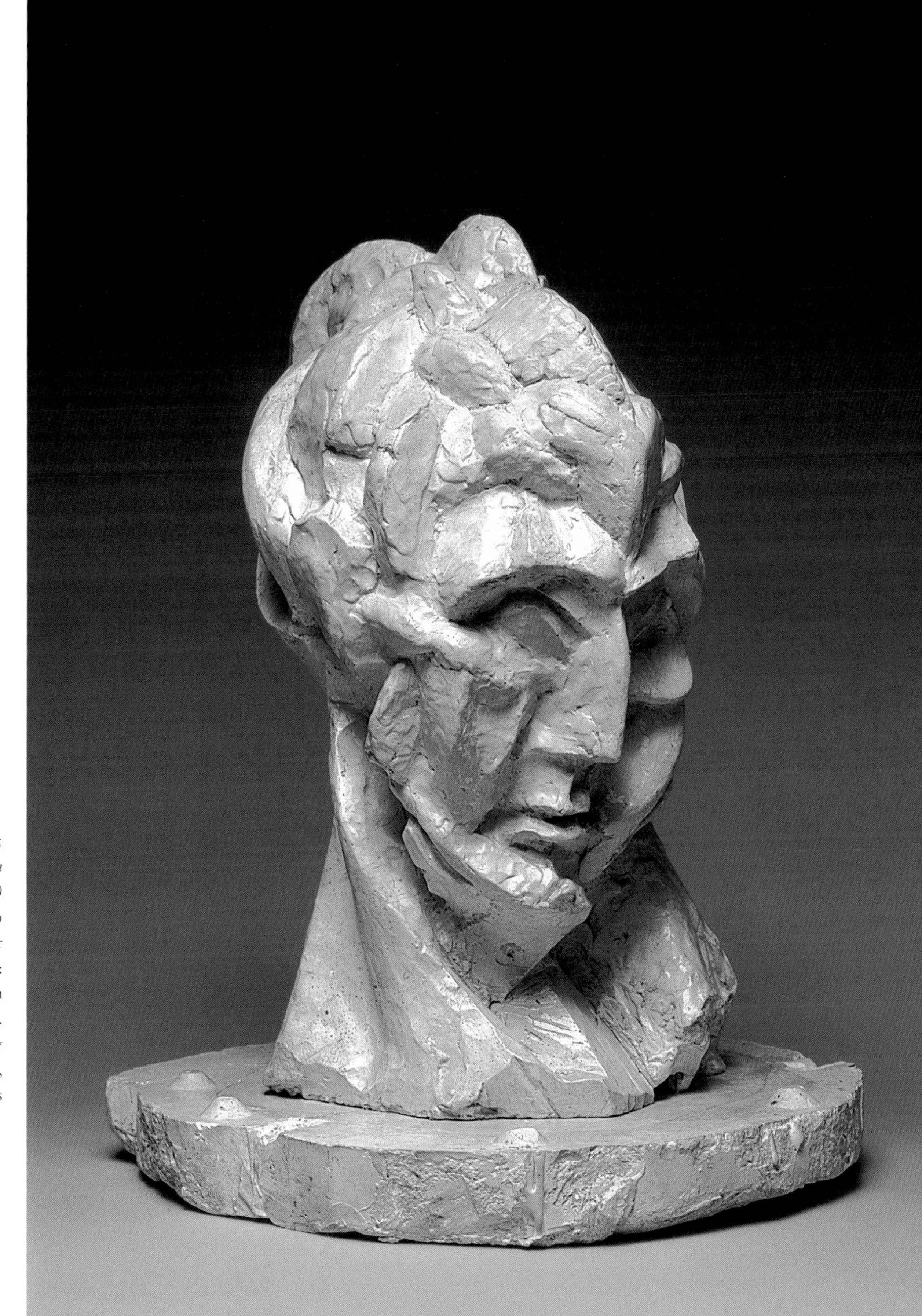

65
Head of a Woman (Fernande)
Paris, fall 1909
plaster
head (without base):
42 × 23.5 × 28.3 cm
16 9/16 × 9 1/4 × 11 1/8 in.
Raymond and Patsy Nasher Collection, Dallas, Texas

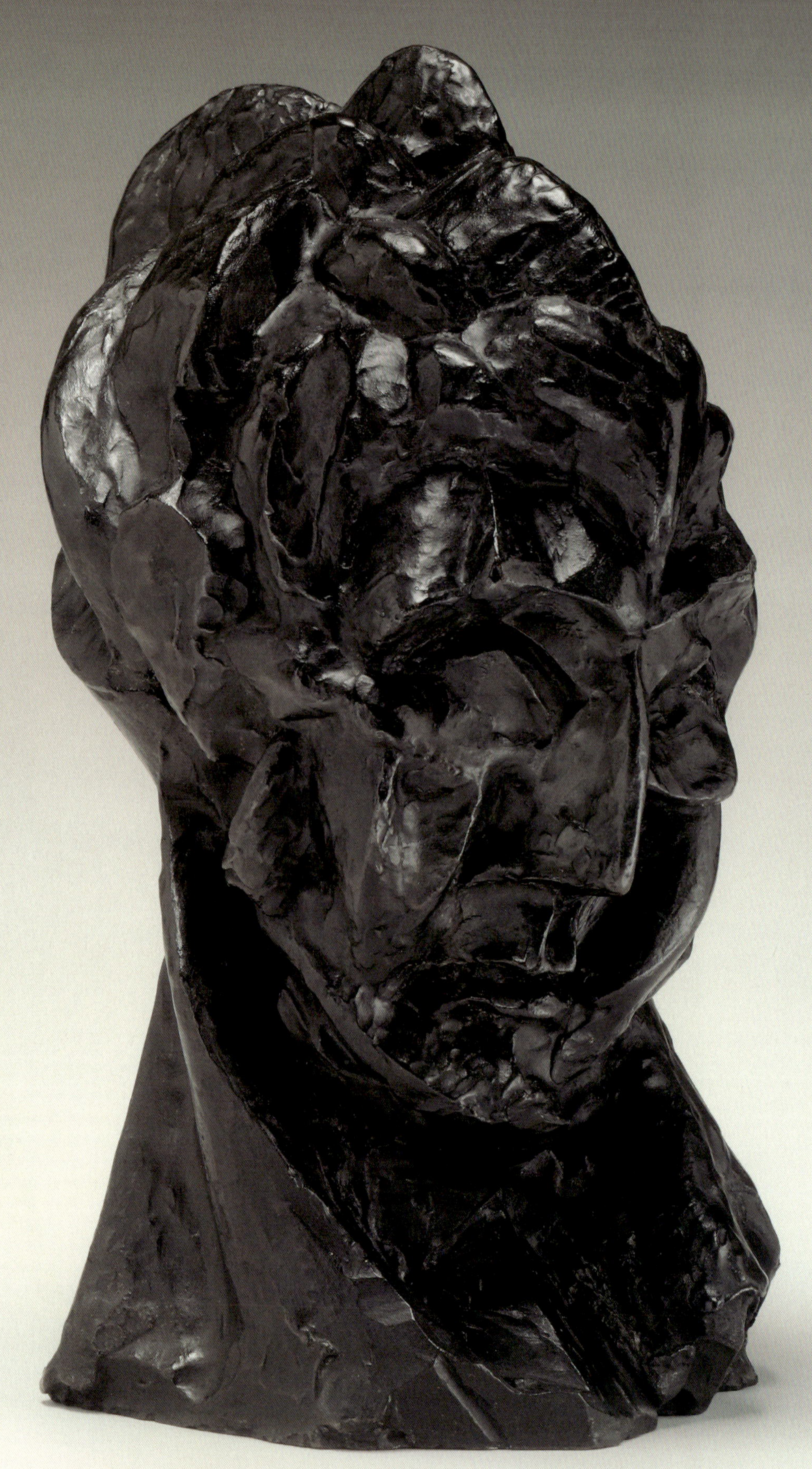

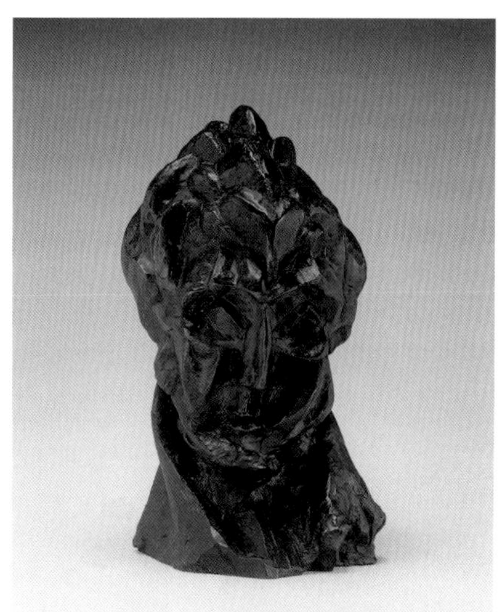

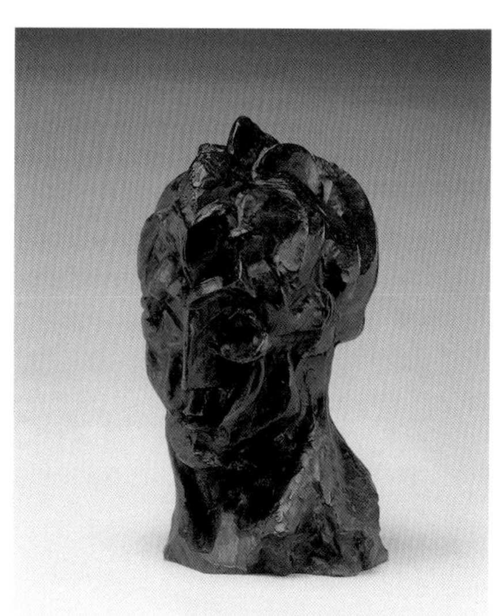

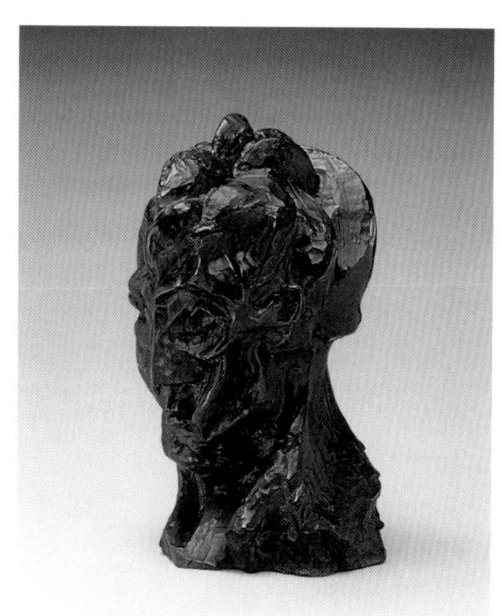

66
Head of a Woman (Fernande)
model 1909,
cast before 1932
bronze
41.2 × 20.5 × 25.5 cm
16¼ × 8 1/16 × 10 1/16 in.
National Gallery of Art, Washington, Patrons' Permanent Fund and Gift of Mitchell P. Rales

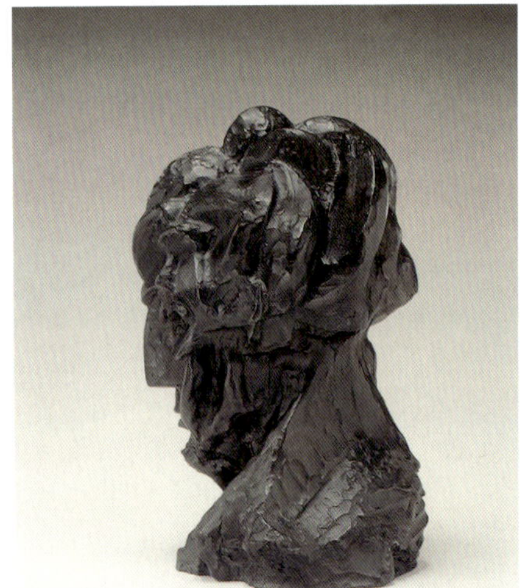

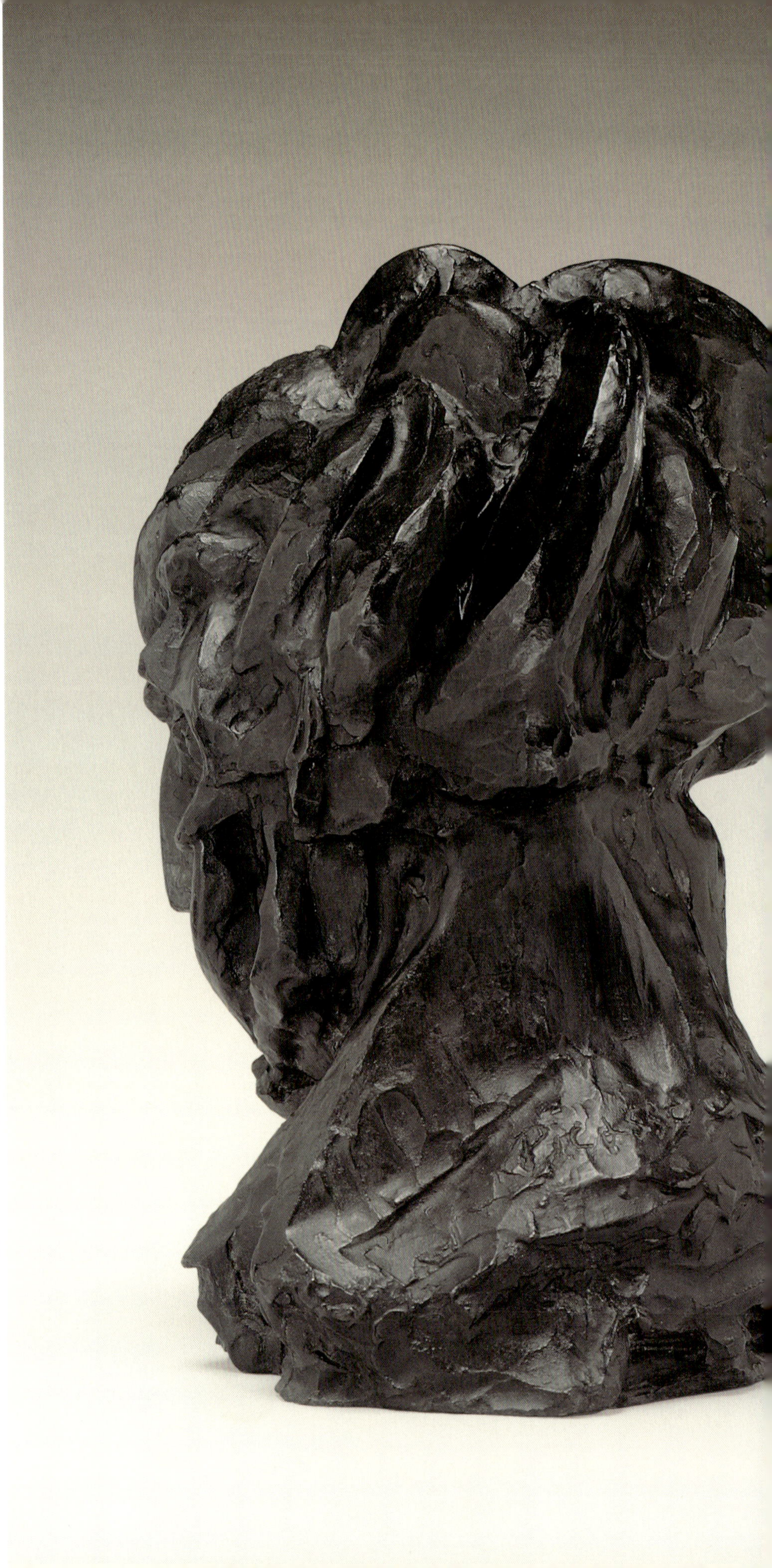

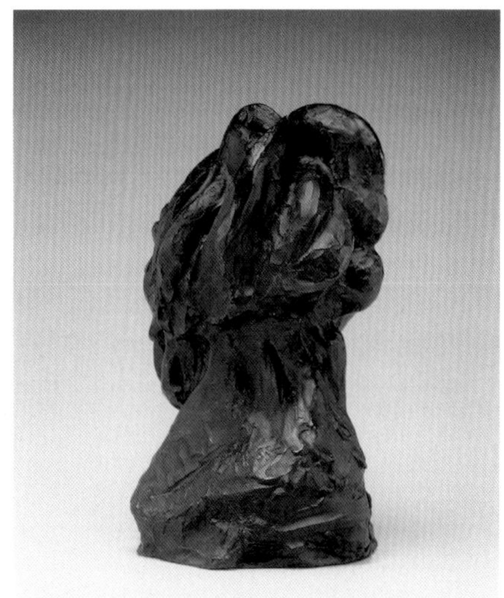

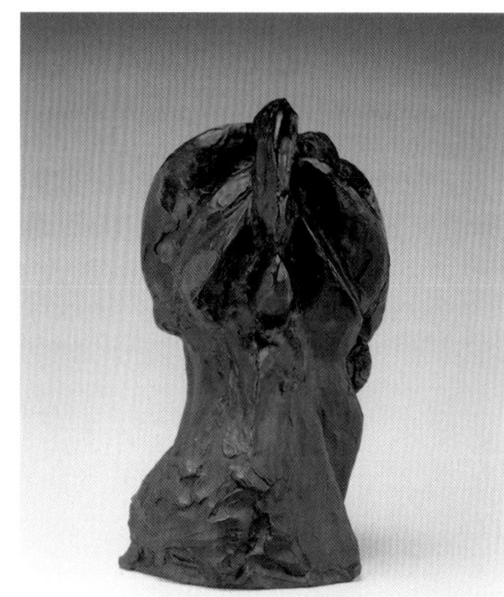

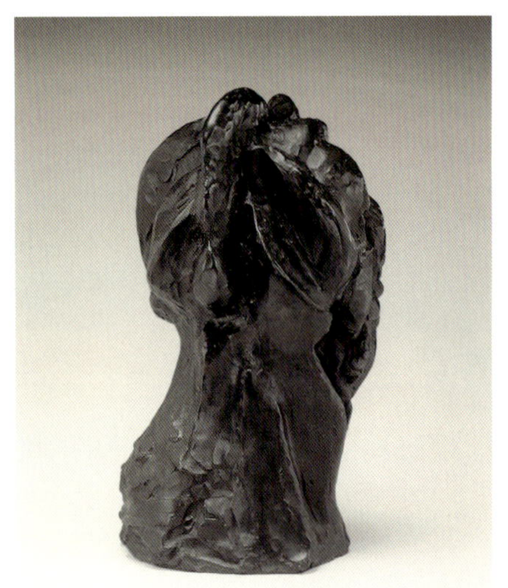

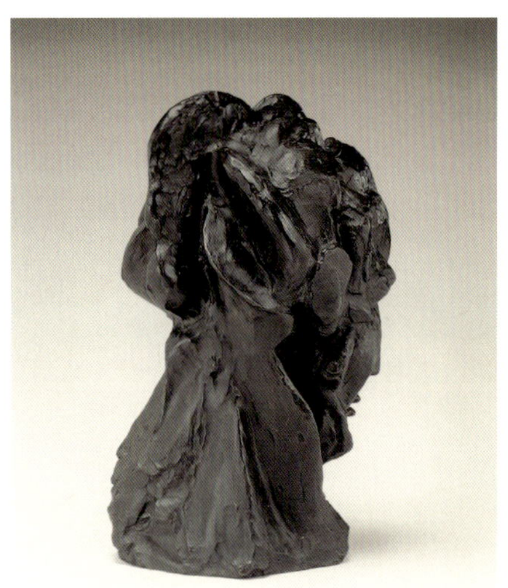

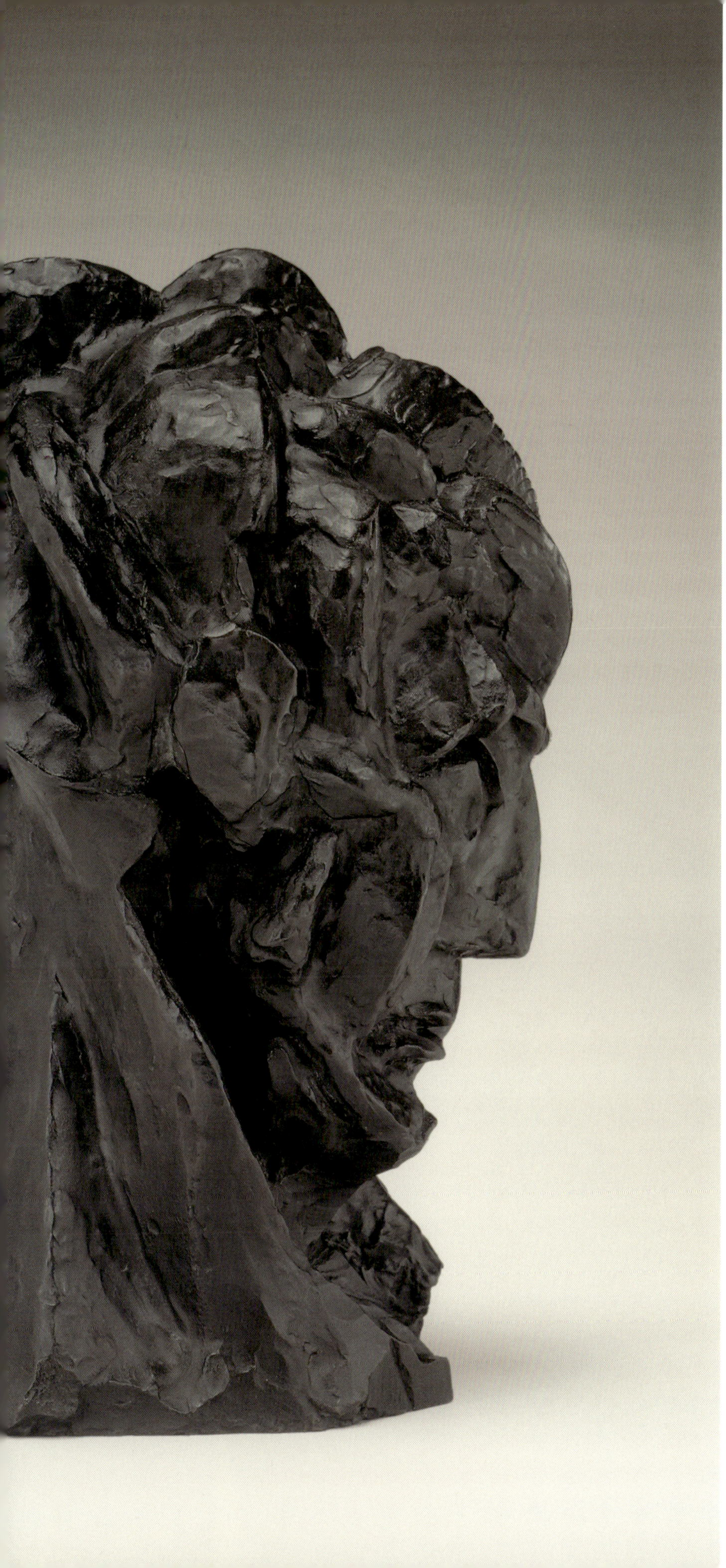

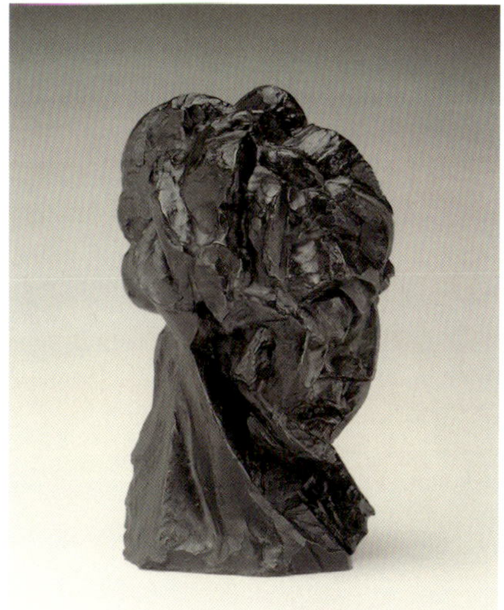

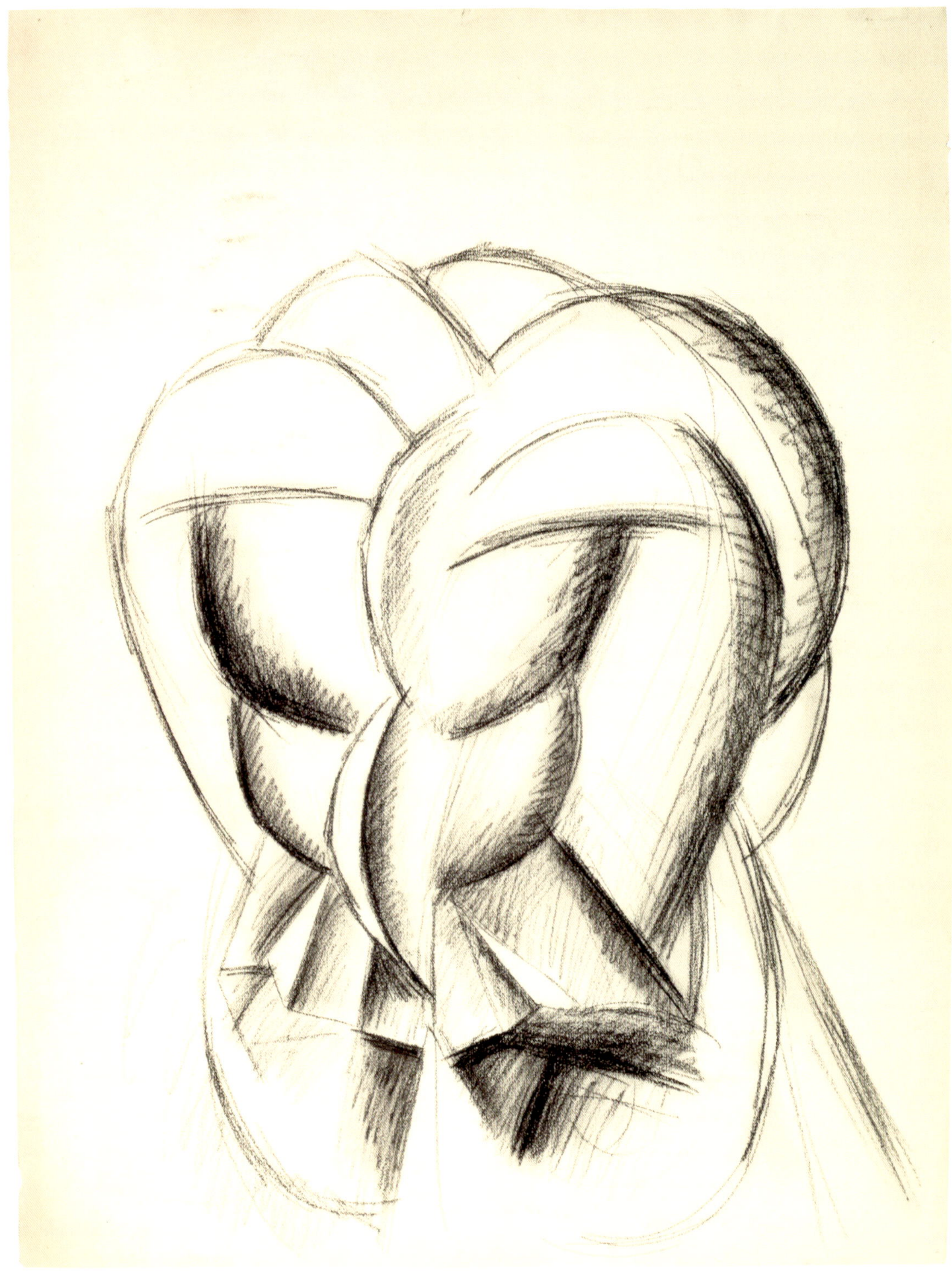

67
Study for Head of a Woman (Fernande)
1909
charcoal with black pencil highlights on paper
63.2 × 48 cm
24⅞ × 18⅞ in.
Musée Picasso, Paris

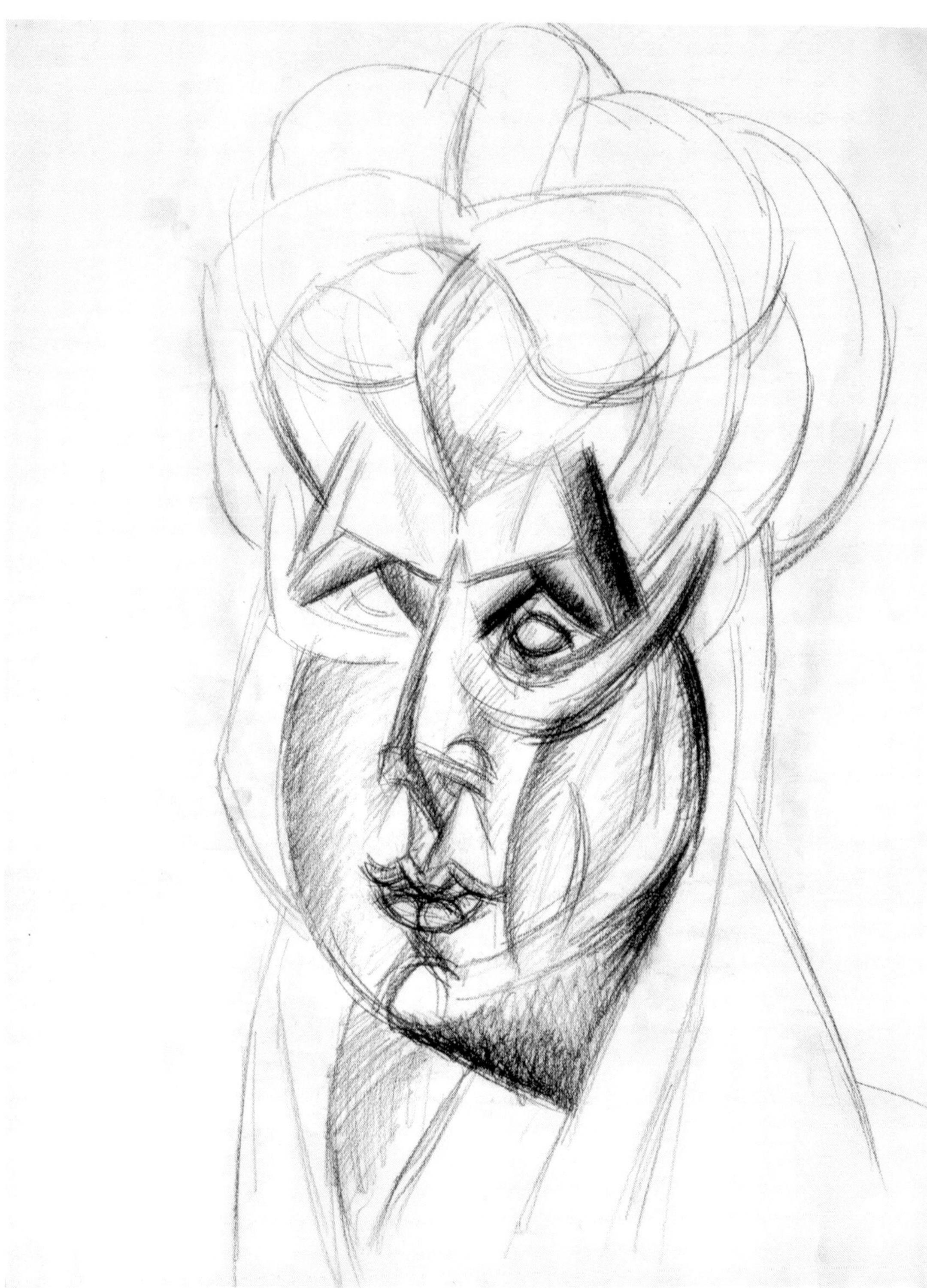

68
Study for Head of a Woman (Fernande)
1909
black pencil on paper
62.8 × 48 cm
24 3/4 × 18 7/8 in.
Musée Picasso, Paris

69
Head of a Woman
Paris, fall 1909
black pencil on paper
63 × 45.5 cm
24 13/16 × 17 15/16 in.
Albertina, Vienna

70
Woman in Green
Paris, fall–winter
1909–1910
oil on canvas
100.3 × 81.3 cm
39 1/2 × 32 in.
Van Abbemuseum,
Eindhoven

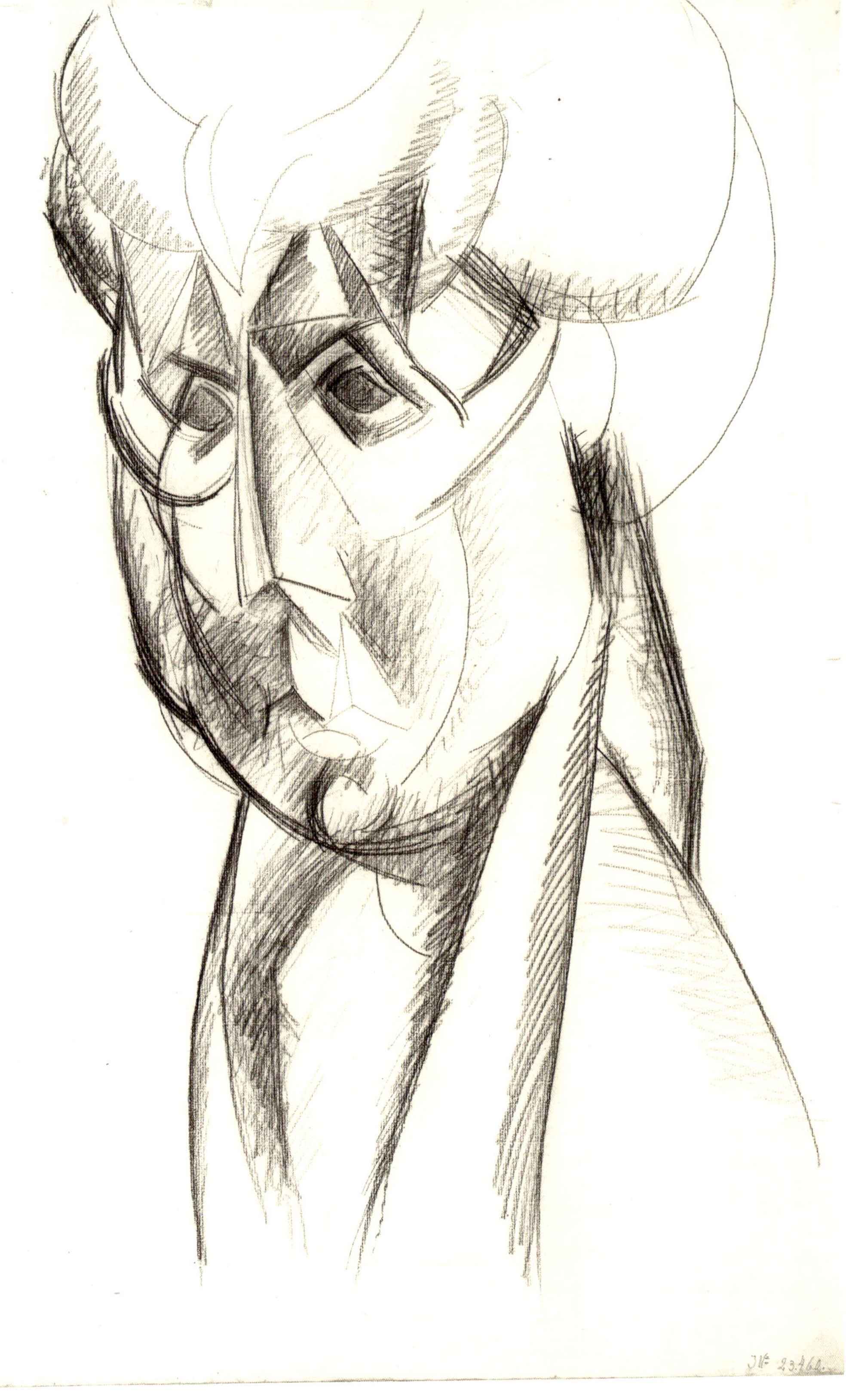

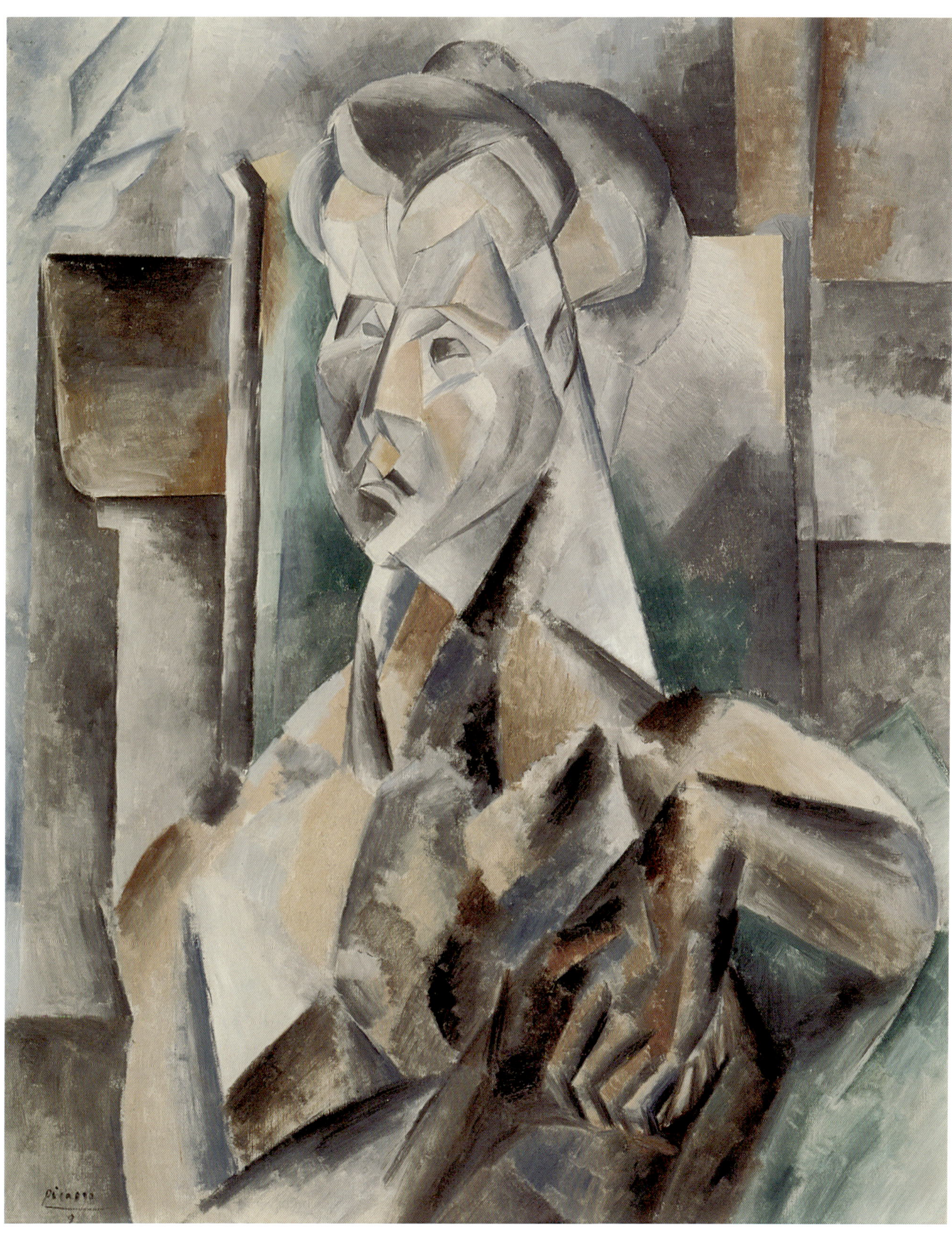
Picasso

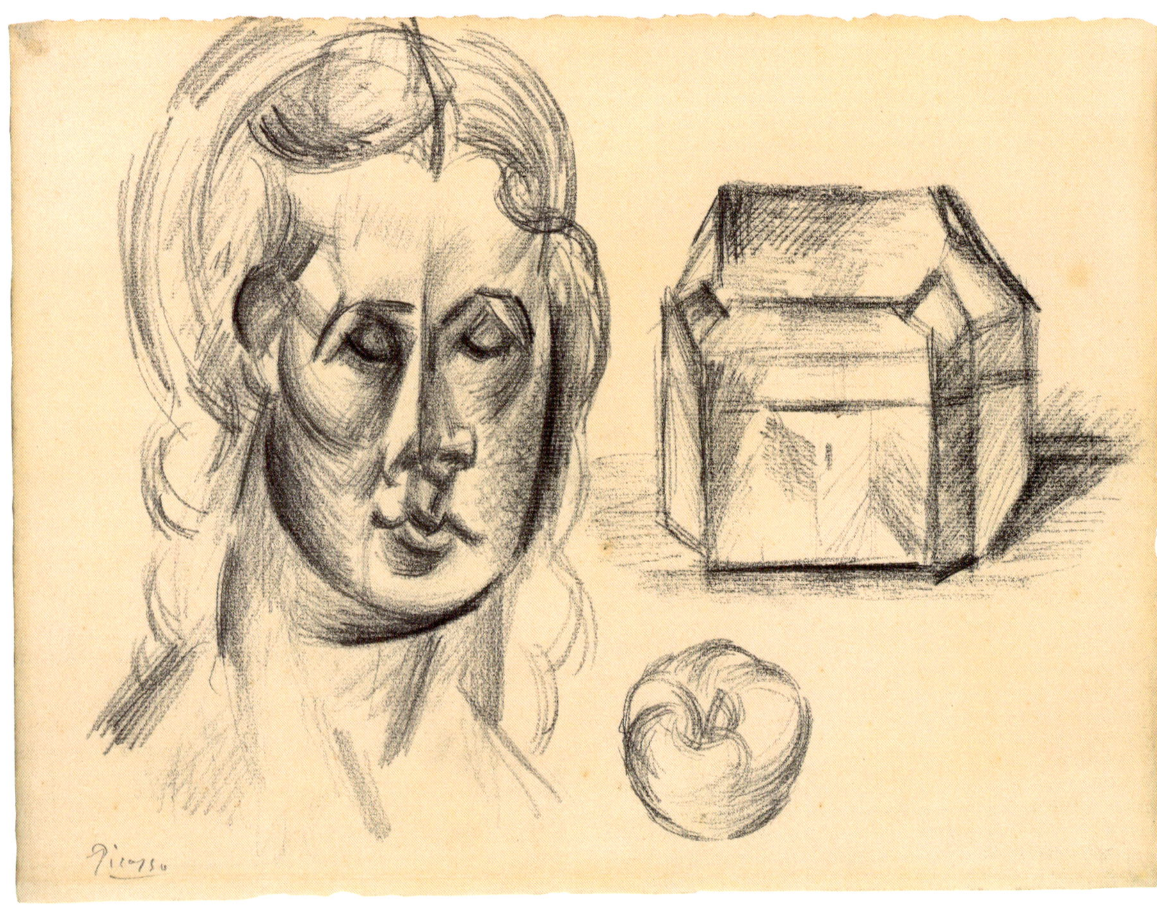

71
Head of Fernande, Casket and Apple
Paris, fall 1909
pencil on paper
23.5 × 31.8 cm
9 1/4 × 12 1/2 in.
Arne and Milly Glimcher

72
Woman with a Mustard Pot
Paris, winter 1909–1910
oil on canvas
73.2 × 60.2 cm
28 13/16 × 23 11/16 in.
Gemeentemuseum Den Haag, The Hague

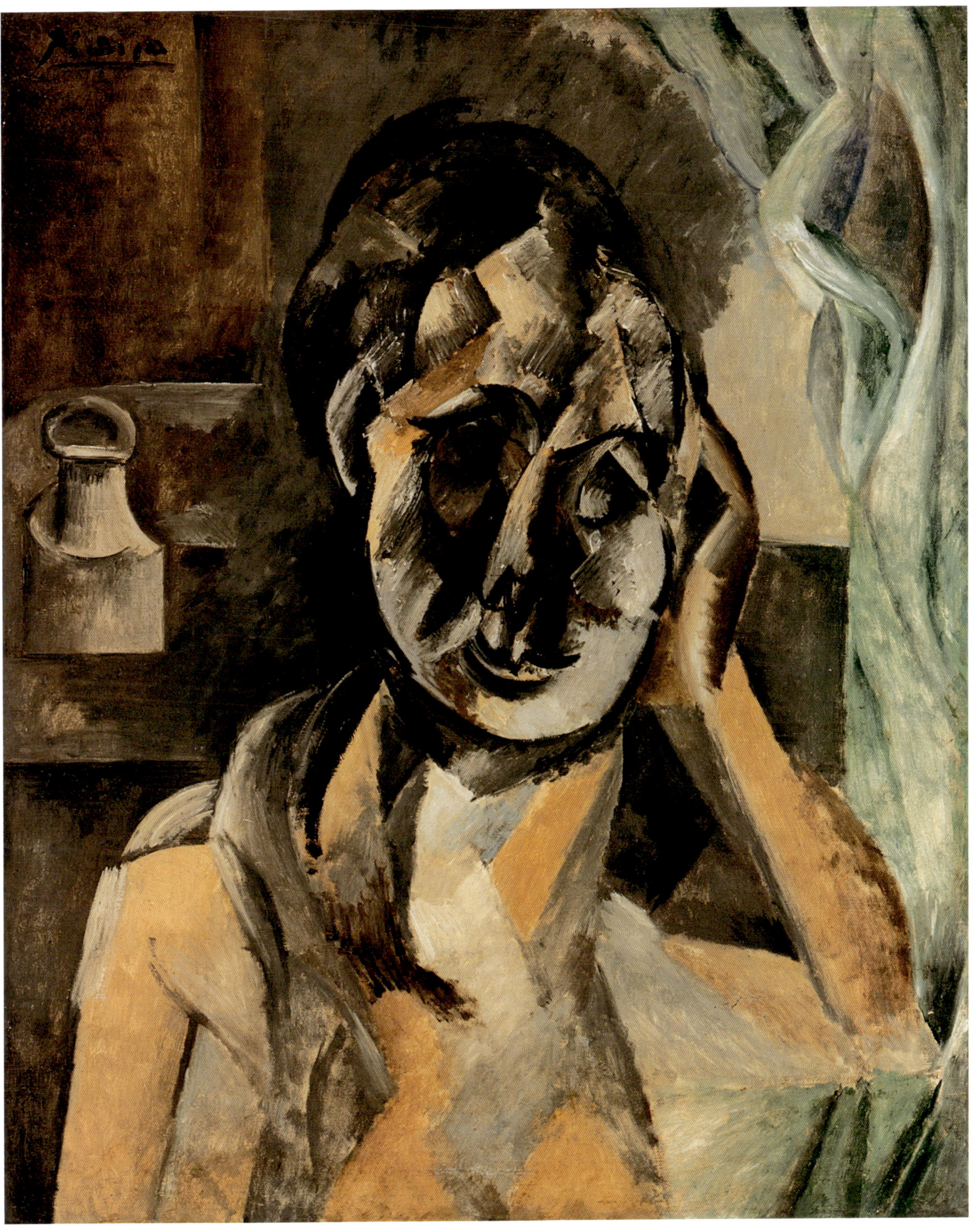

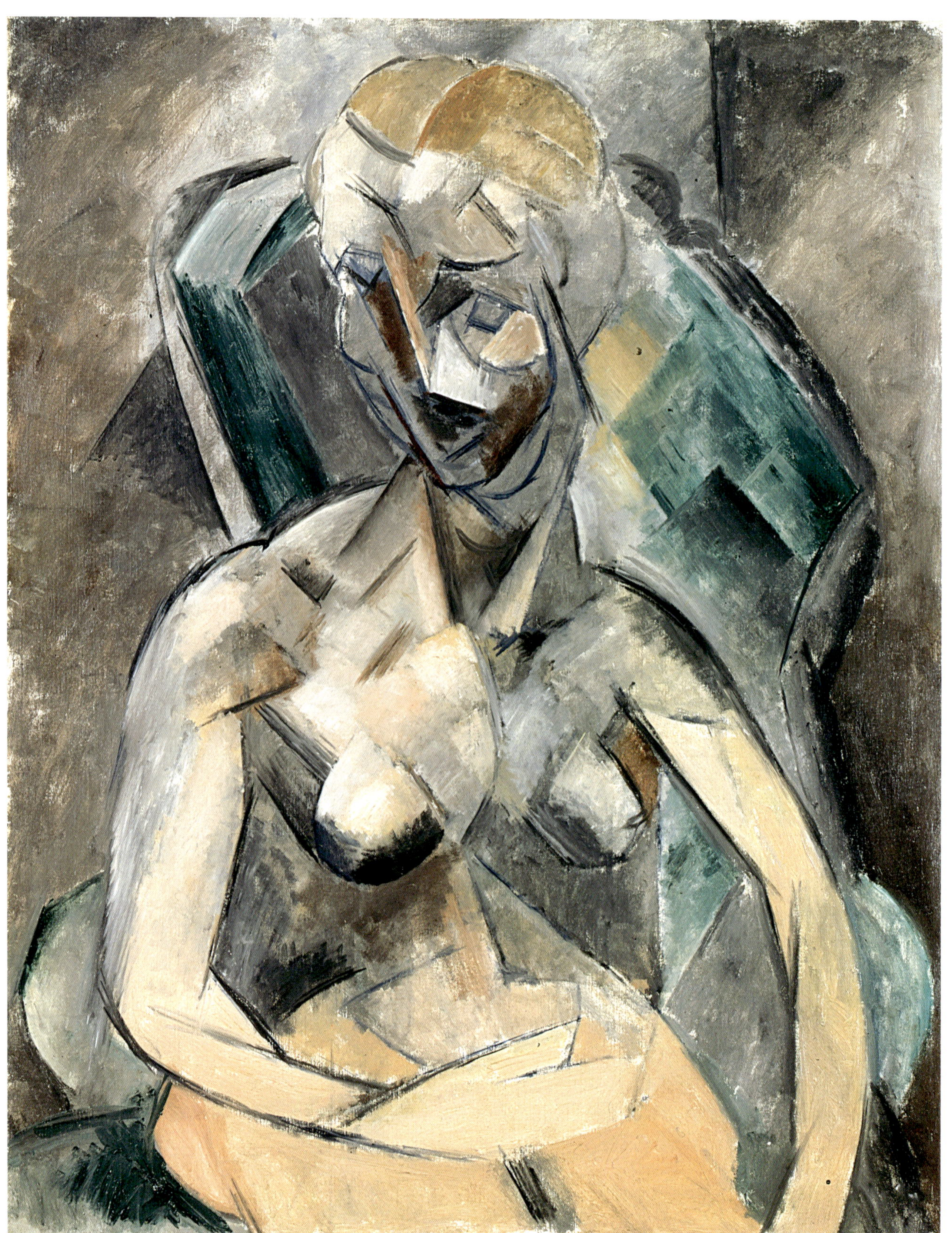

75
Woman in an Armchair (Young Woman)
Paris, winter 1909
oil on canvas
91 × 72.5 cm
35 13/16 × 28 9/16 in.
The State Hermitage Museum, Saint Petersburg

76
Woman in an Armchair
Paris, winter 1909–1910
oil on canvas
100 × 73 cm
39 3/8 × 28 3/4 in.
Centre Georges Pompidou, Paris, Musée national d'art moderne / Centre de création industrielle

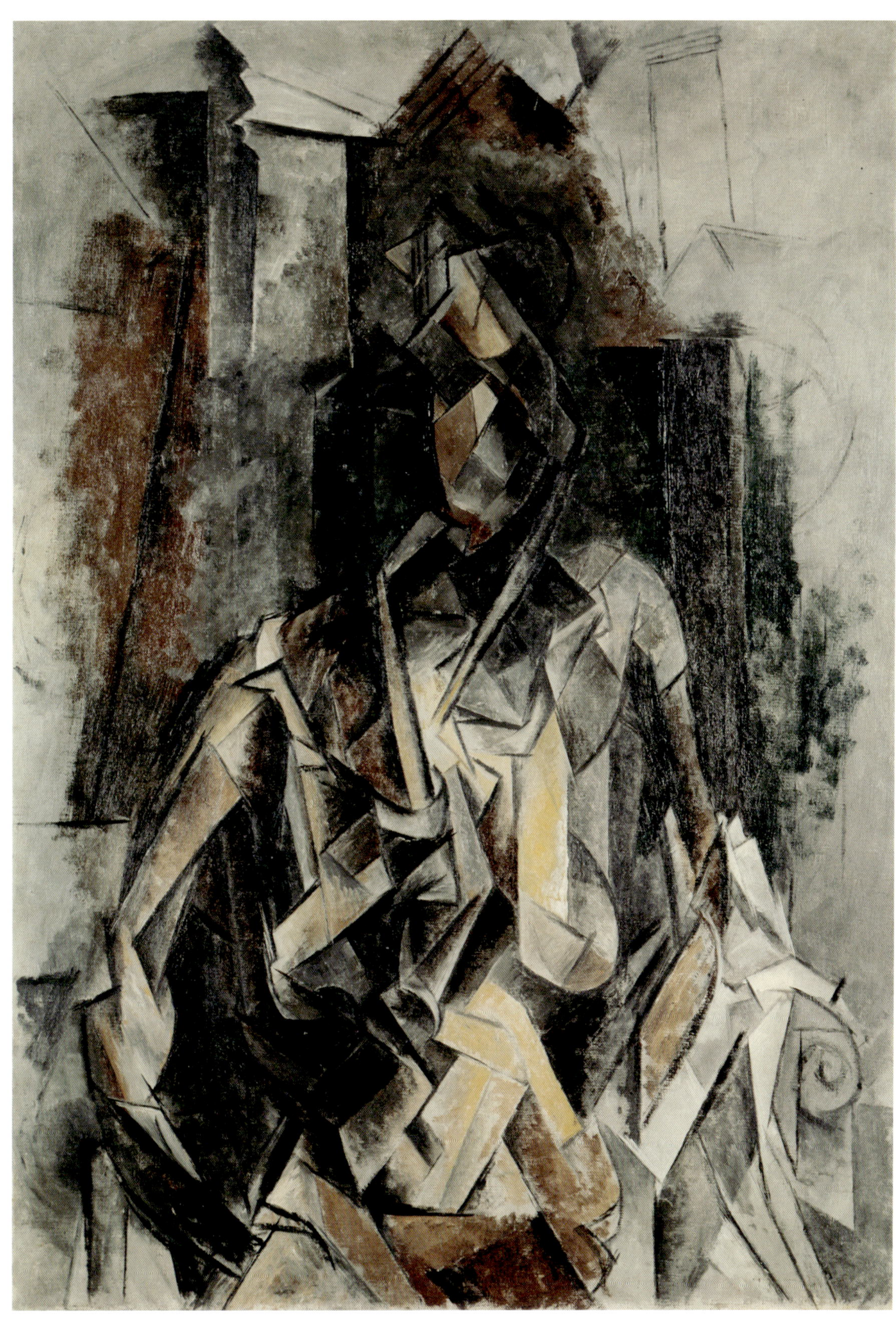

77
Seated Female Nude
Paris,
winter 1909–1910
oil on canvas
92.1 × 73 cm
36¼ × 28¾ in.
Tate, purchased 1949

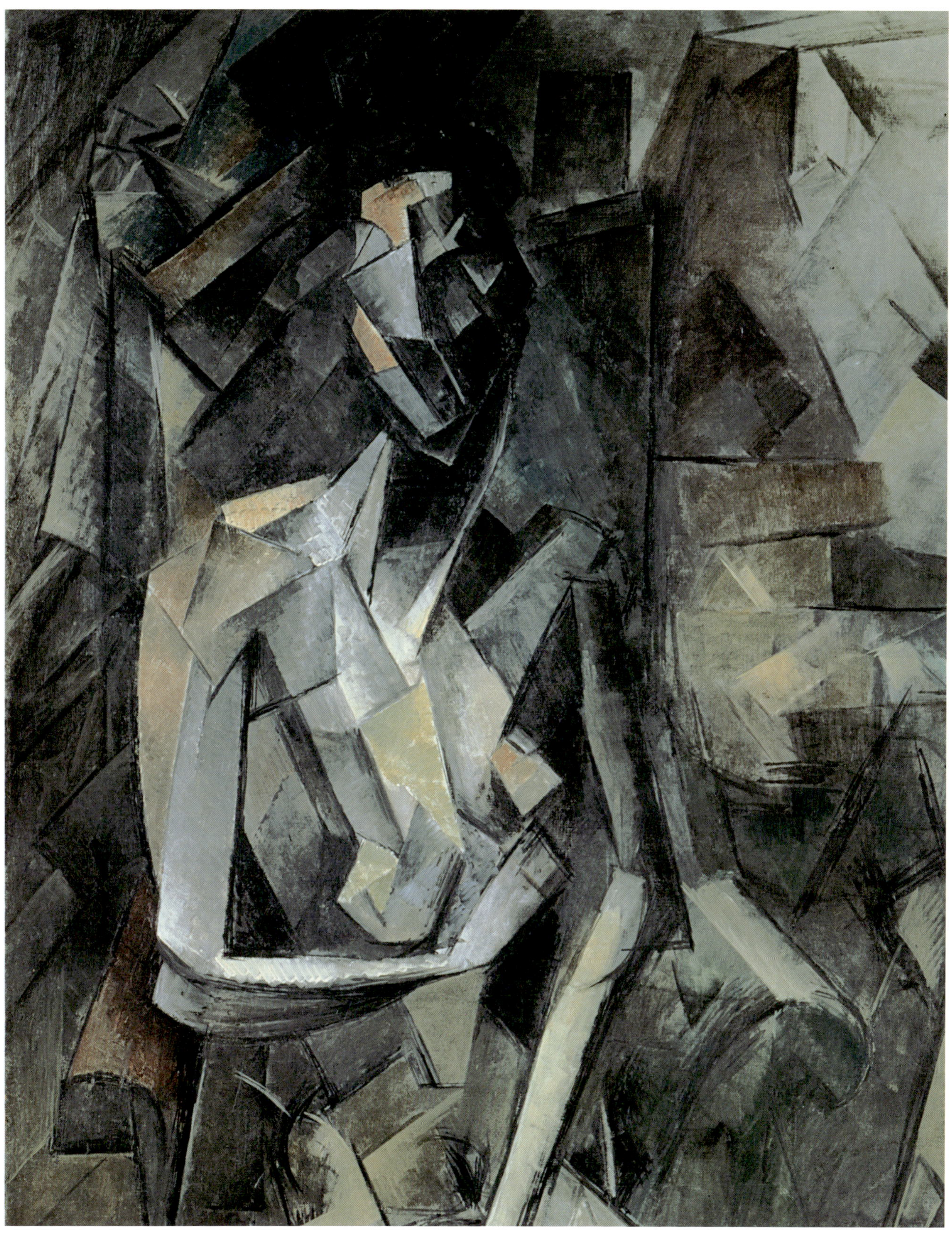

La Peau de Chagrin

Kathryn A. Tuma

Melancholy has always cleaved to the surface of modernist art, from the bituminous shadows of Gustave Courbet to the saturnine luminosities of Mark Rothko. Yet histories of modern art, and particularly narratives of the evolution of early twentieth-century abstraction, have tended to neglect the palpable affective residue that attaches to so many works' forms and surfaces.[1] Despite the resolute formal preoccupation of these narrative histories, metaphors of melancholia and the deep, abiding anxiety that binds to it continue to appear in the language of those accounts, as they do reflexively in certain forms and figures that have preoccupied modernism from early on. In the history of artistic production, that figural intertwining of form and melancholic affect manifests itself chiefly in the domain of the depiction of the human body. The rhetorical legacy of this association, too, is principally anatomical. It surfaces not only in metaphors of partition—the loss of likeness, for instance, as a kind of shattering fragmentation or amputation of parts—but also in metaphors of an even more agonizing excoriation, a protracted stripping of surfaces from the world of bodies and objects toward the ultimate disappearance of the figure.

Here, for example, is the critic Clement Greenberg's description of the rise of cubist techniques out of the lessons of the past. Allegorizing the process by which cubist abstraction renounced the ostensible "opticality" of nineteenth-century impressionism, Greenberg writes, "The world was stripped of its surface, of its skin, and the skin was spread flat on the flatness of the picture plane. Pictorial art reduced itself entirely to what was visually verifiable, and Western painting had finally to give up its five hundred years' effort to rival sculpture in the evocation of the tactile."[2] The logical paradox intrinsic to the evolution of abstraction Greenberg openly admits to; indeed, that paradox is the driving force behind his conception of modernist painting.[3] Yet as modern art gradually sloughed figurative likeness in pursuit of a more exacting pictorial radicalism, a disorienting loss precipitated. The road to abstraction that followed was a path pursued with acute ambivalence and no small degree of anxiety among artists of the prewar period, and Greenberg's metaphorization of this process as an excoriatory experience is apt. The critic's metaphor is all the more fitting in the case of the cubism of Pablo Picasso, whose artistic imagination invited such metaphors, and did so from early on. Almost certainly known to Greenberg, Guillaume Apollinaire, for instance, friend of Picasso and early chronicler of cubism, anticipated Greenberg's conceit in 1912 and again in 1913 when the poet described Picasso as a

1. One monumental exception—and it is a formidable one—is T. J. Clark's *Farewell to an Idea: Episodes from a History of Modernism* (New Haven, 1999). Clark's chapter on Picasso's cubism, "Cubism and Collectivity," 168–223, also addresses the issue of melancholy.

2. Clement Greenberg, "On the Role of Nature in Modernist Painting," in *Art and Culture: Critical Essays* (Boston, 1961), 172.

3. Greenberg 1961, 171, begins his essay: "The paradox in the evolution of French painting from Courbet to Cézanne is how it was brought to the verge of abstraction in and by its very effort to transcribe visual experience with ever greater fidelity."

4. Guillaume Apollinaire, "Du sujet dans la peinture moderne," in *Les soirées de Paris*, vol. 1 (Geneva, [1912]; 1971), 4. This metaphor is repeated in Apollinaire's treatise on the cubists, *Les peintres cubistes*, new ed. (Paris, [1913]; 1980), 79.

5. For the purposes of distinguishing cubism from its historical antecedents, Picasso's dealer and historian of cubism, Daniel-Henry Kahnweiler, *The Sculptures of Picasso* (Paris and London, 1949), n.p., characterizes impressionism as having "contented itself with conscientiously recording particular optical impressions." Picasso also defined cubism as a reaction against impressionism: "We were trying to move in a direction opposite to impressionism. That was the reason we abandoned color, emotion, sensation and everything that had been introduced into painting by the impressionists, to search again for an architectonic basis in the composition, trying to make order of it." Picasso, quoted in Albert Elsen, "The Many Faces of Picasso's Sculpture," *Art International* 13 (Summer 1969), 26.

"surgeon" in his artistic method, the artist studying "an object like a surgeon dissects a cadaver."[4]

Histories of modern art have primarily focused on the rivalry Greenberg and other modernist critics have established between painting and sculpture. The dynamic tension between these two models of representation has functioned as a way to allegorize the organizing dialectic of the evolution of modernist painting. Within these histories of modernism, it has long been Paul Cézanne's immense artistic achievement that has provided the pivotal axis supporting the turn from the ostensibly "pure" opticality of impressionist painting—a characterization to which Picasso and his colleagues largely subscribed[5]—to what Greenberg and others have interpreted as cubism's "restoration" of the traditional basis of Western art in the form of a more "sculptural illusion."[6] That the lessons of Cézanne somehow issued forth Picasso's cubism is conventional to histories of modern art, and the idea is foundational to Greenberg's account. How those lessons did so, and of what precisely they were comprised, has nonetheless remained a driving question behind modernism's master narratives.

The notion that Cézanne's art irrevocably altered the aesthetic horizons of painting was a suspicion that had already emerged by the end of the nineteenth century. During the 1890s, when an ever-increasing range of Cézanne's work was available to be seen and studied, artists and critics alike began to infer from Cézanne's pictorial strategies and techniques that a whole new universe of artistic possibility was opening up, even as those same artists and critics also suspected that they were only beginning to comprehend the aesthetic ramifications of his vision. In words that would later sound prophetic, the critic Gustave Geffroy saw Cézanne already by 1893 as "a sort of precursor of another art."[7] For those looking back over the art of the early twentieth century, few would oppose the view that the fulfillment of Geffroy's prophecy came in the form of the cubism of Picasso and Georges Braque. Even Picasso, ever wary of framing his relationship to Cézanne in too overtly oedipal terms, anointed Cézanne "father" to his generation.[8]

Cézanne's achievement in painting left behind an artistic legacy of formal innovations and unresolved pictorial problems that focused, preoccupied, and galvanized the attention of almost every young artist who came across his work during the early years of the twentieth century. The young Picasso, living in Paris and visiting, among other places, the gallery of Cézanne's dealer Ambroise Vollard (who would later, along with Daniel-Henry Kahnweiler, become one of Picasso's

6. Greenberg 1961, 171.

7. Gustave Geffroy, "L'impressionisme," *La Revue encyclopédique* (15 December 1893), cited in Françoise Cachin and Joseph J. Rishel, *Cézanne* [exh. cat., Philadelphia Museum of Art] (Philadelphia, 1996), 30. Geffroy was almost certainly echoing Joris-Karl Huysmans, who five years earlier had delivered the backhanded compliment that Cézanne was "an artist with diseased retinas who, in his exasperated visual perceptions, discovered the premonitory symptoms of a new art." Joris-Karl Huysmans, "Trois peintres," *La Cravache* (4 August 1888), cited in exh. cat. Philadelphia 1996, 27.

8. Picasso also called Cézanne his generation's "mother." To Kahnweiler Picasso said, "Cézanne was to us like a mother who protects her children," and to the photographer Brassaï, "He was like our father. It was he who protected us...my one and only master." Daniel-Henry Kahnweiler, *My Galleries and Painters* (New York, 1971), 55; and G.H. Brassaï, *Picasso and Company* (Garden City, N.Y., 1966), 79. Both as cited in Leo Steinberg, "Resisting Cézanne: Picasso's *Three Women*," *Art in America* (November–December 1978), 123. Henri Matisse echoes the idea of Cézanne as "father": see Alfred H. Barr Jr., *Matisse: His Art and His Public* (New York, 1951), 87.

principal dealers), was no exception among them.[9] Artists of Picasso's generation experienced Cézanne's work where they could. Prior to 1895, when Vollard staged the first great one-man exhibition of Cézanne's painting at the dealer's gallery in Paris, examples of Cézanne's art were such a rarity that some even doubted the artist truly existed.[10] Even after Vollard's show, the work was difficult to find. For the first decade of the twentieth century, revelations of the power and depth of Cézanne's art were made possible primarily by exhibitions at the Salon d'automne in Paris, in addition to an extremely influential show of seventy-nine of Cézanne's watercolors at the gallery Bernheim-Jeune in 1907. The first Salon exhibiting Cézanne's work took place in 1904, where the thirty-one of Cézanne's paintings displayed sent shock waves throughout early avant-garde artistic circles. While a smaller share of Cézanne's work was also on view at the Salons of 1905 and 1906, the more momentous upheaval occurred at the Salon of 1907, mounted the year after Cézanne's death, when Cézanne's artistic legacy was cemented as the most consequential influence in the contemporary art world. Broadly conceived as a memorial exhibition, the Salon d'automne of 1907 featured fifty-six oil paintings, including a wide spectrum of the work Cézanne had produced during the last decade of his life. There, artists like Picasso and Braque found themselves confronted for the first time with the magnitude of the achievement represented by Cézanne's late work.[11] In the eyes of the younger generation of artists, it was confirmed: with Cézanne had arrived "an absolute overturning of the art of painting."[12]

The work Cézanne executed between 1895 and 1906 has without question had the most profound impact on later artists, both stylistically and thematically. Curiously, however, the manifest affective tenor of Cézanne's oeuvre, especially the profound melancholy of his late work, has played an almost negligible role in the narratives of cubism's unfolding. Quite the contrary, for some writers the exclusion of affect has become a defining characteristic of the cubist project of Picasso and Braque.[13] Yet while Picasso himself would openly credit the art of Cézanne for having laid the ground for his own breakthrough into abstraction,[14] Picasso also underscored the core of anxiety that aggravated his imagination as he moved toward the revolution in forms we now call cubism. When Picasso later cast a retrospective eye over his formative years as an artist, he looked for a way to distill the essence of how Cézanne's legacy had shaped almost an entire generation of artists.[15] For Picasso, the notion of Cézanne's "anxiety" was the key: "It's not what an artist does that counts, but what he is. Cézanne's anxiety is what interests us. That is his lesson."[16]

9. William Rubin, "Cézannisme and the Beginnings of Cubism," in William Rubin, ed., *Cézanne: The Late Work* [exh. cat., The Museum of Modern Art] (New York, 1977), 181, dates Picasso's earliest interest in Cézanne to 1901, when Picasso would have been able to see a number of Cézanne's paintings at Vollard's gallery in Paris.

10. The painter and critic Maurice Denis famously describes how Cézanne had at the time attained an almost mythic reputation, leading Denis and others to question the painter's genuine existence. See Maurice Denis, "Cézanne," *Théories, 1890–1910*, 4th ed. (Paris, 1920), 246.

11. Cézanne's late portraits are saturated with melancholy, and at the Salons d'automne Picasso would have had the opportunity to see quite a number of them: *Madame Cézanne in a Yellow Armchair*, 1888–1890 (Rewald 655), *Madame Cézanne in a Green Hat*, 1891–1892 (Rewald 700), *Madame Cézanne in the Conservatory*, 1891–1892 (Rewald 703), *The Smoker Resting on His Elbow*, c. 1891 (Rewald 757), *Portrait of Gustave Geffroy*, 1895–1896 (Rewald 791), *Old Woman with a Rosary*, 1895–1896 (Rewald 808), *Man with Crossed Arms*, c. 1899 (Rewald 851), *Portrait of the Gardener Vallier*, 1902–1906 (Rewald 948), and *Portrait of the Gardener Vallier Seen in Profile*, 1902–1906 (Rewald 951), as well as both the London (Rewald 855) and Philadelphia (Rewald 857) versions of *The Great Bathers*.

12. Thadée Natanson, "Exposition: Théodure Duret," *La revue blanche* 30 (April 1894), cited in exh. cat. Philadelphia 1996, 32.

Cézanne himself felt acutely that he was only ever on the verge of beginning his work in painting, and the artist often despaired that he would not live long enough "to realize the dream of art I have pursued my entire life."[17] Burdened by chronic doubts that he would not survive to achieve his goals, Cézanne had also long sensed that his work marked not the end of an older tradition but the birth of a new one. During the last decade of his life, Cézanne—frequently, and perhaps unfairly, characterized as a misanthrope and recluse—demonstrated a remarkably tender commitment to developing younger artists who would paint pictures Cézanne knew he would not live to see. Although his letters betray black moods and a lacerating loneliness, they are also filled with painstakingly attentive advice to members of the next generation of painters. In one such letter—unaddressed and never sent—Cézanne wrote to an unidentified young artist: "I have perhaps come too late. I was a painter more of your generation than of mine. You are young, you have vitality, you will imbue your art with a force that only those who have real feelings can give. As for me, I am old. I will not have time to express myself. Let us work."[18]

If it is Cézanne's anxiety that is most forcefully communicated through his letters, it is a powerful melancholy that best characterizes the affective mode of his late paintings. That twinned affective resonance is a palpable feature inextricable from his pictorial vision and his artistic legacy, and it was a quality to which the young Picasso immediately, and perhaps intuitively, responded. Yet while the thematic sobriety and stylistic austerity of Picasso's Blue period of late 1901 to mid-1904 has been interpreted as an early response to Cézanne's art, it is arguable that Picasso's engagement with Cézanne's legacy remained largely iconographic until relatively late.

The young Picasso nonetheless remained acutely aware of the presence of Cézanne's work as an ineluctable vicissitude of the history of art as well as a valuable resource for his own innovative vision, and over the course of the earliest years of the twentieth century he continued to make explicit reference in his work to paintings by Cézanne. Through a shared vocabulary of bathers and still lifes, Picasso continuously, if episodically, indexed his ongoing dialogue with the painter. The juxtaposition of two icons of early modernist painting, Picasso's *Boy Leading a Horse* of early 1906 and Cézanne's *The Great Bather* of c. 1885 (Rewald 555), both of which now hang in the Museum of Modern Art in New York, is of course a canonical example.[19] While it is difficult to establish for certain which specific canvases Picasso may have seen—*The Bather,* for instance, despite the conventionality of its comparison to Picasso's *Boy Leading a Horse,* was a canvas not exhibited

13. Werner Spies with Christine Piot, *Picasso: The Sculptures* (Ostfildern-Ruit, Holland, 2000), 65, for instance, argues that what he calls "psychological representation" is excluded from cubist portraiture. He adds that "this, in fact, seems to emerge as the aesthetic boundary line of cubism."

14. In 1930 Picasso stated, "Around 1906 Cézanne's influence gradually flooded everything, and the knowledge of composition, of the polarity of forms and of the rhythm of the forms was open to all.... I realized that painting had an intrinsic value, detached from any actual portrayal of objects ...." Picasso, quoted in *Picasso* (Basel, 1967), 32, as cited in Steinberg 1978, 123.

15. I thank Jeffrey Weiss for pointing out to me that this remark was made in the context of a conversation with Christian Zervos in 1935, at a moment when Zervos was working toward the publication of the catalogue raisonné of Picasso's early work. Picasso may therefore have felt obliged to establish for historical record precisely what effect Cézanne's art had had on his own during the formative years of his career.

16. Picasso, quoted in Christian Zervos, "Conversations avec Picasso," *Cahiers d'art* 10 (1935), 178.

17. Cézanne, letter to Roger Marx, 23 January 1905, in *Correspondance,* ed. John Rewald (Paris, 1978), 311–312.

18. Cézanne, letter to an unknown young artist, date unknown, in Rewald 1978, 256.

19. Paintings by Cézanne are referenced parenthetically within the text according to the catalogue numbers in John Rewald with Walter Feilchenfeldt and Jayne Warman, *The Paintings of Paul Cézanne: A Catalogue Raisonné,* 2 vols. (New York, 1996).

20. Rubin in exh. cat. New York 1977, 157. See also John Golding, *Cubism: A History and an Analysis, 1907–1914*, 3d ed. (Cambridge, Mass., 1988), 39, who describes Cézanne's influence as having been "of the most general kind."

21. Picasso was living and working in Spain at the time and would not have seen this particular painting in 1895.

22. For a thorough archaeology of the allusions in this painting, see William Rubin's "From Narrative to 'Iconic' in Picasso: The Buried Allegory in *Bread and Fruitdish on a Table* and the Role of *Les Demoiselles d'Avignon*," *The Art Bulletin* 65 (December 1983), 615–649.

until much later—Cézanne's bathers had a pervasive, if broadly typological, influence on early twentieth-century treatments of the figure. Most scholars will admit that the link between Cézanne's bathers and early masterworks by Picasso like *Les Demoiselles d'Avignon* of 1907 and *Three Women* of 1908 (fig. 1) is qualified at best by a "diffused" or generalized influence.[20] It remains indisputable, however, that Cézanne's bathers haunt the vast majority of Picasso's treatments of the nude, and especially those of the female figure.

Picasso's own uncompromising ambition is always at stake in such allusions, and in 1909 he executed a still life that would openly throw down the gauntlet. Picasso's *Still Life with Hat (Cézanne's Hat)* (fig. 2) features a large black Kronstadt hat, the same type that Cézanne depicted himself wearing in several of his self-portraits, as he does in *Cézanne Wearing a Soft Hat* of 1894 (fig. 3) (Rewald 774), a canvas exhibited at Vollard's landmark one-man exhibition of 1895.[21] The biographical anecdote that stands behind this picture reveals an amplification of Picasso's decisively competitive stance vis-à-vis Cézanne. Picasso had obtained the hat on a recent visit to the studio of his associate Georges Braque. Out of his profound admiration for Cézanne, Braque had sought out and purchased the hat in a desire to emulate the master. Picasso, however, promptly seized the hat for himself in order to include it in his painting. In both the story that informs it and the picture itself, Picasso's message was clear: he intended to take the hat not only off the heads of his contemporaries but also right off the head of Cézanne.

Around this time, Picasso was also working on the monumental statement *Bread and Fruit Dish on a Table* of early 1909 (fig. 4). This large canvas issues a confident proclamation of the painter's prodigious control over references not only to Cézanne but also to the simplified forms of the primitivism of *Le douanier* Henri Rousseau. By early 1909 Picasso's familiarity with the range of Cézanne's work had grown both keener and broader. An artist whose work frequently displays a sharp visual wit, Picasso devised *Bread and Fruit Dish* as a veritable pastiche of diverse subjects within Cézanne's corpus. In this single picture Picasso layers references to Cézanne's *Cardplayers*, 1892–1893 (Rewald 710), *The Temptation of Saint Anthony*, c. 1877 (Rewald 300), and *Afternoon in Naples*, 1876–1877 (Rewald 291), as well as more generically to the painter's still lifes, many of which depict long loaves of bread and bowls of fruit.[22] In a conspicuous display of bold allusiveness, Picasso moves pieces of the history of art around with virtuoso ease. There is no question that the complex strategies of referential concealment and revelation

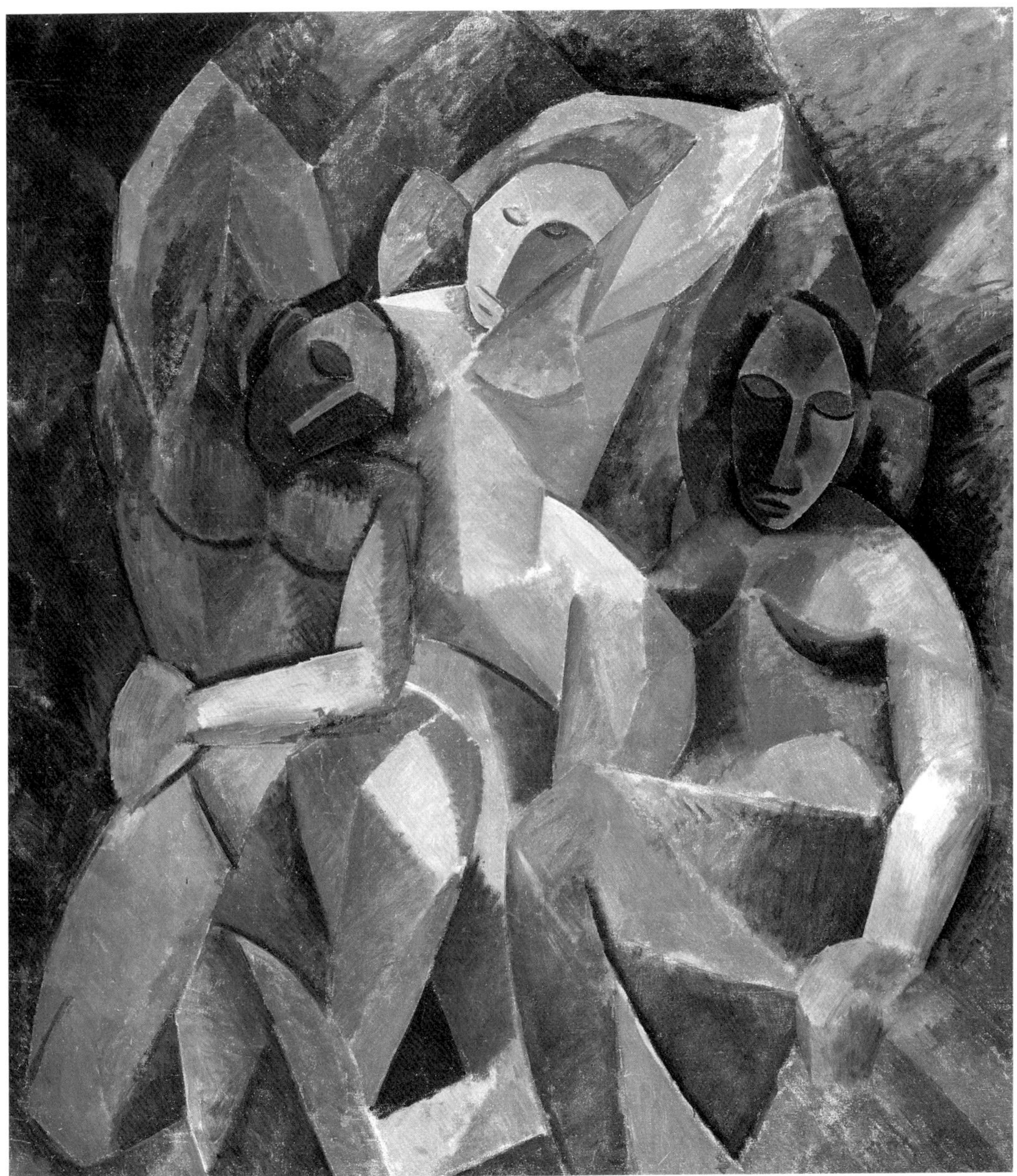

1

Pablo Picasso, *Three Women,*
Paris, begun early summer 1908;
reworked between November 1908
and January 1909, oil on canvas,
The State Hermitage Museum,
Saint Petersburg

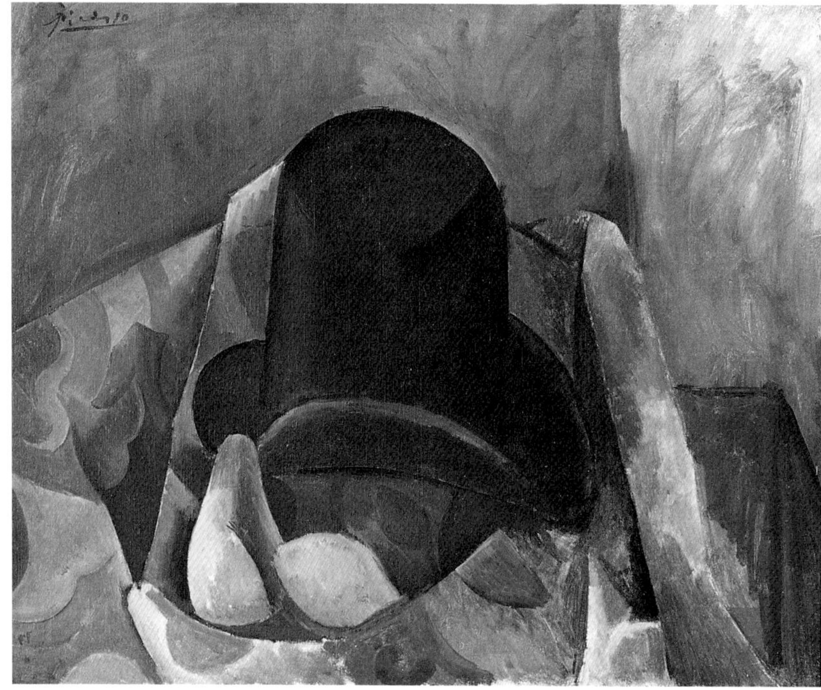

2

Pablo Picasso, *Still Life with Hat (Cézanne's Hat)*, Paris, early 1909, oil on canvas, Private collection

3

Paul Cézanne, *Cézanne Wearing a Soft Hat*, 1894, oil on canvas, Bridgestone Museum of Art, Ishibashi Foundation, Tokyo

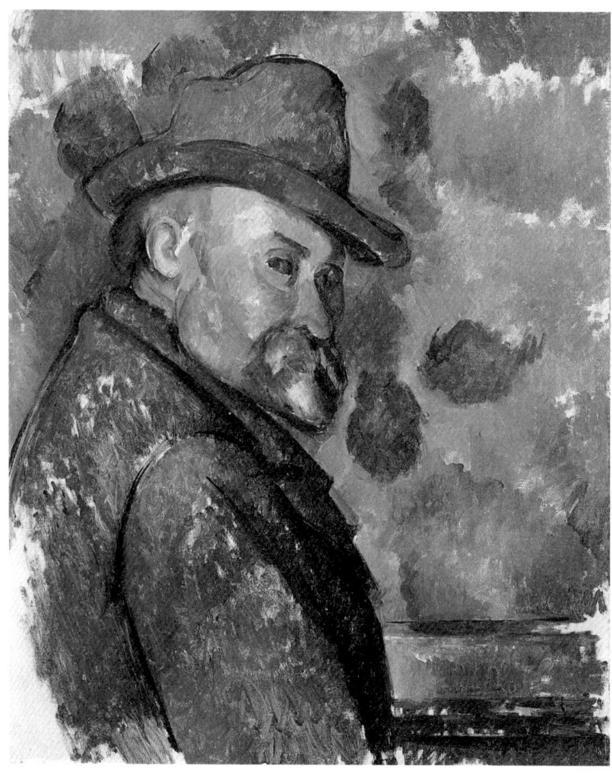

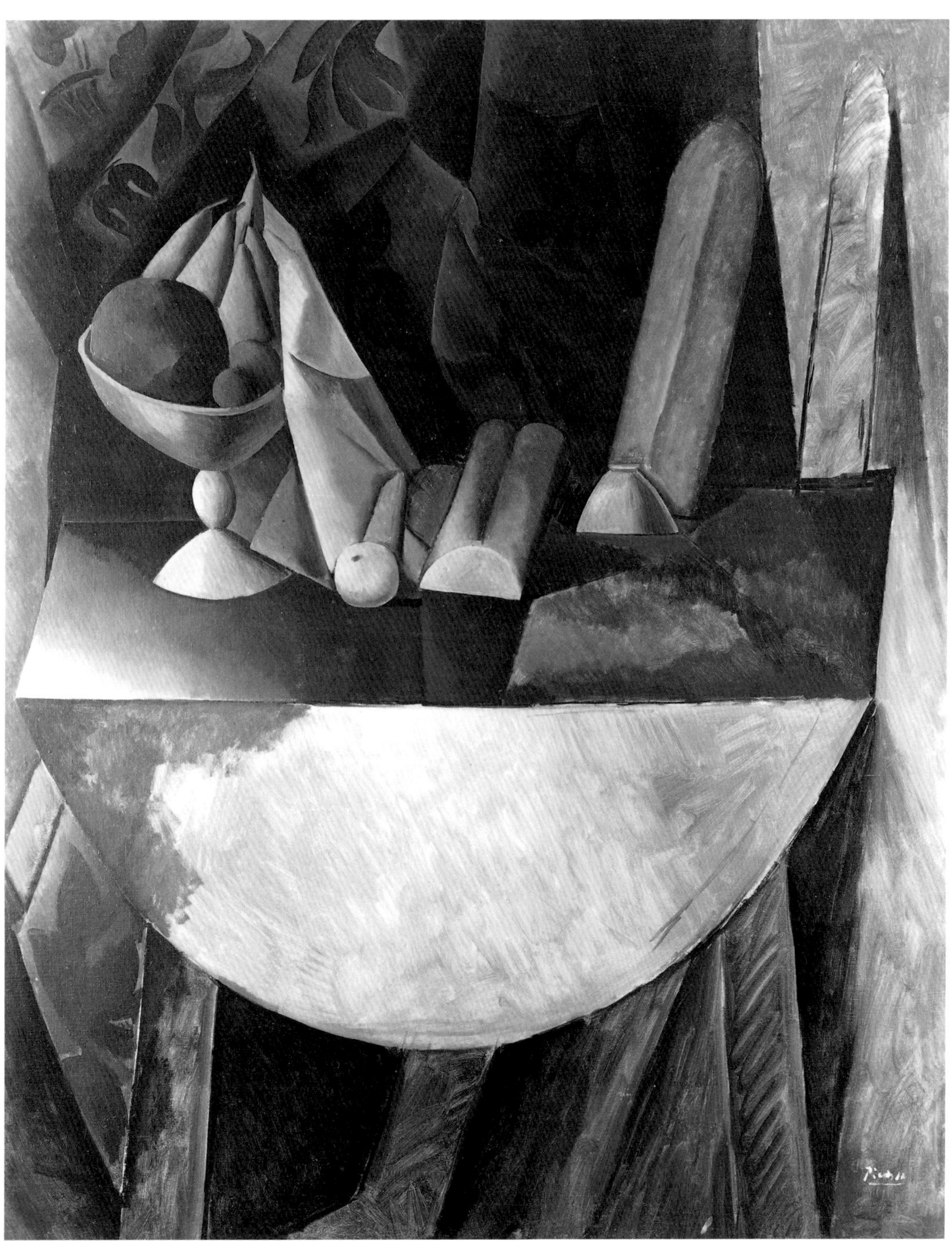

4

Pablo Picasso, *Bread and Fruit Dish on a Table,* Paris, early 1909, oil on canvas, Öffentliche Kunstsammlung Basel, Kunstmuseum

comprising this picture secure its position as one of Picasso's early masterworks. Yet while elements of the painting's construction are undoubtedly intended to signal a *cézannisme* in composition and style—from the high perspective of the table, for instance, to its somber and reduced color scheme—the lessons in technique and pictorial mechanics Picasso ostensibly draws on from Cézanne are neither especially sophisticated nor deep.[23] Above all, what this painting registers is Picasso's impressive and precocious mastery over the picture's sources. In *Bread and Fruit Dish* we witness Picasso deftly spin and toss references around as if they were juggler's balls, his complex, layered allusions to two of the towering masters of late nineteenth-century French painting achieved with the apparent ease of legerdemain.

However cursory the technical *cézannisme* of these two paintings, the pair, both executed during the initial months of 1909, augur the artist's intensifying ambitions to rival and supersede the reputation of Cézanne. Alongside Picasso's deepening involvement with Cézanne's art also comes a notable shift in the affective tone of his pictures. I am thinking, for instance, of Picasso's *Bust of a Woman* of early 1909 (cat. 1), a painting that follows narrowly on works like *Bread and Fruit Dish* and *Still Life with Hat*. *Bust of a Woman* distinguishes itself, I believe, as one of the most profound artistic responses to the shattering melancholy of Cézanne's *Old Woman with a Rosary* of 1895–1896 (fig. 5) (Rewald 808), a work that stopped the breath of those who saw it at the Salon of 1907, and a canvas of such poignancy that it has continued to reduce the most eloquent of critics to silence ever since. A remarkable achievement in and of itself, Picasso's *Bust of a Woman* stands as virtually exceptional in the artist's oeuvre up to this point in its maturity of content as well as its ambitions of style, and it heralds a new and increasing depth of artistic engagement with the legacy of Cézanne.

. . .

Over the course of the year 1909 Picasso's engagement with Cézanne radicalized, reaching a critical moment at Horta de Ebro, where Picasso spent the summer season with his lover Fernande Olivier. Having rapidly absorbed what there was to be learned from his colleague Braque's efforts to digest specific, if idiosyncratic, formal strategies he derived from studying the landscapes of Cézanne,[24] Picasso diverged from the course his friend was pursuing. Returning meaningfully to the genre of portraiture as well as to landscape painting during the spring of 1909 and into the summer at Horta, Picasso began to explore at an unprecedented level of

23. Even Rubin 1983, 620, in his analysis of this picture's complex allusions to Cézanne, admits as much in the end: "Although Cézanne's influence on the style of *Bread and Fruit-dish* was critical, it was neither as deep nor as pervasive as in some other paintings of the winter 1908–1909."

24. See the famous exchange between William Rubin and Leo Steinberg: Rubin in exh. cat. New York 1977, 151–202, and Steinberg 1978, 114–133; Leo Steinberg, "The Polemical Part," *Art in America* (March–April 1979), 115–127; and William Rubin, "Pablo and Georges and Leo and Bill," *Art in America* (March–April 1979), 128–147.

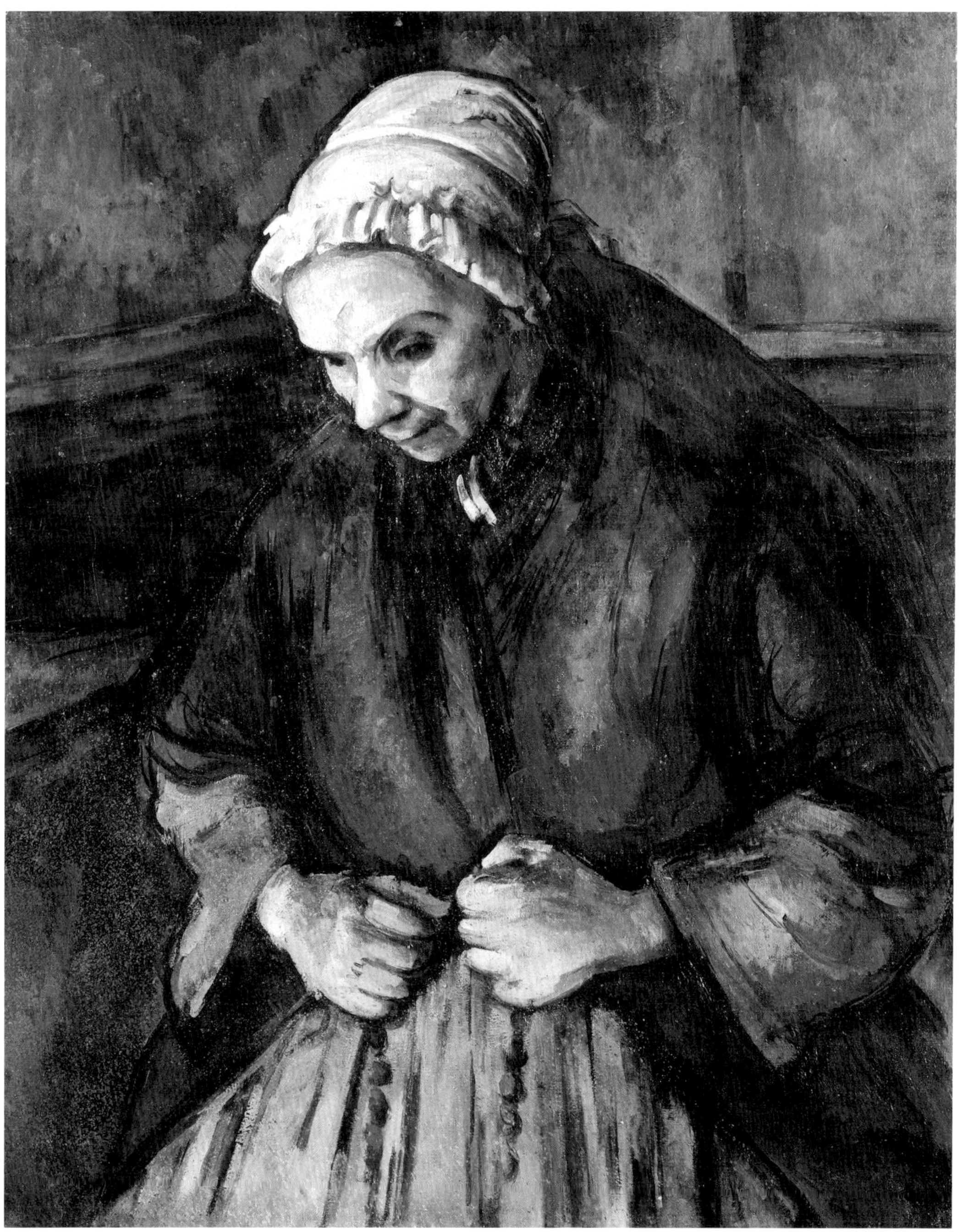

5

Paul Cézanne, *Old Woman with a Rosary*, 1895–1896, oil on canvas, National Gallery, London

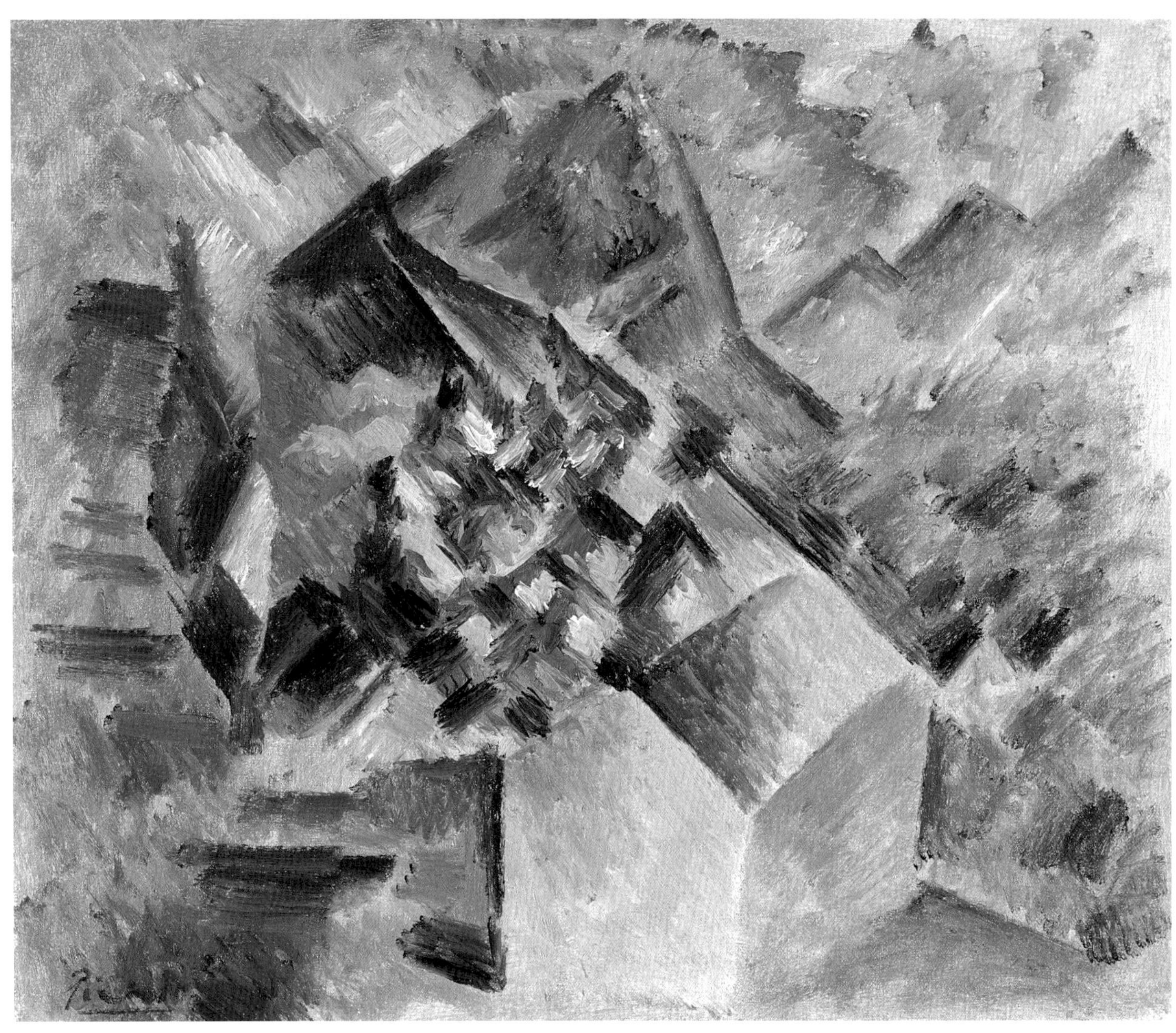

6

Pablo Picasso, *Landscape (Mountain of Santa Bárbara),* Horta de Ebro, summer 1909, oil on canvas, Private collection

depth what I am arguing is an inextricable enmeshment of pictorial innovation and melancholic affect in Cézanne's art.

Much of Picasso's work in spring 1909 nonetheless also continued along the vein of an iconographic involvement with Cézanne's traditional motifs. The pictures Picasso produced are typified by a refinement of, as well as subtle commentary on, Braque's *cézanniste* manner. Like *Bread and Fruit Dish*, some of the paintings are quite bold—and at times openly confrontational—statements about his work's relationship to Cézanne's legacy. Early in Picasso's stay at Horta, for instance, the artist paints *Landscape (Mountain of Santa Bárbara)* (fig. 6), an unmistakable reference to the familiar motif of Cézanne's beloved Mont Sainte-Victoire. The prominent "reversible cube" in the foreground—a figure that appears in turn to project out from and recede into pictorial space—is one of the most common and recognizable *cézanniste* devices Braque developed and codified in his ruminations on the nature of spatial ambiguation in Cézanne's landscapes. Picasso hyperbolizes the trope; in magnifying the cube and placing it at the heart of the foreground, the artist broadcasts his rivalrous competition with both Braque and Braque's version of Cézanne. That "cube" famously migrates through Picasso's pictures of this year, landing at one point on the brow of Fernande (cat. 35). This figure tends to be read as a crucial sign tracing cubism's *cézanniste* lineage—even if, as a motif, that cube finds at Fernande's forehead a kind of final resting place. Later that summer Picasso also paints *Head of a Woman (Fernande Olivier)* (cat. 39), a picture that revises and restates one of the underlying messages of the body of work from this period. In this painting, Picasso lays bare his summer's ambitions: that in and through the series of the portraits of Fernande on which he was furiously working he intended effectively to displace the legacy of Cézanne and supersede his predecessor's reputation as the true progenitor of modern art.

Yet during Picasso's summer at Horta de Ebro, on the eve of a revolution in the history of form that would shake the traditions of Western painting to their core, the work Picasso executed betrays little of the brash aesthetic confidence and technical bravura one associates with the artist up to this point. The paintings he produced possess little of the monumental power of *Three Women* or the declarative gravitas that characterizes *Bread and Fruit Dish*. By any account, Horta was an excruciating ordeal for Picasso, a period plagued with self-doubt, punctuated by artistic missteps and sudden retreats. Hardly an artistic refuge where the artist could work and meditate in tranquility, Horta proved to be for Picasso a crucible in

25. See Fernande Olivier, *Loving Picasso: The Private Journal of Fernande Olivier*, trans. Christine Baker and Michael Raeburn (New York, 2001), 227–250.

which elements from past and present ambitions combined to forge new and even more intense aesthetic pressures. Those pressures nonetheless resulted in one of the most stunning series of portraits in the history of modern art.

Stunning in part, however, because they are so troubling, in both form and content. Much of the work Picasso produced at Horta is, to put it bluntly, quite ugly. Testifying to a fiercely agitated imagination, Picasso's Fernande series reveals an artist searching with a sometimes wildly careening rhythm not only for answers to pictorial problems but also—even more anxiety-provoking for Picasso—for guidance toward a path pursuing the right formal questions. Broadly ignored, or sidestepped with an embarrassment and critical awkwardness uncharacteristic of the historiography on cubism, the portraits of Fernande have perpetually unsettled mainstream literature on cubism's evolution. The work at Horta appears to make little sense as a stepping-stone toward what, with the privilege of historical hindsight, we know was so shortly to come. Recalcitrant to the logic of progress, offering little support for the notion of cubism's incremental development over the course of these important years, this moment in Picasso's career is one most critics opt to pass over with dispatch.

Jarring to the eye, the portraits of Fernande are equally disquieting for the sheer rawness and potency of their emotional range. Some images, and especially the drawings—a medium conducive to the revelations of deep privacies—confront us like the visual equivalent of expletives. Appearing as though more scarified than drawn, the faceted flesh depicted there looks at times gouged out of the surface support with an aesthetic violence that can give rise to some degree of aversion. It is surely not a coincidence that the principal subject to absorb Picasso at Horta was a person deeply unhappy, as we know from the letters Fernande wrote back to Paris that summer.[25] Picasso's personal struggle with the woman who had once been known as *la belle Fernande* certainly must, on some level, have informed the velocity of her pictorial transformations from a figure of crushing sadness (cat. 2) to one smoldering with persecutory wrath (cat. 10). Yet while the temptation to read much of the summer's work through the lens of dynamic psychology is compelling, that critical perspective does little, in the end, to elucidate the sheer magnitude of this body of work's aesthetic ambitions.

One striking aspect about the series of portraits of Fernande is how little they have in common with what would be an intuitive antecedent, the portraits of Cézanne's wife. In part this quality is curious because Picasso's engagement with Cézanne had, up to this point, been so heavily informed by an inclination toward iconographic allusion. Although the representations of the two women do bear some resemblance (a similar manner of wearing their hair, a common roundness of face), and although other background features of Picasso's pictures are surely meant to reference Cézanne in some way (the sitter at times positioned in an armchair [cat. 45], the occasional inclusion of flowers or fruit in the background [cat. 27], or certain passages of drapery [cat. 35]), Picasso's Fernande exudes intensities of affect that are nowhere to be found in Cézanne's pictures of his wife. Instead, Picasso's engagement with Cézanne occurs on a deeper level, latent in the enmeshment of form and affect I described earlier—a level Picasso's inestimable competitiveness leads him simultaneously at pains to explore as well as to obscure. In this, I think Picasso's plumbing investigation of specific pictorial problems, while they do take place in the arena of portraiture, nonetheless may have less to do with the specific genre of portraiture and its immediate iconographic precedent in Cézanne's late work than with some more pervasive trouble left unresolved by it.

. . .

Some time during the 1890s Cézanne confessed to his old friend Auguste Renoir that it had taken him forty years to learn that painting was not sculpture.[26] These words, uttered by a man esteemed above all as the consummate painter's painter, by an artist whose reputation towers over the history of modern art largely due to the incomparable steadfastness and narrowed specificity of his explorations in the medium of paint, qualify as surprising indeed. His remark is unexpected, too, given the painter's lack of interest in sculpture in even less metaphorically dense ways: Cézanne was an artist never known to have possessed even a hint of interest in taking a hand to a lump of clay or chisel to a block of stone. Notably, as well, sculpture is almost entirely lacking as a motif in paintings throughout the course of his career. Clues to what Cézanne may have meant by his enigmatic statement can be uncovered in part by inference from features of his work specific to the period. While it is possible Renoir heard the comment in 1891, I think it more likely that it was expressed during an extended visit Renoir made with Cézanne in Aix in 1895, when the two spent several weeks painting side by side. If this supposition is correct, then what Cézanne meant when he said he had, finally, learned that "painting is not sculpture" may prove a crucial point for understanding some of the bases informing the unprecedented transformations in Cézanne's painting around the mid-1890s. For 1895 is a signal moment in Cézanne's development: it has enduringly

26. Cézanne, quoted in John Rewald, *Cézanne: A Biography* (New York, 1939), 170: "It took me forty years to find out that painting is not sculpture." Rewald does not cite the source of the quotation, nor does he date the remark more precisely than to the 1890s.

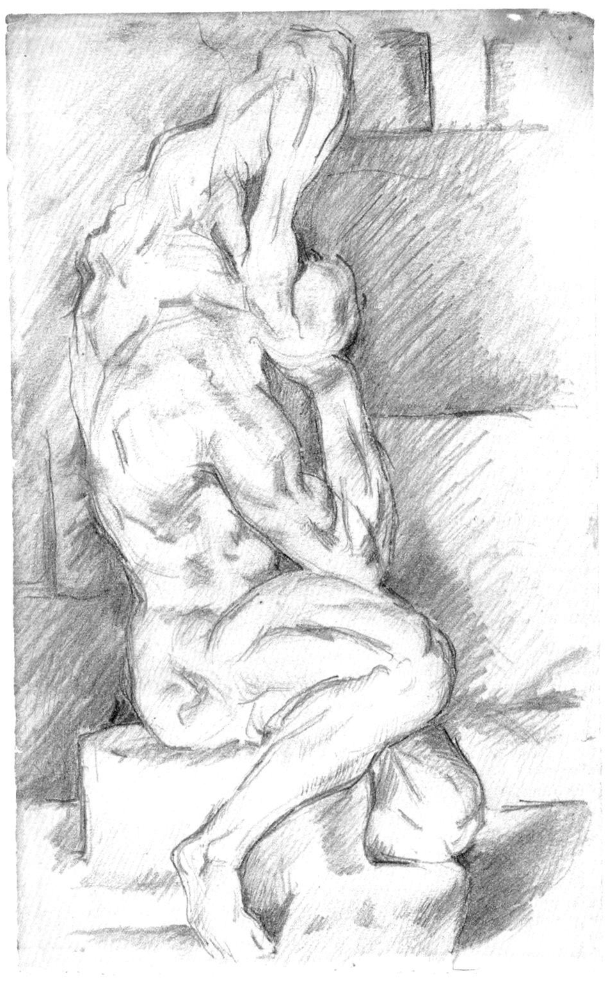

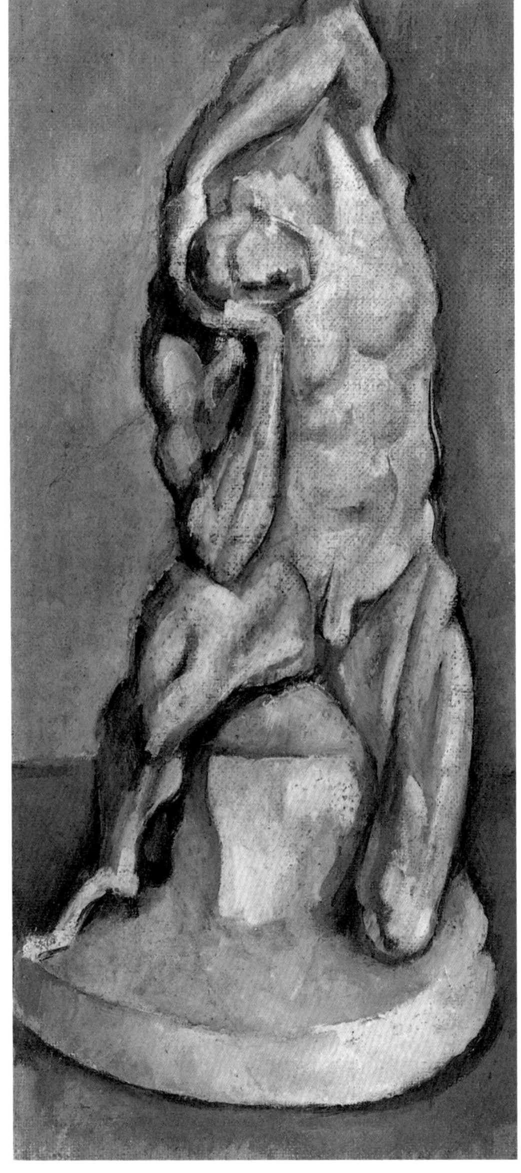

7

Paul Cézanne, *After "l'Écorché,"* 1881–1884, graphite on a page from a sketchbook, The Cleveland Museum of Art, Bequest of Leonard C. Hanna Jr.

8

Paul Cézanne, *The So-called Écorché of Michelangelo,* c. 1892, oil on canvas, Andrea Woodner and Dian Woodner, New York

demarcated the watershed year in Cézanne's career announcing the inauguration of the phase of his incomparable late work.

That something profoundly transformational was occurring in Cézanne's conception of painting as it related to sculpture is corroborated by the work he was producing at the time. For although Cézanne demonstrated a conspicuous lack of interest in painting from sculpture, his sketchbooks nonetheless reveal an abiding interest in drawing from it. This interest markedly increased during the 1890s. Around the time Cézanne made his confession to Renoir, his sketchbooks show Cézanne repeatedly turning to sculptural models as subject matter in his drawings. Of particular interest to the artist were a number of marbles he returned to in the galleries of the Louvre, from the antique marble *The Roman Orator* (Chappuis 993) to Pierre Puget's *Milo of Crotona* (Chappuis 976–978) and his *Hercules at Rest* (Chappuis 1057–1060).[27] At home Cézanne also drew multiple series of studies from two small sculptural figures he owned: a plaster cupid, attributed at the time to Puget,[28] and an *écorché*, a model of a flayed man used in standard academic training in human anatomy. We know from the evidence of an earlier painting dating to c. 1867, *Plaster Cupid* (Rewald 33), that the cupid had been in Cézanne's possession for nearly thirty years. As was true of the cupid, Cézanne also owned a copy of the *écorché*, thought at the time to have been originally modeled by Michelangelo. Common to the period,[29] this particular *écorché* was known not only to Cézanne's early hero Courbet but also to Vincent van Gogh and Henri Matisse, all of whom included the figure at one point in at least one painting.[30] While we do not know when Cézanne procured the model, it had been in his possession at least since the late 1870s, when the first extant drawings from the model were executed (Chappuis 565–573). In that series of drawings, from a sketchbook now at the Art Institute of Chicago, Cézanne gradually turns from an attention to the relationship between the model's face and body wrenched in pain to a meditation on the *écorché* from the back. In this and a related drawing from 1881–1884, the features of the anguished face are concealed, the affective force of the image now transmitted exclusively through the modeling of the figure (fig. 7) (Chappuis 574).

Cézanne executed a finished painting of the flayed man only once, in the early 1890s (fig. 8) (Rewald 785). A small canvas of 35 by 16.5 centimeters, it is tall and narrow, closely framing a frontal view of the model. While this painting after the *écorché* is unique, the 1890s mark a moment when the figure returns deeply to

27. Drawings by Cézanne are referenced parenthetically within the text according to the catalogue numbers in Adrien Chappuis, *The Drawings of Paul Cézanne: A Catalogue Raisonné*, 2 vols. (Greenwich, Conn., 1973).

28. At the time the cupid was thought to have been originally sculpted by the seventeenth-century Provençal artist Pierre Puget, whom Cézanne greatly admired. More recently, alternative attributions have been proposed, including François Duquesnoy and Nicolas Coustou. See exh. cat. Philadelphia 1996, 389.

29. This *écorché* was one of a group of anatomical models standard to the period. See, for example, Mathias Duval and Edouard Cuyer, *Histoire de l'anatomie plastique* (Paris, 1898), 66–67.

30. Gustave Courbet did so at least twice, and this may have inspired Cézanne to procure a copy of the *écorché*, not unlike the manner in which Braque demonstrated his admiration for Cézanne by purchasing a Kronstadt hat. Theodore Reff, "The Pictures within Cézanne's Pictures," *Arts Magazine* 53 (1979), 104 n.58, lists the following images depicting this *écorché*: Gustave Courbet, *Backgammon Game*, 1844; Vincent van Gogh, *Plaster Statuette: Man Kneeling*, 1887; and Henri Matisse, *Still Life with Aubergines*, 1911. Michael Fried, in *Courbet's Realism* (Chicago, 1990), 74, also identifies this same figure on the table at the left in Courbet's *Man with the Leather Belt*, 1845–1846.

31. Joachim Gasquet, *Cézanne*, new ed. (Paris, 1988), 33.

32. There is, however, a medallion with what appears to be a unique example of a bas-relief: a portrait of Dr. Paul Gachet rendered by Cézanne's friend Philippe Solari and depicted in *Still Life with Medallion of Solari*, c. 1872 (Rewald 211).

33. Meyer Schapiro, "The Apples of Cézanne: An Essay on the Meaning of Still-Life," *Modern Art, 19th & 20th Centuries* (New York, 1982), 11, reads the picture of the *écorché* at the top as a drawing and not as a painting. It is possible that Schapiro was not familiar with the painted version of the *écorché*.

engross the artist in his practice of drawing. The second principal series of sketches after the *écorché* dates to the mid-1890s and exists now as separate sheets, some of which were removed from sketchbooks of various sizes (Chappuis 1086–1089). That these surviving drawings likely represent only a small portion of Cézanne's studies after the *écorché* is suggested in a remark made by Joachim Gasquet, a young writer and poet who befriended the elder artist around this time. Gasquet attests that during this period Cézanne was drawing from the *écorché* ritually, possibly as frequently as every morning: "Until his very last day, every morning, like a priest reads his breviary, he drew and painted for an hour from all its aspects the *écorché* of Michelangelo, and I remember with what respect he frequently evoked the image of *père* Ingres going to the Louvre, under his umbrella, at sixty years of age, saying, 'I am going to learn to draw.'"[31]

Cézanne's interest in these two figures culminates in one of his most conceptually dense paintings of the decade, *Still Life with Plaster Cupid* of c. 1895 (fig. 9) (Rewald 786), now at the Courtauld Institute Galleries in London. This seminal picture represents an almost unprecedented incorporation of sculpture in Cézanne's painting: with the exception of earlier versions of the Courtauld *Still Life*, the *Plaster Cupid* of 1867 had previously stood as the most recent painting of a sculpture in Cézanne's oeuvre.[32] A veritable dissertation on the complex games pictorial illusionism can play, *Still Life with Plaster Cupid* depicts an illogical and irresolvable space, one where an onion on the table next to the cupid fuses with a contiguous onion painted in the canvas propped up behind it, even as yet another at the right of the cupid also merges with the floor—as if the floor, too, were now doubling as the face of a canvas, a disproportionately large apple in the background seeming to confirm the frontal planarity of that ground. Rife with illusionistic ploys of this kind, the canvas also meaningfully incorporates representations of both sculptural models. In part an allegorical meditation on the relationship between painting and sculpture, Cézanne's *Still Life with Plaster Cupid* utilizes the two figures as metaphors for two different modalities of sculptural representation. The cupid we observe is a painting of a sculpture (qualified by the fact that the cupid's torso is framed by a canvas leaning on a wall behind it, as if the cupid were a painting of a sculpture within a painting) and occupies the vertical center as this canvas' featured object. The *écorché*, however, is a painting of a painting of a sculpture, and proves a more complex metaphorical case.[33]

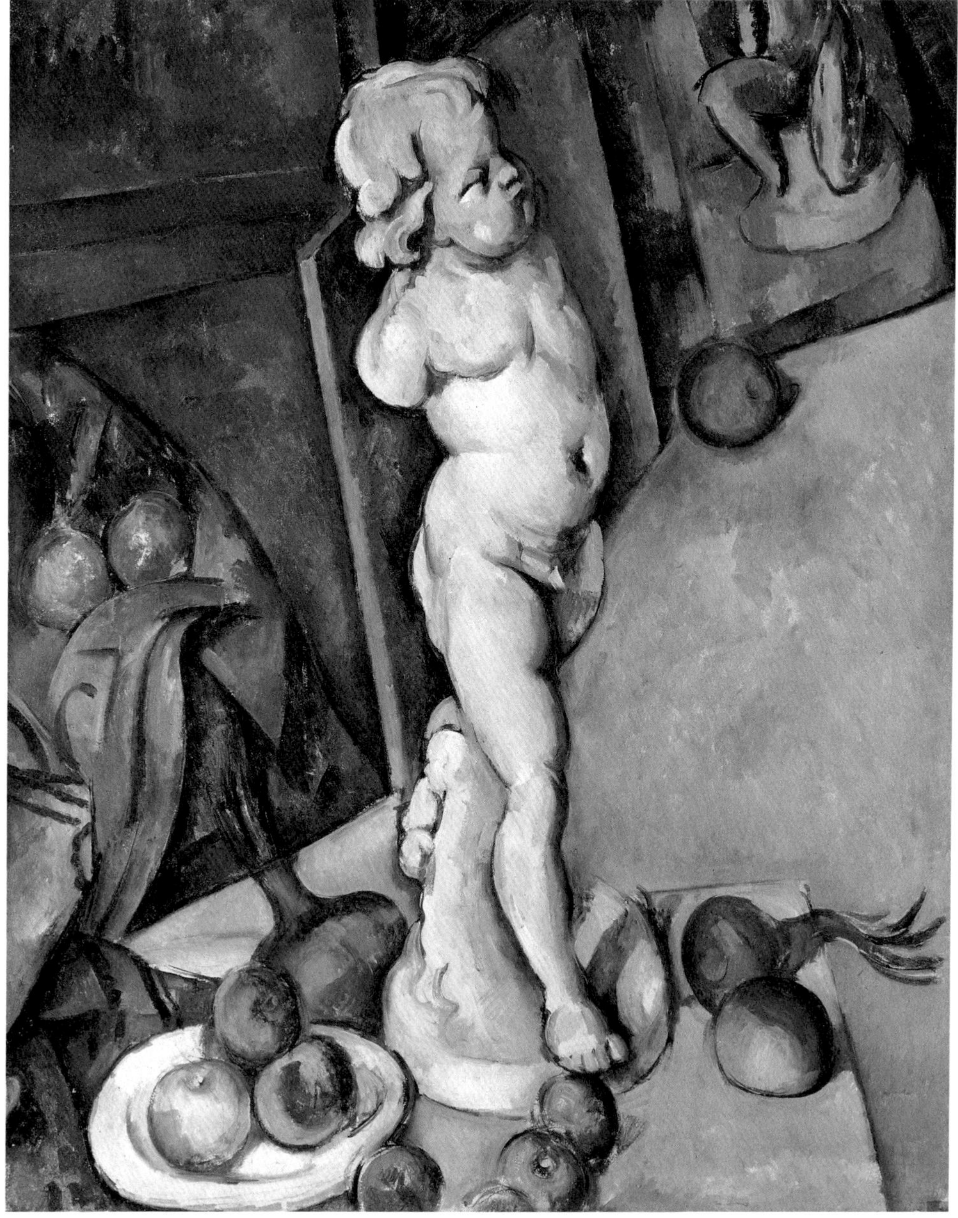

9

Paul Cézanne, *Still Life with Plaster Cupid*, c. 1895, oil on canvas, Courtauld Institute Galleries, London (The Samuel Courtauld Fund)

34. Renoir, quoted in Rewald 1939, 170–171.

For Cézanne, in the process, perhaps, of learning that "painting is not sculpture," sculpture appears now in this picture to be subordinated to painting as image. When Renoir took the time to record Cézanne's remark, he also noted his own immediate thoughts on what Cézanne had meant: "That means that at first he thought he must force his effects of modeling with black and white and load his canvases with paint, in order to equal, if he could, the effects of sculpture. Later, his study brought him to see that the work of the painter is so to use color that, even when it is laid on very thinly, it gives the full result."[34] Renoir analogizes the impasted thickness of paint to the dimensionality of sculptural volume. This assessment participates in a conventional comparison of the differing attributes of the two mediums, a comparison that has long served as the basis for the argument about the greater "naturalism" of sculpture in contrast to painting's reliance on the mechanisms of illusionism as its means to evoke depth and volume. In certain ways Renoir's analysis would serve as a fair-enough description of the aspirations of Cézanne's early work, especially in its indebtedness to the realism of Courbet's painterly style. In the *Plaster Cupid* of 1867, with its palette knife–applied impasto, the thickness of objects in the still life visibly protrudes from the surface of the canvas in a luscious texture of paintedness. In some sense, modernism begins here: in its efforts to "rival" sculpture—as Greenberg put it—painting from this moment gradually devolves to an ever-increasing pictorial self-reflexivity about the paintedness of painting. A more uncompromising abstraction waits nascent.

While this nexus of ideas may seem initially to support the prejudice of modernist criticism in its reliance on the duality of painterly and sculptural representation as a way to account for the conceptual development of modernism, that formal predisposition ignores a crucial feature of Cézanne's work as it is intimated in the subtleties of this canvas around the figure of the *écorché*. For the Courtauld *Still Life* functions not merely as a proposition about painting and sculpture in the terms figured by the central cupid; there remains the additional enigma of the meaning transmitted through the peculiar placement of the *écorché*. Not only is the model of the flayed man set at a greater conceptual remove by virtue of its multiple mediations as a painting of a painting of a sculpture, there is also something about the *écorché* that eludes the painting—something this canvas confesses cannot be contained within its frame. The top of *Still Life*'s frame slices through the image of the painting of the *écorché*, dissecting the figure's body mid-torso and occluding the torment of the *écorché*'s stricken face. The complex play of illusionism's tricks

35. Fried 1990, 312 n.19.

36. Roger Fry, *Cézanne: A Study of His Development* (New York, 1958), 7. This anecdote is almost certainly taken from Gasquet's narrative of Cézanne's childhood experience: Gasquet 1988, 19.

37. Rainer Maria Rilke, as quoted in Maurice Blanchot, *The Space of Literature*, trans. Ann Smock (Lincoln, Nebr., 1982), 153.

is the foregrounded subject of this painting, yet the melancholic affect communicated through the face of the *écorché* has been pressed out of the picture. A residual affect nonetheless dissolves and diffuses throughout the painting—as will be the case in so much of Cézanne's late work. What Cézanne abandons here, bound up with the traditional terms of the rivalry between painting and sculpture, is the representation of melancholy through its imaging, particularly through its dependence on the face as the primary locus of affective expression. Cézanne does so in the service of an even greater pictorial ambition.

The metaphorical associations of the *écorché* were for Cézanne both private and conventional. In the case of Courbet's inclusion of this model in his own paintings, the *écorché* has been interpreted as a figural "surrogate" for the artist.[35] Such an identification would also be highly appropriate in the case of Cézanne: a metaphor for the anxiety and suffering of the artist, the flayed man was a figure with whom Cézanne had been identified since childhood. Lacking "that excellent rhinoceros hide which protected Courbet," as the early formalist critic Roger Fry writes, Cézanne was "so far indeed...from possessing any sort of hide, that his fellow students nicknamed him '*l'écorché*,' the man without any skin to protect his sensitiveness from the strokes of fate and the malice of his fellows."[36] Cézanne, the artist without skin, susceptible to anxiety without protection or defense, was also possibly on the poet Rainer Maria Rilke's mind when he characterized the artist as "A being with no shell, open to pain, / Tormented by light, shaken by every sound."[37] Perhaps not coincidentally, it has been proposed that Michelangelo, too, portrayed himself as a flayed man on the wall of the Sistine Chapel: in the *Last Judgment,* Saint Bartholomew, who was martyred by being flayed alive, holds up a skin bearing what many believe is a distorted portrait of the artist himself.

A hidden allegory of the artist, the *écorché* also serves as an allegory for the procedures of modernist picture-making, especially as it functions in its semi-occluded yet superintending position in the Courtauld *Still Life*. While Cézanne painted an identifiable representation of the figure only once in the relatively minor canvas previously mentioned, I believe the artist was nonetheless enduringly preoccupied by the metaphorical implications of this figure and disguised it behind other figures far more common in his oeuvre: his bathers. One of the characteristic features of the *écorché* is its peaked elbow, stretched taut above the figure's head in an attitude of torment, his efforts to find bodily and spiritual relief futile. This identical gesture recurs in Cézanne's representations of bathers, both male and female.

Although for the most part masked as a prototype, in one canvas from the early 1880s, *Five Bathers* of 1880–1882 (fig. 10) (Rewald 449), we see a standing male bather toward the right whose face closely resembles several muddled attempts to render the face of the *écorché* in the sketchbook at the Art Institute of Chicago—a sketchbook that dates precisely to the moment Cézanne was working on this painting (fig. 11) (Chappuis 571).

This gestural attitude, too, is adopted by Picasso in numerous depictions of female figures. Picasso's *Three Women* of 1908 occupies a key position in cubism's early evolution. Indeed, the painting has at times been nominated as the movement's true point of departure. Initiated in the summer of 1908, the canvas was extensively reworked in the late fall and early winter after the artist had the opportunity to study Braque's *cézanniste* paintings executed over the course of his summer at L'Estaque.[38] Far more than any other work Picasso would undertake until 1909, *Three Women* represents the moment of Picasso's most intense engagement with the formal legacy of Cézanne. Leo Steinberg, in his trenchant and moving analysis of this painting's troubled relationship to Cézanne, draws particular attention to a striking feature linking *Three Women* to the iconographic tradition of Cézanne's bathers: what Steinberg calls the "peaked" or "hoisted" elbow. That this feature was an important hinge for Picasso is clear; all known studies for *Three Women*, as Steinberg points out, "preserve Cézanne's obsessively repeated gesture of the peaked elbow"[39]—a gesture that importantly carries over from the thunderbolt that struck the history of art in 1907, Picasso's *Demoiselles d'Avignon*.

Isolating one charcoal study for the figure at the left in *Three Women* (fig. 12), Steinberg proposes multiple possible sources for the gesture, from Michelangelo's *Dying Slave* to the Greek marble *Dying Niobid* to El Greco's *Agony in the Garden*. Steinberg and others have also nominated various specific bather paintings by Cézanne as likely references, yet few of the Cézannes enlisted as sources provide an especially satisfying point of comparison.[40] What this figure indeed resembles is Cézanne's kneeling *écorché*, with an arm raised in a tight peak. Picasso could have seen Cézanne's painting of the *écorché* at the gallery of Vollard, who eventually acquired the picture.[41] He most certainly saw Cézanne's *Five Bathers* (Rewald 449) at the Salon d'automne in 1904, that same canvas from 1880–1882 in which the face of the standing bather most closely resembles the Art Institute of Chicago drawings of the *écorché*. Picasso also had the opportunity to see multiple versions of this gesture in numerous bather paintings of the 1890s and 1900s (Rewald

38. See Rubin's thorough account of this painting's execution and its relationship to Braque's landscapes of the previous summer in exh. cat. New York 1977, 184–188.

39. Steinberg 1978, 116.

40. None of the bather sources that has been suggested shows the figure with the hoisted elbow balancing on one knee. In at least one proposed source, none of the figures bears the gesture of the hoisted elbow at all (Rewald 360), or if so, the figure is positioned with both hands behind the head (Rewald 553, 667) or with one elbow above the head and the second arm draped in front of the chest (Rewald 554)—gestures with very different valences and pictorial traditions.

41. Cézanne's sketchbooks including drawings of the *écorché* were, for the most part, in the hands of Cézanne's son early in the century.

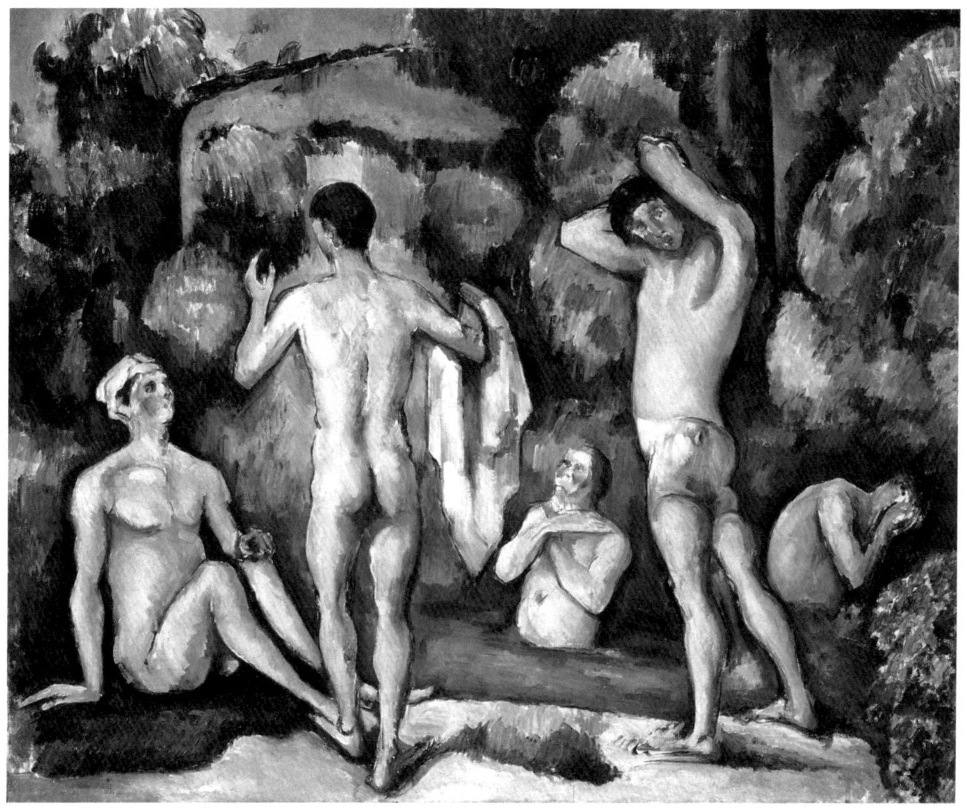

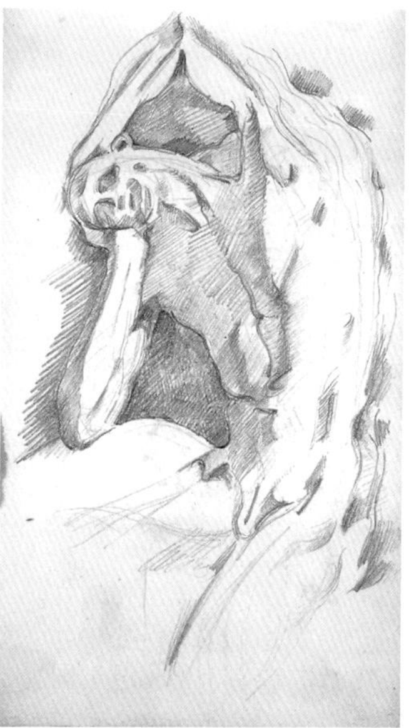

10

Paul Cézanne, *Five Bathers,* 1880–1882, oil on canvas, Private collection

11

Paul Cézanne, *After "l'Écorché,"* 1879–1882, graphite, The Art Institute of Chicago, Arthur Heun Purchase Fund

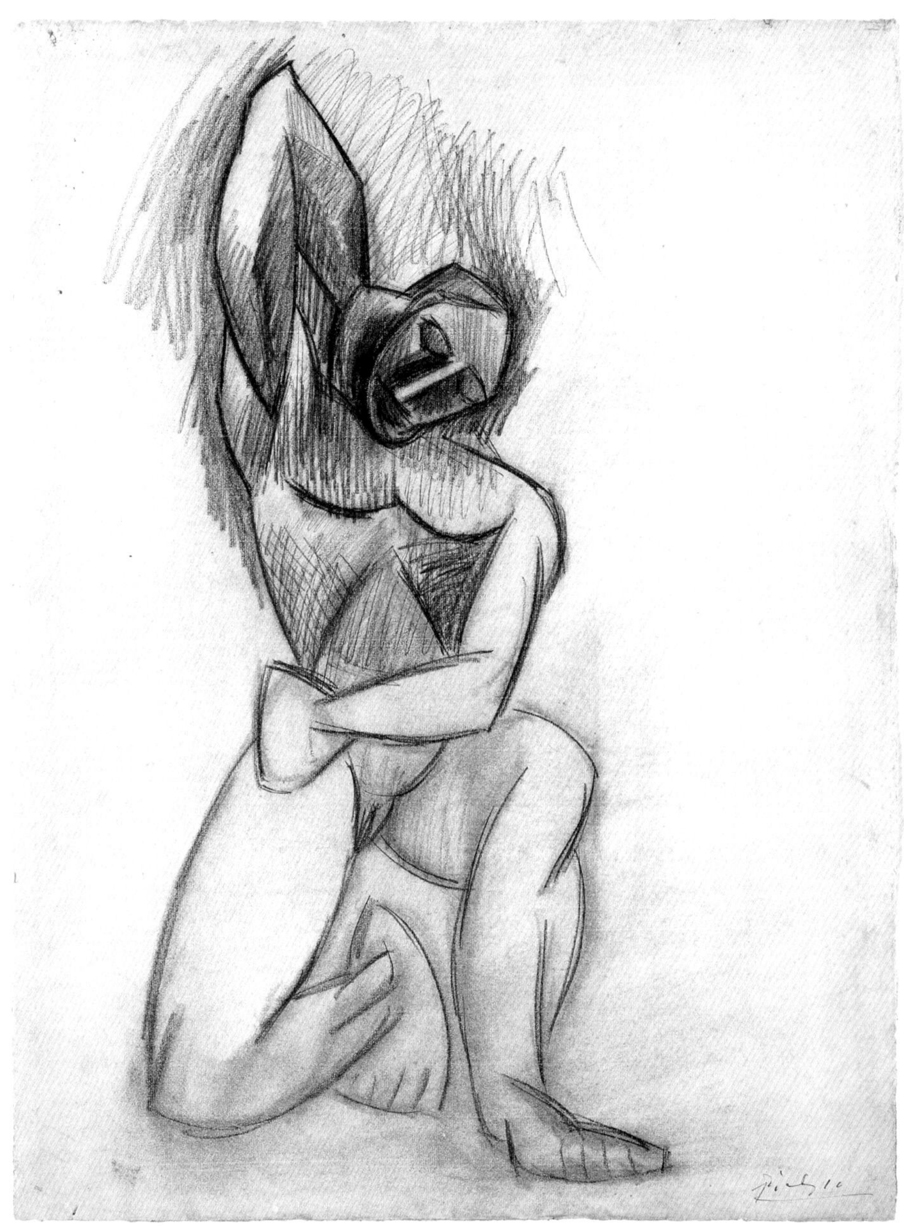

12

Pablo Picasso, *Kneeling Nude,* Paris, fall 1908, charcoal, The Metropolitan Museum of Art, New York, Jacques and Natasha Gelman Collection, 1998

747–753, 755, 860–864), one of which became part of the collection of Leo and Gertrude Stein, whose home Picasso frequented.[42] Whether or not Picasso had occasion to see Cézanne's *écorché* or to observe its disguised genealogy in the gesture of particular bathers, the resemblance between the studies for the left-most figure in *Three Women* and Cézanne's *écorché* remains intriguing. Cézanne carefully conceals this archetype: never noted until now, the identity of the originary *écorché* has remained all but entirely obscured. The hiddenness of the archetype is consistent, and perhaps exigent: the outward expression of agony transmitted through the face of the original model was not Cézanne's primary interest.

. . .

Generated with a fevered and anxious energy unequaled since Picasso's preparatory studies for *Les Demoiselles d'Avignon,*[43] Picasso's portraits of Fernande have consistently evinced associations to flayed figures, inspiring writers to remark on the "skinned effect" of their depiction, where the surface of Fernande's face and neck appears to have been stripped away to reveal tendons and exposed flesh (cat. 35).[44] The neck that is of such keenly preoccupying focus to Picasso is frequently the feature that most insists on the metaphor (cat. 34). The motif of the *écorché* is not new to Picasso's work up to this point. Just as Cézanne's *écorché* lurks as the disguised archetype behind his bathers with the peaked elbow, the unusual and precarious forward-lunging pose of Picasso's *The Dryad* of 1908 (fig. 13) has been linked to the precedent of an earlier *écorché*, a sixteenth-century woodcut by Andreas Vesalius depicting a flayed figure strung up to a supporting shaft by a rope threaded through its eye sockets, the tortured posture enabling the artist more effectively to expose the musculature of the neck (fig. 14).[45] Nominal "cadaver" or not, as in the case of Cézanne's *écorché* this figure's living agony transmits powerfully through the body, from the tensed quadriceps of the legs to the arms outstretched in a gesture of supplication, the neck thrown back in utter vulnerability to the torment. Picasso's *Dryad,* while substantially transformed, retains the affective tenor of its source. That affect is quieted, perhaps, by virtue of the figure's lumbering awkwardness—the picture mollified overall by the dusky sobriety of its color scheme—yet a tempered despair pervades the work, as it will in so many of the portraits of Fernande.

Picasso's biographer John Richardson suggests that Picasso may have seen a reproduction of Vesalius' *écorché* of 1543 in Apollinaire's personal library, which included a number of antiquarian medical books. If true, this connection may have tacitly informed Apollinaire's choice of metaphors in describing Picasso's "surgical"

42. *Bathers* of 1898–1900 (Rewald 861) was acquired by the Steins in October 1904. In addition, most of Cézanne's bather paintings from the later years of his life passed early on through the hands of Vollard, where Picasso would have been able to study them at length.

43. Picasso's friend, André Salmon, described the artist's great restlessness of mind as he prepared to paint the *Demoiselles:* "Picasso was unsettled. He turned his canvases to the wall and laid down his brushes.... During long days and as many nights, he drew, giving concrete expression to the abstract ideas and reducing the results to their fundamentals. Never was a labor more arduous, and it was without his former youthful enthusiasm that Picasso began on a great canvas that was to be the first result of his researches." André Salmon, *La Jeune peinture française,* 42, as cited in Golding 1988, 34–35.

44. Spies and Piot 2000, 60. Golding 1988, 81, may also have had something like an *écorché* in mind when he describes the necks of the Horta figures, "where the area between the projecting tendons appears to have been cut back into a deep recess."

45. John Richardson with Marilyn McCully, *A Life of Picasso, 1907–1917,* 2 vols. (New York, 1996), 2:89.

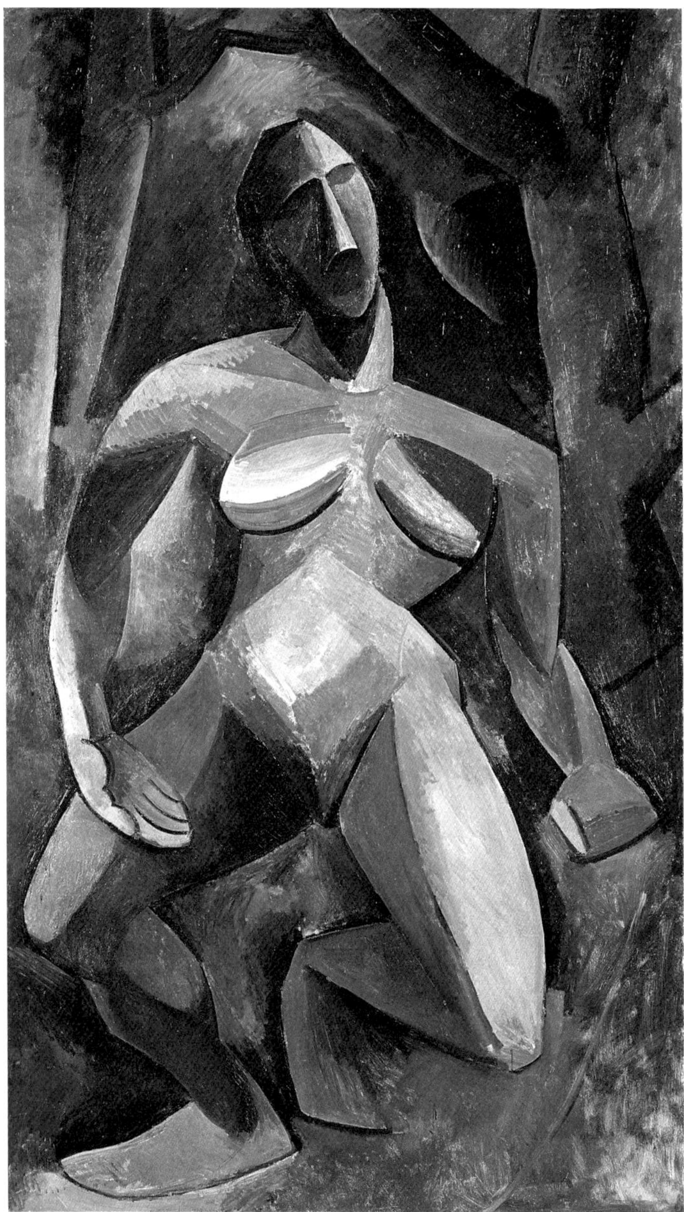

13

Pablo Picasso, *The Dryad,* Paris, fall 1908, oil on canvas, The State Hermitage Museum, Saint Petersburg

14

Andreas Vesalius, seventh plate of the muscles from the second volume of *De humani corporis fabrica* (1543), National Library of Medicine, Washington, DC

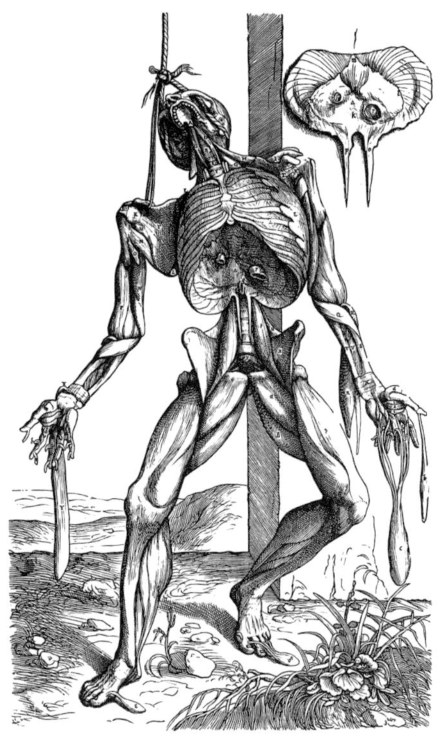

46. Apollinaire 1980, 79.

attitude toward the rendering of the human figure. What Apollinaire's metaphor occludes, however, is the extent to which Picasso's interest in the *écorché* revolves as much around the problem of human anatomy—the possibility of reducing it, for instance, to a concatenation of pulley- and jointlike elements—as it does around the intense affective registers that the figure so potently evokes. Far from surgical, far from the dry intellectualism often attributed to Picasso's cubist devices, what is happening to the human figure as it is "stripped down" to its component parts does not result in a cold abstraction but in something more like an anguished expression of exposure and loss. A year later, in 1913, when Apollinaire repeats and elaborates his conceit, he writes: "And besides, anatomy, for example, no longer really existed in art; it had to be reinvented and its assassination needed to be carried out with the science and the method of a great surgeon."[46] We are meant to hear the ambiguity of what is being "assassinated" here, be it art or anatomy or both. Above all, Apollinaire's revised statement of Picasso's method now communicates the violence wrought in the dispositions of the new artistic style. It was not only that anatomy had to be "reinvented"—the task would also be achieved by artists other than Picasso—but that the metaphors of the attending annihilation that the new cubist methods conjured up had also become palpably part of the picture.

The body of traditions that make up Western pictorial illusionism is not treated as a lifeless corpse to dissect. In this Apollinaire drew his metaphor in a direction Picasso's pictures do not support, especially in the case of the Fernande series, which has always troubled writers on cubism. With Picasso the activity of stripping illusionism down to an essential core of procedures likens itself more to a vivisection, or a living excoriation. In the portraits of Fernande, the corporal vulnerability of the suggestively "exposed" musculature of her figure that results from Picasso's pictorial investigations is transposed as a body of affect we experience as proper to the interiority of the sitter, even as the individualism of that sitter—over the course of the numerous depictions Picasso executed in this series—gradually transforms by virtue of that seriality into a figural typology: one could say, for instance, into a kind of *écorché*. In the activity of stripping illusionism down to its basic mechanisms something more meaningful transpires pictorially than merely the disappearance of a figurative skin. For what surfaces in Picasso's operations is not so much a more clarified disclosure of pictorial illusionism's elemental underpinnings as the unexpected emergence of the affective traces of his procedures' effects.

The Fernande series invites us to focus on Picasso's relentless experimentation with ways to break the body down and put it back together again in accordance with forms strictly subordinated to an idea of the basic mechanics of pictorial illusionism. Indeed, the evidence is there on the surface: the interlocking musculature of *Female Nude with Raised Arm* (cat. 12), a relatively early drawing in the series, readily elicits comparison to the exposed flesh of an *écorché*. There, the multiple outlines embodying her limbs almost begin to suggest striations of muscular fibers, standing in marked contrast to the abstracted hatchings of some of Picasso's previous work. Deprived not only of protective skin but also of skeleton and ligament, the figure reveals Picasso searching for means of compositional balance not dependent on or extrapolated from metaphors of the body. His effort is not entirely successful, and this particular path is soon abandoned as the artist proceeds to other alternatives.

Attempts to resolve pictorial problems under the rubric of a reduction of illusionism's basic devices led to numerous geometric stylizations, ranging from interlocking ovoid shapes (cat. 12) to concatenations of tubes and nodules (cat. 15) to complex pictorial textures composed of tangent triangles and rhomboids (cat. 46). What matters as much as the particularities of the shapes, as Picasso continues his search for some stable technical principle out of which to "reinvent" the human figure, is the way that in each case—whether it was Picasso's express purpose or discovery after the fact—the so-called mechanics of formal reductions produce affective intensities that could not have been predicted in advance. A shifting around of tubes and nodules to manufacture arms generates a collapsed chest and dislocated shoulders registering despair, compounded by the figure's lumpen balloon breasts that rhyme with her belly bulging out of the base of her abdomen (cat. 18). Or look at the way the repeated curves of the cheek, hair, and ears in another group in the series swell out to a goitered throat and jowly chops, Fernande's face inflated, her body tumid with bloat (cat. 29); or how the hard-edged angular shapes Picasso manipulates so expertly not only skew to a crustacean Fernande, all scaly exoskeleton and loricate breastplate (cat. 38), but also—via related devices—deliver the Fernande of the hollowed eyes, with her plangent, vacuous stare emanating from emptied sockets above flintlike features, her fragile cheekbone ready to snap at a touch (cat. 69). These are tough pictures. But is the sometimes harrowing affective range they manifest the cause or the effect of the formal principles of the experiment?

Little of this ever seems to have settled into a code or a stable syntax Picasso could rely on. Nor did it become a system of semiotic equivalents, where edges equal bones and surfaces skins. This instability and unpredictability may well have been part of Picasso's problem and the reason he kept working fast and furious only abruptly to abort a given path. Whether intentionally or through slow discovery—and I suspect it was a mixture of both—Picasso gradually began to uncover over the course of the summer some more deeply ingrained knottiness to the structures by which pictorial illusionism bodied forth bodies. The reinvention of anatomy would not be so simple as a nip and a tuck, and the surgery menaced as potentially lethal to the body as a whole. When Picasso began to realize that what had looked like surface operations in fact cut much deeper into the body of illusionism's traditions, the artist frequently retreated—I think at times in horror. It is almost as if with the stripping down of illusionism's mechanisms what was revealed to Picasso were not its deepest secrets but something else—something unexpected and dark. Far from full possession and reinvention of the figure, Picasso discovered, over and again, how much kept slipping out of his grasp.

The *écorché* is useful as an allegory for a certain procedure of picture-making that peels away at the anatomy of illusionism to expose intensities of a more deeply embodied affect. It is not so much that the picture is allegorized as a body with a skin—although one can read these pictures partially from that vantage. There is something that exceeds the sheer mechanicity of the metaphor, which wants to encapsulate the pure structuralism of the body's scaffolding as mere flesh and bone. For it generates, too, something like a melancholic skin that adheres to the pictorial surface—a *peau de chagrin,* one could say. As we learned in Cézanne's *Still Life with Plaster Cupid,* these are not simply mechanical problems with logical outcomes. However one wishes to metaphorize the procedure, that affective quality becomes an ineradicable part of Picasso's work for the next couple of years. Indeed, I think it becomes an endemic part of cubism.

. . .

What tends to be foregrounded in discussions of the transformations in Picasso's style over the course of the years leading up to analytic cubism, especially as those transformations are allied with the artist's early *cézannisme,* is principally formal and technical. Whether the discussion focuses on the example of the landscapes, still lifes, or portraits, scholars predominantly hone in on what appears to be an increasingly specific and refined set of pictorial devices and techniques used by Picasso. Cézanne's painting is said to have spawned those devices, ultimately adding up to a new language or "syntax" from which cubism derives.[47] The reversible cube usually ranks high on the list of examples, as do *passage* and multiple perspective.[48] The *cézannisme* of these devices functions as a fulcrum in the teleology of those modernist narratives that turn on a sense of the inevitability of cubist abstraction—an inevitability driven by the "logic" or "organic necessity"[49] of the so-called Cézannist syntax that fundamentally informs a cubism propelled toward the ultimate dissolution of likeness.[50]

If one goes looking for these tropes in Picasso, one will find them without difficulty. One can certainly see them in the series of portraits of Fernande. The reversible cube deposited in the forehead of Fernande is hard to miss. One will find examples of *passage*, a term used to describe the elision of planar distinction along the line at which facets abut. One will also find the notorious wedge at the side of Fernande's throat, a feature interpreted as evidence of Picasso's explorations of what is sometimes called multiple perspective, considered by some historians of cubism to be "one of [its] fundamental features."[51] One finds these *cézanniste* devices, along with broken contours, a continuation of a loosely Cézanne-inspired palette of ochers, dark greens, and rusts, as well as an array of pears and apples and *cézanniste* rooftops. But does all this in the end help us get to the bottom of these strange and haunting pictures? Do such features prove adequate to address the question we have been circling around all along: does Picasso's engagement with Cézanne only go this far?

I realize what I am saying goes against the grain of much that we think we know about modernism's evolution. Nominally *cézanniste* tactics are evident in Picasso's work of this year; this much remains indisputable. Yet what is also present is the displacement of affect across the surface effects of those techniques deployed. The motivation for interpreting the meaning of Cézanne's work as hinging strictly on a solution to the pictorial problems of painting's "rivalry" with sculpture, however, serves a greater purpose. William Rubin, for instance, characterizes Cézanne's late work as a "simulacrum of bas-relief"—a conceptual halfway point between impressionism and cubism's sculptural architectonics.[52] Devices such as *passage* are interpreted as "logical coefficients"[53] of the simulacrum of bas-relief model; they are said to "logically derive" from Cézanne's pictorial vision. What this "controlling principle"[54] helps establish is a sensible genealogy of cubist devices coming out of

47. Rubin in exh. cat. New York 1977, 166: "Braque arrived at cubism by a direct extrapolation of the means of Cézanne." In Rubin 1979 the author restates his argument: "I tried to show how Braque's profound and single-minded involvement with Cézanne in 1907–1908 had led him—through a process of reduction, extrapolation and inventive conceptualizing—to formulate in the summer of 1908 the basic syntax or structural framework of early analytic cubism," 131.

48. Elizabeth Cowling and John Golding, *Picasso: Sculptor/Painter* [exh. cat., Tate Gallery] (London, 1994), 20, for example, claim: "It was Braque who brought Picasso back to a more thoughtful study of Cézanne's painting with its implications of a shifting, mobile viewpoint."

49. Robert Rosenblum, *Cubism and Twentieth Century Art* (New York, 1960), 36, cited in Rubin 1979, 129.

50. Rubin 1979, 142, describes Braque's as "the formal definition of a new style in terms of a Cézanne-derived syntax."

51. Golding 1988, 79.

52. Rubin 1979, 131.

53. Rubin 1979, 132.

54. Here the phrase "simulacrum of bas-relief" is picked up by Steinberg 1979, 119.

a *cézanniste* "syntax" that will ultimately serve to explain the emergence of analytic cubism.[55] This narrative offers something important, and it has remained compelling: above all, we get a consistent story with an internal logic. For Greenberg, Cézanne's could be described as a "sculptural" impressionism.[56] Hence the remark Cézanne once made about having wanted to make something "solid" and "durable" out of impressionism is frequently rehearsed in the literature on modernism.[57] As we have learned, however, Cézanne also stated to Renoir that he was forsaking sculpture as a model for the solution to his pictorial problems, and there is more than one way to interpret Cézanne's attitude toward the problems posed by impressionism than having recourse to a solution based on sculpture.[58] Be this as it may, the traditional story of the evolution of modernist art relies on the codification of Cézanne's "sculpturalism" in order to underwrite the emergence of certain stylistic features of cubism. Later, the dialectic collapses back on itself in the increasing "painterliness" of cubism's analytic phase:[59] this the finale, too, of Greenberg's narrative, where painting gives up not only on the devices of sculptural illusionism but also on likeness itself.

All this makes a great deal of logical sense, yet the story manifests its limitations when we find ourselves confronted with the legacy of late portraits like *Old Woman with a Rosary* or even with the didactic lessons of the Courtauld *Still Life*. Few of the techniques typically associated with cubism have ever proved especially satisfactory in accounting for the achievement of Cézanne. Most scholars, even as they insist on the *cézannisme* of cubism's devices, will also confess that Cézanne at best used those devices infrequently and inconsistently, or even that in the hands of Picasso and Braque, while such devices are present, they are ultimately all but unrecognizable as Cézanne's.[60]

There are nonetheless good reasons to imagine that something was troubling Picasso in the wake of Horta and that the artist sought to solve, or at least to explore, possible solutions to those problems through a meditation on the relationship between painting and sculpture. On his return to Paris after the season at Horta de Ebro, Picasso began working on a sculptural project, *Head of a Woman (Fernande)* (cat. 66), a work pivotal in discussions about the relationship between painting and sculpture in his work of this period. Picasso's return to sculpture has, in the principal narratives of cubism, broadly reframed the interpretation of the previous summer's pictorial efforts. Functioning as a retroactive qualification of the Fernande series, Picasso's *Head* has prejudiced writers about the significance of

55. Rubin 1979, 131.

56. "Cézanne," in Greenberg 1961, 53.

57. Cézanne, quoted in Denis 1920, 250.

58. I have discussed an alternative interpretation at length in my "Cézanne and Lucretius at the Red Rock," *Representations* 78 (Spring 2002), 56–85.

59. See, for instance, Rubin 1979, 135.

60. When pressed, for example, Rubin 1979, 139, makes the startling confession: "Braque's *passage*, being a cubist usage, is more abstract and conceptualized; it is not intended to look like Cézanne's." See also Steinberg's efforts to parse the proliferation of definitions of *passage* in Steinberg 1979, 121–123.

Picasso's two-dimensional work with the consequence of a widespread interpretation of the Horta pictures as having revolved largely around issues of "translatability" or "transferability" of pictorial forms and techniques to sculpture.[61] The pictures have thus been discussed as "studies" for sculpture;[62] at times some of the Fernande portraits have even been mistaken as actual renderings of Picasso's *Head of a Woman*.[63] With few exceptions, Picasso's *Head* is judged in terms of its relationship to painting, both to what preceded it and to what was shortly to come. Its importance measured by the standard of what it nominally fails to do, that "failure" invariably turns on the painterly techniques Picasso engaged at Horta[64]—techniques, we have been told, that derive originally from Cézanne.

Head of a Woman is the best-known of Picasso's sculptural projects of fall and winter 1909, but it is not unique. There is another from the same period: Picasso's *Apple* (fig. 15).[65] As mentioned, over the course of 1909 Picasso's work continued to allude to Cézanne. One recurring motif is Cézanne's iconic apple: in Picasso's art, it is typically a single apple, excised from the larger context of Cézanne's painting. The simultaneity of concerns with Fernande and the apple is evidenced by the pencil drawing, *Head of Fernande, Casket and Apple* (cat. 71). The rendering of the apple is schematic, the face of Fernande an uneasy hybrid of several different pictorial strategies. In his drawing of both the head of Fernande and the apple Picasso regresses to certain elements of naturalism—the artist even takes care to draw at the apple's top a tiny stem. Later studies of the apple focus on planarity (fig. 16); like so many of Picasso's studies of Fernande, the artist seems to be searching for a way to break objects down into hard-edged facet planes, on the order, for example, of a casket, frequently the third object in these drawings.

Picasso's interest in the apple culminates in the plaster executed at the end of the year. It is a regressive object. At 11.5 centimeters high, the plaster is about half a size larger than a standard variety of the fruit. Although it has been modeled in the round, the object has been flattened on the bottom so that it rests stably on a support: like a real apple, it is meant to sit on a table. The visible surface of the apple is composed of a play of planes and edges, most of which are linear, although rounded arcs also serve to define a partial contour suggestive of the more natural curvature of an apple's shape. Trebly displaced—from Cézanne's oeuvre, from its essential relatedness to other apples depicted there, and from its native medium of paint—Picasso's *Apple* proposes itself as an essential reduction of the artist's meditations on Cézanne. In this, Picasso participates in propagating a

61. See, for example, Elsen 1969, 25; Spies and Piot 2000, 57; or Roland Penrose, *The Sculpture of Picasso* [exh. cat., The Museum of Modern Art] (New York, 1967), 19.

62. See, for instance, Cowling and Golding in exh. cat. London 1994, 20; or Penrose in exh. cat. New York 1967, 23.

63. See Spies and Piot 2000, 57, for the decisive dating of the sculpture as following on the work at Horta.

64. See, for instance, Alan Bowness, "Picasso's Sculpture," in *Picasso in Retrospect*, ed. Sir Roland Penrose and John Golding (New York, 1973), 130.

65. According to Penrose in exh. cat. New York 1967, 19, two plaster apples were made, both of which he dates to 1910. Spies and Piot 2000, 57, revise the dating to the end of 1909 and list only one plaster apple in the catalogue raisonné of the sculptures. William Rubin, *Picasso in the Collection of the Museum of Modern Art* [exh. cat., The Museum of Modern Art] (New York, 1972), 203, also lists only one plaster *Apple* but dates it to early 1910.

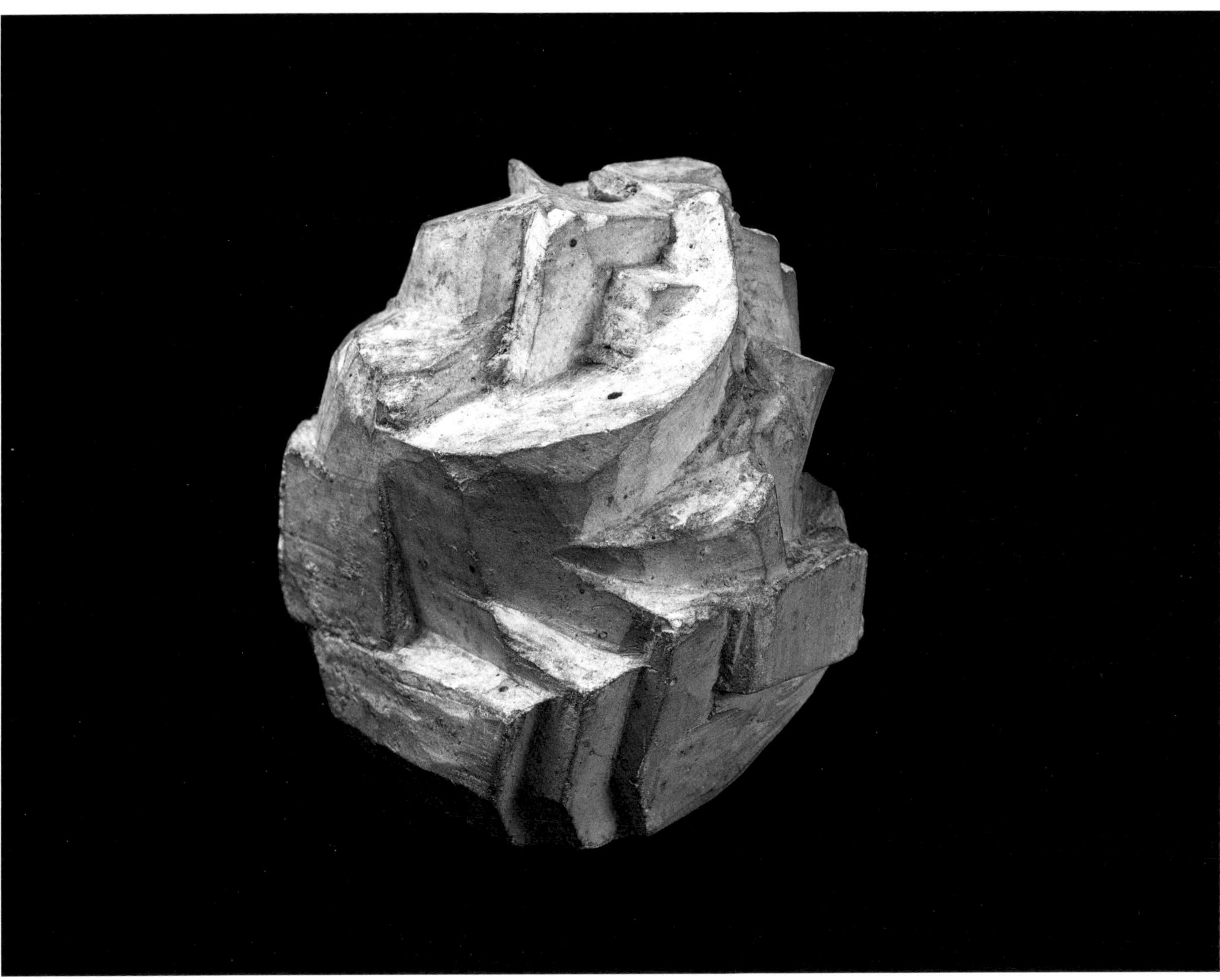

15

Pablo Picasso, *Apple,* Paris, 1909, plaster, Musée Picasso, Paris

66. Louis Vauxcelles, *Gil Blas* (18 March 1910), cited in Golding 1988, 5.

version of Cézanne whose pertinence is strictly limited to formal problems of painting in relation to sculpture. While I do not doubt the sincerity of Picasso's effort, I think it would be a mistake to take this apple as a metaphor for Picasso's relationship to Cézanne at face value. Indeed, I think that as much of a failed sculptural object as *Apple* may be, it ultimately encapsulates one of the most extraordinary achievements Picasso had gradually managed to solidify over the course of 1909.

Despite Picasso's *Apple*, the greater evidence of the art produced at Horta and after points to the artist's growing realization that what Braque's idiomatic *cézannisme* offered was limited. If I had to make a general claim for what I think was happening over the course of 1909—that transformational year leading up to Picasso's break into analytic cubism—I would say that Picasso, even as he chose to foreground certain technical devices conspicuously linked to Cézanne (at least via Braque), was nonetheless also working through the complexities of some other order of struggle with Cézanne—and that he was doing so behind precisely that same curtain before which he stood so openly confirming his own *cézanniste* genealogy. As we recall from *Bread and Fruit Dish* and the evidence of so many other major works, Picasso is a master of disguise and displacement, an adept at strategies of revelation and concealment. Throughout 1909 Picasso foregrounds the weight of his *cézannisme* in those devices that the history of art—following Picasso's lead—has typically read as Cézanne-derived. In doing so, Picasso accomplishes two important things. Not only does he divert attention from certain deeper points of his connection to the painter, but Picasso's flaunted *cézannisme* also actively revises the idea of what had, in fact, preceded his own art. What we are left with is the notion that Cézanne somehow "anticipated" cubism. Yet the picture Picasso draws with such subtlety also simultaneously impugns Cézanne for having failed to arrive at the inevitable conclusions to his own proposals: Cézanne's greatest "failure," in other words, was that he never discovered cubism. The reading of Cézanne's pictures as "simulacra of bas-relief" is one powerful rhetorical effect of Picasso's revisionism. The idea that Cézanne was "responsible" for cubism of course goes way back. As early as 1910 Louis Vauxcelles, a critic disparaging of the new "cubism," laid blame for the movement at the doorstep of Cézanne and called his artistic progeny "ignorant geometricians, who reduce scenery and the human body to dull cubes."[66]

For any artist seeking to break free of the traditions of past generations, what may have appeared to be the liberation of artistic possibility that arrived

67. Clark 1999, 174.

68. Gertrude Stein, quoted in Harold Acton, *More Memoirs of an Aesthete* (London, 1970), 175, cited in Richardson 1996, 50. Richardson suggests that Stein's remark "sounds suspiciously like Picasso."

with Cézanne's achievement was harnessed as much with a profound aesthetic burden as it was with a generative release of the imagination. To put it another way, with Cézanne's influence also came the impossibility of getting out from under it, because of the incomparable magnitude of his originality and vision. For Picasso this situation was all but unbearable, and much of the anxiety of his summer at Horta certainly qualifies as an "anxiety of influence." Perhaps as a defense against too complete a submission to Cézanne's preeminence did Picasso seek to deflect attention from the deeper drafts he was drinking from Cézanne's fountain. *Apple* is, after all, unsuccessful as an object in part because it is so inert, lifeless, dumbly impassive—stripped of all those essential qualities related to form and affect Picasso had been exploring during the summer and fall. Having begun to absorb the lessons of Cézanne's "anxiety," Picasso built on the foundations of Cézanne's own lifelong struggle. Picasso's retention of the essence of that struggle, even if it cannot properly be characterized as a repetition, persists in the transmission of the quality of melancholy—the pictures' suffusion with an "impacted, melancholic severity," as T. J. Clark puts it.[67] Not a reducible language, not a syntax, not a toolbox of techniques for spatial ambiguation like *passage* or the reversible cube, the melancholy abides. The gloomy luminosity of a work like Picasso's *Seated Female Nude* of 1909–1910 (cat. 77), the stunning picture that teeters on the edge of analytic cubism and all but puts an end-stop to the series of portraits of Fernande, radiates nothing so much as this melancholic affect.

Apple is thrown out as a decoy, along with the other trappings of Picasso's *cézannisme,* and the history of modernist art that emerged out of Cézanne's vision would henceforth be an art that commenced just at the point where Cézanne had failed. Not only does Picasso's work propagate this view, his friends did it for him as well. Gertrude Stein, likely repeating Picasso's own words, once advertised: "All modern painting is based on what Cézanne had failed to do, instead of on what he nearly succeeded in doing. To show what he could not achieve had become Cézanne's obsession and that of his followers."[68] At Horta de Ebro, however, Picasso produced pictures quietly confessing that the "Cézanne" over whom he had earlier announced his triumph in pictures like *Three Women, Bread and Fruit Dish,* and *Still Life with Hat* was not in fact Cézanne but a *cézanniste* Braque, serving as a surrogate for the master. The pictures of the summer at Horta testify to the ways Picasso came to struggle with a more worthy opponent in the contest for his very identity as an artist who would—and did—again change the course of

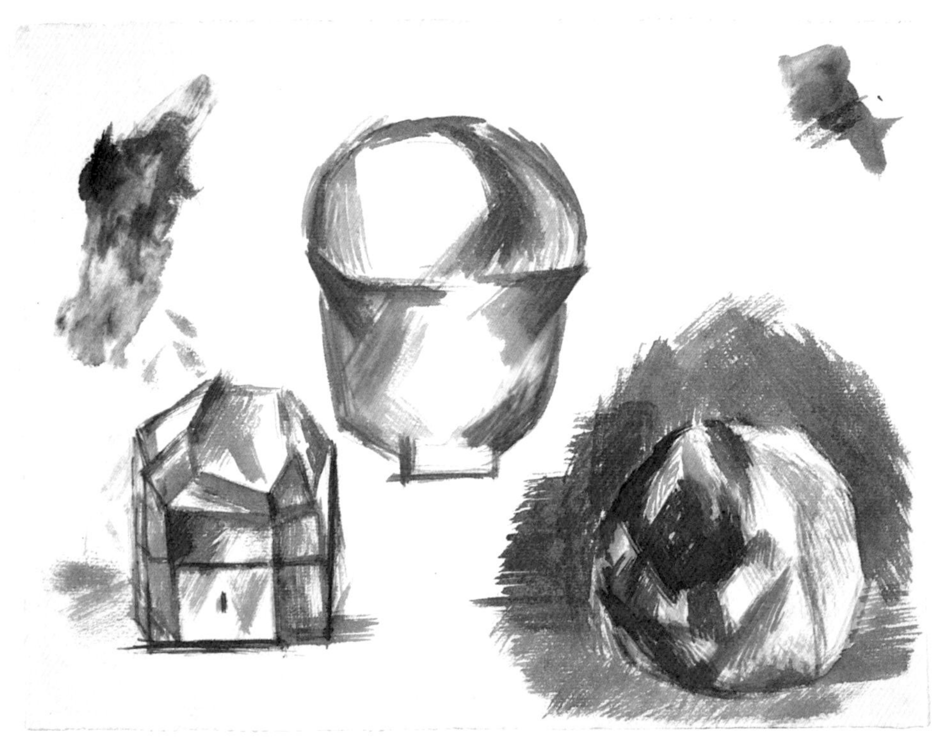

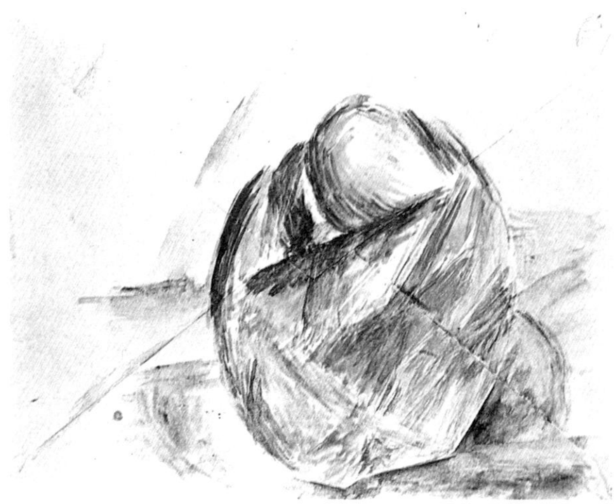

16

Pablo Picasso, *Casket, Cup, Apple,* Paris, fall 1909, ink and wash on paper, The Museum of Modern Art, New York, Gift of Justin K. Thannhauser

17

Pablo Picasso, *Apple,* Paris, fall 1909, watercolor on verso of envelope, Private collection

the history of modern art. That Picasso admits partial failure is betrayed not so much in the terms and techniques of a set of proposals for the revolutionary new forms of analytic cubism, but rather under the thick skin of one of the other most significant feats of twentieth-century painting: Picasso's ingenious invention of a version of a proto-cubist "Cézanne" so effectively convincing, so rhetorically persuasive, that the history of art would for decades hence confuse the one with the other.

. . .

Among the drawings Picasso executed of apples toward the end of 1909, one the artist rendered on the back of an envelope (fig. 17). In this watercolor we see Picasso privately slip into conversation with what had been isolated from Cézanne's original vision all along: the deep matter of luminous color without which Cézanne's art might be reduced to sheer schema. Like the letter Cézanne never sent to the anonymous young artist, Picasso's envelope, too, remains closed. Unaddressed, both private and public, the image of the apple is crossed with the folds of the envelope's paper, as if both to center it and to annul it. If we could say that Picasso wishes us to believe he chose not to unsheathe the contents of Cézanne's communications, their primary force was nevertheless carried on the outside of the envelope, right there on the surface all along. The means of transmission sealed and thus preserved, refused and yet also serving as the platform for Picasso's response, Cézanne's enfolded message was delivered.

Process and Technique in Picasso's *Head of a Woman (Fernande)*

Valerie J. Fletcher

Pablo Picasso's *Head of a Woman (Fernande)* ranks among those works that have attained iconic status in the history of modern art. Since its creation nearly one hundred years ago, this sculpture has received so much attention from artists, scholars, curators, and critics that few experts can contend with it all. The present exhibition offers several new perspectives on the sculpture's place in Picasso's oeuvre and on its aesthetic and perceptual ramifications. This essay focuses on the physical making of the sculpture, from the artist's own hands in 1909 through the production of two editions in bronze from 1910 to 1960.

My research began more than twenty years ago as I was documenting the history of the Hirshhorn Museum's bronze from the second edition; I returned to the subject recently when the National Gallery decided to acquire a bronze from the first edition. My goal was to compile and assess the known data and sources (acknowledging when information is contradictory or lacking) and to make deductions. My methods rely on traditional connoisseurship and scholarly research: visually examining the sculptures themselves, reviewing documentation, evaluating hearsay accounts, and consulting with conservators. As I struggled to arrange the pieces of this puzzle, I realized that it was important to provide technical information—situated within its historical context—and to clarify the provenance of each cast. As in any major undertaking, I am greatly indebted to other experts who have generously shared their observations and research, and to publications by eminent Picasso scholars.[1] One caveat to bear in mind is that no scientific analyses have been done on any of the individual works discussed—perhaps my efforts here will engender such examinations in the near future.

During his early years, Picasso created few sculptures: only twenty-six of his nearly seven hundred were made before 1912. He worked on them in the studios of friends, where traditional materials were available. In Barcelona during 1902 and 1903 he used clay for *Seated Woman* and *Mask of a Picador with a Broken Nose*.[2] In Paris in 1905 he created *Head of a Jester* in wax.[3] Then in 1906, working in the studio of his friend the ceramist Paco Durrio, he used clay in producing three further works: *Head of Fernande, Woman Combing Her Hair,* and *Head of a Man,* all of which Durrio fired in his kiln.[4] Picasso tended to sculpt quickly; for example, he completed *Head of a Jester* within two days.[5]

Picasso's first deviation from academic materials and methods occurred from late 1906 through 1907 when, inspired by Paul Gauguin's Tahitian sculptures and West African tribal carvings, he made some primitivist wood carvings. This proved

1. See especially the catalogue raisonné of Picasso's sculptures: Werner Spies with Christine Piot, *Picasso: The Sculptures* (Ostfildern-Ruit, Holland, 2000).

2. Daniel-Henry Kahnweiler, *The Sculptures of Picasso* (Paris and London, 1949), n.p. See Spies and Piot 2000, nos. 1, 3. The term clay is here used in its broadest definition, intended to encompass water-based earthen clay as well as oil-based plastilene. Plastilene, which had been invented in the 1890s, gradually entered sculptors' studios, becoming widespread by the 1920s. Artists preferred it because it remained malleable without drying out and cracking as readily as water-based clay.

3. See Spies and Piot 2000, 24, no. 4. Spies suggests that Picasso learned of wax as a sculptural medium from Degas' works. Degas' wax sculptures, however, were not widely known at the time, although some intimates (including the dealer Ambroise Vollard) saw them in the artist's studio. Many other sculptors used wax in various ways, from the precise realism of Ernest Meissonier to the impressionism of Medardo Rosso.

4. Kahnweiler 1949, n.p. See Spies and Piot 2000, nos. 6, 7, 9.

5. Picasso began it as a portrait of Max Jacob one evening and revised it the next day, according to Roland Penrose, *La Vie et l'oeuvre de Picasso* (Paris, 1961; rev. ed. in English, Berkeley, Calif., 1981), 116.

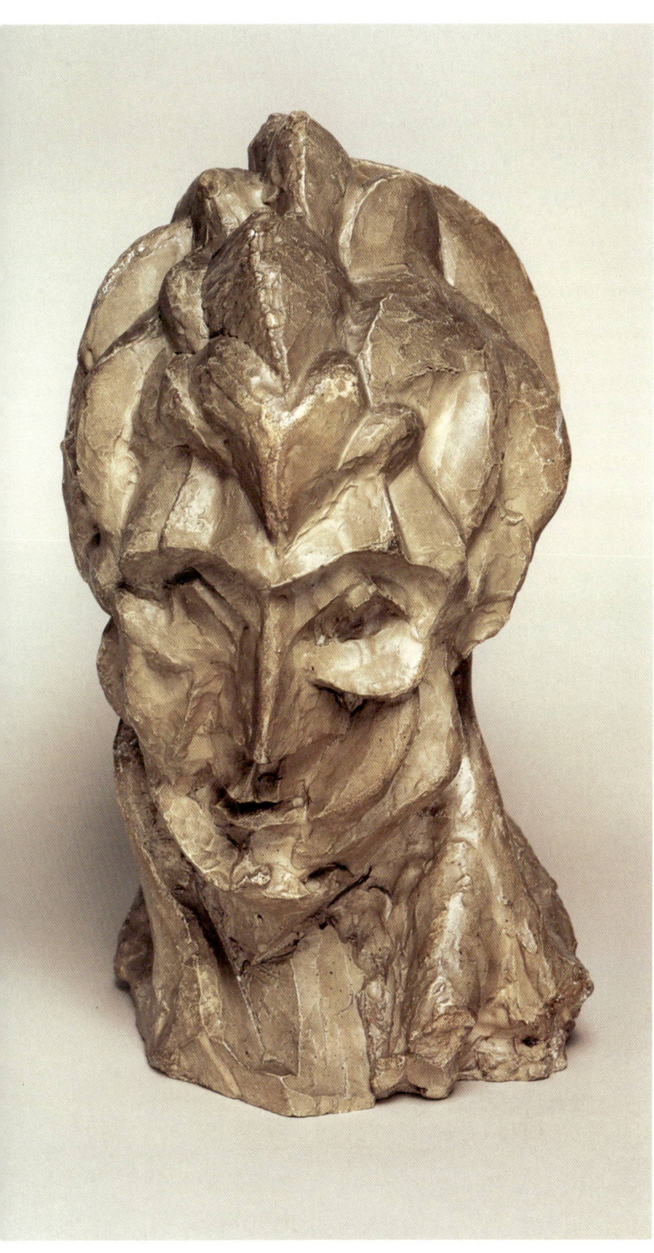

1

Pablo Picasso, *Head of a Woman (Fernande)* (cat. 64), Paris, fall 1909, plaster with shellac coating, Latner Family Collection, Toronto

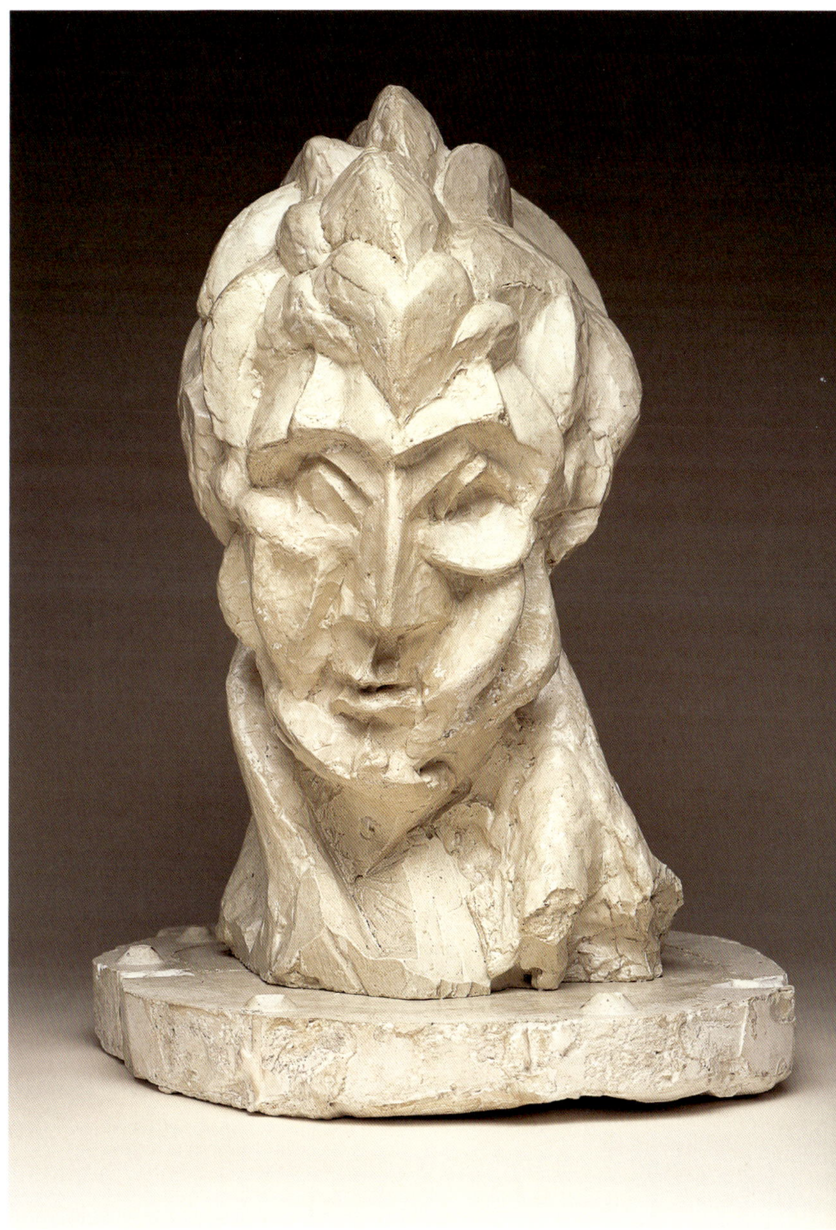

2

Pablo Picasso, *Head of a Woman (Fernande)* (cat. 65), Paris, fall 1909, plaster, Raymond and Patsy Nasher Collection, Dallas, Texas to be only a temporary change of technique. When he returned to sculpture in the autumn of 1909, he worked again in clay and plaster for the little-known *Head*, the small *Apple*,[6] and the large *Head of a Woman (Fernande)*, which was the most impressive sculptural work of his formative years.

According to Picasso's scrawled inscription on the back of a photograph, he made the original *Head of a Woman* in the studio of the Catalan sculptor Manolo (Manuel Hugué). A member of the Quatre Gats group in Barcelona, Manolo had come to Paris in 1901 and was one of Picasso's closest friends. They saw each other often, although less so in the summer of 1909, when Picasso was in Horta de Ebro while Manolo stayed in a town in the French Pyrenees. After their separate returns to Paris in mid-September, Picasso went to Manolo's studio. Most scholars therefore date *Head of a Woman* to late September or sometime in October.[7]

Although the original does not survive and is apparently not documented in photographs, the shapes and surfaces of the two surviving plaster casts readily confirm the use of clay for creating *Head of a Woman* (figs. 1, 2). Most of the forms in the sculpture are fluid, organic, and somewhat irregular, although this observation is not normally applied to the work because its style was revolutionary in its reduction of natural physiognomy to geometric shapes. Few photographs capture the subtle modulations made by the artist's fingertips across the surfaces. Nonetheless, close examination of the facial features and hair reveals that they were formed by the artist pressing and manipulating the malleable clay. This becomes remarkably clear when the sculpture is examined by feeling the surfaces rather than by merely looking. Something indefinable takes place between an artist's mind and hands when modeling. The element of touch comes into play as the artist's fingers shape, tweak, gouge, smooth, even caress the pliant clay. Modeling incorporates a tactility of almost primal instinct; forms emerge and are altered as much by feeling as by visual analysis. To the few who have had the privilege of exploring the plasters by touch, the extent to which Picasso's finger marks are still evident is remarkable. The area where thumb and forefinger firmly pinched the lips into sharp organic ridges (fig. 3), the row of indented thumb marks in the proper-left rear neck, and the horizontal finger swipe across the back (figs. 4a, b) all capture the touch of the artist.

The forms of *Head of a Woman* are not as straight, smooth, or cleanly angular as those in many of the related drawings and paintings. Modeling in soft clay is intrinsically both an additive and subtractive method: the artist begins by

6. Spies and Piot 2000, nos. 25, 26.

7. Picasso made the annotation "fait dans l'atelier de Manolo" on a photograph of the bronze reproduced in Jean Cassou, *Picasso* (Paris, 1940); my thanks to Elizabeth Cowling for this information. Picasso confirmed to Spies that he had sculpted *Head of a Woman* in Manolo's studio after his return from Horta de Ebro (Spies and Piot 2000, 57). According to Judith Cousin, "Documentary Chronology," in William Rubin, *Picasso and Braque: Pioneering Cubism* [exh. cat., The Museum of Modern Art] (New York, 1989), 362–363, Picasso returned from Horta de Ebro before 13 September and created the sculpture in October. John Richardson with Marilyn McCully, *A Life of Picasso, 1907–1917*, 2 vols. (New York, 1996), 2:139, states, "As soon as he was back in Montmartre, he went to his sculptor friend Manolo's studio ...and modeled this head." Richardson (interview with the author, 3 December 2002) noted that Picasso would not have returned to Durrio's studio to sculpt, as he had done in 1905–1906, because Durrio vehemently disapproved of Picasso's cubism. Manolo himself left no information on Picasso's creation of *Head of a Woman*.

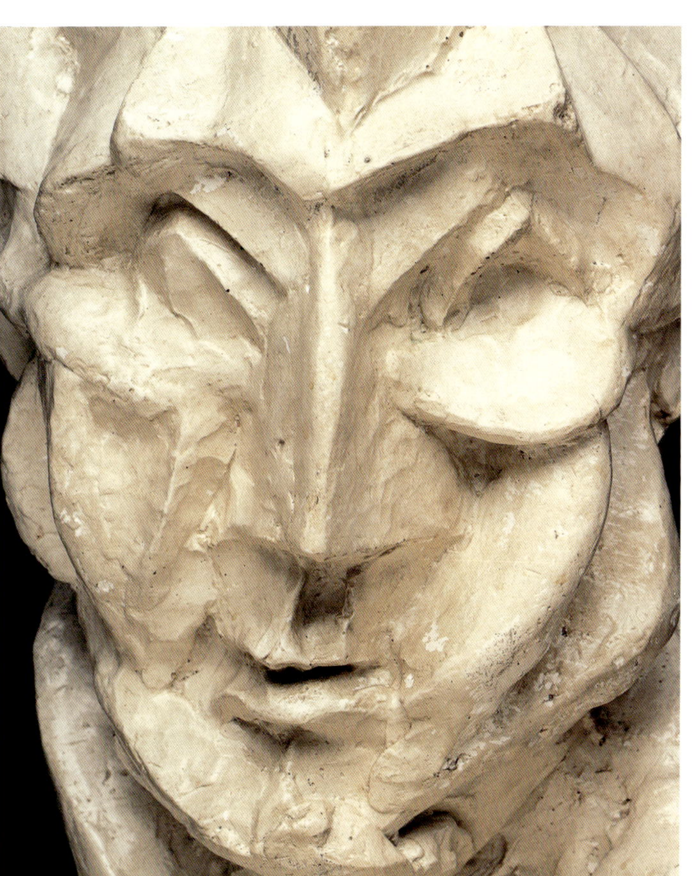

3

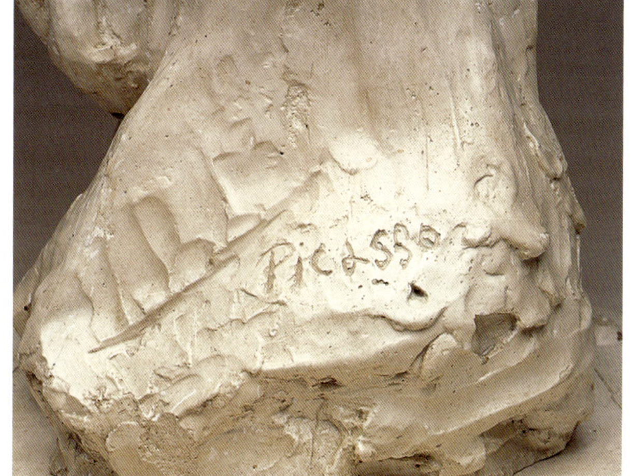

4a

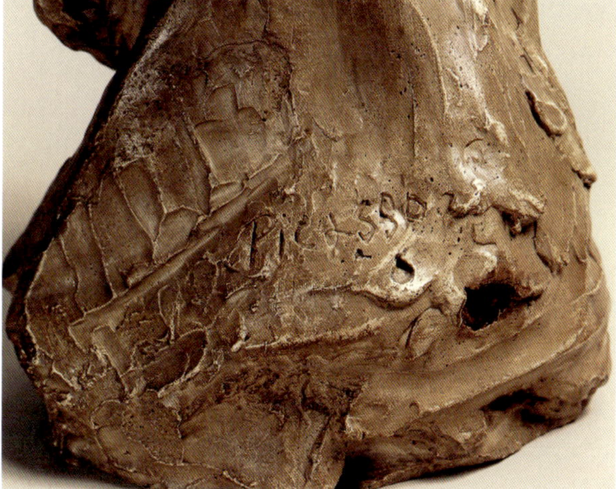

4b

3
Detail of cat. 65, Pablo Picasso, *Head of a Woman (Fernande),* Paris, fall 1909, plaster, Raymond and Patsy Nasher Collection, Dallas, Texas

4a
Detail of cat. 65, Pablo Picasso, *Head of a Woman (Fernande),* Paris, fall 1909, plaster, Raymond and Patsy Nasher Collection, Dallas, Texas

4b
Detail of cat. 64, Pablo Picasso, *Head of a Woman (Fernande),* Paris, fall 1909, plaster with shellac coating, Latner Family Collection, Toronto

5a | **5b**

Details of cat. 65, Pablo Picasso, *Head of a Woman (Fernande)*, Paris, fall 1909, plaster, Raymond and Patsy Nasher Collection, Dallas, Texas

6

Auguste Renoir, *Portrait of Ambroise Vollard* (holding a statuette by Maillol), 1908, oil on canvas, Courtauld Institute Gallery, Somerset House, London

5a

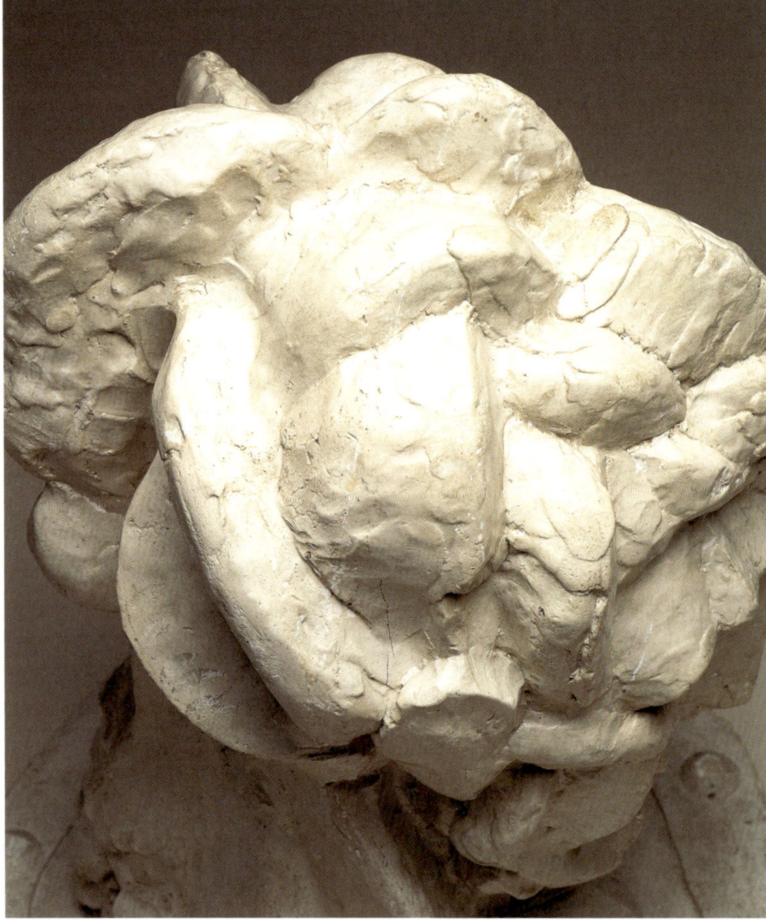

5b

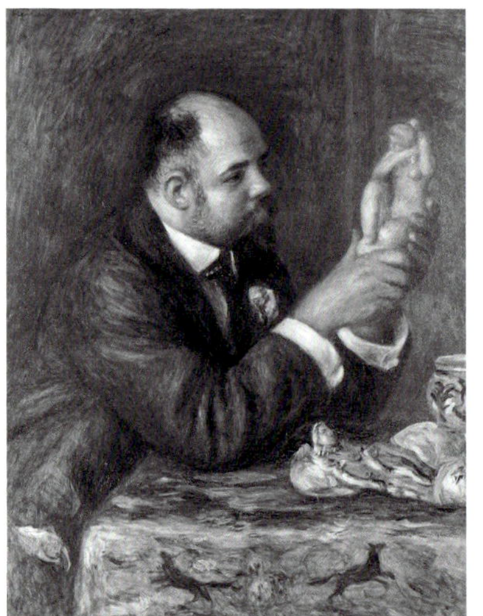

6

building up a monolithic mass, then selectively removes material to create hollows or recesses, and, if desired, can easily add more clay to enlarge or build up forms. This process, which can be repeated indefinitely, is analogous to painting; if the artist did not like an effect, he could scrape it off or cover it up and start again. As an example, in *Head of a Woman* Picasso heightened the top-center forms of the hair (figs. 5a, b) by applying a row of clay pellets in parallel strips and then smoothing them once, enough to flatten and attach the pellets but not enough to meld them completely into the underlying shapes (like pentimenti left visible). Thus modeling in clay was the ideal method for experimenting with positive and negative forms—actual forms rather than those depicted illusionistically in drawings and paintings. Picasso's choice of clay as a modeling medium suggests that his intention was to explore and formulate anew. Had he wanted merely to reproduce in three dimensions the forms already defined in certain paintings and drawings at Horta de Ebro, the ideal medium would have been plaster. It dries with minimal risk of cracking (as clay tends to do) and would have been ready for bronze casting.

The clay original of *Head of a Woman* may have remained indefinitely in the artist's studio had it not been for the perspicacity of the art dealer Ambroise Vollard. Vollard had come to Paris from the remote island of La Réunion and had gained fame in the late 1890s as a dealer of postimpressionist canvases, especially those by Paul Cézanne and Auguste Renoir. Soon after meeting Picasso in 1901, Vollard exhibited his paintings and continued to buy works regularly for the next decade.[8] Before long, Vollard had competition from the young Daniel-Henry Kahnweiler, who bought forty works from Picasso in 1907 and then avidly sought to become the artist's exclusive representative, which he would be from 1912 to 1914.[9]

Although Vollard entitled his memoirs *Recollections of a Picture Dealer,* he was also passionate about prints, commissioning superb lithographs, etchings, and engravings from contemporary artists. In 1899 the dealer launched into sculpture by purchasing nine terracotta figurines from Aristide Maillol to cast into bronze for sale (fig. 6). This profitable experience whetted Vollard's ambitions; he also tried, unsuccessfully, to persuade Edgar Degas to have his sculptures cast into bronze.

In 1910 Vollard bought five original sculptures from Picasso: *Woman Combing Her Hair, Head of a Man, Head of a Jester, Head of Fernande,* and the cubist *Head of a Woman.* Although no record of this transaction survives in the Vollard archives, other sales receipts convey an idea of Picasso's terms, which

8. See Vollard's memoirs, *Recollections of a Picture Dealer* (London and Boston, 1936; Paris, 1937). See also Una E. Johnson, *Vollard Editeur: Prints, Books, Bronzes* [exh. cat., The Museum of Modern Art] (New York, 1977), and Hans Bolliger, *Picasso for Vollard* (New York, 1956), v–xv.

9. Richardson 1996, 34–36, 47–48, 71, 107–108, 268–269, 313–316. See also Isabelle Monod-Fontaine, *La Donation Louise et Michel Leiris: Collection Kahnweiler-Leiris* [exh. cat., Centre Georges Pompidou] (Paris, 1984).

10. Ambroise Vollard archives (private collection, Paris); microfilm in the archives of the Musée d'Orsay. Among the documents from 1906 through 1911 few are from Picasso; the only receipts are for paintings and prints. Two receipts from 1910 for sixteen paintings stipulate that the sales included rights of reproduction.

11. Fernande Olivier, *Picasso and His Friends* (New York, 1965), 143–144. My thanks to Jessica Stewart for this reference. See Cousin in exh. cat. New York 1989, 368, for dates of Vollard's portrait.

12. André Salmon, "Courier des arts," *Paris-Journal* (5 September 1910), announced the forthcoming exhibition. Vollard's calendar notes an appointment with the artist on 2 November 1910, but this date seems late to purchase uncast sculptures for an exhibition that would open seven weeks later. Vollard 1937 mentions Picasso's portrait of him but not the sculpture *Head of a Woman*.

included all rights of reproduction.[10] Clues in the Vollard archives suggest when the sale may have occurred. The dealer's calendar recorded an appointment with the artist on 5 November 1909—soon after the sculpture was made. The following year Vollard was in almost daily contact with Picasso, spending months posing in the artist's studio for his portrait. The work was intense in early June and again in September 1910 before and after the artist's summer stay in Cadaqués (fig. 7). Vollard may have purchased the sculptures at any time during those months. In her memoirs Fernande Olivier remembered only that "One day, when he needed a pretty large sum of money, he sold his sculptures to Vollard....It was at about this time that he began to paint cubist portraits [of Uhde, Vollard, and Kahnweiler]. He spent a long time...especially on the one of Vollard which dragged on several months."[11] Quite probably the sale took place in or soon after September 1910, when Kahnweiler decided not to buy Picasso's most recent paintings. Vollard took them instead and immediately announced plans for an exhibition of Picasso's works from 1900 to 1910. The show would open in December. Making selections for that important exhibition would have meant combing through the studio, and it seems likely that the five sculptures were purchased during that process.[12] Astute dealer that he was, Vollard intended to reveal Picasso's sculptural talents to the world. Although the Spaniard's paintings were gaining fame, none of the artist's previous exhibitions—including the most recent one at Wilhelm Uhde's gallery in May 1910—had featured sculpture.

The clay original *Head of a Woman* now entered the complex process of bronze casting. A sculpture of unbaked clay cannot serve directly as the basis for making a bronze; the first step is to make a plaster cast. This is difficult because the moist clay tends to stick to the mold—technical expertise is needed to avoid damage. It is highly unlikely that Picasso made a plaster cast himself. Presumably, Vollard sent the clay original to a foundry in the Paris area, where experienced technicians were able to deal with the work properly. French foundries at that time—including Barbédienne, Bingen, A.A. Hébrard, Alexis Rudier, and Susse—ranked among the best in the world.

The standard procedure was to make a "waste" mold. After inserting thin metal shims in a vertical line around the sculpted clay head, the technicians would cover the sculpture in liquid plaster. Once the plaster dried, the shims were used to pry the whole object apart, destroying the clay original. The plaster mold was then carefully cleaned out, coated with a slurry as insulator, and filled with plaster.

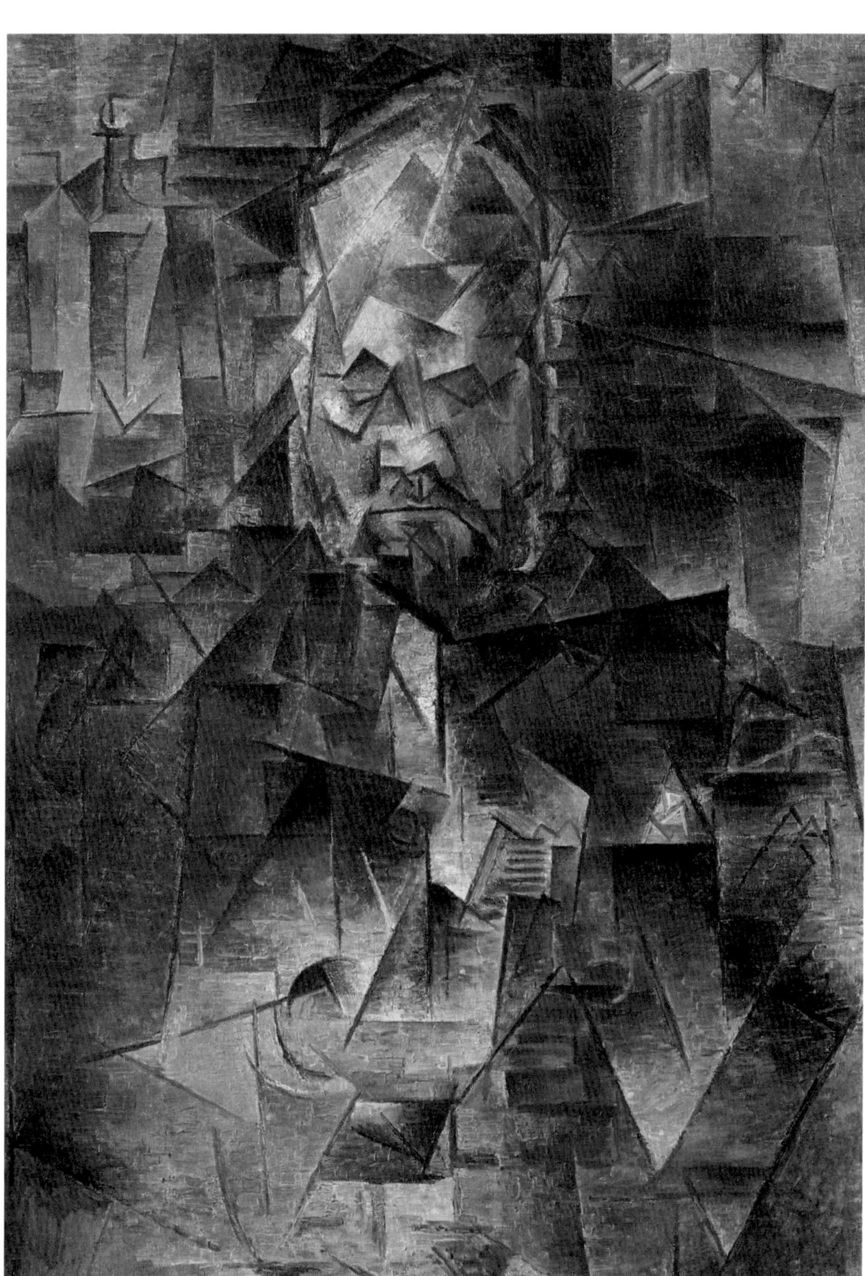

7

Pablo Picasso, *Portrait of Ambroise Vollard,* 1910, oil on canvas, Pushkin Museum of Fine Arts, Moscow

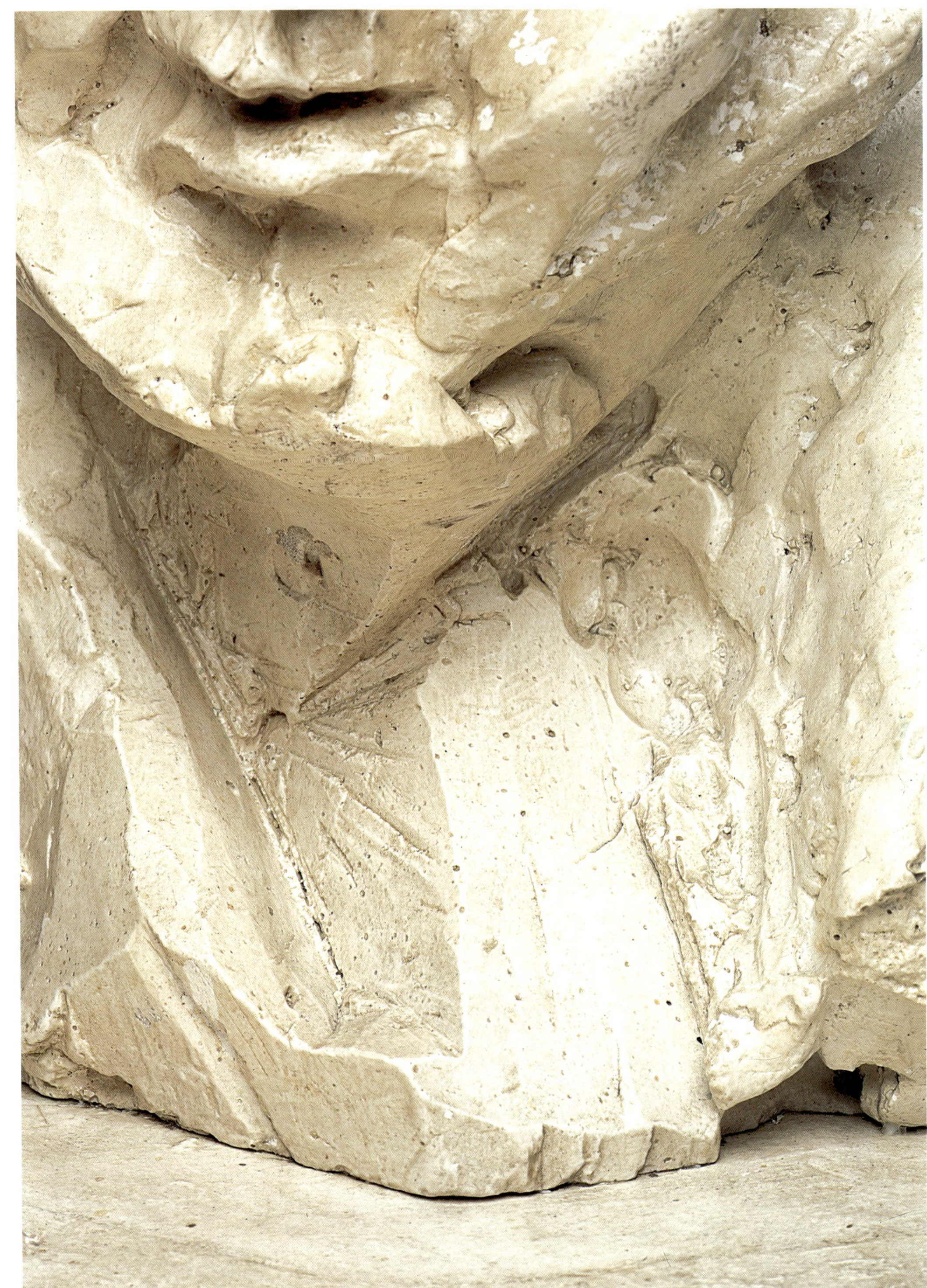

8
Detail of cat. 65, Pablo Picasso, *Head of a Woman (Fernande)*, Paris, fall 1909, plaster, Raymond and Patsy Nasher Collection, Dallas, Texas

After the new plaster set hard, the mold was prized off; this process usually destroyed the plaster mold. The "positive" plaster cast—virtually identical to the lost clay original—was known as the "master plaster" or "modèle."[13]

Forty-five years later Picasso would tell Douglas Cooper and John Richardson that he had "sharpened the working plaster at the foundry" in order to reduce the modeled aspect and to make the angles more acute.[14] As this was Picasso's first hands-on experience with the casting process, he was not familiar with technical terms. To him, the master was a "working plaster" because it was not an end in itself and because the artist did, in fact, work on it. Picasso's recollection is confirmed by an examination of the sculpture, particularly as seen in the two extant plasters. Areas in the front of the neck have been cut harshly with a blade (fig. 8). Those forms, which presumably had been convex, were sliced off and flattened into planes with sharp edges. In one area the knife seems to have scraped somewhat, and a blade can still be slightly inserted into one long cut.

What motivated this dramatic alteration, so different from the tactile modeling that characterizes the rest of the *Head*? Although the exact date on which the master was cast is not documented, it was probably in late autumn 1910, shortly before Picasso's exhibition was set to open at Vollard's gallery. In the year between modeling the clay and inspecting the plaster, the artist had developed his style toward greater abstraction. The difference becomes clear when comparing *Woman with Pears* (cat. 35) with *Portrait of Ambroise Vollard* (see fig. 7). The dealer's image is distinctly less volumetric and more hermetic, barely recognizable as a figure at all. A daring and sophisticated column of angular planes disregards any organic resemblance to the model. When Picasso saw the plaster *Head of a Woman* at the foundry, probably in the company of Vollard, he wanted to improve it by incorporating his recent innovations. Curiously, Picasso did not extend the radical sharpening beyond the neck. The individual facial features remain subtly irregular and "pliable" (albeit physically hardened in plaster), flowing organically in a rhythm of alternating concave and convex forms. A few small ridges, such as that over the proper-right eye, may have been discreetly accentuated with the tip of the knife. Despite Picasso's intention to make the sculpture more angular and abstract, he remained content with the face and hair, choosing to retain their sensitive, hand-modeled tactility.[15]

Prior to 1910, Picasso seems to have had no direct experience with bronze casting. The reasons why he had not personally made the effort to cast his early

13. My thanks to Derek Pullen, sculpture conservator at the Tate Modern (conversation with the author, 20 August 2002), and Scott McKee, specialist in plaster casting (conversation with the author, 7 November 2002), for explaining the process to me.

14. Richardson to Elizabeth Cowling, published in Elizabeth Cowling and John Golding, *Picasso: Sculptor/Painter* [exh. cat., Tate Gallery] (London, 1994), 255, and Richardson 1996, 137.

15. This experience of carving plaster was not unique; see the small *Apple* (fig. 15 in Tuma essay). Picasso had carved a real apple, which he gave to Vincenc Kramář (Richardson 1996, 140), then took a lump of plaster and cut into it to make the small cubist sculpture.

sculptures into bronze are uncertain. Perhaps he lacked the time or money to initiate the complex and expensive process, or perhaps he was not interested in bronze as a sculptural medium (which would be the case later in his career).[16] It is significant that Picasso made the trip to the foundry in 1910 to review the master prior to the bronze casting. Many sculptors at that time would not have bothered to do so. During the late nineteenth century it had become standard practice for artists to delegate the making of bronzes to foundries, and the expertise of Parisian foundries was well known. The technicians were fully capable of executing what was, for them, a routine job. Between 1912 and 1914, Picasso and a few other vanguard sculptors would reject this mass-production approach, but in 1910 the young artist was concerned about the transition from clay to plaster to bronze. He wanted to ensure that his sculptures be revealed to the public without aesthetic or technical weaknesses.

After Picasso had revised the master at the foundry, it could have been used directly to make bronzes, and this may indeed have been the case. Most foundries, however, prefer not to do this, because the elaborate physical processes of bronze casting pose serious risks of damaging the plaster, now the "original." Therefore, the foundry technicians usually make a secondary or "working" plaster.[17] A thin coating of gelatin would be applied to the master and left to dry. When carefully peeled off, that flexible mold could be used to cast a new "working" plaster. For centuries, gelatin molds had been made from natural materials that typically yielded only one new cast. In the late nineteenth century, synthetic gelatin and rubber-based materials came into use, allowing for more than one cast.[18]

The two existing plasters are today in the Latner Family Collection in Toronto (on loan to the Tate Gallery in London since 1994) and in the Raymond and Patsy Nasher Collection in Dallas. Neither was much seen in Picasso's lifetime; for many years, the artist himself did not know their location.[19] Proponents of each plaster advocate its primacy—both are very impressive. Several scholars and conservators—including myself—have examined the two plasters separately and have formed tentative opinions, but at the time this catalogue went to press, the two plasters had not yet been examined side by side, and the available technical evidence is insufficient to definitively identify either as the master. The physical nature of plaster itself can make a determination difficult. Comparing the size of one plaster to another is not as useful a criterion as it is for bronze casts. Unlike bronze, which shrinks about two percent in volume as it cools,[20] plaster hardens

16. According to Richardson (interview with the author, 4 December 2002), Picasso in the 1950s considered bronze "too museum-y" and too academic—which it certainly was by then. Spies (interview with the author, 4 December 2002), based on conversations with Picasso in the 1970s, said that the artist much preferred plaster to bronze.

17. See Arthur Beale, "The Search for the Lost Modèle," in Richard Kendall, *Degas and the Little Dancer* [exh. cat., Joslyn Art Museum, Omaha] (New Haven and London, 1998), 97–108. Beale's pioneering essay, "A Technical View of Nineteenth-Century Sculpture," in Jeanne L. Wasserman, ed., *Metamorphoses in Nineteenth-Century Sculpture* [exh. cat., Fogg Art Museum] (Cambridge, Mass., 1975), 29–55, provides basic explanations of mold-making. For further technical information on molds and casting around the turn of the last century, see Henry Lie, "Technical Features in Rosso's Work," and Derek Pullen, "Gelatin Molds: Rosso's Open Secret," in Harry Cooper and Sharon Hecker, *Medardo Rosso: Second Impressions* (New Haven and London, 2003), 69–97.

18. My thanks to Dick Polich of Polich Art Works for pointing out that gelatin molds made of bone marrow and other substances were used in the Renaissance. Casting expert Scott McKee believes that in France gelatin molds were widely used for casting plasters by the 1880s. Gelatin molds cannot be used on clay originals, as the materials are incompatible.

through crystallization, which entails very little shrinkage. Also, because plaster of fine quality can reproduce very subtle details, a plaster that was meticulously cast from another plaster may have only the slightest diminution of quality.

Both plasters of *Head of a Woman* are hollow casts made from mold(s); each has a raised mold-seam line running along the center (left, right, and top). Examined separately, the plasters appear nearly identical in specific forms and surface details, such as the row of parallel strips on the topmost-center form of the hair, the small recess in the inner corner of the proper-left eye, an irregular sharp bump on the chin, a row of fingertip indentations in the proper-left neck above a defined ridge, and the horizontal finger swipe on the rear neck. The artist's signature on the proper-left rear neck appears identical in both plasters; he probably incised "Picasso" into the original clay (as suggested by the raised edges in the signature). Both plasters even have the same technical defects, including the numerous tiny air-bubble holes scattered over the front and back of the neck (see figs. 4, 8), a keyhole-shaped hole beneath the second "S" in the signature, and a larger air-bubble cavity in the back of the neck.[21] The latter two details seem somewhat sharper in the Latner plaster, suggesting that it may be the master. A firm determination will be possible only after the two plasters are brought together for this exhibition. Although we examined them separately, sculpture conservator Derek Pullen and I believe that the Latner plaster may be more precise in many small aspects. Pullen believes the Nasher plaster could have been cast from the Latner plaster but not vice versa.[22]

The "twin" nature of the two plasters is reinforced by their shared provenance. According to verbal accounts—unsubstantiated by early documentary proof—each was purchased by separate dealers at different times from Jacques Ulmann in Paris, who had acquired the works from Vollard's estate. The dispersal of Vollard's extensive estate is not well documented. During his lifetime, the dealer never kept a complete list of his holdings, and no inventory was done after he died in July 1939. According to various sources, Vollard's will divided the estate among several heirs, one half to be apportioned equally among his brother Lucien in Paris and his two sisters in La Réunion, and the other half to be shared by Vollard's longtime love, Mme de Galea, and her two sons. When the Germans invaded France in May 1940, the heirs had to hide the works of art as best they could under difficult circumstances—on Lucien's behalf, the dealer Martin Fabiani illegally exported more than five hundred paintings. After World War II, the heirs gradually dispersed the

19. According to Richardson (interview with the author), Picasso did not own a plaster when one (now in the Nasher collection) was brought to his attention by Heinz Berggruen in 1959. The catalogue raisonné by Spies and Piot lists only one plaster as an "intermediate," without specifying to which one this refers.

20. Beale in Kendall 1998, 97–108. Using specific reference points, the Hirshhorn Museum's bronze *Head of a Woman* (41.6 × 22.8 × 26.4 cm) from the second edition is appropriately smaller than the Nasher plaster (42 × 23.4 × 27 cm) from which it was cast. The first-edition bronze now belonging to the National Gallery of Art is slightly larger than the Hirshhorn Museum's, although not as large as the Nasher plaster. This raises intriguing possibilities, but until the Latner plaster and the other earliest Vollard casts can be measured in the exact same way, no firm conclusions can be drawn.

21. According to Scott McKee, and Beale in Kendall 1998, 103, the pattern of tiny air bubbles formed when the technicians poured plaster into the mold(s). This tends to happen when the mold is not first coated with a thin layer of plaster before pouring the rest. The air bubbles then rise to the outer surface.

22. E-mail from Pullen to the author, 28 January 2003.

assets of the estate, but little documentation seems to exist on these transactions. Édouard Jonas, a former antiques dealer and politician, traveled to La Réunion to purchase the Vollard sisters' share of the estate (which they had never seen). Back in Paris he negotiated with the de Galeas and Lucien Vollard on the division of the estate, receiving among other items a number of Renoir bronzes. After Lucien Vollard died on 1 February 1953, Jonas seems to have become his executor ("légataire universel") and sold works from the estate through at least 1956, often to Americans. The de Galeas tended to sell their works discreetly, one or two at a time, from the 1950s through the 1970s. In short, no one knows exactly which works had been in Vollard's hands nor how those works were distributed after his death.[23]

Jacques Ulmann, who owned a department store in Paris, purchased works from the Vollard estate, including several original Picasso sculptures. In the mid-1950s John Richardson saw a plaster cast of Picasso's *Head of a Woman* in Ulmann's living room; at that time its color was a slightly yellowed white and it had no circular base. Ulmann did not display or mention a second plaster.[24] In 1959 the art dealer Heinz Berggruen purchased a plaster *Head of a Woman* from Ulmann, giving it to Picasso the following year. After the artist's death in 1973, it was inherited by Marina Picasso, exhibited in 1981 and 1986, and then sold by the Galerie Jan Krugier to Raymond and Patsy Nasher.[25] Meanwhile, in 1968 the Swiss dealer Ernst Beyeler purchased a plaster from Ulmann and sold it to the Latners. At the same time, each purchaser believed their plaster to be the "original."[26]

Both plasters have been used for casting at one time or another. Each has several very thin, parallel, incised cuts ("release" lines) that run vertically along the left and right sides and over the top.[27] Such incisions are made when a plaster is removed from a sand-casting bed or when a gelatin mold is removed from a plaster. These cuts typically occur on the sides of a sculpted head, as no experienced foundry technician would risk marring the face. The same processes can be repeated for multiple sand-casts or multiple gelatin molds. Each plaster also has areas expressly for fitting or "keying" mold equipment. The Latner plaster has recessed dimples in the bottom, while the Nasher head is attached to a circular plaster base with raised keys for supporting a "retainer mold" that fit over the entire sculpture. This base, attached to the bottom and inside of the head with white plaster, was presumably added for the second bronze edition in 1959.

23. Published information is very limited; see Lynn H. Nicholas, *The Rape of Europa* (New York, 1994), 92–93, 304–305. Some documents exist in the National Archives, Washington, D.C.; see "Art Looting Investigation Unit Final Report," record group 59, box 10. The Vollard archives provide scattered bits of information, such as Lucien's ownership of Vollard's six-story building, and letters from Jonas, who described himself as a former *Député* (congressman), former president of the Committee of Public Works, and former president of the National Center of Tourism. Jonas had also catalogued works in the Musée Cognacq-Jay in 1930. Among other works, he owned the wax original of Picasso's *Head of a Jester*; see Andrew C. Ritchie, *Sculpture of the Twentieth Century* [exh. cat., The Museum of Modern Art] (New York, 1952). I am indebted to Richardson (interview with the author, 4 December 2002), who kindly provided details on Jonas and the de Galeas.

24. Richardson interview, 4 December 2002.

25. See Heinz Berggruen, *J'étais mon meilleur client* (Paris, 1996), 99–102. Berggruen previously had provided the provenance to William Rubin and Alicia Legg at the Museum of Modern Art, New York, who in turn informed Steven Nash at the Dallas Museum of Art (recorded in his memorandum of 18 April 1987). Olivier Berggruen, letter to Elizabeth Cowling (spring 1994) and conversation with the author (1 August 2002), said that in 1959 his father had seen only the one plaster in

Ulmann's collection. This corresponds with Richardson's account. The plaster was first exhibited in Werner Spies, *Pablo Picasso: Werke aus der Sammlung Marina Picasso* [exh. cat., Haus der Kunst] (Munich, 1981), 244, cat. 66, using a photograph of a bronze.

26. Letter from Gallery Beyeler to author, 10 April 2003.

27. See Beale 1975, 30, figs. 4a and 4b, for photographs of similar cut lines.

28. He wanted his plasters to remain pristine white even after use for bronze casting.

29. Johnson 1977, 43. Vollard's ledgers confirm that he sold a great many Maillol bronzes from 1921 to 1932. Yet Castleman in Johnson 1977, 15–16, notes that Vollard "sold only what he wanted to sell to collectors he deemed worthy." The catalogue raisonné by Spies and Piot unhelpfully cites only "quelques épreuves" (a few casts) by Vollard; this information is repeated in many other publications. From 1979 to 1980, when I first compiled a list of the known Vollard bronzes, I arrived at a total of twelve to fourteen. I shared this information with Olivier Berggruen in 1991; three years later he had accounted for fifteen. In our joint review in August 2002, we concur on at least eighteen, subject to the variables outlined in this essay, and agree that a few more may yet emerge from private collections.

The Latner head has a brown coating typical of the shellac used by foundries to protect plaster surfaces during the process of making a gelatin mold or sandcast bronze. Minute traces of a reddish material remain in several small crevices, evidence that at least one flexible mold was prepared from this head. The red remnants, however, have not yet been scientifically analyzed, and their age is unknown. In comparison, the Nasher *Head of a Woman* has a thin, transparent, slightly yellowed protective coating, possibly a thin shellac or acetate. This appearance corresponds with Richardson's memory of the plaster he saw in Ulmann's collection in the mid-1950s. The coating covers most but not all of the surface, including the base and the "release" cuts, indicating that it may have been applied after, not before, the mold-making process. Unlike the Latner plaster, there are no remnants of mold material in the crevices, although traces of silicone rubber remain inside. The pristine appearance of this plaster suggests that it may have been cleaned at some time. Because the plaster was to be given to Picasso after the second bronze edition was completed in 1959 (see explanation below), it may have been cleaned then by the foundry or later for the artist, as Picasso preferred that all his plasters remain white.[28] All this is supposition, however. The clean state of the Nasher plaster leads some viewers to assume it is much newer than the Latner one, while the dirty appearance of the Latner plaster reinforces an impression of age. Such conclusions are risky, as it is very difficult to determine the age of modern plasters.

One question has perplexed scholars for decades: how many bronze casts of *Head of a Woman* did Vollard actually cast and sell after he bought the original? Many publications by eminent scholars, including William Rubin and Werner Spies, state that only "a few" were cast. Una Johnson, in her study of the dealer's editioning practices, noted: "It is doubtful that Vollard himself knew the total issue of each. His practice was to keep in his shop an example of each of the bronzes. When a collector or dealer wished to obtain one, Vollard would order a cast made. Being a good businessman, he never had more on hand than he could sell." Johnson further pointed out that although Maillol stipulated a maximum of ten bronze casts of each terracotta, Vollard ignored the artist's wish, leading Maillol to say, "Well, he made ten casts, all right, except they turned out to be ten thousand."[29] As a dealer who owned the sculptures outright, Vollard was not obligated to limit the edition. He also knew not to advertise its unlimited extent, because large editions tend to lower the market value. Consequently, Vollard did not have the bronzes numbered;

30. Ludovico de Cristofaro, letter to the author, 9 January 2003. Émile added the lost-wax method to the Godard foundry's methods in 1962; he died in 1971. Cristofaro joined the staff in 1976 and the foundry has since systematically marked its bronzes.

many artists at that time did not bother to do so. The Vollard bronzes also do not have foundry marks, which was less usual but not uncommon.

With so many excellent foundries operating in or near Paris, Vollard could have worked with one or with several. Factors such as price, location, and time constraints can determine the selection of a foundry. Generally, artists and dealers have found it easier and more effective to leave the working plaster at one foundry, where bronzes could be made when needed and where the technicians would be familiar with the sculpture. If Vollard used several foundries over a span of nearly thirty years, this would account for the disconcerting range of quality found among the bronzes. Some casts have superb surface articulation while others are less crisp, even slightly blurry. Patinas also vary from monochrome dark brown to almost black, some with subtly colored nuances.

Recent access to the Vollard archives has shed new light on the foundry question. Bookkeeping entries in the dealer's accounts payable and receivable are meticulous. Unfortunately, the ledgers from 1908 to 1921 are missing; as a result, no documentary proof exists of which foundries he used or which sculptures he sold during that time. The ledgers from late 1921 to early 1939, however, offer excellent evidence for those years and establish a pattern from which it is possible to deduce what may have occurred during the undocumented earlier years. These ledgers confirm that Vollard ordered a few bronze casts whenever he needed them and that he made payments to only one bronze caster, listed simply as "Godard." According to Ludovico de Cristofaro, the current director of the Émile Godard foundry, Vollard had initially used several small, commercial (rather than fine-art) foundries in Paris because he sought the lowest price. Cristofaro believes that those foundries, which applied no identifying marks, produced poor results. Désiré Godard opened his fine-art foundry in Malakoff (in the Île-de-France region outside Paris) in 1918. Vollard turned to this foundry in 1921, but Godard did not keep records on which works were cast or how many. Using only the sand-cast method, Godard was known for the fine quality of his work, although he rarely marked any bronzes with the foundry name. Cristofaro notes that Désiré's brother Florentin Godard had his own foundry in Paris, where he made casts of even higher quality, including many Maillol bronzes; Florentin usually marked his casts. Vollard's association with Désiré Godard ceased in 1932, although the foundry continued and Désiré's son Émile later did some work directly for Picasso.[30]

31. Reviews by Salmon (22 December 1910) and Bidou (14 January 1911) do not mention sculpture.

32. Anne Baldassari, *Picasso photographe 1901–1916* [exh. cat., Musée Picasso] (Paris, 1994), 207, fig. 152; she dates the photograph to fall 1910. Pepe Karmel dates it to early or mid-1911, based on one of the paintings in the photograph (communication to Jeffrey Weiss, 2002).

33. The Czech painter Emil Filla, in a letter from Paris to Kramář, 25 April 1913, confirmed that Vollard still had "la tête de Picasso" on view inside the gallery. I am grateful to Hélène Klein for this information.

I believe that in late 1910 two bronzes of *Head of a Woman* were cast by an unknown foundry: one for the artist to keep and one for display in the exhibition at Vollard's gallery (20 December 1910 to February 1911). Because the exhibition had no catalogue, we cannot confirm that the dealer displayed all five sculptures, but he surely featured the impressive cubist *Head of a Woman*.[31] One of the artist's own photographs establishes that he received his bronze *Head of a Woman*, along with casts of *Head of a Jester* and the *Head of Fernande*, by early 1911. The sculptures appear neatly lined up (as if recently delivered en bloc) in the lower left of a photograph taken around that time in the studio at 11 Boulevard de Clichy (fig. 9).[32] This "artist's proof" of *Head of a Woman* is now owned by the Musée Picasso in Paris. When examined side by side with the Latner plaster, details of this bronze match closely (although the large air-bubble hole in the center-rear neck was partially filled in as a routine matter during the bronze casting). This cast has a thick, unmodulated dark-brown patina, which was probably not the result of a deliberate aesthetic choice by Picasso or Vollard. Patination is a highly specialized skill, utilized only by sculptors and foundries experienced in the ways of finishing bronze casts. Both Picasso and Vollard lacked such expertise, and the dealer did not encourage artists' intervention in the editioning of sculptures. Neither Picasso nor Maillol directly participated in casting or finishing bronzes for Vollard. When no specific instructions are given, foundry technicians provide a basic patina, usually dark brown or black with a few color nuances, depending on the foundry and the era. Picasso's "artist's proof" casts of *Head of a Jester, Head of Fernande,* and *Head of a Woman* all have the same matte dark-brown patina, tending toward black. Compared to the bronzes personally patinated by Maillol from 1896 to 1900 (Musée Maillol, Paris), the difference is remarkable. Maillol's own patinas range from warm honey-brown and earthy reddish brown to acidic green, forest green, and blue-green over black. The nondescript coloration of Picasso's bronzes probably disappointed the innovative artist and would affect the treatment of his next bronze sculpture, the *Absinthe Glass* (see fig. 19 in Weiss essay). When Kahnweiler had that wax original made into a bronze edition in spring 1914, Picasso insisted on hand-painting each cast differently.

Vollard featured *Head of a Woman* in the front window or inside his gallery for the next several years as the public and artistic debate over cubism reached its zenith.[33] The sculpture's impact was immediately apparent in works by Alexander Archipenko, Umberto Boccioni, Raymond Duchamp-Villon, Otto Gutfreund, Henri

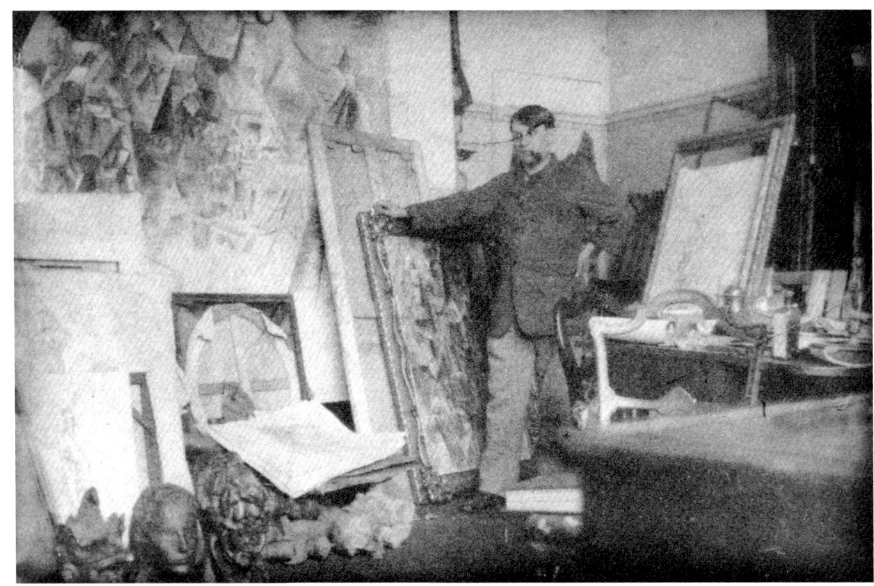

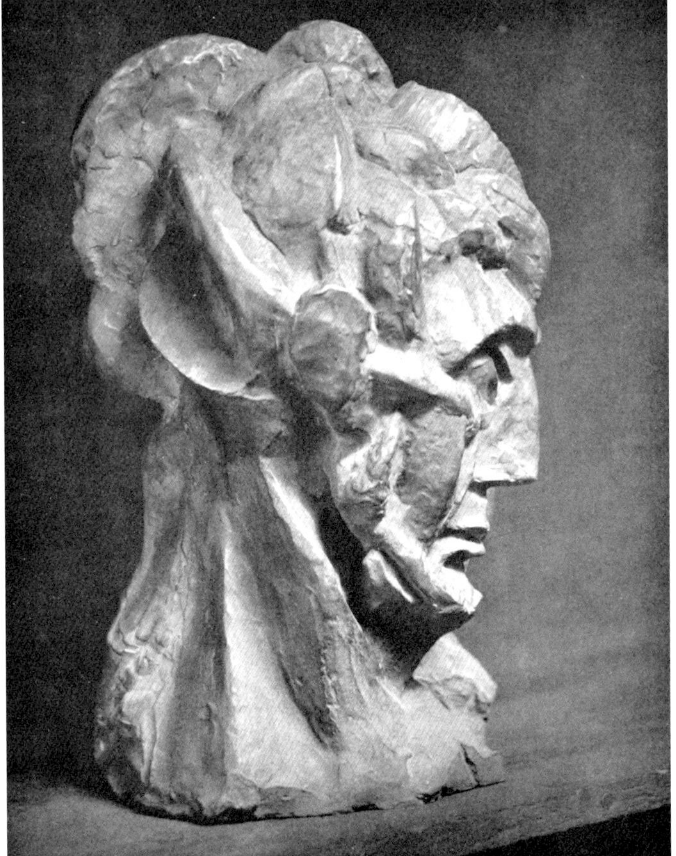

9

Pablo Picasso, Self-portrait in the studio at 11 Boulevard de Clichy, early 1911

10

Alfred Stieglitz, *Picasso: Sculpture*, photograph of bronze *Head of a Woman*, published in *Camera Work*, special number (August 1912)

Laurens, Jacques Lipchitz, and others who saw it in 1911 and 1912. It is not known whether Vollard kept the same bronze cast throughout his lifetime and sold others, or if he sold that first one and periodically replaced it with newer casts when sales were brisk.

Soon after the exhibition Vollard sold two bronzes to collectors from other countries. In May 1911 one went to Vincenc Kramář in Prague. Kramář paid 600 francs, Vollard's standard pre-World War I price for Picasso bronzes (about one-third the price of a painting).[34] That cast now belongs to the National Gallery in Prague. In January 1912 Vollard sold a cast to Alfred Stieglitz, who would bequeath it to the Art Institute of Chicago in 1949. Stieglitz took beautiful photographs of his bronze for publication in *Camera Work* (August 1912)[35] and then lent the work to the notorious Armory Show in 1913. Although rarely seen today, Stieglitz's black-and-white photographs present the *Head of a Woman* with great subtlety and sensitivity (fig. 10). He perceived the work as a three-dimensional piece with its own merit, not merely as a solidified version of a cubist painting. Stieglitz was the first photographer—and one among few—to feature a profile view of the head as well as a frontal view. He showed the head's proper-right side, which is executed with greater refinement than the left. The solid shape and curvature of the ear provide a central focus and balance for the complexity of the facial contours. Stieglitz emphasized the play of light and shadow on the surfaces, highlighting nuances of organic forms and sharp edges. Skillful use of lighting, film exposure, and darkroom printing allowed him to overcome the dull, dark-brown patina, making the bronze appear almost like a plaster or clay, thus intuitively re-creating Picasso's original version.

Subsequent publications did not follow Stieglitz's inspired example. The Picasso catalogues published by the Museum of Modern Art (MoMA) in New York from 1936 on, Walter Chrysler's collection catalogue in 1941, Carola Gidion-Welcker's book on modern sculpture in 1955, and others invariably featured only a single-view photograph from a frontal or three-quarter viewpoint. Although this angle shows the head to great advantage, it also tends to reduce the form to a pictorial entity, akin to the painting *Woman with Pears* (cat. 35). The pouting lips, the strong curvature of a cheek, the brooding angularity of the brows, the beaky profile of the nose, and the unevenly pointed chin all recede into the geometry of the whole.

It is virtually impossible to know how many other casts of *Head of a Woman* Vollard sold before 1922. Between February 1912 and November 1913 the dealer

34. Sales receipt dated 26 May 1911 (Kramář archives, National Gallery, Prague); my thanks to Hélène Klein for this information. Kramář's bronze was featured in the *Third Exhibition of Plastic Artists* in Prague in May–June 1913. The bronze, which I have not seen personally, is illustrated in color in *Vincenc Kramář: From Old Masters to Picasso* [exh. cat., National Gallery, Prague] (Prague, 2000).

35. In spring 1911, Stieglitz had presented a Picasso exhibition of eighty-three drawings and watercolors (organized by Edward Steichen and Manolo, among others) at his "291" gallery (Little Galleries of the Photo-Secession, 28 March–25 April 1911). Vollard's daily calendar for 15 January 1912 documents the sale of *Head of a Woman* to Steichen, who was acting on Stieglitz's behalf. This bronze was shipped to Stieglitz two weeks later. His photographs appear with Gertrude Stein's essay "Pablo Picasso" in *Camera Work*, special number (August 1912), 41, 43.

shipped three Picasso bronzes to German dealers, including Alfred Flechtheim and the Thannhauser galleries, but he did not identify them by title.[36] Art sales increased strongly after the hiatus of World War I. Vollard's accounting ledgers document his success in selling sculptures, especially those by Maillol. For example, during 1924 and 1925 he paid the Godard foundry thirty-six times; the first twenty-one payments were for sixty-one bronzes by Maillol. In contrast, from 1921 through 1925 Vollard sold only paintings and prints by Picasso. A sudden spate of activity followed: between July 1926 and July 1927, Vollard sold and shipped fifteen bronzes by Picasso, each now selling for 8,000 francs. Unfortunately, the dealer recorded them simply as "head" or "bust," only twice specifically mentioning a "tête cubiste." In February 1927 he sold a "buste de Picasso tête de femme" to E. Weyhe in New York. All these bronzes must have been cast by Godard, as Vollard paid no other foundry during those years. According to his ledgers, Vollard continued to sell bronzes by Maillol prolifically in 1928 and 1929 (at least twenty-eight payments were made to Godard), but none by Picasso, despite the fact that *Head of a Woman* appeared in two prestigious publications in 1928.[37] These bits of information indicate that during the 1920s Vollard may have sold as few as three or as many as a dozen bronze casts of *Head of a Woman.*

Art sales dropped off drastically during the Great Depression. Although Vollard sold major paintings by Cézanne and Renoir, he recorded only two sales of sculpture by Picasso during the 1930s. Even the large Picasso exhibition at the Galeries Georges Petit (16 June to 30 July 1932), which included four Vollard bronzes, did not stimulate sales.[38] Perhaps Vollard no longer bothered to keep accurate records or perhaps he did not bother to sell; he had long been sufficiently affluent to choose what he sold and to whom.

Vollard's death in a car crash in July 1939 brought his career to an end. Less than a year later, the Nazi invasion of Paris halted most art transactions and bronze casting in France. In October 1941 the Germans even authorized melting down some bronze sculptures so the metal could be used for munitions.[39]

A few sales during the war have been documented, particularly in New York. Dealers with previous connections to Vollard sold three *Head of a Woman* bronzes to Americans in 1940. The one owned by Weyhe was included in two major exhibitions at MoMA, *Cubism and Abstract Art* in 1936 and *Picasso: Forty Years of His Art* in 1939. Weyhe then sold the bronze to a private collector, not to the museum, as is widely believed. After several changes of ownership, this cast

36. Two went to Flechtheim, who at that point was primarily a collector; he opened his gallery in Frankfurt in November 1922. In *Alfred Flechtheim: Sammler, Kunsthändler, Verleger* [exh. cat., Kunstmuseum, Düsseldorf] (Düsseldorf, 1987) no Picasso sculpture is mentioned, although a 1929 photograph of his collection, on page 55, shows the closely related *Woman with Pears* (cat. 35). The huge Picasso exhibition at the Thannhauser gallery in Munich in February 1913 consisted only of paintings, watercolors, drawings, and prints, although the Vollard sales account suggests that a sculpture could have been included at the last moment and not been recorded.

37. Adolphe Basler, *La Sculpture Moderne en France* (Paris, 1928), 42, ill.; Christian Zervos, "Sculptures des Peintres d'Aujourd'hui," *Cahiers d'Art* 7 (1928), 286, ill.

38. *Exposition Picasso* [exh. cat., Galeries Georges Petit] (Paris, 1932), 71–72, nos. 224–228. The catalogue entries were highly inaccurate, dating all the sculptures to c. 1900 and misidentifying the cubist one as *Head of a Man*. The credit line for each clearly stated, "Éditions Ambroise Vollard, Paris."

39. Steven Nash, "Chronology," in *Picasso and the War Years 1937–1945* [exh. cat., Fine Arts Museums] (San Francisco, 1998), 212.

eventually came to the collection of Leonard Lauder in New York.[40] It has crisp surface textures and a blackish-brown patina nuanced in some areas with an earthy red. Meanwhile, MoMA bought a different cast in 1940—the first to enter a museum anywhere—from the German-born, New York–based dealer Curt Valentin.[41] During the late 1920s and early 1930s he had worked for Flechtheim in Berlin and had come to know many artists personally before fleeing the Nazis. From 1938 until his death in 1953, his Buchholz Gallery in New York exhibited and sold sculptures by Ernst Barlach, Edgar Degas, Käthe Kollwitz, Laurens, Lipchitz, Maillol, Henri Matisse, Henry Moore, Picasso, and many others. Although Valentin's name is not widely familiar today, the dealer was very well connected and knowledgeable about modern European sculpture; his sources included Flechtheim, Vollard, Kahnweiler, Paul Guillaume, and Degas' niece.[42] In May 1940, the same year he sold a cast to MoMA, Valentin sold still another bronze *Head of a Woman* to Walter Chrysler, who was forming a major group of Picasso's works.[43] That cast has the unmodulated dark-brown patina of most Vollard casts and seems to have been finished in a hurry. File marks are in evidence—Vollard was not known for being attentive to such matters. The Chrysler bronze was auctioned in 1989 to a private collection in New York, making that city a nexus for early casts of Picasso's famous cubist sculpture.

Only the bronze casts mentioned above have provenances that can be clearly traced to Vollard. Other casts may well have passed through his hands but no evidentiary proof survives. In the upheaval and devastation of World War II many documents were destroyed, including sales records and other transfers of art. As any experienced provenance researcher knows, it is extremely difficult to establish thorough histories for works of art made before 1940. The problem becomes infinitely more difficult with multiple bronzes and almost impossible with an unnumbered edition, turning provenance verification into a matter of probability rather than certainty.

The history of two other bronze casts of *Head of a Woman (Fernande)*—one of many European works of art to surface in Switzerland during the war—can be traced almost to Vollard. The Kunsthaus Zurich purchased its *Head of a Woman* from the Galerie H.U. Gasser in Zurich in 1944. The provenance of the bronze *Head of a Woman* now owned by the Museum of Fine Arts, Boston, can be traced to an excellent source: the dealer Kahnweiler (Galerie Simon) in Paris well before 1952.[44]

40. Weyhe's cast went to Mrs. Ralph Heinz, Chicago, then to Robert Pirie in Hammondton, Massachusetts, and then to its current owner in New York.

41. William Rubin, *Picasso in the Collection of the Museum of Modern Art* [exh. cat., The Museum of Modern Art] (New York, 1972), 203, published the provenance as Weyhe. On 8 December 1986, MoMA curator Alicia Legg wrote to Olivier Berggruen, providing the corrected source as Valentin. Care should be taken when using MoMA's cast to compare other bronzes, as it no longer has its original patina. According to a receipt in the museum's files, the sculpture was repatinated by independent restorer Joseph Ternbach in 1956; no reason was recorded (Lynda Zycherman, sculptor conservator at MoMA, telephone conversation with the author, 21 January 2003). At some point, mounting flanges were added to the inside of the museum's cast.

42. Valentin's gallery was named Buchholz Gallery until 1951. He exhibited a *Head of a Woman* in *Sculpture* (26 September–14 October 1949), and another in *Picasso: Paintings, Sculpture, Drawings* (February–March 1952). Valentin's records are preserved in the archives of the Museum of Modern Art; at the time this essay was written they were temporarily inaccessible.

43. *Collection of Walter P. Chrysler, Jr.* [exh. cat., Virginia Museum of Fine Arts] (Richmond, 1941), 90–93, nos. 160–165; the "cubist head" is ill. 163.

44. The bronze is recorded as the Galerie Simon's stock no. 03895, photograph no. 52167; it passed to the Galerie Louise Leiris-Kahnweiler, where it was sold in 1952 to the Svensk-Franska Konstgalleriet, Stockholm. Theodore Ahrenberg in Stockholm owned it until 1968. After passing through several dealers, the bronze was purchased in 1976 and given to the Museum of Fine Arts, Boston (1976.821).

45. René Gaffé, "Sculpteur Picasso?" *Artès* 3–4 (1947–1948).

46. Letter from Karin Lindegren, curator, Moderna Museet, to Henry Hopkins, Fort Worth Art Museum, 30 December 1970.

47. Steven A. Nash, *Paintings and Sculpture from Antiquity to 1942* [exh. cat., Albright-Knox Art Gallery] (New York, 1979), 431.

At least two casts belonged to collectors who knew Picasso and were actively acquiring from the 1920s through the 1950s, although the actual dates of purchase were not recorded. René Gaffé (Belgian, 1887–1968) had his cast by 1948, when he published an article on it;[45] it seems reasonable to conclude that his bronze probably came from Vollard before 1940. That cast, recently acquired by a private collector in the United States, is now on loan to the Philadelphia Museum of Art. Another bronze *Head of a Woman* belonged to Rolf de Maré, who had been the impresario of the Swedish Ballet of Paris and a friend of Georges Braque. He met Picasso in the 1920s, again a reasonable indication that his cast came from Vollard before the war. De Maré later became director of the Moderna Museet in Stockholm and bequeathed his cast to the museum in 1964.[46]

Within a few years after World War II, the art market revived and thrived. With most of Europe in economic ruin, the primary venue was the United States. Art of all kinds emerged from European collections, and dealers sold works to a new generation of eager Americans. Half a dozen casts of *Head of a Woman* changed hands between 1948 and 1952. In November 1948, R.H. Norton bought one cast from Julius Thannhauser in New York; this may have been the one Vollard had sold to the Thannhauser gallery in Germany in December 1926. Norton's cast, with its deep-brown patina, now belongs to the Norton Gallery in Palm Beach, Florida. In 1948 the Art Gallery of Ontario in Toronto purchased its bronze *Head of a Woman* from the Zwemmer Gallery in London, and that same year the Albright-Knox Art Gallery in Buffalo bought another cast from Valentin in New York.[47] Samuel and Florene Marx acquired their cast from the same dealer in 1951. It now belongs to the Metropolitan Museum of Art in New York; its patina has more reddish areas than other early casts. In 1952 the Portland Art Museum in Oregon also purchased a cast from Valentin, bringing his sale total of *Head of a Woman* bronzes to at least five within eight years. For the Portland sale, Valentin gave his source as Lucien Vollard. Lucien's heirs were cited as the provenance for still another cast, formerly in Germany, which was sold at Christie's in November 2000 (private collection, California).

At this point, although not specifically in reference to any of the casts listed above, I feel obliged to mention the possibility—or probability—that some of the "Vollard" bronzes may have been made after the dealer's death. After the French postwar economy began to revive in late 1946 and 1947, many artists or their agents resumed bronze editions begun earlier, as did Alberto Giacometti, the Laurens heirs,

Matisse, and the Musée Rodin. Dealers and collectors who owned original sculptures by Honoré Daumier, Duchamp-Villon, Paul Gauguin, and others commissioned new bronze editions. This phenomenon was not limited to France: Moore in England and the Barlach and Kollwitz heirs in Germany did likewise. In the United States, where copyright laws were rarely applied to sculpture, foundries were also very busy. The demand for prewar sculpture steadily increased and rising prices encouraged more casting, so the trend continued. Considering these circumstances, it would have been entirely apposite for the Vollard heirs to produce more casts, just as Georges Petit printed the 1939 Vollard suite of Picasso etchings in 1950. Legally the heirs had the right to do so, for they had inherited not only the plasters but also the reproduction rights.[48] If made at a good foundry, such casts would be equal—or possibly superior—in quality to those made during Vollard's lifetime. It should be borne in mind that Picasso himself never worked on any of the casts, regardless of when they were made.

Although I have not seen all the above-mentioned casts, several with secure provenances provide consistent physical evidence. The bronzes belonging to the Musée Picasso, the Art Institute of Chicago, and the Museum of Fine Arts, Boston, and the one formerly owned by Gaffé are all sand-casts with residues of reddish-gray sand and similarly made core pins (fig. 11).[49] Sand-casting was widely used in Europe for nearly three hundred years, reaching its apogee in France during the late nineteenth and early twentieth century. The process entails placing a plaster sculpture in a two-part, boxlike framework, which is filled with a densely packed sand mixture (industrial-grade silica with various binders). When the sand has set firmly, the box is carefully opened and the plaster original removed, leaving a precise imprint in the sand. The box halves are rejoined and molten bronze is poured in. After the metal has cooled, the box is opened again and the sand, which has also hardened, is broken away to remove the bronze cast. Thus the sand mold is destroyed each time a bronze is made; the plaster original must be repacked into fresh sand for each cast. Depending on the foundry technician's skill, the sand mold could be packed very finely or less so. If the same technician made multiple bronze casts, they tended to be identical or to become progressively better, but if bronzes were made by different technicians at different times, the precision of surface details could vary.

Such physical criteria can help authenticate Vollard casts that lack documentary proof of a Vollard provenance. The *Head of a Woman* bronze now owned by the National Gallery of Art has been traced back only to the mid-1950s, when it

48. When Picasso granted Berggruen permission in 1959 to make a new edition of the 1906 *Head of Fernande*, he stipulated that this permission was conditional on the dealer obtaining the reproduction rights from Ulmann along with the sculpture itself (see Berggruen 1996 for a photograph of Picasso's written authorization). This was before laws were enacted in France granting greater control to all artists concerning the use of their works.

49. My thanks to Derek Pullen and Dominique Dupuis-Labé for their help in examining the Musée Picasso bronze at the Tate Modern on 20 August 2002. Thanks also to Shelley Sturman at the National Gallery of Art and to others for sharing photographs of the interiors of the Chicago and Boston bronzes (shown to the author 7 July 2002).

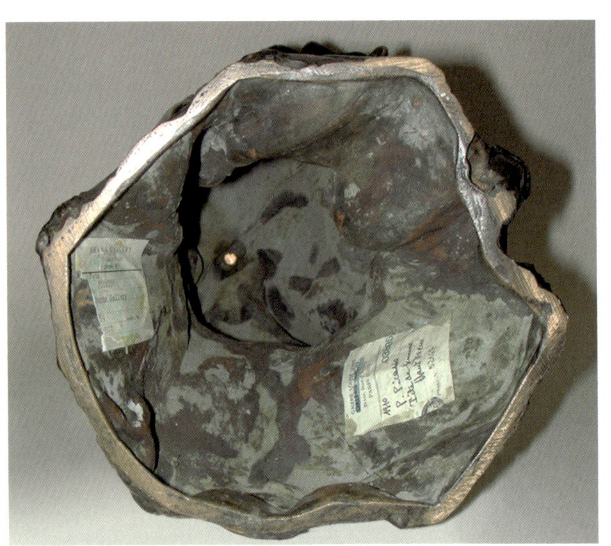

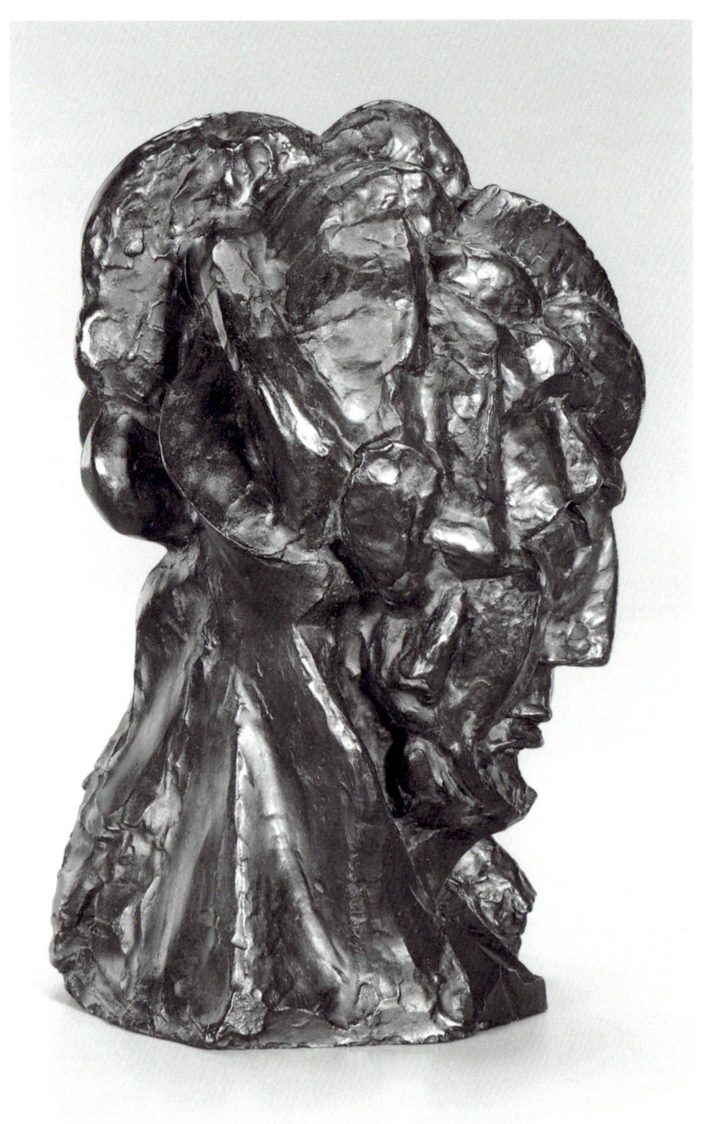

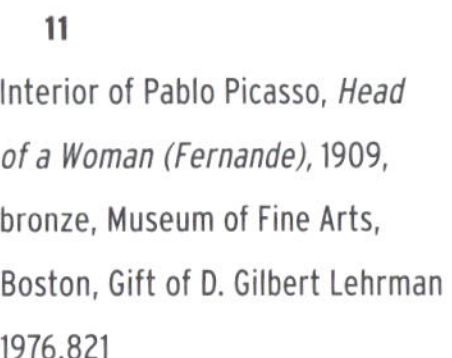

11

Interior of Pablo Picasso, *Head of a Woman (Fernande)*, 1909, bronze, Museum of Fine Arts, Boston, Gift of D. Gilbert Lehrman 1976.821

12

Pablo Picasso, *Head of a Woman (Fernande)* (cat. 66), model 1909, cast before 1932, bronze, National Gallery of Art, Patrons' Permanent Fund and Gift of Mitchell P. Rales

belonged to a private collection in Stockholm.[50] The technical quality of this cast is superb, with surface details very crisp and tactile (fig. 12). The artist's finger marks on the proper-left neck, the clearly defined "pellets" on the top-center hair form, and the angular forms of the front neck are comparable to the plasters and to the bronze formerly owned by Weyhe. The cast's dark-brown patina with subtle areas of deep green is superior to the monochrome patina on the cast in the Musée Picasso and contributes to the work's powerful sculptural presence. The National Gallery's bronze must have been produced by a highly skilled foundry technician, probably one who had benefited from the experience of making previous casts, as would have been the case at the Godard foundry when Vollard's sales were brisk in 1926 and 1927. Although no documentary proof exists, this cast was probably one of those personally made by Désiré Godard.

As Picasso's fame and the market for his works steadily increased in the 1950s and 1960s, several dealers became interested in making new editions of the sculptures formerly owned by Vollard. When Heinz Berggruen purchased the plaster *Head of a Woman* from Ulmann in 1959, he acquired the reproduction rights, which had been handed down with the sculpture from the Vollard estate. Berggruen obtained Picasso's permission to cast from it an edition of nine new bronzes. As before, the artist took no active role in the casting or patination process. By this time, forty-five years after he had hand-painted each bronze cast of the *Absinthe Glass,* Picasso was accustomed to leave the mechanics of bronze casting to others. The plasters created at Boisgeloup in 1931, for example, were cast under the eye of Jaime Sabartés, and later sculptures such as *Man with Goat* and *Woman with Baby Carriage* were handled by Kahnweiler. As part of the deal for *Head of a Woman* in 1959, Berggruen agreed to give the plaster to Picasso, along with three of the bronzes.[51] Berggruen entrusted the casting work to the C. Valsuani foundry, which had specialized in the lost-wax method since the 1920s.

The success of synthetic gelatin molds encouraged many foundries to move away from sand-casting to lost-wax casting in the early and mid-twentieth century.[52] In this method a liquid mixture is applied to the plaster; when dried, the gelatin is peeled off and used to make bronze casts. Because the gelatin mold is so flexible, it is supported externally by an enveloping "retainer mold" and internally by a "core." The gelatin mold is filled with molten wax. When cooled, the wax cast is removed; it is a replica of the plaster original. The wax is covered in plaster and heated, causing it to melt and drip out. Molten bronze is then poured into the

50. The owner, Charles Nilsson, purchased his cast from a Frenchman named D'Arquian, who ran the Galerie d'Art Latin. Nilsson's son believes that D'Arquian acquired it in Switzerland or Holland just after World War II (letter from Charles Nilsson Jr. to Henry Hopkins, Fort Worth Art Museum, 25 January 1971). Nilsson lent his cast to the exhibition *Picasso* [exh. cat., Svensk-Franska Konstgalleriet] (Stockholm, 1959), cat. 40, ill.

51. See Berggruen 1996. Ulmann told Berggruen that he had not made any bronzes from the plaster (Olivier Berggruen, conversation with the author, 1 August 2002). From Ulmann Berggruen also bought the original terracotta *Head of Fernande,* c. 1906, to make a second bronze edition in 1959. *Woman Combing Her Hair* would be cast in a numbered edition of ten in 1968.

52. According to Pullen and others, the use of synthetic flexible molds for bronze casting possibly migrated to France from Italy (where Medardo Rosso sent his delicate sculptures to be cast). An Italian named Paolozzi may have brought flexible-mold technology with him when he joined the Hébrard foundry in Paris in 1904 (to cast Rembrandt Bugatti's sculptures). Paolozzi's work, which culminated in the Degas posthumous bronze edition in the 1920s, inspired other technicians, who helped spread lost-wax bronze casting to other French foundries.

plaster. After the bronze has cooled, the plaster is chipped away to release the cast. The process can be repeated several times using the same flexible mold. Such molds eventually become worn and desiccated and must be replaced from time to time. Bronzes cast from an old mold may have blurred surfaces. As with sand-cast bronzes, the surface is "chased" (details sharpened and defects filed off) and chemically patinated.

The nine Valsuani bronzes were clearly numbered and marked with the foundry stamp. Because the edition was made within the span of only a few months, the casts are consistent in the articulation of surface details and the unmodulated black patina. Most have been located:

1/9 Hirshhorn Museum and Sculpture Garden, Smithsonian Institution, Washington, DC (given by Joseph H. Hirshhorn, 1966)

2/9 Los Angeles County Museum of Art (given by Mr. and Mrs. Nathan Smooke, 1978)

3/9 Norton Simon Art Foundation, Pasadena (purchased from Stephen Hahn, 1969)

4/9 Private collection (formerly Max Rayne, sold at Sotheby's, London, 27 June 2000)

5/9 Private collection (one of the three given to the artist in 1959)

6/9 Stiftung Kulturbesitz Berlin (acquired from Heinz Berggruen)

7/9 Museo Nacional Centro de Arte Reina Sofía, Madrid (gift from Caja de Ahorros y Monte de Piedad, 2001, purchased from Christie's; formerly David L. Kreeger, Washington, DC, 1962–1976)

8/9 Location unknown (one of the three given to the artist in 1959 but not in the estate inventory)

9/9 Private collection (one of the three given to the artist in 1959)

Having compiled data that suggest at least eighteen Vollard casts (including any that may have been cast by his heirs) and nine Berggruen casts, I would like to raise a difficult issue: that of possible other casts. In the mid-1980s, while researching the editions of Picasso's *Head of a Jester*, I encountered disconcerting complexities and discrepancies regarding authenticity and quality. Examining two proven Vollard casts side by side, the difference in surface articulation was noticeable. When another purported "Vollard" cast was brought in for comparison, it was demonstrably a *surmoulage*, meaning a bronze made from a mold taken from another bronze rather than from an original plaster. At least three other bronzes in reputable collections also turned out to be *surmoulages*. I was told by several sources (although without any documentary evidence) that all the bronzes in the unnumbered second edition of the *Head of a Jester* were *surmoulages* authorized by Picasso in 1958 because the wax

53. See "Le Casse-tête du faux en sculpture," *Le Figaro* (13 April 2001), 27, and Nicholas Powell, "The $60 Million Scam," *Art News* (September 2001), 158–160. Many unauthorized casts of works by Daumier, Gauguin, Rodin, and other artists have been seized by authorities in Europe in the last decade.

54. Spies and Piot 2000, 344 n.14.

original was not available. Furthermore, some illegal secondary *surmoulages* were made in the 1970s, taken from a bronze in the second edition. According to one source, Picasso once even authenticated a *Head of a Jester* with the signature misspelled "Piccasso."

The circumstances for *Head of a Woman* may not be that intricate, but nonauthentic bronzes do exist. Every expert I consulted acknowledged having seen at least one bronze whose technical quality was adequate but not wholly persuasive. Authentication is a delicate matter and even experienced connoisseurs do not always agree. Unless seen side by side with an authentic bronze, a well-crafted *surmoulage* can be difficult to distinguish. Because the clarity of surface details and textures varies somewhat even among provable Vollard casts, cautious scholars may be reluctant to tarnish the reputation of a work that just might be the result of careless workmanship at a foundry. Some forgers compensate for blurred surfaces in *surmoulages* by adjusting details in the mold before casting or on the bronze afterward. Dimensions are useful only if taken and compared methodically. Because molten bronze shrinks as it cools, a *surmoulage* will be about two percent smaller than an authentic bronze and four percent smaller than the original plaster. Measurements must be taken from identical points of reference. Height alone is not adequate; not only can it legitimately vary from cast to cast (depending on how the foundry technicians filed the bottom of each cast), but some forgers have also learned to enhance the bottom.

Two scandals that emerged in the 1990s give an inkling of how sophisticated forgers have become. One person fabricated sculptures with the Alberto Giacometti signature and then planted false provenance evidence in several archives. From 1988 to 1993 a dealer in Paris used the Georges Rudier foundry to make hundreds of unauthorized casts and *surmoulages* of works by Rodin, Maillol, and ninety-six other artists. Georges Rudier marked the bronzes as having been made by his uncle, Alexis Rudier, who had died in 1953. The bronzes were of such good quality that they entered many museum and private collections.[53] According to Spies, Picasso in later years sometimes sent plasters to be cast at the Rudier foundry.[54] So, what are we to think of a cast of Picasso's *Head of a Woman* that existed before 1980 and bears the Alexis Rudier mark? Or what about a lost-wax bronze with no foundry mark that appears somewhat blurry in surface articulation but has an attractive patina? An inaccurately formed detail in the hair, a signature that has been improperly enhanced, an undocumented provenance—such factors raise doubts that may never be resolved.

Early spring

Picasso paints *Woman in an Armchair* (Daix 269)[1] and sends a postcard of this work, which appears to be postmarked 23 March, to his patrons, Gertrude and Leo Stein.

In his Bateau Lavoir studio at 13 Rue de Ravignan, Montmartre, Paris, Picasso photographs his dealer Clovis Sagot both frontally and in profile and soon paints Sagot's portrait (Daix 270).

Picasso decides to spend the summer away from Paris and to return to the remote Spanish mountain village of Horta de Ebro,[2] the site of an extended visit from summer 1898 through early 1899. (That stay—with his friend from the Barcelona art school La Llotja, Manuel Pallarés, and Pallarés' family—had been a formative one, with Picasso later stating, "all that I know, I learned in Pallarés' village."[3]) Picasso's companion, Fernande Olivier, who accompanied him in 1909 and on other sojourns, wrote, "Each year he spent several months in Spain. He would come back refreshed, having made quantities of studies which expressed some new interest."[4]

May

On Monday, 10 May, Picasso writes to his close friend, the poet and critic Guillaume Apollinaire, that he and Fernande are leaving for Spain Wednesday evening and that he would like to see Apollinaire before they depart.[5]

On 12 May, after a send-off by friends at the station, Picasso and Fernande embark on their journey by train, arriving in Barcelona on the evening of Thursday, 13 May. The date is confirmed by a letter of 16 May from Fernande to Gertrude Stein in Fiesole, Italy, declaring that they "arrived in this horrible town of Barcelona on Thursday..."[6] and were planning to stay "perhaps another week" before leaving for Horta de Ebro. Their departure on the arduous trip to Horta, with the last twenty-five miles to be traveled on mule back and on foot, is delayed when Fernande becomes ill. She is later diagnosed with a kidney infection that will plague her throughout the summer. In a note card postmarked 26 May, Picasso writes to Leo Stein in Fiesole that they are still in Barcelona and are waiting for Fernande's health to improve before leaving for the country. In the same note, Picasso refers to the "certitude" of the Steins' visit to Spain that summer. The artist also sends several postcards to Apollinaire. While in Barcelona, Picasso is reacquainted with old friends, including Vidal Ventosa and Manuel Pallarés (who is now teaching at La Llotja, with Picasso's father). Throughout their visit, the couple stays at the Grand Hótel d'Orient, and Picasso executes six renderings of the view from their window before their departure. Working in Pallarés' studio, he also paints a portrait of Pallarés (Daix 274). On 31 May, Fernande sends a postcard to Alice Toklas—Gertrude Stein's secretary and companion, to whom Fernande had been teaching French—who remained in Paris for the summer. Fernande indicates that she has been sick and bedridden and confesses, "We're still in Barcelona because of this."

June

Picasso and Fernande depart Barcelona in early June, likely on the fourth, staying for one night at an inn in Tortosa (where they send postcards to Apollinaire and Alice Toklas), and the next day traveling to Horta de Ebro, a six-hour walk.

On 15 June, Fernande writes to Alice Toklas from Horta, giving their address and stating that ten days have passed since their arrival and that she is still "unwell and miserable." She continues, "Pablo is in the loft. He's working," and adds that because of his camera, "the people here thought we were photographers...."

On 24 June, Picasso writes to the Steins that Fernande has been ill but he has been working, although "not much," and has "begun two landscapes and two figures—same thing as usual." He adds, "I'm thinking of taking photographs of here. I'll send them to you when I have them. The countryside is very beautiful."

In a letter of 26 June to Alice Toklas, Fernande mentions that the sculptor Manolo (Manuel Hugué) and Frank Burty Haviland, a painter and collector of Picasso's work, may be coming to see them. She adds that she would be "very happy" if Alice could visit, and tells her that the Steins have written and that they "are supposed to come here in September."

July

In a letter to the Steins likely dating from this month, Picasso suggests arrangements for their visit to Horta, Madrid, and Toledo, and asserts that he is working and has made some studies.

In letters of mid-July, Fernande expresses to Alice Toklas that she was "too ill" to write earlier, and to Gertrude Stein that "for the two months I've been in Spain I haven't had one complete day's respite." Not long afterward, however, she writes again to Alice, conveying that she has been feeling better and that "Pablo is working. He has been given the use of a room in the baker's house, as there was no room to spare here. Over there he has an empty room and peace and quiet."

Following the extensive 11 July call-up of military reservists from Barcelona for active duty in Morocco, numerous demonstrations and a socialist appeal for general strikes ensue. An insurrection erupts in the Catalan port on 26 July. This "social revolution" is eventually suppressed; martial law is declared throughout Spain on 28 July and the last resistance overcome by the army on 31 July. The series of events will become known as "Tragic Week."

August

In separate letters to Alice Toklas and to Gertrude Stein, Fernande announces that her health has improved and refers to having received a letter from Apollinaire and to the possibility that he might visit.

The first reference in their correspondence to the repercussions of Tragic Week appears in Fernande's postscript to a letter from Picasso to the Steins (dated only "Saturday" and revisiting their proposed travel to Barcelona, Madrid, and Toledo, but apparently not Horta), in which she describes the "grave" political situation in Spain and their ten-day isolation. Perhaps the same day, Fernande writes to Alice, "We've been cut off from the whole world for some ten days without letters or newspapers, as nothing was allowed to come in from Barcelona."

In another letter to the Steins from the same period, Picasso yet again addresses the Steins' intended visit, declaring, "it has been a long time that I have wanted to see Greco again in Toledo and Madrid." He states that he is working and intends to send the photographs he has taken of the region and of his paintings the next day.

Picasso sends three photographs (of four of his paintings) to the Steins with a letter indicating others will follow soon. He further inquires of their plans for travel to Spain but describes "une grande revolution maintenant."

On 18 August, Picasso's sister Lola is married in Barcelona to Dr. Juan Vilató Gómez, a neurologist. As Fernande divulges in a letter to the Steins written several days later, Picasso "managed quite easily to avoid the chore of attending the ceremony." She also mentions their receipt of a letter from Leo and notes that the Steins will be in Paris long before they will. It appears that Leo Stein's letter confirmed he and Gertrude would not be visiting Spain after all, as Fernande avows, "we'll come back next year, and you'll come with us...." She describes their plan to depart from Horta in ten days, traveling to Barcelona to spend two weeks there and then perhaps to Bourg Madame to see Manolo and Haviland, who had not come to Horta.[7] In the same letter, Fernande again attests that "Pablo is working" and refers to "letter after letter" they have received from Picasso's dealer, Daniel-Henry Kahnweiler, regarding an intended September visit.

In a letter acknowledging that the excursion to Madrid and Toledo will not take place that summer but the following year, Picasso also references Kahnweiler's proposed September visit, which he says "irritates" him, and inquires whether the Steins have received the photographs of "four of my paintings." He vows, "One of these days I will send others of the landscape and my paintings. I am continuing to make studies and working quite regularly."[8] Over the course of the summer Picasso would execute cats. 20 through 58 and the following canvases, as well as related watercolors and drawings: *Landscape (Santa Bárbara Mountain)* (Daix 275), *Landscape (Santa Bárbara Mountain)* (Daix 276), *The Oil Mill* (Daix 277), *Houses on the Hill, Horta de Ebro* (Daix 278), *Factory at Horta de Ebro* (Daix 279), *The Reservoir, Horta de Ebro* (Daix 280), *Head and Shoulders of a Man* (Daix 296), *Head and Shoulders of a Man* (Daix 297), *Carafe, Jug, and Fruit Bowl* (Daix 298), and *Bottle of Anís del Mono* (Daix 299). A number of these works appear in the studio photographs; see cats. 51 through 58.

On 28 August, Picasso writes to the Steins that he is sending some photographs of his paintings and that he is thinking of leaving within several days to spend time in Barcelona with his parents, returning to Paris afterward.

September

On 7 September, Picasso sends a postcard to Apollinaire, confirming he and Fernande have arrived in Barcelona and will be in Paris in a few days. That same day, Fernande writes to Gertrude Stein (who is now in Paris) on stationery from the Grand Hótel d'Orient, telling her that she and Picasso reached Barcelona on the sixth and that they plan to stay five or six days "at most" before taking the eighteen-hour express train back to Paris.

On 8 September, a Wednesday, Fernande reports to Alice Toklas that they plan to "be in Paris on Saturday morning... we're taking the express from Barcelona on Friday at around 3 o'clock."

Picasso and Fernande likely did arrive in Paris on Saturday, 11 September. Writing to Apollinaire on the fourteenth, the artist confirms that he has been in Paris "two or three days," and in a letter postmarked 13 September, Picasso invites the Steins to a "vernissage" of the Horta paintings at his studio on Wednesday afternoon, 15 September. This viewing, however, is later postponed to the following day. The Steins would add two of the views of Horta (Daix 278 and 280) and cat. 28 to their collection of Picasso's work, while Frank

Burty Haviland acquired *Factory at Horta de Ebro* (Daix 279), and Picasso's dealer Ambroise Vollard ultimately purchased a number of the other Horta works.

Fall

In late September or early October, Picasso models *Head of a Woman (Fernande)* (see cats. 64–66) in Manolo's studio. In addition to this work, the artist created two smaller sculptures during the fall, another *Head* and *Apple* (Spies and Piot 25, 26). While these works (one in clay and one in plaster) were never cast in bronze, Picasso would sell *Head of a Woman (Fernande)* and four earlier sculptures to Vollard—who proceeded to cast them—the following year. Fernande reveals in her memoir that "one day, when he needed a pretty large sum of money, he sold his sculptures to Vollard."[9]

The 1909 Salon d'automne, which opens 1 October, includes *Figures de Corot*, a retrospective of twenty-four works by Jean-Baptiste-Camille Corot, which Picasso sees. He would soon acquire a small Corot figure painting from Wilhelm Uhde, in exchange for his portrait of the dealer (Daix 338).

According to Fernande's memoir, during their journey back from Horta Picasso "finally made up his mind" to move.[10] By early October, they have moved from the Bateau Lavoir—where they met in 1904—leaving the two studio spaces they had occupied there since 1905. Their new apartment at 11 Boulevard de Clichy, near the Place Pigalle, has a large studio and room for a live-in servant.

On 10 January 1910 Picasso writes to Apollinaire that Fernande had an operation that morning and is doing well. Despite her signature, "Fernande Picasso," in a letter of 29 December 1909 to Gertrude Stein, the couple never married, but they would stay together until 1912.

Compiled by Jessica Stewart

. . .

This chronology is based primarily on the letters from Picasso and Fernande Olivier to Gertrude and Leo Stein and to Alice B. Toklas, which are housed at the Yale Collection of American Literature, Beinecke Rare Book and Manuscript Library, Yale University. Other sources include Judith Cousin's "Documentary Chronology," in William Rubin, *Picasso and Braque: Pioneering Cubism* [exh. cat., The Museum of Modern Art] (New York, 1989), and those that follow in the notes.

1. Paintings and works on paper by Picasso are referenced parenthetically in this chronology and in the plate section according to the catalogue numbers in Pierre Daix and Joan Rosselet's catalogue raisonné, *Picasso: The Cubist Years, 1907–1916* (Boston, 1979).

2. The name of the village was changed to Horta de Sant Joan after 1910.

3. See Jaime Sabartés, *Picasso: An Intimate Portrait* (New York, 1948), 43.

4. See the memoir Fernande Olivier—a former artists' model whose given name was Amelie Lang—published in 1933 of her years with Picasso, *Picasso and His Friends*, trans. Jane Miller (New York, 1965), 93.

5. See *Picasso/Apollinaire: Correspondance* (Paris, 1992), 71-75, for all references to Picasso's correspondence with Apollinaire during this period.

6. All translations of Fernande's letters are from Fernande Olivier, *Loving Picasso: The Private Journal of Fernande Olivier*, trans. Christine Baker and Michael Raeburn (New York, 2001), 227-250.

7. My thanks to the Vilató family—and Lluís Bagunyá of the Museu Picasso—for confirming the date and location of the wedding. According to John Richardson, Manuel Pallarés, who "materialized a day or two before the artist left," was their only visitor during the summer. Richardson with Marilyn McCully, *A Life of Picasso, 1907–1917*, 2 vols. (New York, 1996), 2:135.

8. Picasso presumably did send his photographs of Horta to Gertrude Stein, as she had several in her collection. Stein later wrote that "Picasso in 1909 was in Spain and brought back with him some landscapes which were, certainly were, the beginning of cubism. These three landscapes were extraordinarily realistic and all the same the beginning of cubism. Picasso had by chance taken some photographs of the village that he had painted and it always amused me when every one protested against the fantasy of the pictures to make them look at the photographs which made them see that the pictures were almost exactly like the photographs." See Gertrude Stein's 1938 "Picasso," in *Gertrude Stein on Picasso* (New York, 1970), 14.

9. Olivier 2001, 251. See Valerie Fletcher's essay in this volume regarding this sale and the casting of the works.

10. Olivier 1965, 143.

Photographic Credits

Every effort has been made to locate the copyright holders for the photographs used in this book.

Fleeting and Fixed: Picasso's Fernandes

fig. 1, Digital Image © 2003 The Museum of Modern Art, New York / Licensed by SCALA / Art Resource, New York
fig. 5, Réunion des musées nationaux / Art Resource, New York
fig. 8, © Antonella Vigliani Bragaglia
fig. 9, © 2003 Artists Rights Society (ARS), New York / VG Bild-Kunst, Bonn
fig. 10, Bildarchiv, Österreichische Nationalbibliothek, Vienna
fig. 11, Réunion des musées nationaux / Art Resource, New York
fig. 17, © 2003 Artists Rights Society (ARS), New York
fig. 21, Art Resource, New York

Catalogue

cat. 1, © Succession Picasso / DACS 2003 / Tate 2003
cat. 5, Digital Image © 2003 The Museum of Modern Art, New York
cat. 7, © Rheinisches Bildarchiv, Cologne
cat. 10, © The Art Institute of Chicago
cat. 17, © Images Modernes, photograph by Marc Domage
cat. 18, © Photographie ImageArt Antibes, France
cat. 20, photograph by Vladimir Vukadinovic
cat. 27, photograph by Walter Klein, Düsseldorf
cat. 28, © The Art Institute of Chicago
cat. 30, photograph by Schecter Lee
cat. 32, © Images Modernes, photograph by E. Baudouin
cat. 33, © Images Modernes, photograph by E. Baudouin
cat. 35, Digital Image © The Museum of Modern Art, New York / Licensed by SCALA / Art Resource, New York
cat. 38, photograph by Becket Logan
cat. 39, © Blauel / Gnamm-Artothek
cat. 40, © Images Modernes, photograph by Marc Domage
cat. 41, © Images Modernes, photograph by Marc Domage
cat. 42, © Images Modernes, photograph by Marc Domage
cat. 47, Courtesy Galerie Gmurzynska
cat. 48, © Robert Lorenzson
cat. 49, © Images Modernes, photograph by E. Baudouin
cat. 59, © Photographie ImageArt Antibes, France
cat. 61, Prudence Cuming Associates, Ltd., London
cat. 63, © The Art Institute of Chicago
cat. 64, © Succession Picasso / DACS 2003 / Tate, London 2003
cat. 66, © 2003 Board of Trustees, National Gallery of Art, Washington, photograph by Lee Ewing
cat. 74, © Images Modernes, photograph by E. Baudouin
cat. 76, © CAN / MNAN / Dist. Réunion des musées nationaux / Art Resource, New York
cat. 77, © Succession Picasso / DACS 2003 / Tate, London 2003

La Peau de Chagrin

fig. 1, © SCALA / Art Resource, New York
fig. 2, photograph by Bernd Kirtz BFF, Duisburg, Germany
fig. 4, photograph by Martin Bühler
fig. 6, photograph by Bob Kolbrenner
fig. 7, © 2003 The Cleveland Museum of Art
fig. 9, © SCALA / Art Resource, New York, photograph by Erich Lessing
fig. 10, © Christie's Images, Ltd.
fig. 12, photograph by Malcolm Varon
fig. 13, © SCALA / Art Resource, New York
fig. 15, © Réunion des musées nationaux / Art Resource, New York
fig. 16, Digital Image © 2003 The Museum of Modern Art, New York

Process and Technique in Picasso's *Head of a Woman (Fernande)*

fig. 1, © Tate, London 2003
fig. 2, photograph by Tom Jenkins
fig. 3, photograph by Tom Jenkins
fig. 4a, photograph by Tom Jenkins
fig. 4b, © Tate, London 2003
figs. 5a, b, photographs by Tom Jenkins
fig. 6, © 2003 Artists Rights Society (ARS), New York
fig. 7, SCALA / Art Resource, New York
fig. 8, photograph by Tom Jenkins
fig. 9, private collection
fig. 11, photograph by Pam Hatchfield

Other illustrations

page ii, cat. 67
page iii, cat. 68
page iv, cat. 69
page v, cat. 70
page ix, *top:* Portrait of Picasso (self-portrait?), 1908–1909, photograph, Réunion des musées nationaux / Art Resource, New York; *bottom:* Pablo Picasso, Portrait of Fernande Olivier, 1908–1909, photograph, Yale Collection of American Literature, Beinecke Rare Book and Manuscript Library
page x, cat. 53
page xiv, see fig. 4, Weiss essay
page 198, Pablo Picasso, Portrait of Fernande Olivier, 1908–1909, photograph, Yale Collection of American Literature, Beinecke Rare Book and Manuscript Library

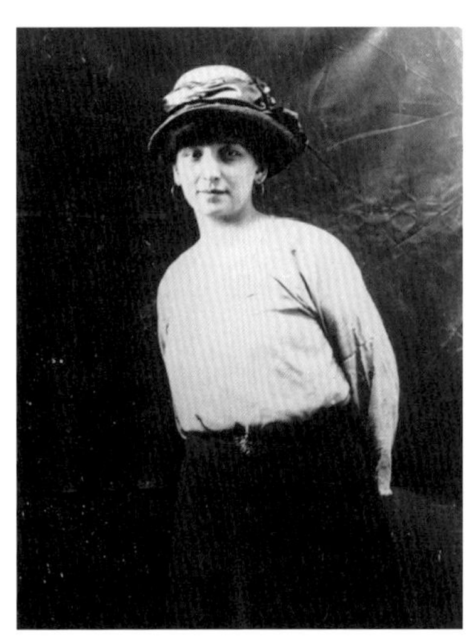